AFFIRMING
DIVERSITY

AFFIRMING DIVERSITY

The Sociopolitical Context of Multicultural Education

Sonia Nieto

University of Massachusetts

Longman

New York & London

AFFIRMING DIVERSITY: THE SOCIOPOLITICAL
CONTEXT OF MULTICULTURAL EDUCATION

Longman, 10 Bank Street, White Plains, N.Y. 10606

Associated companies:
Longman Group Ltd., London
Longman Cheshire Pty., Melbourne
Longman Paul Pty., Auckland
Copp Clark Pitman, Toronto

Senior editor: Naomi Silverman
Production editor: Marcy Gray
Cover design: David Levy
Cover photos: David Zuccalo
Production supervisor: Anne Armeny

Library of Congress Cataloging-in-Publication Data

Nieto, Sonia.
    Affirming diversity : the sociopolitical context of multicultural
education / by Sonia Nieto
        p.   cm.
    Includes bibliographical references and index.
    ISBN 0-8013-0529-2
        1. Intercultural education—United States—Case studies.
    I. Title.
    LC1099.3.N54 1991
    370.19′341—dc20   91-21254
                                                              CIP

6 7 8 9 10-CRS-97 96 95 94 93

In loving memory of
Esther Mercado Cortés and Federico Cortés

Contents

Case Studies

Foreword

It takes more than a little courage these days to write a book on multicultural education. Since its heyday in the late 1960s and early 1970s, the concept and implementation of multicultural education has been attacked by both sides of the political spectrum. It has been assailed from the ''left'' for its focus only on superficial aspects of cultural diversity and for its failure to address the institutionalized racism that is embedded in the structures of our societies. The marginal status assigned to issues of language within much multicultural education theorizing and its ambivalence with respect to bilingual education have also been subject to criticism. Several writers (including myself) have viewed multicultural education as a stage that some societies have already passed through in their attempts to address issues of diversity and equity. The focus on surface manifestations of culture has given way to two parallel thrusts: on the one hand, an antiracist focus designed explicitly to promote equity through removing structural barriers to children's achievement; on the other, an internationalist focus that recognizes the cultures and languages of children as collective resources that have enormous individual and national relevance in a rapidly shrinking world.

While multicultural education has been viewed from the left as imposing little more than a veneer on the structure of inequality, it has been taken far more seriously by those on the right of the political spectrum. Together with bilingual education, it has been viewed as legitimating the maintenance of cultures and languages other than those of the dominant group and, as such, constituting a real threat to national unity. Perhaps the most coherent expression of this viewpoint is E. D. Hirsch's insistence on ''cultural literacy'' as a major goal of education. Needless to say, the cultures, knowledge, and values of groups that have been historically subordinated by the dominant group are notably absent from the list of ''facts'' that the ''culturally literate'' American needs to know.

A major reason why multicultural education has been subject to such different interpretations is that the construct has not been adequately grounded in a causal analysis of school failure among subordinated group students. Thus, any form of intervention that purports to promote respect for cultural diversity could legitimately claim to represent multicultural education.

Sonia Nieto's book is the first that I have read that provides a comprehensive framework for analyzing the multiple causes of school failure among subordinated group students and, on the basis of this analysis, suggests creative intervention strategies that are supported by research and theory. The collectivity of these educational strategies are labelled "multicultural education" which is viewed as an umbrella term encompassing more specific programs and pedagogical orientations such as "bilingual education," "antiracist education," "critical pedagogy," etc. Viewed in these terms, the construct of multicultural education is rescued from the perception that it concerns itself only with the surface manifestations of culture divorced from societal power relations; multicultural education, on the contrary, becomes a central and essential element in any consideration of educational reform. As expressed in *Affirming Diversity,* "the alternative to multicultural education is *monocultural education.*" The incisive analyses of this book make very clear that a monocultural education is an inferior education that ill prepares students to function either in the broad arena of a democratic society or in the more narrow confines of an employment market that is increasingly oriented to the vast cultural diversity of our "global village."

The reader is left in no doubt as to what multicultural education entails. It entails a direct challenge to the societal power structure that has historically subordinated certain groups and rationalized the educational failure of children from these groups as being the result of their inherent deficiencies. Multicultural education as conceptualized here challenges all educators to make the schools a force for social justice in our society.

This book should be viewed not only as another contribution to the field of multicultural education, but as a much needed extension of the field of critical pedagogy into the areas of culture, race, and language. Unlike many contributions in the fields of critical pedagogy (and multicultural education), students' voices occupy a central place in this book. They complement and illustrate the theoretical analyses and remind us that the interactions between educators and students dramatically affect not only the acquisition of knowledge and skills but the creation of identity.

Affirming Diversity challenges us, as educators, to make explicit the image of our students and of our society that is implied in our interactions in the school context. Students who are currently in the early years of elementary school will graduate in the next millenium; what kind of people do we hope they will be? What kinds of abilities and knowledge are we giving them the opportunity to acquire? What kind of society do we hope they will create? The answers to all these questions are written in the daily record of our interactions with our students. Our interactions with students and communities constitute a moral enterprise, whether we define it as such or not.

Viewed in this light, all the major studies of classroom interactions carried out during the past decade (e.g. John Goodlad's *A Place Called School*) paint a somewhat depressing picture. They demonstrate clearly the predominance of transmission models of pedagogy that reduce students to passive receivers of inert facts. The curriculum has been sanitized to such a point that opportunities for critical reflection on personal and collective identity and on issues of social justice are minimized. The image of our students and society implied by this pedagogical orientation is an image of compliant consumers who will gratefully accept their place within the existing power structure and who can easily be manipulated to exercise their democratic rights to preserve that power structure.

A radically different image is implied by the pedagogical orientations articulated in *Affirming Diversity*. Students are viewed as critical thinkers capable of, and responsible for, creating change through action both in their own lives and in the broader society. Their interactions in school provide opportunities to collaborate across cultural and linguistic boundaries in the generation, interpretation, and application of knowledge. The curriculum orients students towards critical reflection on issues of social justice and of identity (both personal and collective). The image of students and society implied in these educational interactions is an image of individuals who have developed respect both for their own cultural identity and for the identities of others; who are capable of collaborating with others in the democratic pursuit of social justice; and who see themselves as members of a global community with shared economic, scientific, and environmental interests. As such, the directions highlighted in *Affirming Diversity* respond much more adequately to the challenges of the 21st century than the introverted xenophobic focus of many of the current reports on "educational reform."

Jim Cummins
Ontario Institute for Studies in Education
July 1991

Acknowledgments

No book is fully complete without an author's reflection on how others have contributed to its development. There are many people who have been involved with this book—from the days when it was just an idea to the final revisions shortly before its last editing—to whom I owe a tremendous debt of gratitude. My friend and mentor, Bob Suzuki, was an inspiration to me when I was a graduate student and first started on this multicultural road. I hope his presence can be felt in this book. Years later, initial conversations with James Banks, Patti Ramsey, Chris Bennett, Carlos Cortés, and Maddie Marquez helped me to formulate what I wanted this book to be about. Their collective vision was instrumental in motivating me to begin. My friend and colleague David Bloome spent many hours helping me organize my thoughts about the project. His creative ideas, boundless energy, and faith in my ability were invaluable to me in those early months. I am most grateful to the graduate students, colleagues, and friends who found and interviewed the students for the case studies. Carlie Collins Tartakov, Paula Elliott, Haydée Font, Maya Gillingham, Mac Lee Morante, Diane Sweet, and Carol Shea not only found extraordinary young people to interview but also provided contextual information and valuable insights that were crucial in understanding the students' stories. I want especially to thank the ten students who agreed to discuss their experiences, perspectives, and hopes for the future. Although I did not meet them all in person, I fell in love with each of them. As I pored over transcripts and listened to their voices, I found myself moved to laughter, tears, and sadness. When I finished the case studies, I came away with a tremendous sense of power and surge of hope for them and for all of us.

I want to thank the following friends and colleagues who have read and commented on the manuscript: Meyer Weinberg; Carolyn O'Grady; Maya Gillingham; Manuel Frau; and Lydia Cortés. Others to whom I am grateful assisted me with helpful resources, bibliographic information, or editorial help: Diane Sweet; Youngro Song; Peter Kiang; Dick Barbieri; Masha Rudman; Roberto Marquez; Jules Chametsky; Ellen Daniels; Alberto Morales; and Alicia Nieto. All of them, along with the anonymous reviewers selected by

Longman, provided a helpful critique that was instrumental in improving the book. I cannot thank them strongly enough. I am also grateful to Jim Cummins, a colleague whose work I admire and from whom I have learned a great deal, for the foreword. It has meant a great deal to me to have his voice here as well. I will always be grateful to my dear friends and program colleagues, Luis Fuentes, Bob Sinclair, and Jerri Willett, for their support and encouragement during this process. They helped to carry the burden of the program leadership while I was completing the manuscript. Their collective commitment to equal education and social justice are an inspiration to me not only in this book but also in the work we do every day. A special word of acknowledgment to all the students I have been privileged to teach over the years and from whom I continue to learn.

Joel Spring, from SUNY at Old Westbury, volunteered to field-test the manuscript when it was far from complete. I want to express my heartfelt gratitude to him and to his students for having given it so much time and consideration. Naomi Silverman, who started out as my editor and became a close friend in the process, has been a source of support and unbridled enthusiasm since before I began to write.

My family, the center of my life and without whom I could not function, has been a constant source of education for me. Angel, el compañero de mi vida, has helped me to think about this book even before I began to think about it; he has been there throughout, reading every word and quietly suggesting needed changes. Finally, my daughters, Alicia and Marisa, have helped to make the writing of this book anything but an academic exercise. Their experiences have forced me to come face to face with the very issues about which I wrote in these pages and prevented me from falling into easy or romantic notions of success. It is to them that I owe the honesty of this book.

Introduction

Over the years, I have made scores of presentations on multicultural and bilingual education in many different school systems. After each session, a number of teachers invariably approach me with the same concern: Why do some of their students (usually their African American, Latino, or Indian students and very often their poor European American students) fail, no matter what they, their teachers, do, whereas other (usually their middle-class European American students and sometimes their middle-class students of other ethnic groups) succeed? Although a small number of these teachers are convinced that their students of color or their poor students are genetically or culturally inferior and simply want verification of their racist and classist beliefs, this is certainly not true in the vast majority of cases. Another group, who may have begun as committed and idealistic teachers, have simply tired of confronting hostile and nonachieving students in their classrooms every day. These teachers genuinely do not want to believe that some children are inferior to others or that the culture of their students is what causes their school failure. Most of them are sincerely interested in exploring ways to meet the educational needs of all their students.

Yet it is not unusual for teachers, after having worked with a great many youths, to start accepting the belief that children from some ethnic or racial groups may indeed be inherently "better" students than others. The cause for failure, they often reluctantly conclude, must be within the children or within the communities from which they come. After all, the schools have tried everything from compensatory education to free lunch and breakfast programs. Nothing seems to work, and the same young people keep dropping out and failing. How can multicultural education help?

WHAT GOOD CAN MULTICULTURAL EDUCATION DO?

Multicultural education cannot be understood in a vacuum but rather must be seen in its personal, social, historical, and political context. Assuming that multicultural education is "the answer" to school failure is simplistic at best, for it overlooks important social and educational issues that affect daily the lives of students. Educational failure is too complex and knotty an issue to be "fixed" by any single program or approach. However, if broadly conceptualized and implemented, multicultural education can have a substantive and positive impact on the educational experiences of most students. That is the thesis of this book.

I have come to this understanding as a result of many experiences, including my childhood and my life as a student, teacher, researcher, and parent. As a young child growing up in Brooklyn, New York, during the 1940s, I was able to experience firsthand the influence that poverty, discrimination, and the perception of one's culture and language as inferior can have. Speaking only Spanish when I entered first grade, I was immediately confronted with the arduous task of learning a second language while my already quite developed native language was all but ignored. Some 40 years later, I still recall the frustration of groping for words I did not know to express thoughts I could very capably say in Spanish. Equally vivid are memories of some teachers' expectations that because of our language and cultural differences, my classmates and I would not do well in school. This explains my fourth-grade teacher's response when mine was the only hand to go up when she asked if anybody in the class wanted to go to college. "Well, that's O.K.," she said, "because we always need people to clean toilets."

I also recall teachers' perceptions that there was something wrong with speaking a language other than English. "Is there anybody in this class who started school without speaking English?" my tenth-grade homeroom teacher asked loudly, filling out one of the endless forms that teachers are handed by the central office. By this time, my family had moved to what was at the time a working-class and primarily European American neighborhood. My classmates looked in hushed silence as I, the only Puerto Rican in the class, raised my hand timidly. "Are you in a special English class?" he asked in front of the entire class. "Yes." I said, "I'm in Honors English." Although there is nothing wrong with being in a special class for English as a second language (ESL), I felt fortunate that I was able to respond in this way. I had learned to feel somewhat ashamed of speaking Spanish and wanted to make it very clear that I was intelligent in spite of it. Many students in similar circumstances who are in bilingual and ESL classes feel guilty and inferior to their peers.

Those first experiences with society's responses to cultural differences did not, of course, convince me that something was wrong with the *responses*. Rather, I assumed, as many of my peers did, that there was something wrong with *us*. We learned to feel ashamed of who we were, how we spoke, what we ate, and everything else that was "different" about us. "Please," I would beg my mother, "make us hamburgers and hot dogs for dinner." Luckily, she never paid attention and kept right on cooking rice, beans, plátanos, and all those other good foods that we grew up with. She and my father also continued speaking Spanish to us, in spite of our teachers' pleas to speak to us only in English. And so, alongside the messages at school and in the streets that being Puerto Rican was not something to be proud of, we learned to keep on being who we were. As the case studies point out, these conflicting messages are still being given to many young people.

Immigration is not a phenomenon of the past. In fact, the experience of immigration is still fresh in the minds of a great many people in our country. It is an experience that begins anew every day that planes land, ships reach our shores, and people make their way on foot to our borders. Many of the students in our schools, even if they themselves are not immigrants, have parents or grandparents who were. The United States is thus not only a nation of immigrants as seen in some idealized and romanticized past; it is also a living nation of immigrants even today.

The pain and alienation of the immigrant experience, however, have rarely been confronted in our schools. This experience includes the forced immigration of enslaved Africans and the colonization of American Indians and Mexicans from within. Because schools have traditionally perceived their role to be that of an assimilating agent, the isolation and rejection that come hand in hand with immigration and colonization have simply been left at the schoolhouse door. Curriculum and pedagogy, rather than using the lived experiences of students as a foundation, have been based on what can be described as an alien and imposed reality. The rich experiences of millions of our students, their parents, grandparents, and neighbors have been kept strangely quiet. Although we almost all have an immigrant past, very few of us know or even acknowledge it.

What the research reported in this book suggests to me is that we need to make this history visible by making it part of the curriculum, instruction, and educational experience in general. Whether through the words of Manuel, who claims that he cannot be an American because it would mean forsaking his Cape Verdean background, or those of Vanessa, who knows nothing about her European American past and even feels uncomfortable discussing it, it has become clear that the immigrant experience is an important point of departure for beginning our journey into multicultural education. This journey needs to begin with teachers, who themselves are frequently unaware of or uncomfortable with their own ethnicity. By going through a process of reeducation about their own backgrounds, their families' pain, and their rich legacy of stories, teachers can lay the groundwork for students to reclaim their own histories and voices.

As an adult, I have come to the conclusion that no child should have to go through the painful dilemma of choosing between family and school and of what inevitably becomes a choice between belonging and succeeding. The costs for going through such an experience are high indeed, from becoming a ''cultural schizophrenic'' to developing doubts about one's self-worth and dignity. This is nowhere more poignantly described than in Richard Rodriguez's painful recollection of growing up as a ''scholarship boy,'' an academically promising student who is doomed to lose his family, culture, and language in the process. His conclusion is that one's public and private worlds cannot be reconciled:

> My awkward childhood does not prove the necessity of bilingual education. My story discloses instead an essential myth of childhood—inevitable pain. If I rehearse here the changes in my private life after my Americanization, it is finally to emphasize the public gain. The loss implies the gain.[1]

Because of his wrenching loss of language and culture, Rodriguez decides that bilingual/multicultural education and affirmative action are all policies that cannot work because they in effect delay the inevitable loss. My conclusion is quite the opposite: *The loss implies the pain.* Just as the title of an important book on the issue asserts (*Minority Education: From Shame to Struggle*[2]), our society must move beyond causing and exploiting students' shame to using their cultural and linguistic differences to struggle for an education that is more in tune with society's rhetoric of equal and high-quality education for all students. That is the fundamental lesson I have relearned while doing the research for this book.

OVERVIEW

Why students succeed or fail in school has been the subject of much research and debate, particularly for students who are from racial, ethnic, linguistic, or social class backgrounds different from the dominant group. In addition, the promise of educational programs and practices such as bilingual and multicultural education has often been unfulfilled and indeed full of controversy because such programs challenge the status quo and even the very premise of much of our educational system.

In this book, I will consider the constant and complex interplay and interactions among personal, social, political, and educational factors in exploring the success or failure of students in schools and the benefits of multicultural education. Only by listening to students can we learn how they experience school, how social and educational structures affect their learning, and what we can do to provide high-quality education for all students.

Educators frequently rely on their own experiences and common sense when they teach. However, educational research (the systemmatic and careful study of how and why students learn) conducted by teachers and others generally provides a better source for educational practice. Rather than relying on convention or tradition or what seems to work, it is more effective to look to research for implications in teaching. Thus, this book is grounded in research. Research gives us a way of understanding what happens in classrooms and has implications for the improvement of education. Although the findings of research are often contradictory and seldom neat and tidy, they nonetheless contribute to our understanding of the complex process of education.

However, I do not mean to imply that research is neutral and objective. We approach each endeavor with a set of assumptions and a philosophical and political outlook. No research can be free of some biases, no matter how neutral it may claim to be. Even the decision to study a particular phenomenon is a political decision and may have unstated agendas, for example, the decision of the federal government to compare *English as a second language* with *bilingual education* and *immersion* (for a review of these terms and the literature associated with them, see the Ramirez study in Chapter 6). In this study, bilingual education proved to be far more effective than the Reagan administration had hoped it would be. When the preliminary results, which were contrary to what had been expected, became apparent, they were withheld from the public for several years. In spite of the fact that no research is truly neutral, however, it can help us by providing a focus for complex issues.

The purpose of this book is to explore the meaning, necessity, and benefits of multicultural education for students from all cultural backgrounds through the following:

1. An investigation of the impact on schooling of
   a. Racism, discrimination, and expectations of students' achievement

    b. Structural factors such as school organization and educational policies and practices

    c. Cultural and other differences such as ethnicity, race, gender, language, and class

2. A rationale for multicultural education based on the preceding
3. Case studies, in the words of a selected group of successful students from a variety of backgrounds, about home, school, and community experiences and how these have influenced their school achievement

This book presents data concerning the multicultural nature of schools and society, including pertinent information about different cultural and linguistic groups, their experiences in schools, and the unique issues and challenges they face. Relevant research on the success or failure of students in schools will also be presented.

The book consists of 12 chapters divided into 2 sections. In the first section, a conceptual framework for multicultural education is developed in a sociopolitical context, and structural and cultural factors in schooling, as well as individual and group responses to education, are emphasized. This first section focuses on understanding the myriad forces that may affect the school achievement of students from a variety of backgrounds.

To provide insights into the interdependent roles of discrimination, structural factors, and culture on the education of students in the classroom, a number of case studies will be presented. These will be incorporated throughout the first section and are meant to highlight salient issues discussed in these particular chapters. The case studies will provide a concrete means for understanding and addressing issues of diversity and success or failure in the schools. It is hoped that the case studies will help the reader understand more fully the lives and school experiences of a variety of young people and provide a description of what social justice in schools would look like.

Part II of the book focuses on the implications of the case studies for teaching and learning in a multicultural society such as ours. A definition of multicultural education emerges organically from the conceptual framework developed in Part I. First, a rationale for multicultural education as a way of equalizing educational experiences is presented. Themes that emerge from the case studies are used as the basis for this section of the book as the many factors affecting learning and school experiences are reviewed. Information concerning the school and home life of each student will be explored to understand the conflicts that may arise between home and school expectations. Areas in which further collaboration is needed for positive student achievement will be pointed out. Second, ways to remove those barriers that inhibit learning will be explored. Suggestions for developing environments that foster high-quality education, concentrating on multicultural education as a process, will be offered. In addition, a model of multicultural education that affirms all the students in our schools will be proposed. Finally, the last chapter will propose a number of approaches and strategies that teachers and schools can use to implement multicultural education.

SOME ASSUMPTIONS

It is necessary to clarify a number of assumptions embedded in the text. The first concerns who is included in multicultural education. My perspective is that multicultural education is for everyone regardless of ethnicity, race, language, social class, religion, gender, or sexual preference. My framework for multicultural education is thus a very broad and inclusive one. Nevertheless, although I refer in the text to many kinds of differences, I am particularly concerned with race, ethnicity, and language. These are the major issues that provide a lens through which I view multicultural education. This perspective is probably based on a number of reasons, not the least of which is my own experience. Another reason concerns the very history of multicultural education. A direct outgrowth of the civil rights movement, multicultural and bilingual education was developed as a response to inequality in education based on racism, ethnocentrism, and language discrimination. Although I believe it is imperative to include other differences, for me it is necessary to approach an understanding of multicultural education with a firm grounding in these three areas.

This brings up another dilemma related to inclusion. It is easier for some educators to embrace a very inclusive and comprehensive framework of multicultural education because they have a hard time facing racism. They may prefer to deal with issues of class, exceptionality, or religious diversity because, for them, these factors may be easier to confront. Racism is an excruciatingly difficult issue for most of us. Given our history of exclusion and discrimination, this is not surprising. Nevertheless, I believe it is only through a thorough investigation of discrimination based on race and other differences related to it that we can understand the genesis as well as the rationale for multicultural education. I will also refer to gender, social class, and exceptionality because these areas provide other important lenses with which to view inequality in education. However, because no one book can possibly give all of these issues the central importance they deserve, I have chosen to focus on race, ethnicity, and language.

Another assumption that guides this book is that teachers should not be singled out as the villains in the failure of so many students. Although some teachers do indeed bear the responsibility for having low expectations, being racist and elitist in their interactions with students and parents, and providing educational environments that discourage many students from learning, most do not do so consciously. Most teachers are sincerely concerned about their students and want very much to provide the best education they can. Nevertheless, they are often at the mercy of decisions made by others far removed from the classroom. In addition, they have little to do with developing the policies and practices in operation in their schools and frequently do not even question them.

Teachers are also the products of educational systems that have a history of racism, exclusion, and debilitating pedagogy. As such, they put into practice what they themselves have been subjected to and thus perpetuate structures that may be harmful to many of their students. Furthermore, the disempowerment felt by so many teachers is a palpable force in many schools. Finally, schools cannot be separated from communities or from our society in general. Oppressive forces that limit opportunities in the schools are a reflection of such forces in the society at large. Thus, the purpose of this book is not to point a finger but to provide a forum for reflection and discussion so that teachers take responsibility for their own actions, challenge the actions of schools and society that affect their students' education, and help effect positive change.

CONCLUSION

Writing a book that can offer interesting and useful insights into education in a highly complex and diverse society such as ours is an exceedingly difficult task. There are numerous pitfalls in such an endeavor. The major one, of course, is presenting information that can be overgeneralized to the point that it becomes just another harmful stereotype. One may reach the conclusion that Vietnamese students such as Vinh, for instance, are always successful in school because their culture reinforces academic success. This, we know, is neither a complete nor a wholly satisfactory explanation for what is a very complex matter because it neglects to explore the role of teachers' expectations and tracking, among many other factors, on school achievement.

Another pitfall, related to the first, is the tendency to oversimplify the experiences of students so that some crucial factors in their schooling are overlooked. We can conclude, for example, that Manuel's ''problem'' was that he did not speak English and therefore had a difficult time adjusting to school and to U.S. society in general. In this case, we may fail to take into account a community's reluctance to accept languages other than English as legitimate, even though a particularly effective bilingual program may be in place.

I have tried in this book to consider schooling as a dynamic process in which competing interests and values are at work every day in complex and often contradictory ways: Students' and community expectations are often pitted against teachers' and school expectations; the structures and organization of schools are sometimes diametrically opposed to what is developmentally appropriate for young people; and racial, gender, class, and language stratification are frequently used to explain the success or failure of students. All of these forces working with and often against one another can help us begin to understand the experiences of students in a multicultural society.

NOTES

1. Richard Rodriguez, *Hunger of Memory: The Education of Richard Rodriguez,* (Boston: David R. Godine, 1982), p. 27.
2. Tove Skutnabb-Kangas and Jim Cummins, eds., *Minority Education: From Shame to Struggle* (Clevedon, Eng.: Multilingual Matters, 1988).

Developing a Conceptual Framework: Multicultural Education in a Sociopolitical Context

OVERVIEW

Multicultural education cannot be understood in a vacuum. Yet it is often presented as somehow divorced from the policies and practices of schools and from the society in which we live. The result is a fairyland kind of multicultural education disassociated from the lives of teachers, students, and their communities. The premise of this book is quite different: *No educational philosophy or program is worthwhile unless it focuses on two primary concerns:*

- *Raising the achievement of all students and thus providing them with an equal and equitable education*
- *Giving students the opportunity to become critical and productive members of a democratic society*

To the extent that it remains education to help students get along or to help them feel better about themselves or to "sensitize" them to one another, without tackling the central but far more difficult issues of stratification, empowerment, and inequity, multicultural education becomes another approach that simply scratches the surface of educational failure. Although we may all want our students to get along and to be sensitive to and respect one another, this by itself will make little difference when it comes to the options they have as a result of their schooling. Because the choices they make are inexorably affected by social and political forces in schools and society, it is necessary to consider them in our understanding of multicultural education.

Equal education in this context goes beyond providing the same resources and opportunities for all students, although this alone would be a crucial step in affording a better education for a wide variety of students. By remaining at this level, however, it completely misses the point that education is a two-way process. That is, education must involve the interaction of students with teachers and schools, not simply the action of teachers and schools on students. Equal education thus also means that the skills, talents, and experiences that all students bring to their education need to be considered valid starting points for further schooling. *Equity* is a more comprehensive term because it includes equal educational opportunities while at the same time demanding fairness and the real possibility of *equality of outcomes* for a broader range of students. Throughout this book, multicultural education will be considered as fundamental to educational equity.

The purpose of Part I is to develop a conceptual framework for multicultural education that takes into account the sociopolitical context in which schooling takes place. In analyzing education within this context, factors that may affect the success or failure of students will be reviewed, including the persistence of racism and discrimination, structural factors within schools, and cultural and linguistic differences. It should be stressed, however, that it is not always easy to ascribe a causal relationship to these factors. That is, we cannot say that racism inevitably leads to educational failure or that the lack of tracking will result in educational success for all students. Educational achievement is a much more complicated issue and cannot be reduced to a simple cause-effect argument. Nevertheless, these factors need to be taken into consideration to understand how they may influence, to varying degrees, the educational experiences of a wide variety of students.

The impact of structural, cultural, and linguistic factors on educational success or failure are highlighted through the ten case studies throughout Chapters 3 to 6 of this section. Case studies are placed within a particular chapter because the themes that emerge from each have relevance for the issues discussed there. Nevertheless, each of the case studies brings up numerous issues discussed in other chapters. Thus, for example, although Linda's case study is placed after Chapter 3 because it focuses on racism and its impact on school achievement, it also concerns such issues as teacher expectations and multicultural curriculum. Although her particular experience highlights one issue for us, no exploration of the schooling experiences of students from diverse backgrounds can overlook any of these overarching dimensions in its analysis.

Our public schools are unsuccessful with too many students, primarily, although certainly not limited to, those from culturally and linguistically diverse and poor families. Why schools fail to meet their mission to provide all students with an equal and high-quality education has been the subject of educational research for some time. Although theories about *cultural deprivation* and *genetic inferiority* no longer hold the great appeal they once did, the subtle implications of these *deficit theories* continue to have an impact on educational policies and practices. *Deficit theories* refer to the assumption that some children, because of genetic, cultural, or experiential differences, are inferior to other children; that is, they have a *deficit*. One problem with such hypotheses is that they place complete responsibility for children's failure on their homes and families, thus removing any responsibility on the part of the school or society. Whether the focus is on the individual or the community, the result remains largely the same: blaming the victims of poor schooling rather than looking in a more systematic way at the schools in which they learn (or fail to learn) and the society at large, which they reflect and with which they interact. All of these factors need to be explored together.

Another problem is that such theories focus on situations that are out of the control of most teachers, schools, and even students. Teachers and schools can do little to alleviate the poverty and other oppressive forces in which their students live. It is more realistic to tackle those problems that they *can* do something about, among them, providing educational environments that encourage all students to learn to the best of their potential.

Part I begins with a rationale for using case studies. In Chapter 1, the case study approach is described and the students in the case studies are briefly introduced. Chapter 2 provides an explanation of the terms used throughout the text. Thus, this chapter underscores the important connection between language use and multicultural education.

Chapter 3 centers on racism, other forms of discrimination, and expectations of student abilities and their influence on learning. Chapter 4 focuses on structural factors within schools that may affect learning: tracking practices; discipline policies; the curriculum; and the limited role of teachers, students, and parents. How cultural issues might affect the educational experiences of students is explored in Chapter 5. The final chapter in Part I focuses on linguistic differences. Specifically, it considers bilingual education as a necessary and important component of multicultural education and as one response to linguistic diversity.

CHAPTER 1

Why the Case Study Approach?

Educational researchers, teachers, and policymakers have all had their say in what causes school achievement or failure. The voices of students are rarely heard in the sometimes heated debate surrounding school failure and success. The experiences of students from disempowered and dominated communities are usually even more invisible. Case studies provide an important vehicle for these voices. In the case studies in this book, young people speak freely about their schooling, their families, and their communities. They "think out loud," so to speak, about what they like and dislike about school, teachers who have made a difference in their lives, their culture and language, and what they expect to get out of school. Through the case studies, it is hoped that readers will hear not only the students' pain and conflict but also their determination and hope. The fervor with which these youths speak of their families and communities, the eloquence they display in discussing missed opportunities at such tender ages, and the feeling with which they talk about their future are a confirmation of their soaring ideals and aspirations.

CASE STUDIES: A MOSAIC OF STUDENTS IN U.S. SCHOOLS

The case studies in this book have been carefully selected to give readers a glimpse into the mosaic of the student body in U.S. classrooms, the citizens of the twenty-first century. They represent a number of racial, ethnic, linguistic, and social class groups, as well as both sexes. They live in various geographical locations and in settings as diverse as large cities or small rural areas. They are first-, second-, or third-generation Americans, or their ancestors may have been here for many hundreds or even thousands of years. They range from students from poor families to those from solidly middle-class families. In this way, they provide important dimensions of the diversity in our society. These students, however, share one common characteristic, which may not be true of many of their peers: They can be considered "successful" students. Although there may be disagreements about what it means to be successful (research by Fine and Felice, for example, has suggested that sometimes the most "successful" students are those who drop out of school),[1] the students in these case studies have been able to develop both academic skills and positive attitudes about themselves and about the value of education. They generally have good grades, most have hopes (but not always plans) of attending college, and most have fairly positive perceptions of school.

The students in the case studies are young men and women of high school age who have had a variety of experiences in schools in the United States and, in some cases, in other countries as well. Adolescents of high school age were selected because they are generally able to think about and articulate their own experiences in a more reflective and analytical manner than younger students. In addition, they can discuss not only their present experiences but also those of their past, providing an important continuity. Because most books on multicultural education have been designed with an elementary school population in mind, this has unwittingly reinforced the perception that multicultural education is only for younger children, that it cannot be included in the more "rigorous" requirements of the high school, and that it is a frill unrelated to important curriculum. The focus on secondary school students is a challenge to that perception.

The case studies present ten young men and women from diverse racial, cultural, linguistic, geographic, and economic backgrounds. They were chosen to represent the vastly changing demographics in U.S. society. These changes are important for us to understand in preparing to teach the students of the future. Consider the following:

> Our population is currently over 80 percent White, with 12 percent Black, 6.4 percent Latino, and 1.6 percent Asian. However, by the year 2050, the White population is expected to decrease to 60 percent, with the Black community increasing slightly, Asians increasing tenfold, and Latinos almost tripling in number. By the last quarter of the next century, those who are now referred to as "minority" are expected to be in the majority.

> These changes will be apparent in the schools as well. Right now, 22 of the 25 largest central-city school districts in the nation are already predominately Black and Latino, although only about 27 percent of our public school enrollment is made up of children of color. This percentage is expected to increase substantially by the beginning of the century.

> It is estimated that the number of children who speak a language other than English will rise from just over 2 million in 1986 to over 5 million by 2020.

> The percentage of teachers of color has been decreasing steadily. For example, whereas the percentage of African American students in our public schools is 16.2 percent, only 6.9 percent of the teachers are African American; American Indian and Alaska Native students make up 0.9 percent of student enrollment, with teachers from these groups making up only 0.6 percent of the teaching force. At present, 91 percent of our teaching force is White and English-speaking. This percentage is expected to increase even more.

> Among bilingual teachers, where one would expect to see a large number of linguistic minority teachers, the percentage of those who are of the same national

origin as their students is small. Thus, for example, only about 15 percent of bilingual teachers are Hispanic.[2]

The implications of these changing demographics for teacher education, staff development, and educational reform are enormous. These will be considered at length in the following chapters.

DEFINING THE CASE STUDY APPROACH

The case study approach should be understood within the framework of qualitative research. It is defined by Merriam as "an intensive, holistic description and analysis of a bounded phenomenon such as a program, an institution, a person, a process, or a social unit."[3] She further describes the four essential characteristics of a qualitative case study as *particularistic* (focusing on one person or social unit), *descriptive* (the end product is a rich, thick description), *heuristic* (because it illuminates the reader's understanding and brings about the discovery of new meanings), and *inductive* (because generalizations and hypotheses emerge from the examination of the data).[4] The purpose of using this particular methodology is to gain a deeper understanding of specific issues and problems related to educational practice. Case studies can help us look at particular situations so that solutions for more general situations can be hypothesized and developed. According to Erickson, practitioners can learn from a case study *"even if the circumstances of the case do not match those of their own situation."*[5] Although not meant to generalize to all cases, the particular situations presented and analyzed can help illustrate some general problems in education.

The thoughts and insights of these students are used as the basis for understanding how the presence or absence of multicultural education, as broadly defined in Chapter 8, might affect their educational experiences and those of others. All ten are presented contextually within the cultural and social environment in which they find themselves. Thus, these case studies are *ethnographic case studies*; that is, they use a sociocultural analysis of each of the students.[6] The reader will note, for example, that all of them are described within a variety of settings; home, school, community, and city or town in which they live. By looking at each of these settings, we gain a more complete and contextualized picture of their lives.

The use of case studies is not meant to generalize to all students within schools in the United States. No research, whether qualitative or quantitative, can expect to do so. The issue of *sampling* provides one of the major differences between qualitative and quantitative research. Reginald Clark, in case study research with families of successful and unsuccessful Black students, says that the families he studied represented not a *sample*, as might be the case with quantitative research, but rather *examples* of a wide variety of families. This kind of research provides the possibility of generating sound hypotheses from even a small number of case studies.[7] For example, although James is not meant to represent all Lebanese students in U.S. schools, his lived experience as one such student presented within its sociocultural framework can illuminate our understanding of other Lebanese students. Whereas quantitative methods may yield some important data about Lebanese students in general, it is only through a qualitative approach that one can explore more deeply, for example, the impact that being an "invisible minority" has had on James. Qualitative approaches can sometimes render very distinct but equally important data to influence our educational practice.

It is important to underscore that no case study of a single individual can adequately or legitimately portray the complexity of an entire group of people. Not all Mexican Americans learn cooperatively and not all African Americans perceive school success as "acting White." To reach this conclusion contradicts the very purpose of the case studies, for gross stereotypes are the inevitable result. It is important then, to understand each of the case studies as *one example* of the ethnic experience within the United States rather than as *the model* by which all students of a particular group should be understood. Although it is always easy to overgeneralize, it is hoped that the complexity of the case studies themselves will help to counter this tendency.

CHALLENGING STEREOTYPES

The students in the case studies range in age from 13 to 19. At the time of the study, two were almost graduating from high school, two were in junior high school, and the others were at different levels of high school. There are an equal number of males and females. They range from monolingual, English-speaking youths to fluent bilinguals. Their economic backgrounds range from poor working class to professional middle class. The communities in which they live reflect this economic diversity as well, from poor inner-city neighborhoods in large urban areas to middle-class residential communities in small towns. Their family structures vary from very large (eleven children) to very small (only child), in both one- and two-parent households. Their parents' educational backgrounds vary as well, from no high school education to a doctorate.

These case studies are meant to challenge you to ask questions rather than to make assumptions about what it means to be Vietnamese, African American, Mexican, or anything else. Because it is far too easy to pigeonhole people according to our own predetermined conceptions and biases, the struggle here is to try to understand these young people on their own terms. Some of their experiences, feelings, and statements may surprise you and shake some deep-seated beliefs. So much the better if they do. Some of them may also reinforce some of your own experiences with young people of diverse backgrounds. In either case, what these students say should be understood within the context of the particular school experiences, families, and communities from which they come.

It can be said that the students in these case studies are both typical and atypical of their ethnic, racial, or linguistic group. This is as it should be. The purpose of these case studies is not to perpetuate stereotypes but to question and even shatter them. Nevertheless, because the issues and perspectives that these students present are probably similar to those of other young people of their background, they can help us better understand and appreciate the particular issues they may face on a daily basis. At the same time, each of their experiences is quite unique and should be understood as such. None of these students is a walking stereotype. The purpose is thus not to understand "The Black Experience" or "The Puerto Rican Experience" as an isolated and hypothetical phenomenon but instead to expose us to *one* of the many experiences within that broader context.

FORMAT OF THE CASE STUDIES

Each case begins with a contextual description of the individual under study: a short description of the student's family, school, community, and ethnic group, along with other information that was deemed important. Following are the words of the student, categorized according to themes that were suggested by the interviews. In each case, there are between three and four themes.

After I listened carefully to the tapes several times, I determined the primary themes by thinking about what each student seemed to be saying and what she or he returned to time after time. I divided the case study into these themes and wrote it up in this way. For easier accessibility, I omitted most of the common "fillers," including *well, um, you know, and,* and *but* statements, as well as false starts. I then gave the case study to the person who had actually done the interviews for review and corroboration of the data and themes. When interviewers felt that the student had been appropriately portrayed and that we had caught the essence of his or her message, the case study was completed. The interviewers also made a number of suggestions for revision, inclusion, or removal, most of which were followed. However, although I am most grateful for their recommendations and insights, I myself must take final responsibility for the case studies, especially for any errors or oversights that may be present.

You will notice that the themes are sometimes quite similar across several students and revolve around issues of family, language, culture, and community. The guiding questions used for the interviews centered on these particular concerns to determine how they might affect school experiences and success. The interviews themselves were quite informal, with the suggested questions used primarily as a guide and springboard for further dialogue. Generally, each student was interviewed several times for a total of three to four hours. When the interviews were transcribed, the students' words were clustered according to the themes that emerged in each case. That is the reason for the ellipses that you will see throughout the case studies. They mean that the upcoming statement may not have been made immediately after the preceding one. Thus, when Yolanda discussed family, for example, all of her thoughts on this theme were placed together in the case study even though she may have said things at different times. This method makes clear the concerns each student emphasized.

SELECTION OF STUDENTS

The students in the case studies were selected in a number of ways. Those doing the interviews usually attempted to find students through community or informal channels rather than through the school, although in some cases teachers or counselors were consulted. In addition, most students were interviewed at home or in a community setting, away from school, but this was also not always true. The only requirement in selecting a student was that she or he be from a particular background in order to give us the diversity we were looking for.

All but two of the students are from Massachusetts, although the locations in which they live and go to school are vastly different, ranging from large, urban, ethnically diverse cities to small, rural, and almost totally culturally and socially homogeneous towns.

To maintain confidentiality, pseudonyms are used for the students and for the towns or cities in which they live, unless they are from a large urban area such as Boston. The names of their schools, teachers, and family members have also been changed. Naturally, all of the students and their families gave us permission to tape their interviews and to use the results in this book.

Students were selected for the case studies in a number of what turned out to be serendipitous ways. In one case, for example, Haydée Font, a graduate student at the University of Massachusetts, asked the director of a university tutoring program for linguistic minority students to suggest a Vietnamese student to interview. When she called to get his number, the operator gave her the number of *another* Vietnamese family in town, obviously confusing the last name. The young girl who answered informed Haydée that it was another family she was looking for. However, she suggested that her older brother who was *also* at the high school would be happy to talk with Haydée. This is how Vinh was found. In the case of James, Diane Sweet went to a local Arab American bakery. After speaking informally with the proprietor, she was able to get the name of a local Lebanese family with a son who was studying at a nearby high school. The owner called James's mother on the spot, and she agreed instantly to have James speak with Diane. Linda was found through a local music department at a high school in Boston, and Yolanda was discovered through a high school counselor in southern California.

FOCUS ON SUCCESSFUL STUDENTS

After reviewing the preliminary interviews and transcripts, we discovered that all of the students we had interviewed could be classified as successful. We thought more carefully about what it meant to be successful and determined that we would consider them to be so if most of the following conditions were met:

- They were still in school and were planning to complete high school or in fact had just recently graduated.
- They had good grades, although they did not have to be at or near the top of their class.
- They had thought about their future and had made some plans for it.
- They generally enjoyed school and felt engaged in it.
- They were critical of their own school experiences and that of their peers.
- Most important, they described themselves as successful.

Although most of the students had thought about continuing their education, definite college plans were not considered a prerequisite for classifying them as successful students. For example, Manuel was graduating from high school and thought vaguely about college, but he had no actual plans. Just the fact that he was the first in his family to graduate from high school, the pride he felt in this accomplishment, and the importance he gave to an education were enough to classify him as successful.

This is not to suggest that college attendance is the primary criterion for being a successful, intelligent, or well-adjusted student. Nevertheless, it is an important consideration to keep in mind precisely because so many students of color and poor students have been effectively denied the opportunity to receive a high-quality education or even to dream of going on to college. That many of the students in these case studies have done so in spite of expectations to the contrary is important to explore if we are serious about providing equal educational opportunity to all students. To dismiss college aspirations as a middle-class, White value thus begs the question of why some students remain in school, with high hopes for their future, whereas others drop out, disillusioned and frustrated by an educational experience that has done little to motivate them. The hope for college or for some form of higher learning is one indication that these students believe that they are capable and worthy of the very best education. Thus, it was considered important in an exploration of what it means to be a successful student.

It was also clear that all of these students felt that they were *entitled* to a good education and were working hard for it. Nevertheless, they were all eager to talk about problems with school as well. That is, they felt free to critique their education and that of other students who had not been as fortunate as they had in school. They were anxious to give us examples of what would make school a better and more rewarding experience for all students.

Although it had not been our initial intention to focus exclusively on successful students, it was interesting that all of the students who we sought out and who agreed to speak with us were indeed successful. This fact surprised us somewhat, but on closer reflection it seemed logical that students who are successful in school are more likely to want to talk about their experiences than those who are not. It was at this point that I decided to explore what it was about these specific students' experiences that helped them become successful in school, focusing on home, school, and community resources, attitudes, and activities. The focus on academically successful students emerged as a result of the interviews; it was not an original objective of the research.

By focusing on successful students, we can gain a clearer understanding of the conditions, experiences, and resources in their schools, homes, and communities that have helped them succeed. Because the students represent so many different cultural experiences and values, some of these conditions may be quite different. Nevertheless, most of the students, as you will see, report very similar *conditions*, albeit within a broad range of environments, that seem to have helped them. These environments were explored further in an attempt to reach some conclusions about the conditions for success that families, schools, and communities together can provide.

Another quite unexpected result of the research was that the interviews themselves were empowering to the students. In every case, they looked forward to and enjoyed being interviewed. They eagerly accepted the opportunity to discuss their families, school experiences, and cultures. More than one mentioned that it was the first time anybody had ever bothered to ask these kinds of questions. Interestingly, the questions themselves became sources of dialogue and illumination for the students. When Fern was asked, for example, what was special about being an American Indian, she said, "Getting picked for things like this." After her first interview, Linda said that she couldn't wait for the next one. Some of the students had never considered the issues that emerged through the interviews. James clearly became more aware of the implications of the exclusion of Arab Americans from the multicultural fair at his school although he had not reflected in depth on it before.

The lessons about the empowerment that can take place through dialogue should not be lost on teachers. That is, not only can we learn something from students about their cultures and languages through interviews, but indeed dialogue of this kind can and should become an important pedagogical strategy in itself. This also has implications for using oral histories in the development of literacy and fostering parent and community involvement in the schools.

PLACEMENT OF THE CASE STUDIES IN CHAPTERS

Each of the case studies is included after the end of a particular chapter with an eye toward illuminating problems from the perspective of students who have lived through them. This is not meant to suggest that these young people are unidimensional or that they focused on only one issue. In fact, the interviews revealed a profound awareness on the part of the students of the interplay of factors that have contributed to their success in school as well as those that have held them back from achieving even more. Nevertheless, placing each case study after the end of a chapter helps us to focus on the issues addressed in that chapter.

Following Chapter 3, you will read three case studies. Linda Howard and Rich Miller speak eloquently about how racism, discrimination, and teacher expectations have affected them. This does not mean, of course, that they are unconcerned about other issues. Nevertheless, both expressed more than others the pain, distress, and consequences of racism and discrimination in their lives. You will also find Vanessa Mattison's case study, included here for quite a different reason. In her case, the issues of race, culture, and diversity were so detached from her experience that they became invisible, although she was not unconcerned about them. It was important to place Vanessa's case study in the context of those who have to face the dilemmas of diversity, discrimination, and racism on a daily basis and to explore why their experiences are so different.

The case studies of Fern Sherman and Avi Abramson follow Chapter 4, in which structural factors within schools that help or hinder students' achievement are discussed. Both Fern and Avi reflected carefully on these issues. The concerns are different in each case, however. For example, Avi focused on school structures with a value system profoundly different from his. Fern talked about the isolation of being the only American Indian in her school. In Chapter 5, cultural issues and how these may affect learning are explored. Here, the stories of Marisol Martinez, James Karam, and Hoang Vinh are included. The invisibility of his culture is crucial in understanding James's story. How Marisol's culture has been maligned or denied and her ambivalence toward it is apparent in her case study. Vinh poignantly describes the impact of immigration, separation from family, and cultural clash on his life. How all three of them are nevertheless able to counteract negative messages is important for all teachers to learn.

The tremendous influence of language and linguistic diversity in learning will be considered in Chapter 6. The cases of Manuel Gomes and Yolanda Piedra are included here. Manuel, a Cape Verdean who is the first in his family to graduate from high school, is compelling because of the role that bilingual education and Cape Verdean teachers had in his school success. Yolanda's story is important because it focuses on how her language is seen in a positive light within the school, even though she is not in a bilingual program.

Although the students in these case studies are unique, interesting, and even fascinating, they are not exceptional. In the sense that they are unlike anybody else and may have particular talents and experiences, they are of course different. Nevertheless, they are not exceptional because young people such as these are all around us. We did not have to go to extraordinary measures to find them. They are the girls and boys in our local urban, rural, or suburban schools. They can be found on our sports teams, in our communities, and in our places of worship. They are in our English and math classes, bilingual and monolingual programs, and special education and gifted and talented programs. All we have to do is speak to them and listen to what they have to tell us. Just as you may find the stories of these particular students engaging, the stories of the students in your own classrooms will be just as educational.

It is hoped that each of these stories will be read critically and with an eye toward understanding how the experiences and thoughts of young people can influence classroom discourse and strategies. These ten students demonstrate that all the students in our classrooms are capable of learning and being successful in school. Although their stories prove the indomitable strength of youth, they also demonstrate the tremendous fragility of academic success and how it can be so easily disrupted by a poor teacher, a negative comment, or an environment that denies the importance of one's experiences. In the final analysis, though, all of their voices challenge us as teachers and as a society to do the very best we can to ensure that educational equity is not an illusion but an achievable goal.

NOTES

1. See Michelle Fine, "Perspectives on Inequity: Voices from Urban Schools," in *Applied Social Psychology Annual IV*, ed. Leonard Brickman (Beverly Hills, CA: Sage Publications, 1983); Lawrence G. Felice, "Black Student Dropout Behavior: Disengagement from School Rejection and Racial Discrimination," *Journal of Negro Education*, 50 (1981), 415–424.
2. See *New Voices: Immigrant Students in U.S. Public Schools* (Boston: National Coalition of Advocates for Students, 1988); Ray Valdivieso and Cary David, *U.S. Hispanics: Challenging Issues for the 1990s* (Washington, DC: Population Trends and Public Policy, December 1988); Gary Natriello, Edward L. McDill, and Aaron M. Pallas, *Schooling Disadvantaged Children: Racing Against Catastrophe* (New York: Teachers College Press, 1990); *Hispanic Education: A Statistical Portrait 1990* (Washington, DC: National Council of La Raza, 1990); The Quality Education for Minorities Project, *Education That Works: An Action Plan for the Education of Minorities* (Cambridge: Massachusetts Institute of Technology, January 1990); E. Emily Feistritzer, *Teacher Crisis: Myth or Reality? A State-by-State Analysis, 1986* (Washington, DC: National Center for Education Information, 1986).
3. Sharan B. Merriam, *Case Study Research in Education: A Qualitative Approach* (San Francisco: Jossey-Bass, 1988).
4. Ibid.
5. Frederick Erickson, "Qualitative Methods in Research on Teaching," in *Handbook of Research on Teaching*, 3rd ed., ed. Merlin C. Wittrock (New York: Macmillan, 1986; emphasis added).
6. Merriam, *Case Study Research in Education*.
7. Reginald M. Clark, *Family Life and School Achievement: Why Poor Black Children Succeed or Fail* (Chicago: University of Chicago Press, 1983).

CHAPTER 2

About Language

Language is always changing. It responds to social, economic, and political events and is therefore an important barometer and descriptor of a society at any given point. Language also becomes obsolete; it could not be otherwise because it is a reflection of societal changes. The shift in terminology over the years, for example, from *Negro* to *Black* to *Afro-American* and more recently to *African American*, is a case in point. Such changes often represent deliberate attempts by a group to name or rename itself. This is not only a linguistic decision but a political one as well, and one that responds to the need for self-determination and autonomy. Of equal importance are the changes in the terms describing people that reflect an attempt to be more precise and correct. In this sense, *African American* may be a more accurate term than *Black* because it implies a cultural base rather than only color or racial differences. This term recognizes that race, in spite of its overarching importance in a society rigidly stratified along racial lines, does not define the complexity of a people in the same way as do race and culture together.

Language is particularly important in multicultural education for it describes and defines people of many different groups. It is certainly true that we have not always been appropriate or sensitive in our use of words to describe people. In its most blatant form, this insensitivity can be seen in the racial and ethnic epithets that even our youngest children seem to know. It is also evident in more subtle examples, such as the observation made by Allport many years ago that the refusal of southern newspapers to capitalize *negro* was meant to diminish the importance of Blacks or the stereotypical connotations that certain words unrelated to ethnicity develop over time—*inscrutable* is almost automatically associated with Asians, *rhythm* with African Americans.[1] Although these words are not negative in and of themselves, they become code words for simplifying the experience of and, in the process, disparaging an entire group of people.

MAKING CHOICES ABOUT WHAT TERMS TO USE

In an attempt to be both sensitive and appropriate in the use of language, I prefer and use in this book particular words or terms over others. My purpose here is not to suggest that they are ''politically correct'' or that these are the only terms that should be used but rather to describe my own thinking on the language we use and propose that others go through a similar process in determining what language is most useful, precise, and appropriate for them.

I have generally, although not always, based my choice of terms on two major criteria:

1. What do the people in question want to be called?
2. What is the most precise term?

I have answered these questions by talking with people from the groups in question, reading current research, and listening to debates regarding the use of terms. As our language is always tentative, so are the choices that I have made. New terms may evolve tomorrow. Such is the inexactitude of language that it can never completely capture the complexity of our lives.

In some cases, I have chosen to use two or more terms, sometimes interchangeably, because each may have meanings important in particular contexts. In these and other cases, I have sometimes made choices that I would not have made a decade ago. For example, for years I used only the term *Native American* for the many indigenous nations in the Western Hemisphere. During the late 1960s this seemed to become the preferred term. It reflected a people's determination to name themselves and to have others recognize them as the original inhabitants of these lands.

Nevertheless, the use of this term seems to have declined recently and I have decided to use also the terms *Indian* or *American Indian* within this text. I have done so for several reasons. First, in gatherings of indigenous peoples over the years, I have noted that among themselves, they generally use the term *Indian*. Second, a number of Indian students have directly confirmed its use. It was explained to me that it is not so much that the term *Native American* has been abandoned but rather that some of their communities had never really adopted it. Another student told me that it has become a confusing term because it is often used by others to mean a citizen of the United States whose ancestors came from Europe long ago (i.e., who is now *native* to this land). Nonetheless, you will notice that Fern, one of the young women in the case studies, consciously refers to herself as Native American, thus reminding us that language is never monolithic.

Chicano, a term popular in the late 1960s and early 1970s, was a decidedly self-affirming and political term reflecting the unique culture and realities of urban, economically oppressed Mexican Americans in U.S. society. Its use in the recent past, however, seems to have been largely abandoned by many segments of the community, and the more descriptive but less political term *Mexican American* appears to be back in common use. Although used by scholars and activists, *Chicano* was never wholly accepted in the community. *Mexican*, on the other hand, is used generally to refer to those who are the first generation to come from Mexico. I have decided to use all of these terms within their appropriate contexts because each has connotations that must not be lost.[2] Yolanda, in the case studies, refers to herself as Mexican because she is a first-generation immigrant. Some classmates whose families have been here longer would probably choose other terms.

In this text, the terms *Hispanic* and *Latino* are also used more or less interchangeably to refer to people of Latin American and Caribbean heritage. Although I generally prefer the term *Latino* because it is more inclusive of the African and indigenous heritage and not only the Spanish heritage of these groups, *Hispanic* is more widespread and well known. Unlike *European, African, Latin American,* or *Asian,* however, it does not refer to a particular continent or country (there is no continent named *Hispania*). *Latino,* on the other hand, has the disadvantage of having a sexist connotation when used to refer to a mixed group rather than to a specific man. Neither term, however, is used when the more precise ethnic name is available. For example, Marisol, one of the Latina students in the case studies, is referred to as Puerto Rican; Yolanda, the other Latina, is referred to as Mexican. Whenever possible, these distinctions will be made because otherwise fundamental differences in ethnicity, national origin, self-identification, and length of time in this country are easily overlooked.[3]

White people, as the majority in U.S. society, do not often think of themselves as *ethnic,* which is a term they reserve for other, more easily identifiable groups. Nevertheless, the fact that we are all ethnic, whether we choose to manifest it or not, is undeniable. This is one of the reasons I have opted to use the term *European American* rather than *White* in most cases in this book. Although most Whites do not generally refer to themselves as European American, I have chosen to do so to highlight the ethnicity in us all. Whiteness is an important factor, but it is not an exclusively determining one in defining a group. The term *European American* also implies *culture,* something that many European Americans lament they do not have. This is nonsense, of course. Everybody has a culture, whether clearly manifested in its more traditional forms or not.

Many European Americans are a mixture of several European ethnic groups. A person may be German, Irish, and Italian, for example, and not speak any of the languages or follow any of the rituals associated with those cultures. It is reasonable to ask, in this case, why such people should be called *European American* when in effect they are "as American as apple pie." They may never have even visited Europe, for example, or may not at all identify with a European heritage. Nevertheless, they are European Americans because their habits, values, and behaviors are grounded in European mores and values, although these were later adapted and modified to create a different culture within the United States. Because Whites in U.S. society tend to think of themselves as the "norm," they often view other groups as "ethnic" and therefore somewhat exotic and colorful. This issue is very clear in Vanessa's case study. By using the term *European American,* I hope to challenge Whites also to see and define themselves in ethnic terms.

I have chosen not to use the term *Anglo* or *Anglo-American* except when speaking specifically of those with an English heritage. It is an inaccurate term if used to refer to most Whites in the United States, who are not English in origin but represent a wide variety of ethnic groups from European societies. Classifying all Whites in this way is a gross overgeneralization. If it is used to contrast English speakers from speakers of other languages, it is equally inaccurate because African Americans, among others whose native language is English, are not included in this grouping. Finally, it is a term that is rejected by some, not the least of whom are Irish Americans, who are often understandably offended at being identified with an English heritage.

My choices were not made easily. In the case of race, the concept itself has come in for a great deal of criticism because, in scientific terms, *race* does not exist and is often simply used to oppress further entire groups of people for their supposed racial differences. Yet there is really only one race, and that is the human race. There is no scientific evidence that racial groups differ in any biologically or genetically significant ways. Differences that do exist are primarily social; that is, they are based on one's experiences within a particular ethnic group.

However, the problem with using terms that emphasize *culture* rather than *race* is that they tend to obscure the very real issue of racism in society. My use of language is in no way meant to do so but rather to stress the fact that race alone does not define us. For example, African Americans and Haitians are both Black. They share some basic cultural characteristics and are both subjected to racist attitudes and behaviors in the United States. Nevertheless, the unique ethnicity of each is overlooked or even denied if we simply call both groups Black rather then also identifying them ethnically. This is particularly true of native language use, which is often obliterated when we group people together only by race. However, I have also decided to use terms that refer specifically to race when they are warranted. In speaking of segregated schools, for example, it makes sense to refer to Black and White students rather than to African American and European American students, as race is the salient issue here. In this way, I also hope to underscore the fact that there are always differences of opinion about the use of various terms. This kind of debate is occurring now about the use of *African American* or *Black* as the preferred term in the Black community.

You will notice that the terms *White* and *Black*, when used, are capitalized. I have chosen to do so because they refer to groups of people, as do such terms as *Latino, Asian*, and *African*. As such, they deserve to be capitalized. Although these are not the scientific terms for races, terms such as *Negroid* and *Caucasian* are no longer used in everyday speech or are rejected by the people to whom they refer. These more commonly used words, then, should be treated as the terms of preference.

Another term used in this book is *people of color*. I use this expression rather than *minority* for a number of reasons. First, *minority* is a misnomer. It is never used to describe, for example, Swedish Americans, Albanian Americans, or Dutch Americans. Yet, strictly speaking, these groups, being a numerical minority in our society, should also be referred to as such. The term has historically been used only to refer to *racial minorities*, thus implying a status less than that accorded to other groups. In fact, even when such groups are no longer a "minority," the language by which we describe them becomes convoluted and almost comical in its effort to retain this pejorative classification. Thus, schools in which African American students become the majority are called "majority minority" schools rather than "primarily Black" schools. There seems to be a tenacious insistence on maintaining the "minority" status of some groups even when they are no longer "minority" in fact. The connection between name and low status in the use of this term is quite clear. Given this connotation, the word is offensive.

Although *people of color* is accepted and used by a growing number of African Americans, Latinos, Asians, and Native Americans, it, too, is problematic. It implies, for example, that Whites are somehow colorless; it also negates the racial mixing that is a reality among every ethnic group, no matter how insulated it may seem to be. I am thus not wholly comfortable with its use. Nevertheless, it is at this historical moment probably the most appropriate term and preferable to the others that are available. The expression is used for several reasons, however, and not only because *minority* is rejected. It is a term that encompasses those who have been labeled "minority," that is, American Indians, African Americans, Latinos, and Asian Americans. It is a term that emerged from these communities themselves. It also implies important connections among the groups and underlines some common experiences in the United States. In spite of these connections, whenever possible and for the sake of clarity, I will identify people by their particular ethnic or racial group.

LUMPING GROUPS TOGETHER

The question of lumping together people of similar backgrounds has been mentioned previously. Let me add some other points to that discussion. The term *European American*, for example, brings up a question of appropriate usage. Not all those who are White are European American, such as many Jews and some groups in the Soviet Union. Language still remains imprecise in capturing these differences. Thus, whenever possible, I attempt to use terms that are more specific rather than overarching. Overarching terms cause other problems as well. Although some groups, such as Latinos, share a great many cultural features including language, religion, and values, they are each unique ethnic groups. A Guatemalan and a Dominican, for example, may both speak Spanish, practice the Catholic religion, and share deeply rooted family values. Nevertheless, the first language of Guatemalans is often not Spanish, and Dominicans have an African background not shared by most Guatemalans. These differences, among many others, are often unacknowledged when we speak simply of *Latinos* or *Hispanic Americans*. Within the context of the U.S. experience, it is also necessary to understand differences among Latinos related to race, class, education, and length of time in the country. Each of these issues may make a dramatic difference in understanding the school achievement of children from distinct groups.

The same discussion applies to American Indians. Again, although they may share some basic cultural values and historical experiences, unique ethnic characteristics and historical frames of reference are lost when we refer to them all as *Indians*. The problems inherent in using overarching classifications such as these are evident. Therefore, every attempt will be made to disaggregate groups according to ethnicity whenever possible, that is, to refer to them by national origin. Besides being more accurate, it is also how people prefer to be called. A Bolivian, for example, refers to herself first as a Bolivian and later as a Latina; the same can be said for a Navajo, who identifies first with his Nation and second with Indians as a larger group.

Nevertheless, it is also true that there are many commonalities among all indigenous groups, as there are among most Latin American groups. These may include a worldview, a common historical experience, and shared conditions of life in the United States. Where such commonalities exist, the groups may be called by the more generalized term. In addition, I am restricted by the fact that much of the literature of both Indian and Hispanic groups makes no distinction among the ethnic groups within them. Therefore, I am sometimes obliged to use the generic term in spite of my preference to disaggregate along ethnic lines.

Finally, a word about the terms *America* and *American*. It is important to underscore that *America* refers to the Western Hemisphere, all of the Americas. Thus, whenever referring to our country, *United States* or *U.S.* will be used. *American* refers as well to all the peoples of the Americas, North, South, and Central, although it has been limited by common use to mean only U.S. citizens. Not only is this inaccurate but also it is offensive to millions of Central and South Americans, who are as much *Americans* as those living within the confines of the United States. Nevertheless, and because it is the term in common use in the United States, I have decided to use it to refer to citizens and residents of the United States. Although I considered the idea of using the term *United Stateser*, since this is in fact a more accurate term (and there is a precedent for it in Spanish in *Estadounidense*), I decided in the final analysis to stay with *American* as a more inclusive and still accurate term. That is, not only are we citizens of the United States but also we are Americans, both in the restricted U.S. sense and in the more expansive hemispheric definition.

CONCLUSION

The language choices I have made throughout this book are meant first and foremost to *affirm diversity*. Thus I have attempted, whenever possible, to identify people as they would want to be identified. I have also used terms that call people what they *are* rather than what they *are not* (e.g., I have not used terms such as *non-White* or *non-English-speaking*). I will no doubt change the terms I use in the years to come. Even now, some of them seem inaccurate and imprecise, although they are my best estimate of what is most appropriate. My choices are certainly open for debate, for language can capture only imperfectly the nuances of who we are as people. But language, like multicultural education itself, is a process that is in constant flux. We therefore need to pay close attention to the connotations and innuendos of its daily use.

NOTES

1. Gordon W. Allport, *The Nature of Prejudice* (Reading, MA: Addison-Wesley, 1954).
2. For a discussion of this issue, see Concha Delgado-Gaitán, ''Parent Perceptions of School: Supportive Environments for Children,'' in *Success or Failure? Learning and the Language Minority Student*, ed. Henry T. Trueba (Cambridge, MA: Newbury House, 1987).
3. See Gerardo Marín and Barbara Vanoss Marín, ''Methodological Fallacies When Studying Hispanics,'' *Applied Social Psychology*, 3 (1983), 99–117, for an explanation of a number of fallacies that researchers fall into when studying Hispanics that are relevant to this discussion (such as, ''When you've seen one, you've seen them all'').

CHAPTER **3**

Racism, Discrimination, and Expectations of Students' Achievement

In this chapter, we will explore the impact that racism, other forms of discrimination, and expectations of student abilities may have on achievement. These are inextricably connected with other structures, such as the policies and practices of schools including tracking, testing, and irrelevant curricula, which will be considered in Chapter 4. Cultural and linguistic differences that students bring into the school will be the subject of Chapters 5 and 6.

Separating structural issues from cultural and linguistic concerns may unfortunately create the false impression that they are unrelated phenomena. On the contrary, they play interconnected and complementary roles in the schools. Let us take the example of children who enter school speaking a language other than English. The fact that they do not speak English cannot be separated from the way in which the language they speak is viewed by the larger society or from the programmatic options the school offers, whether these be *submersion, ESL, immersion, transitional bilingual education,* or *maintenance bilingual education.* More will be said about these terms in Chapter 6. For now, we need to remember that each of these structural options has an underlying philosophy and approach with important implications for the academic achievement or failure of students with limited English proficiency. Existing societal inequities, the structure of the schools, and the culture of students and their communities must be understood in tandem. A review of research in these areas will demonstrate that children are educated differently by our schools; in addition, the differences that children bring to school have a profound effect on what they gain from their educational experiences.

In the ideal sense, education in the United States is based on the values of democracy, freedom, and equal access. In a break with the rigid systems of class and caste, on which education in most of the world was and still is founded, our educational system proposed to tear down these barriers and to provide all students with an equal education. Education was to be, as Horace Mann claimed, "the great equalizer."[1] This is a process that began in earnest in the nineteenth century through the legislation of compulsory education and that continues today through such policies as desegregation and nonsexist education. In spite of the many criticisms leveled against our educational system, it must be recognized that legislation and policies have often been aimed at eradicating many existing inequalities. The role of resistance has been equally crucial in effecting reforms in the schools. For instance, schools were not racially desegregated only because the courts ordered it, and gender-fair education was not legislated simply because Congress decided it was a good idea. In both cases, as in many others, educational opportunity was expanded because many people and communities engaged in struggle, legal or otherwise, to bring it about. Although in theory education is no longer meant to replicate society but to transform it into a true democracy, we know that such is not always the case in reality. Our schools have consistently failed to provide an equitable education for many students. The purpose of this chapter is to explore a number of reasons for this failure.

THE PERSISTENCE OF RACISM
AND DISCRIMINATION

Schools are institutions that respond to and reflect the larger society. It is therefore not surprising that racism and discrimination find their way into schools in much the same way that they find their way into other institutions such as housing, employment, and the criminal justice system. Racism and other forms of discrimination, particularly sexism, classism, ethnocentrism, and linguicism,[2] have a long history in our schools.[3] Each of these forms of discrimination is based on the perception that one ethnic group, class, gender, or language is superior to all others. In the United States, the norm generally used to measure all others is European American, upper-middle class, English-speaking, and male. Discrimination based on perceptions of superiority is part of the structure of schools; the curriculum; the education most teachers receive; and the interactions among teachers, students, and the community. Overt expressions of racism may be less frequent in the contemporary classroom than in the past. Nonetheless, no matter how infrequent, subtle, or unintentional, the effects of discriminatory attitudes and behaviors are always negative.

To separate racism and discrimination as distinct structural issues is somewhat artificial, as they affect and are related to many school practices and policies such as tracking and testing. In one study, for example, it was found that tracking and ability grouping are most commonly found in large, racially diverse, and poor communities.[4] That is, policies most likely to jeopardize students at risk of educational failure are most common precisely in the institutions in which those students are found. It is thus sometimes difficult to separate what is racist or discriminatory from what is structural.

To illustrate, let us look at a study cited by McDermott.[5] Through filmed classroom observations, it was found that a White teacher tended to have much more frequent eye contact with her White than with her Black students. Was this behavior due to racism? Was it due to cultural and communication differences? Or was poor teacher preparation responsible for her expectations and thus her behavior? These questions are impossible to answer in any clear-cut way; it is probable that all these factors played a role. The result, however, is very clear: In the cited study, the Black children had to strain three times as hard to catch the teacher's eye, looking for approval, affection, and encouragement.

Thus, in spite of the important interconnections that may exist among all of these issues, they are separated here to highlight the far-reaching and often devastating effects of racism and discrimination on students in our schools.

The results of educational achievement cannot be explained solely by family circumstance, race, gender, or language ability. Yet African American, Latino, American Indian, and poor children in general continue to achieve below grade level, drop out in much greater numbers, and go to college in much lower proportion than their middle-class and European American peers. According to a report issued by the National Coalition of Advocates for Students based on extensive hearings across the nation, African American children are three times more likely than European American children to be placed in classes for the educable mentally retarded and only one-half as likely to be in classes for the gifted; Latino students drop out of school at a rate higher than any other major group, and in some places, it is as high as 80 percent; and whereas in 1977, 50 percent of all African American high school graduates went on to college, by 1982, the rate had fallen to 36 percent.[6] If these indicators of educational failure were caused only by students' background and other social characteristics, it would be difficult to explain why they change over time and place and why students with such characteristics are successful in some classrooms and schools and not in others. The role of racism and discrimination in this underachievement cannot be discounted.

Definitions of Racism and Discrimination

Let us begin by briefly reviewing the meaning of racism in order to understand how it operates in the schools. Jones identifies three levels of racism: individual, institutional, and cultural.[7] *Individual racism* is a personal belief that people of one group are inferior to people of another because of physical traits. *Institutional racism* is manifested through established laws, customs, and practices that reflect and produce racial inequalities in society. *Cultural racism* is the belief in the inferiority of the culture of a group of people or even the belief that they have no real culture. Individual and cultural racism are belief systems that are acted on in the personal and individual spheres, whereas institutional racism is demonstrated primarily through the policies and practices of institutions, which directly affect those discriminated against *as a class:* schools, the justice system, housing, the legal system, established religions, and labor unions, for example.

We need to understand the important role that *power* plays in institutional racism. It is primarily through the power of the people who control these institutions that racist policies and practices are reinforced and legitimized. Furthermore, when we understand racism as a systemic problem and not only as an individual dislike for a particular group of people, we can better understand the negative and destructive effects it can have. For example, many testing practices in schools have been called racist and ethnocentric because students from dominated groups are often stigmatized and labeled as a result of their performance on these tests. What places these students at a disadvantage is not that particular teachers or even school systems may have prejudiced attitudes about them. Rather, the *institutions* of schools and the testing industry have the major negative impact on students from culturally dominated groups. Thus, we need to understand that it is in the interaction of all three levels that racism is most destructive. Indeed, it is sometimes difficult to separate one level of racism from the others, as they feed on and inform one another.

Whereas *racism* is specifically directed against racial groups, *discrimination* is a more general term and will be used here to mean the same kind of belief systems and behaviors, both personal and institutional, directed against individuals or groups based on their gender (sexism), ethnic group (ethnocentrism), social class (classism), language (linguicism), or other perceived differences. These include anti-Semitism, which is discrimination against Jews; anti-Arab discrimination, directed against Arabs; ageism, discrimination based on age; heterosexism, discrimination against gay men and lesbians; and ableism, discrimination of people with disabilities. Allport, in his seminal and comprehensive work on the nature of prejudice, quotes a U.N. document defining discrimination as "any conduct based on a distinction made on grounds of natural or social categories, which have no relation either to individual capacities or merits, or to the concrete behavior of the individual person."[8] This definition, although helpful, does not go nearly far enough in describing the impact of racism because it fails to imply that discrimination is harmful conduct through which some groups are denied life's necessities. In addition, it obscures the institutional nature of discrimination. That is, racism and other forms of discrimination are practiced not simply by individual people but instead are harmful policies and practices within institutions that are aimed at certain groups of people by other groups of people.

Although he does not support the hypothesis that prejudice is simply a general personality trait, Allport cites extensive research that demonstrates that personality does in fact play a part in the development of prejudice. One intriguing study, for example, found a high correlation between patriotism and discrimination; that is, the more patriotic the person, the more likely that he or she would be prejudiced. This finding was explained by the fact that the person who rejects "out-groups" is more likely to have a narrowly defined idea of the "national in-group." This is the person who perceives menaces on all sides, feeling that all newcomers or those who are different from the mainstream pose a threat to an idealized and more secure past.[9] The "prejudiced personality" is also more likely to be indiscriminate in negative attitudes and behaviors toward others; anybody perceived as "different," whether through race, religion, or life-style, may be the object of this person's wrath.

Prejudice (an attitude) or discrimination (an action), however, cannot be defined on only the personal level. It is not just a personality trait or a psychological phenomenon but also a manifestation of economic, political, and social forces.[10] Some people and groups benefit from racism, whereas others inevitably lose. Whites, whether they want to or not, benefit in a racist society; males benefit in a sexist society. Thus, discrimination always helps somebody—which partly explains why racism, sexism, and other forms of discrimination continue to exist. Racism is better understood, according to Weinberg, as "a system of privilege and penalty." That is, one is rewarded or punished by the simple fact of belonging to a particular group, regardless of one's individual merits or faults. He goes on to explain, "Racism consists centrally of two facets: First, a belief in the inherent superiority of some people and the inherent inferiority of others; and second, the acceptance of distributing goods and services—let alone respect—in accordance with such judgments of unequal worth." In addressing the institutional nature of racism, Weinberg adds, "racism is always collective. Prejudiced individuals may join the large movement, but they do not cause it. The point, sometimes difficult to grasp, is fundamental." According to this conception, the "silence of institutional racism" and the "ruckus of individual racism" are mutually supportive.[11]

The effects of racism are widespread and long-lasting. The bottom line is that our society, among many others, categorizes people according to visible traits and then uses this classification to deduce fixed behavioral and mental traits.[12] We see this kind of classification all the time, based not only on race but also on ethnicity, gender, social class, and other physical or social differences. Frequently, gross exaggerations and stereotypes result: Girls are not as smart as boys, African Americans have rhythm, Asians are studious, Poles are simple-minded, and poor people need instant gratification. Some of these may be considered "positive" stereotypes, but both "negative" and "positive" stereotypes have negative results because they limit our perspective of an entire group of people. More important, the major problem with categorizing people in this way is that resources, both material and psychological, are doled out accordingly. Schools are not exempt from such practices. A brief review will highlight some of the ways in which racism and other forms of discrimination are manifested daily in schools.

Manifestations of Racism and Discrimination in Schools

The most blatant form of discrimination is the actual withholding of education, as was the case with African Americans and sometimes with American Indians until the last century. To teach enslaved Africans to read was a crime punishable under the law. Teaching thus became a subversive activity and was practiced in numerous ingenious ways.[13] Other overt forms of discrimination include segregating students, by law, according to their race or ethnicity, as was done at one time or another with African American, Mexican American, Japanese, and Chinese students, or forcing them into boarding schools, as was done with American Indian students. Children have been encouraged to adopt the ways of the dominant culture in sundry ways, from subtle persuasion to physical punishment for speaking their native language.[14] This, too, is a legacy of U.S. educational history.

Unfortunately, the discrimination that children face in schools is not a thing of the past. School practices and policies still continue to discriminate against some children in very concrete ways. Studies since the 1980s have found that most students of color are still found in predominately "minority" schools.[15] After the impetus of the civil rights movement, many school systems throughout the country were indeed desegregated. Nevertheless, less than rigorous implementation of desegregation plans, "White flight," and housing patterns, among other factors, have been successful in resegregating many schools. And segregation inevitably results in school systems that are "separate and unequal," providing differential school experiences for students based on their social class, race, and ethnicity. For example, schools that serve students of color tend to provide curricula that are watered down and at a lower level than those that serve primarily White students. In addition, the faculty of these schools tends to have less experience and less education than colleagues who teach in schools that serve primarily European American and middle-class students.[16] Even when they are desegregated, however, many schools continue to segregate students through such practices as tracking and testing. Thus, desegregating schools does not guarantee equity for all students.

School structures have proven to be problematic in terms of gender as well. Thus, they tend to be sexist in their organization, orientation, and goals. Shakeshaft, for example, has concluded that most schools are organized to meet best the needs of White males, that is, that policy and instruction are generally based on what is most effective for their needs, not for the needs of either females or students of color.[17] This organization includes everything from the curriculum, which follows the developmental level of males more closely than that of females, to instructional techniques, which favor competition as a preferred learning style, although it is far from the best learning environment for either females or most students of color. In addition, the very composition of schools is based on the needs of males. Thus, although single-sex schools have proven to be more affective in developing girls' self-esteem, achievement, and participation, most schools are coeducational because boys tend to do better, at least socially, in such settings. The effect that such discrimination has on female students is to reinforce the persistent message that they are inferior. Even superior students learn this message: According to Shakeshaft, high-achieving female students receive the least attention of all from their teachers.[18]

The effect that discrimination has on students is not always clear. However, some recent research points to negative results, particularly on academic success. Gougis, for example, conducted a study to determine the effects of racial prejudice on the academic performance of African American college students. The results confirmed that racism did indeed have an adverse effect on their performance, partly because it increased emotional stress, which in turn reduced motivation to learn.[19] If such results are apparent in a short-term study and with college students, who tend to be less impressionable than younger students, it seems likely that the effects of long-term racism on young children are even more severe.

Racism and discrimination, intentional or not, can be seen in the quality of the educational experience itself. Ortiz, for example, found that the quality of education for Hispanic students tends to be inferior than for non-Hispanic students, as was evident in numerous ways: Instructional programs for Hispanic children tend to be remedial; tracking more adversely affects Hispanic than non-Hispanic students; teachers do not believe that Hispanic children are capable of academically demanding work; and finally, teachers tend to avoid interaction, including eye contact and physical contact, with their Hispanic students more often than with others.[20]

Relationships between teachers and students also bear out these findings. A number of studies have documented that teachers tend to pay more attention to their White students than to their students of color.[21] Teachers praise their White students more, direct more questions specifically at them, have more cognitively demanding expectations of them, and offer more explicit encouragement. Similar research has documented that boys get much more attention, both positive and negative, than do girls.[22] That is, boys are expected to be more verbal and active and are both praised and reproached more often by their teachers. As a result, girls become invisible in the classroom. They are singled out neither for praise nor for disciplinary action. They are simply expected, as a group, to be quiet, attentive, and passive. More will be said about this issue when we explore teachers' expectations of students' abilities.

The way in which language development is evaluated has been found to be discriminatory as well. In one study, it was found that different methods of language assessment revealed dramatically different results. Although according to objective linguistic measures, African American and Mexican American students equaled or exceeded their European American age-mates in language development, subjective measures by teachers rated the same children of color as inferior. It has also been found that stereotyping by teachers is based on ethnic and social class variation.[23]

Social class discrimination is also highly apparent in schools. Jean Anyon's important research in this area has documented that the hidden curriculum in schools replicates the stratification of social class in society.[24] The *hidden curriculum* refers to those subtle and not so subtle messages that although not part of the intended curriculum, may nevertheless have an impact on students. These messages may be positive (e.g., teachers' expectations that all students are capable of high-quality work) or negative (e.g., that children from the working class are not capable of aspiring to professional jobs), although the term is generally used to refer to negative messages. Very frequently, these messages are not intentional; in fact, they often contradict schools' stated policies and objectives. In another study, Persell has also found social class to be repeatedly related to how well students do in school.[25] In fact, she found that students are more different from one another when they *leave* school than when they *enter*, thus putting to rest the myth of schools as the "great equalizer." These differences are due in part to the kinds of schools the students attend, the curriculum to which they are exposed, and the length of time they stay in school.

Rather than eradicate social class differences, it appears that schooling reflects them. This is a finding confirmed by Bowles and Gintis in their ground-breaking class analysis of schooling.[26] They compared the number of years of schooling of students with the socioeconomic status of their parents and found that those students whose parents were in the highest socioeconomic group tended to complete the most years of schooling. The same is still true according to a national report.[27] These examples provide evidence that schooling in and of itself does not necessarily move poor children out of their parents' low economic class. More often than not, schooling maintains and solidifies class divisions.

Many times, unintentional discrimination is practiced by well-meaning teachers. Grant and Sleeter, in an ethnography of a junior high school in a working-class community, examined schooling and the quality of teaching in relationship to the cultural, social, and gender backgrounds of the students. They concluded that because teachers were not accustomed to thinking in terms of pluralism, the teachers tended to see it not as an asset but rather as an obstacle to be overcome. In their curriculum, for example, they rarely used students' diversity as a subject of study. They were reluctant to mention a student's race, preferring instead to appear "color-blind." Sometimes, in spite of teachers' best intentions, they help to reproduce the structural inequalities in society.[28]

Differences Among Ethnic Groups in the United States

One of the traditional arguments about differences in school success and failure is that because students of color are the last in a chain of immigrants, it will take them a generation or two to climb the ladder of success, just as it took other immigrants. This argument is a specious one, for both the educational and the historical experiences of

African Americans, American Indians, and Latinos are markedly different from those of other ethnic groups. For one, American Indians, African Americans, and many Mexican Americans can hardly be called new immigrants. Many have been here for generations, and some for millenia. An alternative explanation for this difference has been advanced by Ogbu, who points to the status of groups within U.S. society as either *voluntary* or *involuntary* immigrants, that is, those who come of their own free will as compared to those who have been conquered or colonized.[29] The latter are groups that have been incorporated into society against their will, including Indians, Africans, Mexicans, and Puerto Ricans, among others. According to Ogbu, voluntary immigrants may include all European as well as some Southeast Asian, African, and Central American immigrants, among others. The distinction is not always an easy one to make since who may appear on the surface to be voluntary immigrants may not be so at all. Nevertheless, the distinction may be crucial in explaining the present condition of many groups, including their educational experiences.

It is clear that American Indians, who were conquered and segregated on reservations; African Americans, who were enslaved and whose families were torn apart; Mexican Americans, whose land was annexed and who were then colonized within their own country; and Puerto Ricans, who were colonized and are still under the domination of the United States, represent unique cases of subjugated peoples in U.S. history. In addition and probably not incidentally, they are all people of color, and the issue of race remains paramount in explaining their experiences. These groups have also been called "internal colonies" and "pariah" groups and have been compared to the lower castes of rigidly stratified societies.[30]

Such terms are used in an attempt to explain that the experiences of these groups can be understood only in a sociopolitical context. As peoples whose lives have been controlled in concrete and/or psychological terms by the dominant European American group, the legacy of subjugation can be seen in many arenas, including education. As Pantoja and Blourock explain, groups in the United States are categorized as "preferred" or "unpreferred." The further the group is from the "preferred" ideal, the more marginal is their status. Conversely, the closer they can approximate the European American, male, English-speaking, middle-class, heterosexual, and able-bodied ideal, the more valued is their position in society.[31] It is not their *differences* that make them marginal but rather the *value* that has been placed on those differences by the dominant society.

The history of racism in a society is also a history of racism in its educational institutions. Several extensive reviews have documented that dominated groups have experienced the most severe academic disadvantage *because of* their dominated relationship in society. Research reported by a number of scholars, including Cummins, Ogbu, Saville-Troike, and McDermott, demonstrates that students from particular backgrounds experience a great variability in academic performance and that such variabilities can often be explained by the social and political setting in which they find themselves.[32] Thus, students of Korean descent as well as those from the Buraku caste tend to do quite poorly in Japanese schools. Both are perceived in Japan as less valued than the majority population. Yet when they emigrate to the United States, they are equally successful in school as students from the Japanese majority. In addition, their IQ scores, a supposedly immutable indication of intelligence, also rise when these children emigrate to another society. Their dominated and devalued status in their home country seems to be the deciding factor.

The same phenomenon has been found among Finns, who do poorly in Swedish schools but quite well in schools in Australia. Their history of colonization and subsequent low status in Swedish society seems to be the key factor. This result has also been found in New Zealand among the native Maori, who perform less well in school than immigrant Polynesians, who share a similar language and culture, and among the Samis in Norway and Irish Catholics in Belfast. The point is that those who are in minority positions in their own countries may not be in the same castelike status in another culture and consequently may be more successful in school. It also seems to be true that a minority group, particularly an *involuntary* minority group, is educated for failure.

Similar results have been found closer to home. For example, newly arrived Puerto Ricans and Mexican Americans tend to do better in school and have higher self-esteem than those who were born in the United States.[33] Their self-esteem and school success do not depend on their ethnicity but rather on their interaction with U.S. society, where they are scorned or devalued. The research on the effects of school desegregation on Black students has been mixed. Whereas the benefits of desegregated educational settings have usually been clear, it has also been found that Black students in segregated or predominately Black schools sometimes have higher self-concept scores than White students. Similarly some research has concluded that American Indian students drop out in higher rates from urban, assimilated schools than from Indian reservation schools.[34] Again, the differences seem to be the sociopolitical contexts of schooling. These findings point out the obvious: Simply desegregating schools will not make a difference until the power relations within such settings are challenged. Otherwise, they will continue to be skewed in favor of the dominant group in society.

Most research on school failure, however, has focused primarily on the inadequacy of the students' home environment or culture. Such research has hypothesized that poor children and children of color are deficient in language, social development, and intelligence. More will be said about these deficit theories in Chapter 7. For now, we will mention only some of the implications of this research. Baratz and Baratz, in an early study, reviewed differing streams of research on the poor achievement of Black children in school. Most research attempted to explain it by blaming the children's *poorly developed language* (more concretely, on the fact that they did not speak standard English); an *inadequate mother* (i.e., on the assumption that the mothers of poor Black children are simply poor parents); *too little stimulation* in the home (i.e., their homes lacked environments that encourage learning); *too much stimulation* in the home (their homes were too chaotic and disorganized or simply not organized along middle-class norms); and on a host of other, often contradictory hypotheses. In effect, the homes and backgrounds of children of color and poor children are classified in such research as "sick, pathological, deviant, or underdeveloped."[35]

Such caricatures, which continue to exist, are of little value to teachers and schools who want to provide all children with a high-quality education. One researcher quoted a school counselor who explained why children failed to learn: "We find," he said, "that children in our school who don't learn either are brain-damaged or don't have a father in their home."[36] Describing school failure in such simplistic terms fails to provide a realistic or comprehensive way of looking at the problem. The fault is presented as either genetic or cultural, and solutions are then based on the hypotheses of cultural or genetic deprivation.

These solutions have ranged from Head Start and other "compensatory" programs (programs to compensate for the perceived lack of culture, mothering, stimulation, language development, and so on, in the home) to a serious recommendation by a noted psychologist advocating the *total* removal of Black children to kibbutzlike controlled environments so that the effects of the "negative values and practices of the ghetto" can be overcome.[37] This suggestion implies that the home environment of the majority of these children is so destructive that there can be no possible benefit in leaving them there. The fact that a great many families, although certainly suffering from the negative effects of poverty and discrimination, still manage to provide supportive and loving environments for their children is overlooked. This has been a frequent and consistent practice within Indian communities and has been one of the most destructive forces to the social and emotional development of Indian children. That is, there is a long history of placing American Indian children in boarding schools, often against the wishes of their families, in an attempt to remove them from the community and thus from the supposed negative influences of their family and culture.[38]

Racism and other forms of discrimination play a key role in setting up and maintaining inappropriate learning environments for many students. A related phenomenon concerns the possible impact of teachers' expectations on student achievement.

EXPECTATIONS OF STUDENTS' ACHIEVEMENT

Much research has focused on teachers' interactions with their students, specifically on their expectations. The term *self-fulfilling prophecy*, coined by Merton in 1948, means that students perform in ways in which teachers expect.[39] Their performance is based on subtle and sometimes not so subtle messages from teachers about their worth, intelligence, and capability. The term did not come into wide use until 1968, when the classic study by Rosenthal and Jacobson provided the impetus for subsequent extensive research on the subject.[40] In this study, several classes of children were given a nonverbal intelligence test, which was said to measure the potential for intellectual growth. A random number of students were selected by the researchers as "intellectual bloomers," and their names were given to the teachers. Although their test scores had nothing at all to do with their actual potential, the teachers were told to be on the alert for signs of intellectual growth. Overall these children, particularly in the lower grades, showed considerably greater gains in IQ during the school year than did the other students. They were also rated by their teachers as being more interesting, curious, and happy and thought to be more likely to succeed later in life.

Needless to say, this research caused a sensation in the educational community. From the beginning, the reception to this line of research has been mixed, with both supporters and detractors.[41] Nevertheless, the effect of teachers' expectations on the academic achievement of their students had to be taken seriously for the first time. Prior to this research, students' failure in school could be ascribed wholly to individual or family circumstances. Now, the possible influence of teachers' attitudes and behaviors and the complicity of the schools in this process had to be considered as well. The most compelling implications were for the education of those students most seriously disadvantaged by schooling, that is, for students of color and the poor.

This section will consider the impact of expectations on students' achievement. The term *teachers' expectations*, however, will be downplayed. First, this term and the research on which it is based imply that teachers have an overwhelming, and indeed the sole, responsibility for students' achievement or lack of it. This is both an unrealistic and incomplete explanation for students' success or failure. The previously cited study by Rosenthal and Jacobson, for example, brings up both issues of ethics in research and the disrespect with which teachers have frequently been treated. In addition, the use of *teachers' expectations* takes the school and society off the hook for their own responsibility and complicity in students' failure. It is necessary to understand this research within a broader framework of societal expectations. That such expectations are acted on primarily by teachers and schools may indeed be true. In fact, the majority of research focuses specifically on the classroom level, and the role of teachers must be taken seriously. But by referring only to the teachers' responsibility, we end up placing the blame only on teachers for policies and practices that are frequently out of their control. The purpose of this section is to become aware of how teachers, schools, communities, and society often interact to produce failure.

Research by Rist on teachers' expectations is worth mentioning here. In a groundbreaking study, he found that a kindergarten teacher had grouped her class by the eighth day of class. In reviewing the process by which she had done so, Rist found that she had already roughly constructed an "ideal type" of student, most of whose characteristics were related to social class criteria. At the beginning of the school year, the teacher made subjective evaluations of her students based on this ideal type. By the end of the school year, the teacher's differential treatment of children based on who were the "fast" and "slow" learners became evident. The "fast" learners received more teaching time, more reward-directed behavior, and more attention. The interactional patterns between the teacher and her students then took on a "castelike" appearance. The result, after three years of similar behavior by other teachers, was that this behavior toward the different groups became an important influence on the children's achievement. In effect, Rist found that the teachers themselves contributed in a significant way to the creation of the "slow learners" in their classrooms.[42] More will be said about this research when we turn to tracking in Chapter 4.

In the research by Rist, all the children and teachers were African American but represented different social classes. The overriding issue was therefore social class rather than race. Persell, in a review of relevant research, concluded that if race is not present as an issue, teachers' expectations are often based on the social class of the students. In fact, she found that expectations for poor children were lower than for middle-class children *even when their IQ and achievement scores were similar.*[43] Anyon also reported that in the working-class schools she studied, teachers and schools expected so little of their students that they were glad to get any work out of them at all. One teacher was reportedly told by his principal, "Just do your best. If they learn to add and subtract, that's a bonus. If not, don't worry about it."[44] Teachers' beliefs that their students were "dumb" became a rationale for providing low-level work in the form of elementary facts, simple drills, and rote memorization. Students are not immune to these messages. For instance, research by Everhart based on two years of work with adolescents in a working-class junior high school found that students resented what they felt was "being treated like third graders" and an underestimation of their abilities by teachers.[45]

Other research on expectations of students' achievement focuses on racial differences. In an interesting study several years after the Rosenthal and Jacobson experiment and reported by Milner, Black and White children of comparable ability were represented to their teachers as either "gifted" or "nongifted."[46] The supposedly "gifted" White children were given the most attention by their teachers and considered to be the brightest. In contrast, the "gifted" Black children were treated *worse* than any others by their teachers, even when compared with the "nongifted" Black children. It appears, then, that expectations are not automatic but are mediated by teachers' previously held stereotypes. In this study, the teachers may have resented the "intelligent" Black children, thus explaining their negative reactions toward them.

Research on teachers' expectations is not without controversy. It has been criticized as finding fault only with teachers' expectations while failing to take into account such factors as students' background experiences, malnutrition, and parental involvement.[47] In spite of these criticisms, the validity of the original research remains intact and subsequent evaluations of similar research have demonstrated the salience of low expectations.[48]

Notwithstanding the importance of this research, it is essential to emphasize that it is not *simply* teachers' expectations that cause certain children to succeed and others to fail. Rather, a constellation of attitudes, behaviors, and structures and a mismatch between home and school expectations all work together to produce success or failure. Nevertheless, expectations cannot be dismissed simply because they do not produce failure by themselves. If indeed they are part of the problem, they must also be addressed. In the final analysis, it is sensible to assume, as research by Lightfoot concludes, that teachers' behavior varies considerably, that is, that teachers do not have "typical styles" of behavior that they display equally to all their students.[49] Although differential behavior may be positive in that it takes into account children's individual needs and differences, the risk is that some children, *as a class*, may be unduly jeopardized by the assumptions and subsequent behavior of teachers and schools.

Finally, it is important to understand low expectations as mirroring the expectations of the larger society. It is not simply teachers who expect little from poor, working-class, and culturally dominated groups. Garfield High School in East Los Angeles, a school made famous by the extraordinary efforts of Jaime Escalante and others in propelling an unprecedented number of students to college in spite of poverty and discrimination, was visited by George Bush when he was running for president. Rather than build on the message that college was both possible and desirable for its students, he focused instead on the fact that a college education is not needed for success. He told the largely Mexican American student body that "we need people to build our buildings . . . people who do the hard physical work of our society."[50] It is doubtful that he would have even thought of uttering these same words at Beverly Hills High School, a short distance away. The message of low expectations to students who should have heard precisely the opposite is thus replicated even by those at the highest levels of a government claiming to be equitable to all students.

SUMMARY

Focusing on the persistence of racism and discrimination and low expectations is meant in no way to deny the difficult family and economic situation of many poor children and children of color or its impact on their school experiences and achievement. Romanticizing poverty denies its often devastating results. Racism, discrimination, drug abuse, and other social ills, poor medical care, deficient nutrition, and a struggle for the bare necessities for survival cannot help but negatively influence children's lives, including their school experiences. In addition, poor children and their parents do not have at their disposal the resources and experiences that economic privilege would give them.

Nevertheless, poverty is not an adequate explanation for the wholesale failure of so many students in our schools. Many children from the most economically disadvantaged families reach unparalleled levels of success in school in spite of the tremendous odds against them. For example, Edmonds's research on effective schools found a substantial number of schools in which poor children demonstrated academic achievement as high as their peers in middle-class schools.[51] Research by Taylor and Dorsey-Gaines provides another dramatic example. In their work with poor, inner-city, Black families with academically successful students, they found that these children consistently did their homework, made the honor roll, and had positive attitudes about school. In addition, their parents motivated them to learn and study, had high hopes for their education, were optimistic about the future, and in fact considered literacy an integral part of their lives—this in spite of such devastating conditions as family deaths, no food, no heat or hot water, and a host of other hostile situations.[52] The *Success for All* program, a comprehensive inner-city program designed to bring all children to grade level by third grade, provides another example. First-year results showed substantially enhanced language and reading skills compared to children in other programs.[53] We must recognize that home background can no longer be accepted as the sole or primary excuse for the school failure of large numbers of students. Taylor and Dorsey-Gaines, in fact, conclude that the fragmentation that takes place as these successful children move from the hopes of their families through an education system that "disconnects their lives" is overwhelming. The fact that these children are successful is often in spite of, rather than because of, the school system.[54]

These examples help demonstrate that although poverty is certainly a disadvantage, it is not an insurmountable obstacle to learning.[55] A recent term coined by Wilson, the *underclass*, has replaced the more controversial and dated *culturally deprived*. According to Wilson, it refers to those who remain persistently poor and deprived because of structural changes in the economy.[56] Nevertheless, this term, too, has stirred debate about the inevitability of the persistence of poverty, as seen in recent research on the Latino population in California. Hayes-Bautista has challenged the assumption that poverty inevitably leads to particular behaviors and life-styles that are detrimental and self-perpetuating. Although he found that Latinos in California are indeed poor and educationally deprived, he also found that they do not exhibit many of the health problems or behavior patterns associated with the so-called underclass. For example, they have a higher life expectancy, fewer low-birthweight babies, and lower infant mortality than even European Americans. Contrary to the conventional wisdom, he has found that Latinos have cultural strengths that help them survive the injustices they face in their everyday lives.[57]

This and other research serves to point out that we can no longer insist on blaming the poor and those from dominated racial or cultural groups for their educational problems. Racism and other forms of discrimination play a central role in the process of educational failure, as does the related phenomenon of low expectations. In the next chapter, we will consider how other structural factors, particularly policies and practices within schools, also help to keep some students at a disadvantage for academic success.

TO THINK ABOUT

1. Horace Mann's claim that education is "the great equalizer," has been criticized as overly simplistic or unrealistic. Given differences in social class, race, culture, and individual talents and capabilities, can education claim to be an "equalizer"? If not, what can schools do to fulfill this promise?
2. Think about schools you are familiar with. Have you seen evidence of racism or other forms of discrimination? Was it based primarily on race, gender, class, language, or other differences? How was it manifested?
3. Jones has identified three levels of racism: *individual*, *cultural*, and *institutional*. Think of examples of each from your own experiences.
4. Observe a classroom for a number of days to determine some examples of the hidden curriculum. How does it work in that classroom? What are the messages, unintended or not, that children pick up?
5. Do you think there are fundamental differences between students who are what Ogbu has called *voluntary* and *involuntary* immigrants? If so, what are they?
6. There has been some controversy about research on teachers' expectations. Review some of the debate in the sources cited. Think about your own experiences as a student: Describe a time when teachers' expectations did or did not make a difference in your life.

NOTES

1. For a recent and compelling argument that the agenda of the common school had to do with *control* rather than with literacy or efficiency and that it represents an attempt to assimilate all newcomers to a single national identity, see Charles Leslie Glenn, Jr., *The Myth of the Common School* (Amherst: University of Massachusetts Press, 1988). In addition, Joel Spring, in reviewing the history of the common school, maintains that reformers wanted a common education to reduce friction between capital and labor; see *The American School, 1642–1985* (White Plains, NY: Longman, 1986). Alan J. DeYoung claims that teaching children, particularly those from immigrant families, the values and attitudes necessary for full participation in the growing economy was a major theme in the rise of public education; see *Economics and American Education: A Historical and Critical Overview of the Impact of Economic Theories on Schooling in the United States* (White Plains, NY: Longman, 1989).
2. According to Skutnabb-Kangas, *linguicism* can be defined as "ideologies and structures which are used to legitimate, effectuate and reproduce an unequal division of power and resources (both material and non-material) between groups which are defined on the basis of language (on the basis of their mother tongues)." See "Multilingualism and the Education of Minority Children," in *Minority Education: From Shame to Struggle*, ed. Tove Skutnabb-Kangas and Jim Cummins (Clevedon, Eng.: Multilingual Matters, 1988), p. 13.

3. For a comprehensive history of racism and discrimination in U.S. education, see Meyer Weinberg, *A Chance to Learn: A History of Race and Education in the U.S.* (Cambridge: Cambridge University Press, 1977).

4. Caroline Hodges Persell, *Education and Inequality: The Roots and Results of Stratification in America's Schools* (New York: Free Press, 1977).

5. Cited by Ray P. McDermott, "The Cultural Context of Learning to Read," in *Papers in Applied Linguistics: Linguistics and Reading Series 1*, ed. Stanley F. Wanat (Washington, DC: Center for Applied Linguistics, 1977).

6. *Barriers to Excellence: Our Children at Risk* (Boston: National Coalition of Advocates for Students, 1985), pp. xi, 10, 16; see also *Hispanic Education: A Statistical Portrait 1990* (Washington, DC: National Council of La Raza, 1990).

7. James M. Jones, "The Concept of Racism and Its Changing Reality," in *Impacts of Racism on White Americans*, ed. Benjamin P. Bowser and Raymond G. Hunt (Beverly Hills, CA: Sage Publications, 1981), p. 27.

8. Gordon Allport, *The Nature of Prejudice* (Reading, MA: Addison-Wesley, 1954), p. 52.

9. Ibid., pp. 69–72.

10. David Milner, *Children and Race: Ten Years On* (London: Ward Lock Educational, 1983).

11. Meyer Weinberg, "Introduction," in *Racism in the United States: A Comprehensive Classified Bibliography*, compiled by Meyer Weinberg (New York: Greenwood Press, 1990), pp. xii–xiii.

12. See, for example, Stephen Jay Gould, *The Mismeasure of Man* (New York: Norton, 1981), for a history of racism in intelligence measurement; Milner, in *Children and Race*, does a good review of racial thought in the eighteenth and nineteenth centuries, as does Spring in *The American School*.

13. Weinberg, *Racism in the United States*.

14. Ibid. See also the history of segregated schooling by Spring in *The American School* and the documentation of educational discrimination against Mexican Americans and American Indians by Jim Cummins in *Empowering Minority Students* (Sacramento: California Association for Bilingual Education, 1989).

15. Gary Orfield, *Working Paper: Desegregation of Black and Hispanic Students for 1968–1980* (Washington, DC: Joint Center for Political Studies, 1982); see also *Latino Youths at a Crossroads* (Washington, DC: Children's Defense Fund, 1990).

16. Research by Jean Anyon on the educational experiences of children in four different social class settings is revealing in this regard. Although all public, the schools in each of these communities is unequally endowed, as reflected in their physical structure, the materials with which teachers and children work, the playgrounds, and the quality of the maintenance. The physical condition of the schools correlates with their communities and are therefore appropriate symbols of the social and economic status of each. See Jean Anyon, "Social Class and School Knowledge," in *Curriculum Inquiry*, II, n 1 (1981), 3–41. Similar findings were reported by Kathleen Wilcox, "Differential Socialization in the Classroom: Implications for Equal Opportunity," in *Doing the Ethnography of Schooling: Educational Anthropology in Action*, ed. George Spindler (New York: Holt, Rinehart & Winston, 1982). See also the research reported in *Latino Youths at a Crossroads*.

17. Charol Shakeshaft, "A Gender at Risk," *Phi Delta Kappan*, March 1986, pp. 499–503.

18. Ibid.

19. Reginald A. Gougis, "The Effects of Prejudice and Stress on the Academic Performance of Black Americans," in *The School Achievement of Minority Children: New Perspectives*, ed. Ulric Neisser (Hillsdale, NJ: Erlbaum, 1986).

20. Flora Ida Ortiz, "Hispanic-American Children's Experiences in Classrooms: A Comparison Between Hispanic and Non-Hispanic Children," in *Class, Race and Gender in American Education*, ed. Lois Weis (Albany: State University of New York Press, 1988).

21. See, for example, G. Jackson and C. Cosca, "The Inequality of Educational Opportunity in the Southwest: An Observational Study of Ethnically Mixed Classrooms," *American Educational Research Journal*, II (1974), 219–229; U.S. Commission on Civil Rights, *Teachers and Students: Differences in Teacher Interaction with Mexican-American and Anglo Students* (Washington, DC: U.S. Government Printing Office, 1973).

22. Unpublished research by Patricia C. Campbell, as cited in *Barriers to Excellence*. See also David Sadker and Myra Sadker, *Year III: Final Report, Promoting Effectiveness in Classroom Instruction*, Contract No. 400–80–0033 (Washington, DC: National Institute of Education, March 1984).

23. Cited by Daniel Mejia, "The Development of Mexican-American Children," in *The Psychosocial Development of Minority Group Children*, ed. Gloria Johnson Powell (New York: Brunner/Mazel Publishers, 1983). The studies cited are T. K. Bikson, "Minority Speech as Objectively Measured and Subjectively Evaluted," ERIC 1974, ED 131135; L. B. Rosenfeld, "An Investigation of Teachers' Stereotyping Behavior: The Influence of Presentation, Ethnicity, and Social Class on Teachers' Evaluations of Students," prepared for the National Institute of Education, Washington, DC, ERIC, 1973, ED 090172.

24. Jean Anyon, "Social Class and the Hidden Curriculum of Work," *Journal of Education*, 162, 1 (Winter 1980), 67–92.

25. Caroline Hodges Persell, "Social Class and Educational Equality," in *Multicultural Education: Issues and Perspectives*, ed. James A. Banks and Cherry A. McGee Banks (Boston: Allyn & Bacon, 1989).

26. Samuel Bowles and Herbert Gintis, *Schooling in Capitalist America: Educational Reform and the Contradictions of Economic Life* (New York: Basic Books, 1976).

27. *Barriers to Excellence*.

28. Carl A. Grant and Christine E. Sleeter, *After the School Bell Rings* (Philadelphia: Falmer Press, 1986).

29. John U. Ogbu, "The Consequences of the American Caste System," in *The School Achievement of Minority Children: New Perspectives*, ed. Ulric Neisser (Hillsdale, NJ: Erlbaum, 1986).

30. Cummins, *Empowering Minority Students;* Ray McDermott, "Achieving School Failure: An Anthropological Approach to Illiteracy and Social Stratification," in *Education and Cultural Process: Anthropological Approaches*, 2nd ed., ed. George D. Spindler (Prospect Heights, IL: Waveland Press, 1987): John U. Ogbu, "Variability in Minority School Performance: A Problem in Search of an Explanation," *Anthropology and Education Quarterly*, 18, 4 (December 1987), 312–334; Ogbu, "Consequences of the American Caste System."

31. Antonia Pantoja and Barbara Blourock, "Cultural Pluralism Redefined," in *Badges and Indicia of Slavery: Cultural Pluralism Redefined*, ed. Antonia Pantoja, Barbara Blourock, and James Bowman (Lincoln, NE: Study Commission on Undergraduate Education and the Education of Teachers, 1975).

32. See, for example, the review by Cummins, *Empowering Minority Students*; Ogbu, "Variability in Minority School Performance"; Muriel Saville-Troike, "Language Diversity in Multiethnic Education," in *Education in the 80's: Multiethnic Education*, ed. James A. Banks (Washington, DC: National Education Association, 1981); McDermott, "Achieving School Failure."

33. Joseph O. Prewitt-Díaz, "A Study of Self-Esteem and School Sentiment in Two Groups of Puerto Rican Students," *Educational and Psychological Research*, 3 (Summer 1983), 161–167; María E. Matute-Bianchi, "Ethnic Identities and Patterns of School Success and Failure Among Mexican-Descent and Japanese-American Students in a California High School: An Ethnographic Analysis," *American Journal of Education*, 95, 1 (1986), 233–255; David P. Dolson, "The Effects of Spanish Home Language Use on the Scholastic Performance of Hispanic Pupils," *Journal of Multilingual and Multicultural Development*, 6 (1985) 135–156. See also the research reported by Diane Divoky, "The Model Minority Goes to School," *Phi Delta*

Kappan, November 1988, pp. 219–222. She reports that the San Diego study concluded that Hispanic, Filipino, and Asian immigrants who were just becoming fluent in English were more academically successful than their U.S.-born counterparts.

34. Gloria Johnson Powell, "Coping with Adversity: The Psychosocial Development of Afro-American Children," in *The Psychosocial Development of Minority Group Children*, ed. Gloria Johnson Powell (New York: Brunner/Mazel, Publishers, 1983), p. 53; *Barriers to Excellence*, p. 18.

35. Stephen S. Baratz and Joan C. Baratz, "Early Childhood Intervention: The Social Science Base of Institutional Racism," in *Challenging the Myths: The Schools, the Blacks, and the Poor*, Reprint Series #5 (Cambridge, MA: *Harvard Educational Review*, 1971).

36. Quoted by Charles A. Valentine, "Deficit, Difference, and Bicultural Models of Afro-American Behavior," in *Challenging the Myths: The Schools, the Blacks, and the Poor*, Reprint Series #5 (Cambridge, MA: *Harvard Educational Review*, 1971), pp. 10–11.

37. This recommendation, cited by Baratz and Baratz, "Early Childhood Intervention," p. 126, was made by Bruno Bettelheim.

38. Evelyn Lance Blanchard, "The Growth and Development of American Indian and Alaskan Native Children," in *The Psychosocial Development of Minority Group Children*, ed. Gloria Johnson Powell (New York: Brunner/Mazel Publishers, 1983), p. 53; *Barriers to Excellence*. See also Jeanne Eder and Jon Reyhner, "The Historical Background of Indian Education," in *Teaching the Indian Child: A Bilingual/Multicultural Approach*, ed. Jon Reyhner (Billings: Eastern Montana College, 1986).

39. Robert Merton, "The Self-Fulfilling Prophecy," *The Antioch Review*, 8 (1948) 193–210.

40. Robert Rosenthal and Lenore Jacobson, *Pygmalion in the Classroom* (New York: Holt, Rinehart & Winston, 1968).

41. See, for instance, Richard E. Snow, "Unfinished Pygmalion," *Contemporary Psychology*, 14 (1969), 197–200.

42. Rist, "Student Social Class and Teacher Expectations."

43. Persell, *Education and Inequality*.

44. Anyon, "Social Class and School Knowledge," p. 7.

45. Everhart, *Reading, Writing, and Resistance*.

46. Pamela C. Rubovitz and Martin L. Maehr, "Pygmalion in Black and White," *Journal of Personality and Social Psychology*, 25, 2 (1973), 210–218.

47. Samuel S. Wineburg, "The Self-Fulfillment of the Self-Fulfilling Prophecy: A Critical Appraisal," *Educational Researcher*, 16, 9 (December 1987), 28–37.

48. See Robert Rosenthal's rebuttal, "Pygmalion Effects: Existence, Magnitude, and Social Importance," *Educational Researcher*, 16, 9 (December 1987), 37–44.

49. Sara Lawrence Lightfoot, "The Teacher as Central Figure," in Jean V. Carew and Sara Lawrence Lightfoot, *Beyond Bias: Perspectives on Classrooms* (Cambridge, MA: Harvard University Press, 1979).

50. As quoted in the *Newsletter* of the Tomás Rivera Center, 2, 4 (Fall 1989), 9.

51. Ronald Edmonds, "Characteristics of Effective Schools," in *The School Achievement of Minority Children: New Perspectives*, ed. Ulric Neisser (Hillsdale, NJ: Erlbaum, 1986).

52. Denny Taylor and Catherine Dorsey-Gaines, *Growing Up Literate: Learning from Inner-City Families* (Portsmouth, NH: Heinemann, 1988).

53. Robert E. Slavin, Nancy A. Madden, Nancy L. Karweit, Barbara J. Livermon, and Lawrence Dolan, "Success for All: First-Year Outcomes of a Comprehensive Plan for Reforming Urban Education," *American Educational Research Journal*, 27, 2 (Summer 1990), 255–278.

54. Taylor and Dorsey-Gaines, *Growing Up Literate*, 1988.

55. Herbert Ginsburg, *The Myth of the Deprived Child* (Englewood Cliffs, NJ: Prentice Hall, 1972). In a recent reappraisal of his previous work, Ginsburg did a comprehensive review of

the past 10–15 years of psychological research on the intellectual development and education of poor children and has reaffirmed this position even more strongly. "Poverty of intellect," he concludes, "cannot explain their failure in school." See "The Myth of the Deprived Child: New Thoughts on Poor Children" in *The School Achievement of Minority Children: New Perspectives*, ed. Ulric Neisser (Hillsdale, NJ: Erlbaum, 1986), p. 183.
56. William Julius Wilson, *The Truly Disadvantaged: The Inner City, The Underclass, and Public Policy* (Chicago: University of Chicago Press, 1987).
57. Karen J. Winkler, "Researcher's Examination of California's Poor Latino Population Prompts Debate Over the Traditional Definitions of the Underclass," *The Chronicle of Higher Education*, October 10, 1990, pp. A5, A8.

Linda Howard:
"Unless you're mixed, you don't know what it's like to be mixed."[1]

Jefferson High School is a large, comprehensive high school in Boston. With students from all over the city, it has a highly diverse student population, including African American, Puerto Rican and other Latino, Haitian, Cape Verdean, Vietnamese, Cambodian, Chinese American and other Asian, and European American students. This is the high school from which Linda Howard, a 19-year-old senior, is just graduating. Linda has been awarded a four-year scholarship to a prominent university in New England and is looking forward to her college education. She is already thinking about graduate school, and although she has not yet decided what she wants to study, she is contemplating majoring in education or English.

Frequently taken for Puerto Rican or Cape Verdean because of her mixed parentage (her father is African American and her mother is European American), she resents these assumptions by those who do not know her. Linda's insistence on being recognized as bi-racial and multicultural sometimes puts her in a difficult situation, especially with friends who pressure her to identify with either her Black or White heritage. She remains steadfast in her identity in spite of the pain it has caused her. Her friends represent the varied backgrounds of her school and of the community in which she lives. Her best friend is Puerto Rican and her boyfriend is West Indian.

Linda has had an uneven academic career. At Tremont School, one of the most highly respected magnet elementary schools in the city, she was very successful. The population was quite mixed, with children from diverse backgrounds from all over the city. She loved that school and has good memories of caring teachers there. By the time she reached junior high, she was held back twice, both in seventh and eighth grades. There were two major reasons for this: She had been in an accident and had to be absent from school a great deal in her recuperation, and she disliked the school, Academic High, one of the most prestigious public schools in the city. After the eighth grade, Linda transferred to her present school, which she attended for two years, including summer school. By the end of her second eighth grade, she had improved her grades significantly. She has been a highly successful student for the past several years, although she feels that Jefferson High is "too easy." Although the normal load for most students is four academic courses and two electives, she has taken six academic courses a semester.

Linda has been recognized as a gifted student by her teachers. She is a talented singer and hopes someday to make a living as a musician. She inherited her love of music from her father, who gave up a career in music. The entire family sings together, and Linda claims to be the best singer when her father is not around. She has been a member of the school choir and also studies music on her own. Music gives her a great deal of solace and motivates her to do her best. Besides her musical talent, Linda is also gifted in language. She frequently writes poems to express her feelings.

With her mother, father, one older and two younger brothers, Linda lives in a middle-class, predominantly Black community in Boston. Her family moved from a public housing project 14 years ago and bought their first home two years later. She still calls the housing project and neighborhood where she grew up "part of my community, part of my heritage." Both of Linda's parents are working professionals, although that was not always the case. She is proud of the fact that her father started in the telephone company as a lineman some 20 years ago. He now has a white-collar job. Her mother is a human services administrator.

Being both outgoing and personable, Linda has a great many friends. Showing her more playful side, she says she and some of them frequently "cruise around, find cute guys, and yell out the window, 'Yo, baby!' That's how we hang!" Tyrone is her "very best friend." They have known each other for 17 years and were actually engaged when she was 15. She broke off the engagement because she felt that she had her life ahead of her and needed to plan for college and a career. One month ago, they broke up completely but are still good friends. Linda says that she would do anything in the world for Tyrone. Both of them think that they may end up getting married to each other in the future.

Linda is very aware of her values and of the role of her family in their formation. Her interviews highlighted a number of issues that are central to understanding these values: struggle around identity and racism, the importance of teachers' caring and their role in students' learning, and the great value of education in her life and her parents' influence on this factor.

IDENTITY, RACISM, AND SELF-DETERMINATION

My parents are Black and White American. I come from a long heritage. I am of French, English, Irish, Dutch, Scottish, Canadian, and African descent.

I don't really use race. I always say, "My father's Black, my mother's White, I'm mixed." But I'm American; I'm human. That's my race; I'm part of the human race.

After all these years, and all the struggling, because when [my parents] got married it was a time right before desegregation, people from all sides were telling them, "No, you'll never make it. You'll never make it. White and Black don't belong together in the same house." And after 20 years, they're still together and they're still strong. Stronger now than ever, probably. That's what I like the most about them. They fought against all odds and they won.

It's hard when you go out in the streets and you've got a bunch of White friends and you're the darkest person there. No matter how light you are to the rest of your family, you're the darkest person there and they say you're Black. Then you go out with a bunch of Black people and you're the lightest there and they say, "Yeah, my best friend's White." But I'm not. I'm *both*.

I don't always fit in—unless I'm in a mixed group. That's how it's different. Because if I'm in a group of people who are all one race, then they seem to look at me as being the *other* race . . . whereas if I'm in a group full of [racially mixed] people, my race doesn't seem to matter to everybody else. . . . Then I don't feel like I'm standing out. But if I'm in a group of totally one race, then I sort of stand out, and that's something that's hard to get used to.

It's hard. I look at history and I feel really bad for what some of my ancestors did to some of my other ancestors. Unless you're mixed, you don't know what it's like to be mixed.

My boss, who was a teacher of mine last year, just today said something about me being Puerto Rican. I said, "We've been through this before. I am *not* Puerto Rican. I am Black and White." I may look Hispanic, but this is what I mean. And this is a person who I've known for a whole year and a half now. . . . [I felt] like I was insignificant. If, after all this time, he didn't know and we discussed it last year. . . . It was insulting. I usually don't get insulted by it. I say, "Oh, no, I'm not Spanish. I'm Black and White." And people say, "Oh really? You are?! I thought you were Spanish."

[Teachers should not] try to make us one or the other. And God forbid you should make us something we're totally not. . . . Don't write down that I'm Hispanic when I'm not. Some people actually think I'm Chinese when I smile. . . . Find out. Don't just make your judgments. And I'm not saying judgment as in insulting judgments. But some people, they don't realize that there are so many intermarried couples today. You have to ask people what they are. If you really want to know, you have to ask them. You don't just make assumptions. 'Cause you know what happens when you assume. . . . If you're filling out someone's report card form and you need to know, then ask. . . . Like I said, race isn't important to me. But if you need it for paperwork, or if you need it for something important, then ask. When people are misjudged, especially after you've known them for awhile, and you write down the wrong thing about them, it's kind of insulting. . . .

I don't know how to put this . . . race hasn't really been a big factor for me. Because in my house, my mother's White, my father's Black, I was raised with everybody. Sometimes, I don't even notice. I see people walking down the street, I don't care what they are; they're people.

My culture is my family. I have an enormous family. I have three brothers, two parents, and my father has ten brothers and sisters, and all of my aunts and uncles have children. That to me is my culture. . . . I was born and raised in America. I'm fourth-generation American, so it's not like I'm second generation where things were brought over from a different country or brought and instilled in me. I'm just American and my culture is my family and what we do as a family. Family is very important to us. . . . My family is the center of my life.

I've had people tell me, "Well, you're Black." I'm not Black; I'm Black and White. I'm Black and White American. "Well, you're Black!" No, I'm not! I'm both. It's insulting, when they try and . . . bring it right back to the old standards, that if you have anybody in your family who's Black, you're Black. . . . I mean, I'm not ashamed of being Black, but I'm not ashamed of being White either, and if I'm both, I want to be part of both. And I think teachers need to be sensitive to that.

I would say I have more Black culture than White . . . because I know all about fried chicken and candied yams and grits and collard greens and ham hocks and all that because that's what we eat. . . . My father had to teach my mother how to cook all that stuff [*laughs*]. But that's just as far as food goes. . . . But as far as everything else, my family is my culture.

See, the thing is, I mix it at home so much that it's not really a problem for me to mix it outside. But then again, it's just my mother and my grandmother on the "White side," so it's not like I have a lot to mix.

My [Black] grandmother, I don't think she means to do it, when she talks, she refers to people, she describes them. If she's telling you, "Oh, you know that girl, the White one, with the blond hair and the blue eyes?" Why not "the thin girl with the long hair"? Instead, they have to get you by the color. I don't notice that too much. But it is unusual, because a lot of people I know do it. And I just say, what's that got to do with it?

I don't think it's that big of a problem [interracial identity]. It's not killing anybody, at least as far as I know, it's not. It's not destroying families and lives and stuff. It's a minor thing. If you learn how to deal with it at a young age, as I did, it really doesn't bother you the rest of your life, like drugs. . . .

In the city, I don't think there's really much room for racism, especially anymore, because there's just so many different cultures. You can't be a racist. . . . I think it's *possible*, but I don't think it's logical. I don't think it was *ever* logical. It's possible, it's very possible, but it's sort of ridiculous to give it a try.

I think we're all racist in a sense. We all have some type of person that we don't like, whether it's from a different race, or from a different background, or they have different habits.

But to me a *serious racist* is a person who believes that people of different ethnic backgrounds don't belong or should be in *their* space and shouldn't invade *our* space: "Don't come and invade *my* space, you Chinese person. You belong over in China or you belong over in Chinatown."

Racists come out and tell you that they don't like who you are. Prejudiced people will say it in like those little hints, you know, like "Oh, yes, some of my best friends are Black." Or they say little ethnic remarks that they know will insult you but they won't come out and tell you, "You're Black. I don't want anything to do with you." Racists, to me, would come out and do that.

Both racists and prejudiced people make judgments, and most of the time they're wrong judgments, but the racist will carry his one step further. . . . A racist is a person that will carry out their prejudices.

[Racists have power] only if you let them! We'll stick with [the example of] striped shirts: If I go where everyone is wearing solids, and I'm wearing a stripe, and someone comes up to me and tells me, "You don't belong here; you're wearing stripes," I'll say, "I belong anywhere I want to belong." And I'll stand right there! But there are some people who just say, "Oh, okay," and will turn around and leave. Then the racist has the power.

I wrote a poem about racism. I despise [racism] . . .

Why do they hate me?
I'll never know
Why not ride their buses
In the front row?
Why not share their fountains
Or look at their wives?
Why not eat where they do
Or share in their lives?
Can't walk with them
Can't talk with them unless I'm a slave
But all that I wonder is who ever gave
them the right to tell me
What I can and can't do
Who I can and can't be
God made each one of us
Just like the other
the only difference is,
I'm darker in color.

I love to write. I do a lot of poetry. . . . Poetry is just expression. You can express yourself anyway you want; it doesn't have to be in standard English. . . .

I had a fight with a woman at work. She's White and at the time I was the only Black person in my department. Or I was the only person who was *at all* Black in my department. And she just kept on laying on the racist jokes. At one point, I said, "You know,

Nellie, you're a racist pig!'' And she got offended by *that*. And I was just joking, just like she'd been joking for two days—straight—all the racist jokes that she could think of. And we got into a big fight over it. She threw something at me and I was ready to kill her. . . . There's only so far you can carry this. . . . She started to get down and dirty. . . . She was really getting evil. . . . They locked her out of the room and they had to hold me back because I was going to throttle her.

She thought I was upset because she tossed the water at me. I said, "You know, Nellie, it's not the water. It's all these remarks you've been saying. And you just don't seem to have any regard for my feelings."

I remember one thing she was talking about. She said, "I'm not racist, just because I was jumped by eight Black girls when I was in the seventh grade, I'm not racist." After all these [30] years, why was she still saying they were eight *Black* girls? That to me was insulting. That was then; this is now. I didn't do it to you, I didn't jump you. It wasn't my father who jumped you; it wasn't my aunt who jumped you. . . . I told her I didn't want it taken out on me, that's the thing. I don't want anybody's racism taken out on me.

I've got a foot on both sides of the fence and there's only so much I can take. I'm straddling the fence and it's hard to laugh and joke with you when you're talking about the foot that's on the other side.

She couldn't understand it. We didn't talk for weeks. And then one day, I had to work with her. We didn't say anything for the first like two hours of work. And then I just said, "Smile, Nellie, you're driving me nuts!" and she smiled and laughed. And we've been good friends ever since. She just knows you don't say ethnic things around me; you don't joke around with me like that because I won't stand for it from you anymore. We can be friends; we can talk about anything else—except race.

TEACHERS, ROLE MODELS, AND CARING

My first-grade teacher and I are very close. . . . As a matter of fact, she's my mentor. I'm following in her footsteps. I'm going to study elementary education. . . . She's always been there for me. After the first or second grade, if I had a problem, I could always go back to her. Through the whole rest of my life, I've been able to go back and talk to her. . . . She's a Golden Apple Award winner, which is a very high award for elementary school teachers. . . . She keeps me on my toes. . . . When I start getting down . . . she peps me back up and I get back on my feet. . . .

They're all great. . . . All of my teachers were wonderful. I don't think there's a teacher at the whole Tremont School that I didn't like. . . . It's just a feeling you have. You know that they really care for you. You just know it; you can tell. Teachers who don't have you in any of their classes or haven't ever had you, they still know who you are. . . . The Tremont School in itself is a community. . . . I love that school! I want to teach there.

I knew it [Academic High] would be a hard school, but I didn't know it would be so . . . they're just so *rigid*. The teachers, there's no feeling . . . like I said, the Tremont was a community for me and I loved it. I'm that type of person; I'm an outgoing person and I like to be able to talk to anybody and not feel that I can't talk to someone. If I have to spend six hours a day in school, I want to feel that I can talk to my teachers. At Academic, I didn't feel that at all. I *hated* it, absolutely hated it. They let me know that I wasn't high anymore. I was average. They slapped me with it. My first report card, oh goodness, it was terrible. I don't remember exactly what grades they were; I just do remember it was the first time in my life I had seen an F or a D under my name.

I think you have to be creative to be a teacher; you have to make it interesting. You can't just go in and say, "Yeah, I'm going to teach the kids just that; I'm gonna teach them right out of the book and that's the way it is, and don't ask questions." Because then you're gonna lose their interest. . . . Because I know there were plenty of classes where I lost complete interest. But those were all because the teachers just, "Open the books to this page." They never made up problems out of their head. Everything came out of the book. You didn't ask questions. If you asked them questions, then the answer was, "In the book." And if you asked the question and the answer *wasn't* in the book, then you shouldn't have asked that question!

Mr. Benson, he cared; he was the only one of the two Black teachers [at my high school]. He was not enough. . . . The other Black teacher, he was a racist, and I didn't like him. I belonged to the Black Students Association, and he was the advisor. And he just made it so obvious . . . he was all for Black supremacy. . . . A lot of times, whether they deserved it or not, his Black students passed, and his White students, if they deserved an A, they got a B. . . . He was insistent that only Hispanics and Blacks be allowed in the club. He had a very hard time letting me in because I'm not all Black. . . . I just really wasn't that welcome there.

He never found out what I was about. He just made his judgments from afar. He knew that I was Black and White and I looked too White for him, I guess. But we never discussed it.

At Jefferson, just about the whole school is like a big community. There are very few White, Caucasian, whatever you want to call them, *us* [*laughing*]. There are very few, but they don't cluster together. It's all integrated. . . . Nobody gets treated differently. We're all the same.

I've enjoyed all my English teachers at Jefferson. But Mr. Benson, my English Honors teacher, he just threw me for a whirl! I wasn't going to college until I met this man. . . . He was one of the few teachers I could talk to. . . . Instead of going to lunch, I used to go to Mr. Benson's room and he and I would just sit and talk and talk and talk. . . . My father and Mr. Benson share a lot of the same values. And every time I've heard Mr. Benson talk, all I could think about was Daddy: "Oh, that's exactly what my father says!" . . . "Education, get your education and go far." "Whether you're flipping burgers at the local joint or you're up there working on Wall Street, be proud of yourself. . . ."

'Cause Mr. Benson, he says, I can go into Harvard and converse with those people, and I can go out in the street and rap with y'all. It's that type of thing, I love it. I try and be like that myself. I have my street talk. I get out in the street and I say "ain't" this and "ain't" that and "your momma" or "wha's up?" But I get somewhere where I know the people aren't familiar with that language or aren't accepting that language, and I will talk properly. . . . I walk into a place and I listen to how people are talking and it just automatically comes to me.

Mr. Benson is the same as I am. Well, his mother was Black and his father was White, so Mr. Benson and I could relate on all the problems that you face in the world.

Like when you go to fill out any kind of form and they ask you "Black, White, Chinese, Hispanic, Other," I check off "Other" and I'll write it down. And then Mr. Benson told me that he found out that when you write it down, they put you under "Black" because it all comes back to the old laws about if you had any Black blood in you, you were Black.

I wrote a poem about it. It was just a bunch of questions: "What am I?" I had filled out like a whole bunch of college essays and I was tired of having to write out "Other: Black American and White American." And I went to him and I said, "Mr. Benson, what do you do when you get all these forms and they ask you "Black, White, or Other?" And he said, "You might as well just fill out 'Black' because that's what they'll do to you." That just drives me nuts! And we got on this big conversation about it. . . . But no other teacher ever. . . .

He came from the lower class in Chicago and worked his way, and he studied every night, six hours a night. He got into Harvard and he went to Harvard, and now he's back helping the people who needed help. Because the way he sees it, he could go and he could teach at Phillips Academy and he could teach at Boston Latin, which he did for awhile. But those people don't need his help. That's how he sees it. They're gonna learn with or without him. He wanted to come back to a small community, the underprivileged community, and help those people. That's what made me admire him the most because I like to help people.

The teacher who didn't really help me at all in high school . . . was my computer lit. teacher. Because I have no idea about computer literacy. I got A's in that course. Just because he saw that I had A's, and that my name was all around the school for all the "wonderful things" I do, he just automatically assumed. He didn't really pay attention to who I was. The grade I think I deserved in that class was at least a C, but I got A just because everybody else gave me A's. But everybody else gave me A's because I earned them. He gave me A's because he was following the crowd. He just assumed, "Yeah, well, she's a good student." And I showed up to class every day. . . . He didn't help me at all because he didn't challenge me. Everybody else challenges me; I had to earn their grades. I didn't have to earn his grade. I just had to show up.

I'd do what I've seen teachers who I like or enjoyed do: make the classroom fun; make it exciting. If I were to teach math, I'd turn all the math problems into games. I had a teacher who did that. I hated math up until the second time I was in the seventh grade. . . . I *hated* math; I despised math until I met Ms. Morgan. And from that point on, I have never received less than a B in math. She turned every math problem, every type of math problem was a game.

So that school is never "This is the way it is, and that's just it. Just learn it." I'd make everything exciting and fun, or I'd try to. That makes school enjoyable.

FAMILY VALUES AND EDUCATION

In the Tremont and in the Williams [schools], I was the top of my class, well, not top of my class, but I was very high up in the ranks. . . . That all comes from family. My mother's been reading me books since probably the day I was born, up until school age. . . . Any book with a serious message for children. . . . My mother's always been very big on that, to make sure that reading was important. I still love to read . . . mysteries, human interest stories. . . . It made a difference in elementary school, it really did. And, actually, it made a difference in high school, after I left Academic High, because I graduated first in my class.

My parents know that the further I go in school, the better life I'll have. Because they had to struggle to get where they are today. They had to struggle to make themselves comfortable. Going to school is going to be a struggle. But as long as I'm in school, my parents will always be there for me.

The first five years of your life, that's when you develop the most. Before you go to school, you've already got your personality. If you have parents who are showing you the right values (not "the right values" because everybody's values to them are right . . .), whatever values they've given you are what you carry for the rest of your life.

That's the way my family has raised me. . . . They really taught me not to judge. . . . You just accept [people] the way they are. . . . With my family, if you go to church, you go to church; if you don't, you don't. My grandmother says, "Jesus still loves you and I still love you, whether you go to church or not. . . ." It's that kind of thing. You just learn to accept people. . . .

Sexuality—I don't judge, I try not to, anyway. I'm sure subconsciously I do. . . . I don't come out and say, "Ugh, he's gay." My neighborhood is thoroughly mixed and sexually open. And they're my neighbors. I don't differentiate them. And that's something I wish a lot of people would do. Because I think it's wrong. Because if you were to take people and differentiate because of their preferences, be it sexual or anything, *everybody's* different. I prefer a certain type of music; you prefer a different type of music. Does that mean we have to hate each other? Does that mean you have to pick on me and call me names? That's the way I see it.

I'm not going to be exactly like my parents. I grew up with basic values. And I follow those basic values. And if you think about it, the choices I make have something to do with my values. And the only place I got my values from was here [home]. . . . So, I may change things around, flip them over, just adjust them a bit. But they still come down to my home values, my basic values, and my basic values came from home.

[My parents] have always taken good care of me. . . . They're always there for me, all the time, if I need to talk. And they make it so obvious that they love me, you know, with these ridiculous curfews that I have [*laughs*]. I know it's for the better, although I can't stand it, I know there's a reason behind it, some twisted reason! . . . Just a regular night out, I have to be in at midnight. If it's a party, I don't have to be in till two. All my friends stay out till three and four in the morning. But that's because their parents can go to sleep. My parents can't sleep if I'm not home. That's what I like the most about them.

I was reading an article the other day about how the family dinner has sort of been tossed out the window in today's society. My family sits down to dinner together four out of seven nights a week, all six of us. Dinner's at six. If it's late, then everybody waits. You don't just eat on your own. . . . I've noticed a lot of people, my boyfriend, for one, they never eat together. I've had all kinds of friends who always say . . . "Your family *eats*?" And that's different from other families.

It's very important to my parents and it'll be important to me. Because that's the time when we sit down and say, "How was your day? What'd you do? How are you feeling? Do you have a headache? Did you have a rough day? Did you have a good day?"

You know? And that's about the only time the whole family can sit together and talk and discuss. . . . It's different from other families, because a lot of families, they sort of miss each other. And they say, "Oh, *you* were supposed to pick Johnny up today?" . . . My family never has that problem because we always sit down together and talk.

I have wonderful parents, although I don't tell them [*laughing*]. [Do they know?] Probably.

My father and my mother had to work up. . . . My father has been working for the telephone company for 20 years. He started off cutting lines and working underground. Now he sits in his office. . . . He's a businessman these days and he had to work his way up. Whereas if I go and get myself a college education, I'm not going to have to start splicing lines if I want to work at the telephone company. I'm going to start with the knowledge that I don't have to splice a line. I could start in the office with my father.

A lot of us [Black kids] just don't have the home life. I really do think it begins when you're a baby! My mother, like I said, I believe she read to me from the day I was born; I'm sure of it. A lot of people just didn't have that. Their parents both had to work; they didn't have anybody at home to read to them. They just sat in front of the tube all day. When they came home from school, their homework was just tossed aside and they sat in front of the television until Mom and Dad came home. Then Mom and Dad rushed them through dinner, got them to bed, and this and that. A lot of them just didn't come from the right background to have—not the smarts, but to be educated enough to pass that test [to get into Academic High]. Because the Academic test isn't a test of how much you know; it's more of a test of how well can you solve problems. . . . The Black population wasn't very high there.

I blew two years . . . I learned a lot from it. As a matter of fact, one of my college essays was on the fact that from that experience, I learned that I don't need to hear other people's praise to get by. . . . All I need to know is in here [pointing to heart] whether I tried or not.

It's not the school you go to, it's what you want to get out of it and what you take from it.

If I know I did my hardest, if I know I tried my very best and I got an 'F,' I'd have a beef with the teacher about it, but if that's what I got, that's what I got. If that's seriously what I earned after all my efforts, then I'll have to live with it.

[Grades] are not that important. To me, they're just something on a piece of paper. . . . They [parents] feel just about the same way. If they ask me, "Honestly, did you try your best?" and I tell them yes, then they'll look at the grades and say okay. . . . The first thing my father always looked at was conduct and effort. If all the letter grades in the academic grades said F's, and I had A's in conduct and effort, then my father would just see the F's, and say "Oh, well. . . ."

I love music. Music is life. I sing at the top of my lungs every morning. . . . I'm always going to keep this in my mind: After school, after I go to college, after I get my degrees in what I want to get my degrees in, maybe I'll put all of that on hold. Even if I have a teaching degree, I may never teach. I want to be a singer. I just want to go out there and I want to make myself known and I want to sing to my heart's content. It's just what I love to do! But I always want to have something to fall back on. Singing is not my main career goal because I realize it's a farfetched dream to become a world-famous singer. It's not *too* farfetched, but it is farfetched. . . . Oh, I can do it. I have no doubts

I can do it. I just know it's a lot of work. . . . I do eventually want to be a singer. . . . I can become more famous and you can read about me in the papers and you can see my videos on television and you can see me in interviews on "Good Morning, America" . . . [*laughing*].

[Reason for going to school] To make yourself a better person. To learn more, not only about the world and what other people have gathered as facts, but to learn more about yourself.

The more that there are opportunities for you to learn, you should always take them. . . . I just want to keep continuously learning, because when you stop learning, then you start dying.

I've got it all laid out. I've got a four-year scholarship to one of the best schools in New England. All I've gotta do is go there and make the grade.

If I see the opportunity to become a leader, I'll do it. I'll just go and take over. . . . I like the recognition.

I'm ready now. I can face the challenge. . . . I'm ready to go out in the world and let [that] university know who I am!

COMMENTARY

Being "mixed," as Linda says, is the reality of more and more students in U.S. schools. Yet many schools are unaware of this fact and of the strains and dilemmas it poses for many children. Issues of identity are clearly at the core of Linda's striving to carve out a place for herself in her family, community, and school. Although she has reached quite a sophisticated understanding of race, racial awareness, racism, and identity, some feelings of ambivalence, conflict, and pain are still apparent.

Many people in the United States are probably a mixture of several racial heritages, but this is either not known or readily acknowledged. The term *new people*, used by Williamson, is an apt one for people of mixed African and European ancestry. (The term *mulatto,* which he also uses, in contrast, is charged with negative connotations.) As Williamson says, these "are a new people, new not just in the surface way of a new physical type, but new in the vital way of constituting a new culture that is both African and European, each transformed in America and married to one another."[2] In this sense, virtually all of us are "new persons," because there is no such thing as a pure race. According to some estimates, Blacks in the United States are on the average about 20 percent White, and Whites are about 1 percent Black.[3] Although this assertion is impossible to prove, it is nevertheless true that *miscegenation,* or racial mixing, is far more common than generally admitted in our society. Discomfort with this issue is understandable given the history of rape and subjugation forced on African and African American women, especially during slavery.

We also have a history of classifying people according to their value to the economy. It can be traced back to the so-called "one-drop rule," in which people were considered Black if they had even "one drop of Black blood." This classification has not been true in other societies and was not always the case in the United States either. Rather, it emerged sometime in the early eighteenth century.[4] With this logic, people could still be enslaved even if they were mostly White, and this classification was to the benefit of the institution of slavery. This was a social construction rather than a biological one. By the beginning of the twentieth century, the vast majority of those of mixed African and European ancestry were identifying as Black rather than as White or mixed. In fact, Horace Mann Bond, the renowned sociologist and educator and himself a light-skinned Black, wrote of a blue-eyed and seemingly Anglo-Saxon man who spoke fervently at a meeting about "the necessity that all of us black men in America and the world stand together."[5]

Although interracial marriages in the United States had declined drastically in the first half of the twentieth century from earlier times, they began to increase after the civil rights movement. Between 1970 and 1980, the number of interracial marriages doubled, from 310,000 to 613,000. These marriages still represent, however, a tiny percentage of all marriages. At present, they make up only about 1.3 percent of all marriages recorded in the United States.[6] Linda's parents married at the end of the 1960s in Boston. In spite of its history of racial conflict, Boston also has a distinguished Black legacy going back many years. It also has a history of being the most tolerant large city in America in regard to interracial marriage. From 1900 to 1904, for example, about 14 percent of all Black men married White women, a rather large percentage.[7]

Given the racist underpinnings of self- and group identification in the United States, the dilemmas Linda faces are difficult indeed. The pressure on young people from mixed marriages to identify as one or the other is something that she has lived with since birth. The result can be what Stonequist has called "the marginal man." This is an individual who is "condemned to live in two societies and in two, not merely different but antagonistic, cultures." It is in the mind of the marginal person that "the cultures come together, conflict, and eventually work out some kind of mutual adjustment and interpenetration." The marginal person is, according to him, "the crucible of cultural fusion."[8] Although the image of a person on the outside looking in is not necessarily the case for Linda or other children of racially mixed marriages, it does point out the rejection that she has experienced.

Conflict and antagonism are apparent in Linda, but so are mutual adjustment and negotiation. Linda is steadfast and adamant in claiming both her heritages. As she says, "My culture is my family." And because her family is mixed, so is her culture. This is an extraordinarily courageous stand in a society that forces you either to choose one over the other or fits you into one that you have not necessarily chosen yourself. Linda is certain that although she goes to the trouble of writing "Mixed—Black and White" on college applications and other forms, they automatically place her in the "Black" category anyway.

The role of teachers who have understood and cared for her has been important in Linda's school experiences. Fortunately, there have been a number of such teachers in each of her schools. Although she does not expect all her teachers to be biracial like herself, she nevertheless does expect them to be sensitive and accepting of who she is, rather than imposing their own identity on her. Except for her time at Academic High, where she was made to feel inferior, Linda has for the most part loved her school experiences. Her strong family background has been her first and most important support system. This fact can be seen from what she calls "family jam sessions," in which everybody takes part; the important role of reading; and the centrality of family dinners. Friends are Linda's second strongest support. Her schools have come in a distant third, although there have been stellar teachers who have stood out. These teachers have not only been those with whom she could identify culturally but also those who have made learning fun, interesting, and challenging.

Linda Howard is an extraordinary young woman who is full of ambition, certain of her talents, and ready for the future. Her strong bonds with family, love of learning, and strong identification as Black and White are no doubt all factors in her successful school career. Her teachers and schools have not always been able to understand or support her, underscoring research that has concluded that the social context of the school and the degree to which it insulates students from racism have an important influence on self-esteem.[9] Fortunately, Linda has found great support in her exceptional family. She has, in fact, proven what was suggested by the respected psychologist Alvin Poussaint about research concerning children of interracial marriages: "We have lots of reasons to suspect that an interracial background can be an advantage to children in this society." He adds that these children "may be a more successful group in this society than has previously been believed."[10] Surely Linda has more than proven him right.

TO THINK ABOUT

1. Linda Howard insists on identifying herself as biracial. She also says that she is just "a member of the human race" and that race is not that important to her. Are these assertions contradictory? Why or why not?

2. If you were one of Linda's teachers, how might you show her that you affirm her identity? Give specific suggestions.

3. How have teachers shown that they cared about Linda's education? What kind of teachers most impressed her? Why?

4. Linda's family is, as she says, "the center of my life." How do you think this has helped her to become a successful student?

5. Does Linda's case demonstrate that issues of race and identity should be handled by the school? Or that they are too complicated to be handled appropriately in school? Take a stand one way or the other and defend it.

NOTES

1. I appreciate the time and energy that Paula Elliott put into doing and analyzing the extensive interviews that were the basis for this case study.
2. Joel Williamson, *New People: Miscegenation and Mulattoes in the United States* (New York: Free Press, 1980).
3. Ibid.
4. Ibid.
5. Horace Mann Bond, "Two Racial Islands in Alabama," *American Journal of Sociology*, 36 (1930–1931), 554.
6. Rita J. Simon and Howard Altstein, *Transracial Adoptees and Their Families* (New York: Praeger, 1987). See also Williamson, *New People*, for numbers during previous centuries.
7. Williamson, *New People*.
8. Everett V. Stonequist, *The Marginal Man: A Study in Personality and Culture Conflict* (New York: Russell & Russell, 1961).
9. Christopher Bagley, Kanka Mallick, and Gajendra K. Verma, "Pupil Self-Esteem: A Study of Black and White Teenagers in a British School," in *Race, Education and Identity*, ed. Gajendra K. Verma and Christopher Bagley (New York: St. Martin's Press, 1979).
10. As quoted in "Children of Intermarriage," *New York Times*, June 20, 1984, p. C1.

Rich Miller:
"Self-respect is one gift that you give yourself."[1]

Speaking in a slow and deliberate way, Rich Miller is a young man who thinks carefully about life, education, and family. Rich is 17 years old and a senior in high school. He is Black and has lived in a racially and ethnically mixed community in Boston since he was born. He says that the neighborhood "isn't bad" but laments that it was once much nicer than it is now.

The youngest of three children, Rich lives with his mother, brother, and sister. Both of his siblings are currently in college. His brother is in a public college in the south studying engineering, and his sister is in a private, liberal arts college in New England. They are all close in age, the oldest being 20. Rich's mother is a nursery and kindergarten teacher. She did not attend college until she was an adult and has had to struggle both to get a college education and to develop her professional career. Consequently, she feels very strongly about the need for her children to get a college education. This is a major value in their family. Rich is clearly devoted to his mother and considers himself lucky to be part of his family. Nevertheless, he is also quick to point out that at times his mother, in "getting on his case," can be overbearing.

Rich has had what he considers to be a good basic education. He has always gone to desegregated schools that have "a good mix" and are, he recalls, free of racial tension. At present, he attends a comprehensive high school that he describes as "a pretty good school." He decided not to go to his neighborhood school because his high school offers a number of special programs, including one in music. Almost three-quarters of the students in his school are African American, with about 10 percent Latino, 15 percent White, and a small number of Asians. Rich will be graduating this year, and although he feels that he has gotten a very good education there, he also points out that the teachers' expectations are based on their students' race and background. He plans to go to college to study pharmacology. He has been accepted into a respected program at a good college and is looking forward to his studies.

Rich has been very involved in the music program at school. He has played at graduation and other occasions and has also conducted workshops for other students. He has been studying music (both the violin and the piano) since fourth grade. Music is a big part of his life outside of school, too. He plays the organ at his church, and he and his family frequently take part in church activities. Thus, church is also an important part of his life. Rich is contemplating combining a profession as a pharmacist with teaching music to private students.

Several themes emerged through interviews with Rich. One is his great sense of personal responsibility and independence; another focuses on the expectations and pressures he feels from society and teachers and some of the resultant attitudes he has developed; finally, the third relates to family lessons that he has learned along the way.

PERSONAL RESPONSIBILITY

I'm more or less an independent person. I don't depend on anyone to do anything for me. . . . I don't let dependence stand in the way of anything that has to get done. . . . I don't depend on anyone learning for me or making decisions for me or anything. I just want to see how far I can carry myself and what I can achieve on my own. I'm not saying that I wouldn't accept the aid of others, but just see what Rich can do.

The first year [of high school] that I had was real heavy . . . because I was in that transition going from junior high to high school, and at that particular time, when you have that homework—I had never had this much homework before! . . . My mother stayed on me about that, but then it was *my* decision. That first semester of my first year was, oh, it was terrible. It actually opened my eyes up that it was left up to me; it's up to me to go and get that education.

I'm looking at the future as long as I can just continue right into education and not wait until the latter part of my life. I believe that "business before pleasure," so take care of this now and later I can enjoy the time off; I can enjoy the finer things in life that one wants earlier. . . . Many of us want to go out and get cars, but some things have to give and some things come first. I feel that if I involve myself in a lot of things now within the world, then that may hinder me from getting my education. . . . My future is getting that education. Whatever else happens after that, I won't have that problem or worry about getting a job.

I decided on pharmacy. . . . That's next to being a doctor, so it's just as hard. I decided that I wanted to go into a career that would give me guaranteed bacon. . . . Like with music, there's so much competition out here and no matter how much or how hard you study, there's always somebody better than you are. . . . So I figured there's enough room out here for pharmacists.

I always liked music, but when I was little I never felt there was a place for me in music. Other people are talented and they can just sit down and just actually play. Well, I started from scratch, so I didn't know that there was a place for me. . . . So I began taking lessons . . . and I have stuck with that.

There was a time that I had decided to go into music education. Now, I am going to pursue this career in pharmacy, but I also want to be a music teacher. . . . Now, as far as performance, that's something that has to be worked with. I feel there *can* be a slot for me in music education.

I plan on keeping my music up. I really don't have hobbies and I don't play too many sports or anything like this, so I really think this keeps me going. It gives me something to go for from day to day. And you learn something new all the time.

I'm always looking to learn something new. The music I like playing the most is, well, I like playing between the classical and the gospel music. I learned the classical and I always feel that it's a challenge. That's the first music that I really got into before I began the gospel music. . . . I like gospel music because I like to play for the church.

Getting ahead in life, not letting anyone discourage you in any way [is important]. Say, "Well, I want to go forth and do this. . . ." And then someone might say, "Well, I don't think you can do it; I don't think you can make it." And because of someone saying something, then you decide, "Well, no, I'll leave it alone. . . ." I think no matter what anyone says, if you feel that within yourself you can achieve something, go for it!

I was fairly comfortable in school. I'll admit, I mainly kept to myself. Now, it's not saying that I didn't have any friends or anything like that. I had friends, but I knew how to take relationships up to how far. So I've maintained trust and loyalty to friends. So it's not like I was totally alone. . . . I know how I want my friends to treat me and I treat them how they would expect to be treated.

Friends won't let you down. Friends will be around. My closest friends are there when I can talk to or when I want to go out . . . more so to offer encouragement to get that education. . . . Many of my friends are encouraging me to go on to college. I've have that kind of push from outside just as much as I have from inside.

There's just things that I just want to fulfill for myself, and if it takes the rest of my life, eliminating [plans for a] family and whatever, then so be it. . . . I don't want to take on a million responsibilities at once.

EXPECTATIONS, PRIDE, AND SHAME

I went to the Robert Jennings School where we had an Advanced Work Class. Advanced Work Class was more like an exam school for elementary students. . . . That's when I first became familiar with music. We had a teacher to come in to teach violin and cello and those string instruments. So that's where I first started with music and I began taking violin. My mother asked me did I want to take piano lessons, so that's also when I started taking piano lessons.

I was a good student in the average class, the normal, basic class that everyone has to go through. Now, getting into the Advanced Work Class, *there* there are students who fall behind. And I think that I wasn't really looking to be there. I managed to get myself there, but I don't think I really wanted to be there. And I think that's more what the problem was.

I did act out, as I didn't want to be there. But between my mother and the faculty, I never did get out! So, I managed to be in there up until the end of eighth grade. I was trying to get out by acting out, but they didn't go for that because it was just a show that I was putting on that could be stopped. It wasn't a real disability of not being able to do the work.

There are certain teachers that challenge you to think. There are students who say, "School is really tough and I can't do this and I can't do that, and this is just too hard for me. . . ." Some students get through high school; that's it for education for them. They don't pursue college. They take a trade because they might be better at working with their hands. . . . Then there is a part that helps you to think. Some people like challenging problems. . . . I believe there are parts of school that can promote you to think.

It [chemistry class] was just totally interesting. When I first heard of it, you know, my brother and sister, they had chemistry before I did. . . . To hear them tell it, chemistry was hard and I just knew I couldn't do it. . . . But I did it. . . . I still didn't understand it like I understand music. You can tell me something about music and I can understand it; I can see how you go about it. There were some things in chemistry that I couldn't. I myself personally feel like I need to take it all over again. . . . That's what made up in my mind that anything that you want to do, it can be done. Because I just had in my mind that I couldn't do it. . . . I kept at it, I didn't give up. . . . The teacher just constantly told us that it's not difficult. The only difficult thing is getting that understanding. Once you understand how you do something, you can in fact go on with it.

There were games that go on. Like math classes, when we had math competitions that actually help you to learn. You'd win little prizes, candy prizes, or whatever. It actually made school a bit more interesting. It made learning a lot easier because it was a game.

I would put more activities into the day that can make it interesting. . . . Because the elective, it's up to you what you think you might be interested in. If you think that you're interested in dance, which they had, that would be fun to you, so then you would not look at it as being a math class. Who likes a math class? There are people who do, but who really likes a math class that would go there because they like being there? But for people who like to dance or the physical education class, they would break their neck practically to get into that class.

I believe a teacher, by the way he introduces different things to you, can make a class interesting. Not like a normal teacher that gets up, gives you a lecture, or there's teachers that just pass out the work, you do the work, pass it in, get a grade, good-bye!

My guidance counselor. . . . I didn't know what I wanted to do; I had no *idea*. At least, the majority of students graduating have some idea of what they want to do. I didn't have the faintest. So she put in front of me many different brochures about dental hygienist or pharmacy and other different careers. . . . Well, I didn't hear of too many people in the career of pharmacy, so it's something that I want to try. I feel that if I put forth that effort, there's a chance for me. . . . She was more like you would say a fellow classmate. There's always somebody who knows just a little bit more that can help you out. It wasn't about "Well, make an appointment to come and see me." She was always glad to help, so when she offered or presented you with different things or different ideas, or careers, it was from the heart more so than from "doing my job." It made a difference, because she has a general idea of what you're about and what you might like.

This particular guidance counselor . . . I had her for my sophomore year in high school. And till the end of June, even after graduation, I was still seeing her. . . . We still keep in touch. She's White. . . . She'd probably have in the range of 200 [students]. . . . She gave me ideas. . . . If I didn't have the guidance counselor that I had, then I really don't know what direction I would be in.

I don't think that we [Black folks] do enough to stick out like a sore thumb. I don't think we do enough to put us on top or put us up in a higher league. I don't think many of us are working to the ability that we can. We are settling for the easiest way out as far as working, as far as education. We feel that after high school, that's it for us; we don't have to go on with it. As far as getting a job, some of us even would resort to selling drugs (not only the Black race, but specifically speaking on the Black race); we would even go to sell drugs just to make it easier for us. I mean, selling drugs, you can make more that day than the average person makes a week. We always oftentimes, we set up the limits rather than going on to higher expectations.

It's important to me because I believe that I am no different from anyone else. I believe there is a space for me. And it's up to me as an individual, it's up to others in the Black race, to take on those opportunities to further ourselves education-wise and as far as living is concerned.

I'm not saying that there's not enough of us out there. I mean, let's take a household, for example. Nine times out of ten, out of a family, there may be at least one person that succeeds in life. Well, why can't *everyone* succeed in life? That's the question that I'm asking; why can't everyone?

We're somewhat tacky. We don't act professional at anything. I'm not saying everyone, but there are some of us who just don't want to be professional. We rely on welfare to take care of us. I don't believe that even those that are on welfare, I don't believe that anyone should have to touch welfare. . . . You know, there are some of us who are smart or some of us who are able to either further our education or get a job, and we don't even want to do that much. . . . Lazy. I think lazy, and we get too comfortable. . . . "Well, I won't go today, I'll go tomorrow." And tomorrow never comes. And I think too many of us are just too comfortable at home, comfortable with the way things are, not really struggling, getting this check every month.

See, I believe that you can take a rich White and put him in a poor Black neighborhood, and he would [be] somewhat immune to it. But if you take a Black and put him in a rich White neighborhood, how do you think that Black would act? There are some of us who are classy, but then there are some who like to have those parties, and have everyone over and being loud. . . . They just really can't fit in. . . .

I feel that's something that Black people are doing to themselves. Like, for instance, I find that a White can move anywhere, and a Black, if he wants to get out in a highly suburban area where there are rich White doctors, something like that, and for instance, if that house is $300,000, it might go up $100,000 just so you can't get in there. Because it is known for Blacks to, not necessarily true, but it is known for Blacks to pull down an area.

I believe that we can do something about it as Blacks. Because we buy homes, very nice homes and so forth, but we don't seem to be upkeeping our homes. We just let it fall down to the ground completely. And then we say, "Oh, look at them! They're not taking care of the house," and whatever.

With that [high] school being predominately Black, well, it's natural that you're going to have quite a bit of top Black students. However, if you were to take those top Black students, say you have two top Black students, and you put them in a classroom with 20 top White students, where would you rank? . . . Just how educated do you think you are? You know some of us, because we sit in this class, and we say, "Well, I'm the smartest," just how educated are you?

Most people think of being a [Black] school, it's not being top. . . . I think if we had more White students, Black students would go further. I find that White students want to learn. Most White students wanted to learn as much as they can get. . . . I think standards would be higher [if there were more White students].

Many of the White teachers there don't push. . . . Their expectations don't seem to be as high as they should be. I mean, work that I feel myself, being a teacher, I would give them to promote any kind of high standards. . . . I know that some Black teachers, their expectations are higher than White teachers. . . . They just do it, because they know how it was for them. . . . Actually, I'd say, you have to be in Black shoes to know how it is.

Black teachers are more . . . they want to impress you more about getting an education, you know; they're your own race, more so than the opposite race. Because of back then, segregated times or times when you weren't able to get that education. But I think that it is just important to all teachers and to all students just to teach the curriculum as they would in an all White school or as they would any other student.

My only thing to make it better is just to encourage the teachers to push the curriculum, that's about it.

FAMILY LESSONS

I have one brother, one sister, and my mother. And we're just a happy-go-lucky family. My brother is the oldest; my sister is the second to the last in line. It's okay, because the parent and first child relationship has broken the barrier for the second and the last child. So things that they did, they can expect from the second and the third. So it's not like it's tougher on me.

She [mother] didn't go to college right away . . . so she felt that a lot of what she's doing now, she could've been doing back then. But by not going to school right away, by prolonging that time, "Well, I won't go this year, but I'll go next year," has turned into a matter of years. And she feels that if you go right after school, then things will look up. And then you'll say, "Well, I'm glad I went to school now rather than wait." You see, we don't want to go to school (going to college, I should say) because we've had it with 12 years of school! It's hard; it's dull; it's boring; we don't like the teachers! So this is our option, whether we want to go on to college. And many of us feel that "Well, I'm not going to go right away. . . ." And she didn't want the same thing to happen to us. . . . Even today, she's wondering, "Well, what are you going to do about school? All I want is you kids to go to college and get an education and live a halfway decent life."

It mattered to me, because I used to say to myself, and probably still do, back in my mind, "Well, what's the big deal about going to school?" I'm not going to find a job without going to college.

I like the goals and objectives that she set for herself being a single parent. Things that I would change: She's really bossy. I should say bossy *to her children*, not to everyone else. Because she desires those things for us to go on and gradually be pharmacists and nurses and engineers. So, she's very persistent. . . . It's out of love, but it's really aggravating [*laughs*]. . . . Actually, it is out of love and persistence, so I'm trying to bear with it.

It's wonderful being a member of my family. We have our ups and downs, but every day, I have fun. I enjoy being with my mother, my sister, and my brother. And I don't think I can compare her. I wouldn't exchange her for anyone else's parents. . . . I mean, look at us, we're not out roaming the streets or anything like that.

My sister's going into nursing, so it's the same [field], medicine. So I'm looking to actually learn with her. Because some classes, she already had that I'm going to be taking in the fall. And then some classes we're going to be having together. So I feel that this will be an excellent benefit for the both of us.

I don't want to be a letdown to my family, personally, and to myself. But I feel that if I tried and then failed, then that's a different story. At least, I did put forth that effort. But you never know until you've tried. You don't know what you can do or what you cannot do unless you've tried.

I've learned from my family, I could say how to survive. Now you say, how do you survive? I know I've learned how to work a job, how to stay on the job. . . .

I've learned about being Black . . . that Blacks have to work harder at things. Some things are just harder than others. What I mean by working hard, I say if you work hard now, it'll pay off later, it definitely will. Something good will come in your life. But let's not look at life as a piece of cake, because eventually it'll dry up, it'll deteriorate, it'll fall, it'll crumble, or somebody will come gnawing at it. . . . But we want to build *solid* foundations for ourselves and for our future generations, for our future children.

We find many students saying, "Well, Mom, you didn't go to college. How come you're making me go?" But let's not look at it that way. Let's look at it, "Well, you have the opportunity; you can get scholarships; you can get financial aid." And just pursue it. Do something for yourself. You know, it might be hard trying to help with your parents, but that'll make them happy, by you prospering.

Grades are very important to my family. My mother is the most influential on that, and my sister. . . . At all times, I just look out for what Rich can do, what he can accomplish, how well he can do it. Because I find that when you are competing, sometimes if you're trying just a little too hard, sometimes we try just a little too hard and we end up messing things up for ourselves. So I feel that, don't take it easy, but you know how much you can take and when to let go. . . . I'm comfortable setting my own standards.

I mean, I feel that there's a thing with "very well," "good," "average," and "poor" and "inferior." I believe that everyone should at least be "average." It's all right to come out "good" and it's all right to come out "excellent," but you should try to at least be average.

I'm just looking forward to all of us to be graduates of some college. Even if not my brother and sister, I at least want to do something for myself. . . . As they say, self-respect is one gift that you give yourself. And I feel that I'll be doing something for myself if I go to college. Nobody can't go to college for you; nobody can't get that knowledge and understanding for you but yourself. So I think I'm going to be doing something for myself.

My mother won't always be there. . . . So that's where it's left for you to decide: "Well, what am I going to do? How am I going to avoid this situation?"

I think the only thing that's holding me back from getting a good education might be me. I just have to be ready to accept it. . . . I want to pursue a future the right way . . . and not find myself in a graveyard or in jail somewhere.

COMMENTARY

The three themes revealed above are inextricably linked with one another. Independence and responsibility, for example, are major values in Rich Miller's life. He has learned these by being the son of a strong mother, a woman deeply concerned about the education of her children. The expectations held for him by teachers and society at times counteract this message. What emerges in this case study is a highly complex portrait of a young man who is independent, resourceful, mature; at once proud, and critical of his culture; and always appreciative of his family for their pressure and support. Through the conflicting messages of family, school, and community, Rich has also learned that Blacks have to work harder to get anywhere and that White teachers have lower expectations of Black students.

The sociopolitical context in which Rich has developed his values and learned these lessons cannot be underestimated. For example, Rich's enrollment in an Advanced Work Class placed him with a minority of African American students. Data collected by the U.S. Office for Civil Rights support the contention that African American students do not receive equal educational opportunities but in fact are subjected to what has been called "second generation school discrimination" through practices such as ability grouping, differential disciplinary practices, and lower graduation rates. They are grossly overrepresented in classes for the mentally retarded and grossly underrepresented in classes for the gifted and talented.[2] Thus, although the manifestations of racism may now be different, they are nevertheless apparent.

Another way in which messages are communicated to students is by the student and staff makeup of schools. Rich, for example, has concluded that the presence of more White students would raise standards for all students. It is not simply the *presence* of these students that would raise standards, however, but rather what teachers expect of them. The issue he raises is one of teachers' perceptions as well as of student responsibilities. Even the percentage of Black teachers in a school may make a crucial difference (in his case, for instance, he feels that Black teachers have higher standards for Black students). Yet, the number of teachers of color within public schools is diminishing. In 1987, the percentage of Black students was 16.2 percent and that of Black teachers was just under 7 percent.[3]

The relationship among students, teachers, and communities is also implicitly connected with students' achievements and perceptions of themselves and their people. Cummins, in his research on empowering minority students, has reached the conclusion that educational reform can succeed only when these power relationships are taken into account: "Previous attempts at educational reform have been largely unsuccessful because the relationships between teachers and schools and between schools and communities have remained largely unchanged."[4] In his view, teachers and schools need to change their roles in the classroom, the community, and society to help students become empowered within the school. This message is echoed by a national report of Black educators, who conclude that the "essential problem lies not with the academic potential of Black children but with the unproductive institutional arrangements, lowered expectations, and narrow pedagogical processes that characterize the American educational system."[5] "Unproductive institutional arrangements" refer to structural factors such as tracking, discriminatory disciplinary policies, and testing, and "narrow pedagogical processes" refer to a lack of creativity and critique in instruction. Both of these topics will be considered in Chapter 4.

Rich has benefited academically from school, but in the process he has picked up some disabling messages: that Blacks are lazy, unproductive, and too ready to take "the easy way out." Rich may indeed have had personal experiences in his own community that have reinforced these perceptions, but he presents the problem in broad strokes and includes the majority of Blacks in these generalizations. He has learned to "blame the victim," although he himself becomes one of them.

The issue is not this simple, however. Although Rich may be demonstrating some negative perceptions of his community, he is also tremendously proud of his culture: He loves gospel music and is involved in his church; he wants to "build solid foundations" for future generations; and most important, he feels that Blacks can take control of their lives ("I believe we can do something about it as Blacks"). These fluctuations are influenced by expectations from schools and society and point to their complex role in helping young people develop their self-concepts.

The issue of Black self-esteem has been studied by many researchers. In an exhaustive review of this research, Powell and Fuller reached the conclusion that the "low self-esteem" or "Negro self-hatred" models need to be discarded because they have proven inadequate in explaining Blacks' self-concepts.[6] More recent work by Cross on African American identity may help us understand the many and seemingly contradictory statements made by Rich about his culture, family, and teachers. Cross points out that diversity is at the very core of Black psychology. Although most African Americans have healthy personalities, they may have different ideologies. Cross also challenges the view that "Negro self-hatred" is a thoroughly documented finding or that it explains everything. He proposes that it is a complex, layered, multidimensional construct. In what he calls "The Pre-Encounter Stage" of Black identity, he describes several characteristics and attitudes that are clearly evident in Rich: social stigma attitudes (race is seen as a problem or stigma); anti-Black attitudes (a "blame the victim" prism); and spotlight, or race image, anxiety (anxiety about being "too Black," and consequently not projecting the best racial image).[7] This is evident, for example, when Rich talks about Blacks being loud or not taking care of their property. Cross points out what is apparent in Rich: "A great deal of pain and sorrow can be associated with such behaviors."[8]

The role of parents and family in building strong character and motivating children to succeed in school is equally important. Rich's mother and siblings have provided strong motivation for him to succeed and go on to higher education. It is important to point out, however, that Rich's mother is not unlike other parents in this regard. What makes her different is that *she knows how to go about helping her children get the education they need.* Because she herself went to college, although several years after graduating from high school, she is convinced that a college education is a necessary prerequisite for her children's welfare. Her involvement with her children's education, starting from elementary school, is evident every step of the way. Rich talks of how instrumental she was in keeping him in the advanced class. He also complains, although lovingly, that she is too "bossy." Although she may have come from an economically oppressed family, she learned the hard lesson of the value of an education and passed it on to her children. The fact that she may have been poor or that she is a single parent does not seem to be the crucial issue here.[9]

These family lessons are not always easy to teach. In fact, some of them run counter to the reality that Rich confronts every day and that he will continue to face in the future. For example, in spite of all the talk of the great gains in educational opportunity made in the past 30 years, the fact is that U.S. colleges enrolled fewer Black undergraduates in 1985 than in 1960.[10] The role of a strong family becomes much more crucial in the lives of students like Rich who must constantly buck the tide of expectations and negative images.

Rich Miller is, like all of us, a product both of his environment and of his own doing. He has learned about his worth and about the value of an education from his mother. He has learned about his culture from his family and church. He has learned about the expectations of Blacks from his teachers and from society in general. And he has learned the important lesson that "self-respect is one gift that you give yourself." We are left with the portrait of a young man who defies easy categorization and who challenges us as educators to look beyond stereotypes of students, their families, and communities for the more subtle but complex issues that help explain student achievement.

TO THINK ABOUT

1. What do you think Rich Miller means by "Self-respect is one gift that you give yourself"?
2. Where do you think Rich's independence comes from?
3. How is Rich's determination to get ahead apparent to you? How might this be related to his criticisms of other Blacks?
4. Rich says that "normal teachers" are those that "just pass out the work, do the work, pass it in, get a grade, good-bye." What are the implications for teachers? How might you design a lesson to appeal to Rich?
5. In small groups, work on the following problems:
   • In what ways does Rich blame Blacks for their own problems?
   • Why do you think he does so?

- How do the expectations of teachers and society fit in here?
- What are the implications for schools?

NOTES

1. I am grateful to Paula Elliott for her interviews with Rich.
2. As reported in Robert E. England, Joseph Stewart, Jr., and Kenneth J. Meier, "Excellence in Education: Second Generation School Discrimination as a Barrier," *Equity and Excellence,* 24, 4 (Summer 1990), 35–40.
3. Quality Education for Minorities Project, *Education That Works: An Action Plan for The Education of Minorities* (Cambridge: Massachusetts Institute of Technology, January 1990).
4. Jim Cummins, *Empowering Minority Students* (Sacramento: California Association for Bilingual Education, 1989), p. 51.
5. Committee on Policy for Racial Justice, *Visions of a Better Way: A Black Appraisal of Public Schooling* (Washington, DC: Joint Center for Political Studies Press, 1989).
6. Cited in Gloria Johnson Powell, "Coping with Adversity: The Psychosocial Development of Afro-American Children," in *The Psychosocial Development of Minority Group Children,* ed. Gloria Johnson Powell (New York: Brunner/Mazel Publishers, 1983).
7. William E. Cross, Jr., *Shades of Black: Diversity in African-American Identity* (Philadelphia: Temple University Press, 1991).
8. Ibid., p. 195.
9. This finding supports research on the school achievement of poor Black children by Reginald M. Clark, *Family Life and School Achievement: Why Poor Black Children Succeed or Fail* (Chicago: University of Chicago Press, 1983).
10. As reported by Alex Molnar, "Racism in America: A Continuing Dilemma," *Educational Leadership,* 47, 2 (October 1989), 71–72.

Vanessa Mattison:
"A good education is like growing, expanding your mind and your views."[1]

Although she lives in a small, rural hilltown in western New England, Vanessa Mattison has had a number of experiences that have helped make her far more worldly than others in her circumstances. At 17, she has traveled to Africa, the Caribbean, and Mexico, which opened her eyes to some of the realities beyond Welborn Hills, the town in which she lives.

Welborn Hills is a small community made up of several diverse groups of people: farming families, who have lived in the area for generations; more educated and liberal (some would say "hippie") families, who have come to escape the turmoil of urban areas; and working-class families, who make their living in the retail and light industry of the surrounding towns and small cities. Vanessa's family would probably be considered to be in the second of these groups. For example, they read not only *Newsweek* but also *Greenpeace;* they are vegetarians; they listen to Bob Dylan, Joan Baez, and reggae and blues music; and they have traveled from time to time. Although a number of the other families of Welborn Hills routinely travel outside the country, others have never even been to Boston or New York, both just a few hours away by car. In the town's only elementary school, as well as in the regional secondary school that the town's students attend, the class conflict between the more liberal and educated families and the children whose families have lived here for generations is almost palpable.

Only a tiny minority of the residents of Welborn Hills are people of color. The same is true of Hills Regional High School, a grade 7 to grade 12 school with a population of approximately 700 students, which serves a number of rural towns including Welborn Hills. For many of the European American students, access to understanding cultural differences and to meeting and being friends with people different from themselves goes along with class and educational privilege. That is, only those students who have had the privilege of traveling, as Vanessa has, have any inkling of racism or of cultural differences. Both their class background and rural, White New England culture have had a big impact on their own cultural understanding and perceptions.

Currently taking classes in Spanish, calculus, sociology, humanities, art, and "contemporary problems," Vanessa is clearly on the academic track. She is looking forward to being the first in her family to go to college and is successful and engaged in school. She is socially active, involved in sports, and quite self-confident and open to new ideas. She has many friends, both male and female, from a variety of cultural backgrounds. She enjoys spending time with her friends and describes a good time as laughing and talking with them. Very soft-spoken and thoughtful in all of her replies, Vanessa has deeply held beliefs about the value of all people, peace, and social justice, and she is also interested in environmental issues.

At present, there are just three people at home: Vanessa and both of her parents. Her sister, 21, lives in a nearby town. Her father, who was raised in this area, is a craftsperson; her mother is a paralegal. Although both finished high school, neither went to college. Vanessa sees her family as being different because her parents are still together and everyone is happy and gets along. She takes pride in the fact that her parents stand up for what they believe in. At the time she was interviewed, this quality was taking the shape of protest against the Gulf war, which had just begun. Vanessa and her family live in a modest home and are economically lower-middle class. She works after school in a local store.

Having never had to identify ethnically or racially because she has always been considered the "norm," it became clear from the outset that Vanessa was embarrassed and uncomfortable with the issue of self-identification and culture. In spite of the fact that she is probably more aware of culture and cultural differences than the majority of her peers, it nevertheless was a difficult issue for her. She did want to grapple with it, however. In fact, she agreed to be interviewed precisely because the project sounded "interesting and important," and she made time for it in her busy schedule. Discomfort with issues of cultural, racial, and linguistic differences is the major theme that emerged with Vanessa. The others focused on the promise, sometimes unfulfilled, of education and on what teachers can do to make school more fun for students.

THE DISCOMFORT OF DIFFERENCES

[When asked how she describes herself,] I generally don't. . . . Wait, can you explain that? Like, what you want to know?

Well, I would [describe myself as White], but it doesn't matter to me, so that's why I said it's a tough question. 'Cause I usually just describe myself as like what I believe in or something like that. Rather than like what culture I am, whether I'm Black or White. 'Cause that doesn't matter. . . .

[I'm] . . . well, Scottish, French, and German, I guess. My family all speak English at home, though I'm taking Spanish. I guess I'm middle class or lower class. It depends on how you think of it. I guess the German part might have come in the twentieth century. I'm not really sure, that's just a general guess. . . . I wasn't really interested. I don't really know if we have that many connections back to who was where when and what happened.

I don't have any [religious beliefs]. I've never gone to church. We never like read the Bible as a family or anything. I think both of my parents used to go to church. I think they were Catholic. . . . They probably didn't think it was as important to their life as the people who had wanted them to go. . . . I don't really know much about it. But if I had a choice, I probably wouldn't want to go to church because I think that I'd rather formulate my own ideas than being told that the earth was created in seven days and God did this and he did this. I don't know, he seems like just too almighty of a person to me. I just don't believe it.

I guess obviously I just made it seem like [culture] wasn't [important]. It's just that like all the stuff that's happened to people because of their culture, like the slaves and Jewish people. Culture, what you look like, whether you're Black or White could matter less to me. It's the person who you are . . . it's not what your appearance depicts.

Being a White American, the American society has always been, you had more opportunities and stuff. But I don't really see that as good 'cause it's not fair. . . . You have more opportunities and just more of an equal chance. But I guess "equal" can't really be used there. Less of a struggle.

I don't think it's fair. I don't think that one person should have an easier time just because of the color of their skin or their race or 'cause they belong to a particular church or something.

People like Blacks still don't have as many rights as the White man. I'm saying "man" because women don't have their rights either. The "superiority game" . . . [continues] 'cause people just have it stuck in their head that that's the way it is and . . . I don't really know how to change it. I try and change it, speak out against it.

[Other cultures] are not that well represented [in my school] because there's not that many people who live around here. The majority is probably White. But they're represented in a small margin. . . . [In school], we've read books and we've seen movies. I think we saw part of the freedom marches in the South and stuff like that. And we saw Gandhi, although that isn't really to this culture.

Each of us that go there is important to our school because it adds what you could say would be a *culture*. Just like our community, the school community. . . . Well, I guess people's backgrounds *do* [matter] because that's what makes them what they are.

[Culture] is like a conglomeration of language, the way you speak, the way you are . . . things that are important to you. . . . Well, the culture of the United States is kind of like norms, things that happen a lot. Like if you were to go to another country, it might strike you as weird because you don't do it at home that way.

Well, people in Central Africa, if you go into a store you need to say "hi" to the person who's working there and acknowledge them. Because if you don't acknowledge them, they're not going to acknowledge you and they won't help you and that's really important to them. . . . Like when a woman has a child, they go off with their mother and their aunts and their sisters and stay with them for three months to start to raise the child. Which I don't know if I completely agree with, because it leaves the husband away and detaches him at the very start.

In Mexico, I was in a really big city, quite the change. There's lots of rules there about what women can wear. I know at one time, they couldn't wear shorts. I don't really think that's true anymore. It was weird. . . . The way people did things was really different. . . . Like in Central Africa, people sweep their houses and their yards everyday, but then they'll just throw their junk right off the edge of their property. Which here, it's a little bit more discreet because you throw it at the dump.

I don't agree with a lot of our culture. I don't agree with how it's so rushed and how if you're Black, you're supposedly not as good or you're not as fit for the job or something like that. And if you're a woman, it's the same thing. And like you can't be gay without being put down. I don't know, there's all these underlying rules about if you're not this, you can't do that.

It seems weird . . . because people came over from Europe and they wanted to get away from all the stuff that was over there. And then they came here and set up all the stuff like slavery, and I don't know, it seems the opposite of what they would have done. It was probably like burned into their head already from where they were: If you were lower class, then you usually weren't taught to read or educated. . . . They might not have come over thinking that's what they had in mind, but since that's what they had always known, that's what they did.

When I see racism, I often think that I wish I was Black or I wish I was the group that was being discriminated against. You know how some women say, "I hate men"? I don't know, but I'm sure that Black people said this, when they were slaves, like "I hate White people." I don't want to be thought of like that because I'm not against them. I think they're equal. And also after they've been put through so much awfulness, I think that every White person should be in their shoes. . . .

Like [President] Bush says in his speech a little while ago that "We're doing all we can to fight racism and blah, blah, blah," when the Supreme Court just made the ruling about schools and busing, which was basically turning back a decision they had made a long time ago.

When I was in second grade, there was somebody coming into our class who was going to be Black. He was like a new student and somebody said something about it, and me and a couple of my other friends got really mad at him. "It doesn't matter what color they are. They could be orange or yellow or brown. It doesn't matter, they're just a person."

For strength and inspiration, I usually look to Martin Luther King, Jr.

I like Gandhi too, because I believe in nonviolence. And I believe they helped to strengthen the basis for my belief and they gave specific examples of how it could work. I just believe in nonviolence as a way to get what you want and peace. I don't believe if you punch somebody, then, yeah, they may do what you want them to do, but they're not going to be doing it because they want to. They're just going to be doing it because of fear. I don't think fear is a good policy.

EDUCATION AND VALUES

Supposedly education is what this country is built on, but there's no money for it.

Money is being cut out of all the schools. We lost a bunch of programs. We don't have as many teachers. We're going to lose more money and it seems like the government's always promoting it as this great big deal. Then, where's the money for it? They're not supporting it. . . . They still have, for seventh and eighth grade, sewing and cooking and art. Music is still there and sports was supported by the public this year through bottle drives and a big fund-fest. I don't know what's going to happen next year. I hope it's still supported.

[My parents] feel the same way, that the government needs to step in and help and that it's sad that it's going downhill. I think they think it's important to learn. Because they want me to be able to do what I want to do, and not, as I said before, get locked in a corner.

I've learned [from my parents] a lot of my morals, like nonviolence and expressing myself, and striving for what I want, being able to have the confidence to reach what I want.

They're caring and they're willing to go against the norm. They're willing to protest, that's a good word for it, for what they believe in.

I think he [Dad] values being able to survive on his own. Like moving away from your family and growing up and having your own job and supporting yourself and being able to get around, and not always having to have people do things for you. . . . He's fun and supportive.

She [Mom] also strives for what her goals are and believes in self-support, working for what's yours.

[I would like] a little less pressure . . . like around college and school.

It's not a broken-up family. My parents are together and they're happy and there isn't any fighting. Everybody gets along. A lot of my friends [are from divorced families]. There's a lot of support that I don't see in other families. . . . We don't always go with the flow. You know, like most people supposedly right now are for the war. We're not, so we stand in the minority. . . . I personally don't believe in violence to solve things. I don't think that killing a zillion million people for oil is a good reason either. And you can't bring peace to somewhere that's not your culture and has a different government, and you especially can't do it through war. That's not going to solve things. And it would take a lot of talking and rearranging their entire society to get them to be like us, which I don't think is what they should be 'cause they're not and they never have been and probably won't be. . . . People drive by the [peace] vigils and give us the finger.

[My parents want me to go to school] so I can be educated and get a job. So I can have options and not get stuck. . . . Probably because they didn't go to college and they'd like me to. That's just a guess.

[I want to] go to college to help people. I want to be a psychologist or do social work, work with the environment. I'm not sure. . . . There's a guidance counselor but my parents have done more of that with college. I'm not sure what help I need.

I guess [grades are important] because they've kind of become that way. Once you get into the cycle of being in one place, you kind of stay there. . . . If I get grades that aren't real good, [my parents] are not real excited. And they always make sure that I'm doing my homework. They tell me to get off the phone.

I'm happy. Success is being happy to me, it's not like having a job that gives you a zillion dollars. It's just having self-happiness.

A good education is like when you personally learn something . . . like growing, expanding your mind and your views.

MAKING SCHOOL MORE FUN

[In elementary school, I liked] recess, 'cause it was a break between doing stuff. Everything wasn't just pushed at you. And art, which was really fun. . . . It was a safe place and I liked the teachers and the people that went there. . . . I liked that on Valentine's Day and Christmas and birthday parties they had ones for us. They mixed school and fun.

I did the work, I understood it, and I was interested. I think it's if you learn *personally*. That's not what the school thinks. It's not like if you get an A or an F, but if you learn. It's not just for the grades.

My favorite [subject] is art because of the freedom to express myself, to paint and draw. Humanities is my worst 'cause it's just lectures and tests.

I play field hockey and I've done track and I've done tennis, because it's a way of releasing energy and feeling good about yourself and being in shape. And working with other people. . . . I play sports and I'm in a peer education group. It's a group of 18 seniors who set up programs to educate the other students in the school on issues like alcoholism, drunk driving, stereotyping, a bunch more. It's kind of like, since they're students and they're projecting to a student audience, it's easier for some people to relate.

We did a skit on [stereotyping]. We had like jocks, hippies, snobs, burnouts, and a nerd. And we did these little scenarios like the snob liked this guy who was a hippie and all her friends were like, "Oh, my god! You like *him*?! He's such a hippie!" And then like the hippie friends said the same thing about the snob and then like everything stopped and the two people who liked each other got up and said, "I wish my friends would understand. . . . " And then the person who was narrating said, "Well, here's one way in which the situation could be fixed.'' So they went back where they were and said, ''Okay, yeah, well, I guess we should give them a chance.'' Most of the ideas came from us except for the one I just explained to you. Me and two other people basically wrote the whole skit. We just did it for the seventh and eighth grade. We thought that would be the most effective place 'cause that's where it basically starts. They liked it.

It's important for teachers to get to know all the students and know where they're coming from and why they may react a certain way to certain things because then it'll be easier to get through. And there won't be as many barriers because they'll already know. . . . Maybe if school didn't just start off on the first day with homework, maybe if it started off with just getting to know each other. Even if you're in a class that's already known each other. . . .

Have games, more free time. . . . You could have games that could teach anything that they're trying to teach through notes or lectures. Well, like if you're doing Spanish, you can play hangman or something. You can play word games where you have to guess the word. Like they give you a definition and it makes you remember the words. Or if somebody acts out a word, you remember it better than someone just looking it up or writing it down.

Make it more entertaining 'cause people learn a lot from entertainment. If you see a play, you'll probably remember it more than a lecture, if you see a movie, play a game, or something. . . . Work those more into what they're doing. . . . I think that some books should be required just to show some points of view.

Some [teachers], based on [bad] reputation, may not be as patient with some people. [Students get reputations] basically through grades and troublemaking, like if you get in trouble with the system and get detentions.

[Teachers who are not helpful are] ones that just kind of just move really fast, just trying to get across to you what they're trying to teach you. Not willing to slow down because they need to get in what they want to get in.

[Most teachers] are really caring and supportive and are willing to share their lives and are willing to listen to mine. They don't just want to talk about what they're teaching you, they also want to know you.

COMMENTARY

Having to confront racial, class, cultural, and other differences was difficult for Vanessa. She had never even had to consider many of these questions before. One gets the sense from dialogue with her that "culture," "ethnicity," and "race" are things that *other* people have. Vanessa sometimes seemed offended at having to talk about these issues. It was almost as if it were rude to broach questions of race or culture, that discussing them meant you were a racist. She took the approach that cultural and racial differences are not important to her, that it "couldn't matter less to me." In this, she is simply reflecting the value of being color-blind, which we have all been led to believe is both right and fair. In this framework, differences are seen as a *deficit* rather than as an *asset*.[2] Being White and Christian, she has rarely been confronted with her cultural identity. She considers herself the "norm," "just a person." As is the case for most White Americans, she has the privilege of seeing herself as just an individual, an opportunity not generally afforded to those from dominated groups. Being White in the United States is simply not an issue.

Because culture, race, and other differences are associated by Vanessa, as well as by others from dominant (and dominating) groups, with oppression and inequality, it becomes a difficult subject to address. For one, she sees cultural and other differences as *causing* oppression ("like all the stuff that happened to people because of their culture, like the slaves and the Jewish people"). For another, the fact that some people are penalized for being what they are while others are rewarded for it makes it difficult for her to confront differences. Not wanting to benefit from racism, Vanessa finds it easier to avoid or downplay the issue. Her growing awareness of sexism, revealed through such comments as "I'm saying 'man' 'cause women don't have their rights either" may help her make the connection between the two issues.[3]

Vanessa's ambivalence to racial and other differences and to racism itself can be understood by looking at an analysis of the consequences of racism for White children. Using autobiographical accounts, Dennis attempted to explore what happens to White children in an environment where the ideology of racial supremacy is a main socializing element. He concluded that there are four main effects of this kind of racist socialization. White children tend to develop

- ignorance of people outside their own group
- a double social psychological consciousness (whereby they learn to adjust to a lack of correspondence between principle and action)
- group conformity
- a moral confusion and social ambivalence[4]

Some of these effects are evident in Vanessa. She is grappling with the issues of a "double social psychological consciousness," between the ideals she has been taught and the discrimination she sees around her. She is earnestly attempting to understand the complexity surrounding issues of diversity. She believes in the equality of all people and is beginning to understand the links among peace, social justice, racism, and other forms of discrimination. Although she associates herself with her race only when confronted with the example of other White people being racist, it is at times such as these that Vanessa sees the need for Whites to face up to and take responsibility. She also understands that being White means having more opportunities, which she resents as unfair.

Through dialogue with Vanessa, it became clear that few of these issues have ever been addressed in any of her classes. For instance, when asked if she learns history and other subject matter in school from perspectives of different groups of people, she answered that everything was taught from "a general perspective." What she thinks of as "a general perspective" is in fact a European American, White perspective. Because the viewpoints of others are generally invisible in the curriculum, students begin to think of the one reality that is taught as the "general" reality, whereas the experiences of others become little more than ethnic add-ons to "real" knowledge.

Notwithstanding the lack of awareness of diverse perspectives, Vanessa is becoming keenly aware of and committed to social issues. For example, she says that she speaks out against discriminatory statements and in that way tries to change things. This quality was already apparent in second grade. Even in that incident, however, she and her friends thought that by *overlooking* racial differences, they would be helping the new boy in class. Being color-blind was, in their understanding, the moral imperative.

Vanessa is quite involved in a peer education group and has taken the issues of drug abuse, alcoholism, and others seriously. It was interesting to note the skits they used to educate younger students. To make them more accessible to the experiences of those involved, they centered on social class types in the school ("nerds," "hippies," etc.) rather than race or culture.

It is evident to Vanessa that education should be a major priority in our society if we want to give all students an equal education; yet she is aware that the societal commitment is simply not there. The promise of education for advancement and rewards is important but "not as important as society makes out," she is quick to add. "They want me to go and I have to," she says, referring to the fact that although education is compulsory it is often not engaging. In conjunction with the value of education are the values that Vanessa has learned from her parents: self-reliance, self-confidence, and independent thought. These values have obviously helped her develop her own *persona* in a school setting that may be rigidly conformist and conservative.

The role that her parents play in supporting both her personal choices and her academic success is very clear. Vanessa's parents value education beyond high school for their daughter, understanding very well that it will give her options they themselves did not have. They are involved in school activities (her mother served on the local school committee, and both have volunteered time and attention to the schools) and have demonstrated their concerns in many other ways as well. Their involvement, in Vanessa's words, "shows that they care."

Vanessa is caught in the dilemma of seeing education as important while not getting as much out of it as has been promised. She also wishes it were more interesting and interactive. Her perceptions on the boring and "flat" nature of schooling, especially at the secondary level, corroborates research that has focused on schools around the country.[5] Her suggestions for teachers emphasize making school more entertaining and fun for all students. She is particularly concerned about students who feel they need to drop out because they are so disconnected from the school experience. In relation to this, Vanessa also suggests that clubs, sports, and other activities be continued. She is dismayed that so many of these activities have been removed because of budgetary constraints. In her own case, involvement in a school club and in several sports, as well as her part-time job, seems to have helped her develop in more than just academic ways.

A strong and forthright young woman with deeply held values and beliefs, Vanessa Mattison views education as an important part of everyone's growth and development. Although she is still uncomfortable with issues of diversity in any comprehensive way, she is committed to struggling with them. The interviews themselves seemed to have served as a catalyst to her thinking more extensively about diversity, racism, and identity. For example, after thinking about how *unimportant* race and culture are to her, she quietly admitted that "Well, I guess people's backgrounds *do* [matter] because that's what makes them what they are." Given the strength and support of her family, her searching soul, and her grounding in peace and social justice, she is a wonderful example of a young person ready to, in her words, "expand my mind and my views."

TO THINK ABOUT

1. Do you think that White people in the United States in general do not identify as White? Why or why not? Who might be exceptions?
2. What kinds of experiences might have made Vanessa less uncomfortable in dealing with issues of diversity?

3. As a teacher, what is your responsibility in introducing your students to diversity? What kinds of strategies and activities might you use? How would these differ in a primarily White school from a more culturally and racially heterogeneous school?

4. What is the role of values in education? Should schools teach values? Why or why not? Would some of the values that Vanessa's family believes in be included? Why or why not?

5. Vanessa gave several suggestions to make school more entertaining and fun. What do you think of these? Do they contradict the purpose of school?

6. In a group, develop other suggestions for teachers that would make school more interesting and engaging for students. Focus on a particular grade level and subject area.

NOTES

1. I am grateful to Maya Gillingham for the interviews and the background for Vanessa's case study.
2. For a more detailed discussion of this topic, see Sonia Nieto, "We Speak in Many Tongues: Linguistic Diversity and Multicultural Education," in *Multicultural Education for the Twenty-first Century,* ed. Carlos F. Díaz (Washington, DC: National Education Association, 1992).
3. A particularly helpful piece is Peggy McIntosh, "Understanding Correspondences Between White Privilege and Male Privilege Through Women's Studies Work," paper presented at the National Women's Studies Association Annual Meeting, Spelman College, Atlanta, June 25, 1987.
4. Rutledge M. Dennis, "Socialization and Racism: The White Experience," in *Impacts of Racism on White Americans,* ed. Benjamin P. Bowser and Raymond G. Hunt (Beverly Hills, CA: Sage Publications, 1981).
5. See, for example, John I. Goodlad, *A Place Called School* (New York: McGraw-Hill, 1984); Linda M. McNeill, *Contradictions of Control: School Structure and School Knowledge* (New York: Methuen/Routledge & Kegan Paul, 1986).

CHAPTER 4

Structural Factors in Schools

OVERVIEW

Certain school policies and practices exacerbate the inequities that exist in society. Ironically, some of these have evolved in an attempt to deal more equitably with student diversity; this is true of tracking, which is often meant to help those students most in academic need. Others are so integral to the schooling experience that they are hardly questioned; this is the case with the physical structure and with pedagogy and the compartmentalization of knowledge, especially at the secondary school level. And some may not be official "policies" at all but unacknowledged practices that may lead to disempowerment; this is the case with the limited roles of teachers, students, and parents in the school.

It is important to state at the outset that structures in schools that may affect some students in negative ways may actually help other students. For example, tracking may help some high-achieving students, although the evidence is mixed. The point is that the parents of high-achieving students are often the most reluctant to give up or challenge the policy of tracking because they perceive it as beneficial to their children. If tracking were unanimously criticized as jeopardizing all students, it would have been eliminated long ago. Vested interests, particularly of those most powerful in school systems and society itself, are a crucial factor that we cannot afford to ignore.

Numerous structures may affect student learning in negative ways. The following discussion is not meant to be all-inclusive but rather to provide examples of school policies and practices that may inhibit the educational success of many students and therefore reinforce social inequities. Each of the following will be briefly described and examined:

- Tracking
- Testing

- The curriculum
- Pedagogy
- Physical structure
- Disciplinary policies
- Limited role of students
- Limited role of teachers
- Limited role of parents

TRACKING

One of the most inequitable and, until recently, relatively undisputed practices in schools is *tracking*. Tracking is the placement of students in groups of matched ability, or *homogeneous groups*, within classes (e.g., reading groups in self-contained classes), subject areas (e.g., a low-level math group in seventh grade), or even specific programs (e.g., academic or vocational programs at the high school level). In most schools, tracking is as much a part of school as are bells and recess. It begins with children at the very youngest ages.

In a now classic study that had a great impact on the research on teachers' expectations, mentioned in Chapter 3, Rist reported the results of an ethnographic study of one class of poor Black children during their first three years of schooling. You will remember that the kindergarten teacher in his study grouped the children on the eighth day of school and these groups remained almost intact two years later.[1] The data used by the teacher to make these grouping decisions were all social indices; none was directly related to academic ability. That is, she used such information as preregistration forms, initial interviews with mothers, and her own prior knowledge of which families received public assistance. The results were also social: Most students at Table 1 (the so-called "high achievers") wore cleaner clothes that were relatively new and pressed, had no body odor, spoke more standard English, were generally lighter-skinned, and were more likely to have processed (straightened) hair.

It is clear from this research that grouping decisions are often made on the most tenuous of grounds. Yet such decisions may have a disastrous effect on the lives of children. Goodlad, in a more recent study, found that first- or second-grade children who are tracked by teachers' judgments of reading and math ability or by testing are likely to remain in that track *for the duration of their schooling*. He also found that children of color and poor children in general are predominately at the lowest track levels and that they advance more slowly, develop problems of lower self-esteem, and have higher dropout rates.[2] The Massachusetts Advocacy Center, a Boston-based group, found that in that city's public schools, African American, Latino, and some Asian students are most likely to be categorized by their supposed "deficits" in the early grades, whereas White and other Asian students are most likely to be placed in programs emphasizing their "abilities" or "gifts," especially after the elementary grades.[3] A study of in-class reading groups in an integrated classroom by Collins found that the high-ranked group (almost all White students) received consistently different instructional strategies than did the low-ranked group (primarily Black students). There was an emphasis on decoding skills in the low group versus an emphasis on comprehension skills in the high group.[4] Another study found that the practice of ability grouping for *all* subject areas is more prevalent in schools that have sizable enrollments of African American and Latino students.[5]

At the middle and senior school level, tracking continues to be an insidious practice, with often dramatic effects. Students at the improbable ages of early adolescence are often asked to make program choices, which may result in decisions that virtually chart the course of their lives. It is at this age that students are asked to decide on vocational school, an academic track, a secretarial or "business" track, or what is sometimes called a "general" track. Through these choices, they may pursue a college education, a job as a mechanic, or almost certain joblessness. Young people of 13 or 14 years of age are hardly prepared to make such monumental decisions.

Most schools do not have adequate staffs to help students make appropriate choices. Even when counselors are available, they are generally assigned other responsibilities which preclude their assisting children in these decisions. In schools that do provide guidance counselors in this role, students may nonetheless make poor choices, basing their decisions on what their best friends do or on what is perceived as relevant by their peers. Finally, although students may feel that they themselves are making decisions, these may actually have been made for them years before by the first teacher who placed them in a reading group. The placement of students in certain ability groups may help them develop particular classroom personalities and attitudes that remain with them for a long time. For example, in research by Gouldner on the study reported by Rist, it was found that children became "teachers' pets," "troublemakers," or "nobodies" in the classroom, based on their placement in a particular group.[6] Students began to believe that their placement in these groups was a true reflection of whether they were "smart" or "dumb." The messages that children internalize from grouping practices arc probably more destructive than we realize and their effects more long-lasting than we care to admit.

In spite of the pervasiveness of tracking, its effectiveness is questionable. Based on her research in 25 junior and senior high schools around the country, Oakes has reported the almost exclusively negative results of this practice.[7] She concluded that tracking is not in the best interests of students and that it is unrelated to increasing academic achievement or promoting positive attitudes about school. Even worse, she found that it has especially adverse effects on students already alienated by the school experience, that is, poor children and those from linguistically and culturally diverse families. If the purpose of tracking is to provide access to opportunity for those who have most been denied it, it has failed. Actually, it has had largely the opposite effect. Other research on the effects of tracking has found it to be inadequate and even counterproductive in meeting its stated aims.[8]

Despite the overwhelming evidence that it does not work, tracking continues to shape policy in most schools throughout the country. Many educators sincerely believe that it helps to individualize instruction. Tracking is thus perceived as *promoting* equality. Although its effects may actually be contrary to its stated intended outcomes, it has been a fixed and immutable part of the culture of middle and secondary schools in our society. As has been amply documented, the culture of the school is resistant to change.[9] Once an idea has taken hold, it seems to develop a life of its own, regardless of its usefulness or effectiveness. Moreover, schools respond poorly to pressure for change, particularly if it comes from those most jeopardized but least powerful.

Ability grouping leaves its mark on pedagogy as well. Students in the lowest levels, for example, are those who are most subjected to rote memorization and worn methods, as their teachers often feel that these are the children who need, first, to master the "basics." Until the basics are learned, the thinking goes, creative methods are a frill that these students can ill afford. Poor children and those most alienated by the schools are once again the losers. The cycle of school failure is repeated: Those students most in need are placed in the lowest-level classes and exposed to the drudgery of drill and repetition, school becomes more boring and senseless every day, and the students become discouraged and drop out.

This is not to imply that students at the top ability levels always receive instruction that is uplifting, interesting, and meaningful. On the contrary, they too are exposed to similar methods and materials as those at the bottom levels. Nevertheless, if innovative methods and appealing materials exist at all, they tend to be found at the top levels. Knowledge becomes yet another privilege of those who are already privileged.

It appears that tracking is propped up and sustained by particular class interests. Because it sorts and classifies students, it helps prepare them for similar classification in the larger society. Students in the top tracks generally end up attending college and becoming professionals; those in the bottom tracks, for the most part, drop out or, if they do finish high school, become unskilled workers.[10] Without falling into too mechanistic an explanation for what is a very complex process, it is nevertheless true that some students benefit and others lose because of tracking. Teachers and schools compound the problem by seeing tracking as the only alternative to handling student differences and as a "natural" and even "neutral" practice. As one teacher in a study by Sirotnik and Oakes asked, "After all, who's going to collect the garbage?"[11] It is clear that tracking, senseless and ineffective as it may appear, actually reflects and perpetuates class, race, and gender stratification in our society.

TESTING

Another structural factor that impedes equity in our schools is testing. Originally designed to help identify mentally retarded children, the use of tests expanded greatly after the beginning of the century and its original aims were subverted to include rationalization of the theories of genetic inferiority.[12] Although an extensive review of their use is not called for here, it is important to emphasize that tests, particularly intelligence tests, have frequently been used as a basis for segregating and sorting students. The relationship of testing to tracking has often been a symbiotic one. Lewis Terman, a psychologist who experimented with such tests at the turn of the century, was able to state with absolute conviction after testing *a pair* of Indian and Mexican children, "Their dullness seems to be racial, or at least inherent in the family stock from which they came. . . . Children of this group should be segregated in special classes . . . they cannot master abstractions, but they can often be made efficient workers."[13] The same reasoning was used on other occasions to "explain" the inferior intelligence of Blacks, Jews, and Italians.[14]

The situation today is certainly not as blatant, but the kind and number of tests to which we continue to subject our students are staggering. Fair Test, an organization that monitors standardized testing use, has conservatively estimated that about 100,000,000 such tests are given to the almost 40 million students in our schools yearly. This comes out to an average of 2.5 tests per student per year.[15] Much of the testing frenzy is a result of the "educational reform" movement of the 1980s, in which academic achievement was tied to such variables as test scores, number of days spent in school, and a standardized curriculum. However, the validity and effects of tests are questionable, particularly for children from culturally diverse backgrounds.[16] Increasingly, the results of such reforms are making it clear that poor children and children of color are experiencing even more failure than before the reforms.

America 2000, the Bush administration's education strategy to raise national standards, is also based on the dubious reasoning that more tests will somehow lead to more learning and higher standards. A new and dizzying round of tests for all fourth, eighth, and twelfth grade students in the nation in all five core subjects is proposed, with standards developed by an appointed National Education Goals Panel. The plan gives little mention, however, to changes in curriculum or instructional practices, or to improvements in teacher education.

Testing affects other factors that impede equity. For example, it may have a decided effect on the curriculum. Teachers in schools in which children have poor test scores may be forced to "teach to the test" rather than to create curricula that respond to the real needs of the learners. This in turn affects teacher autonomy for it removes curriculum decision making from the teacher level to the school, district, city, or even state level. And the further the curriculum is from the school level, the less it will reflect the culture of the students in that school.

The stated purposes of achievement testing are often at odds with the way in which such tests are used. That is, although they are ostensibly used to provide teachers and schools with information about the learning needs of students, in fact they are often used to sort students further. In a vicious cycle of failure, students who are perceived as needing more help are placed in classes in which the curriculum is diluted and higher levels of thinking are not demanded, and their academic achievement falls even further behind. Many teachers and schools may sincerely believe that tests provide data for helping those students most in need of academic support. Although this belief may prove true in some schools, it is doubtful that the majority of students benefit from testing.

THE CURRICULUM

The curriculum in many schools is also at odds with the needs of learners. This mismatch is evident in the irrelevance of the content to the lives and life-styles of students and their families. In many places, schools are fortresses, which are separated in more than physical ways from their communities. The life of the school is separate and distinct from the life of the community in ways that are abundantly clear as soon as one steps inside. For example, it is not unusual to see classrooms in which young children learn about "community helpers" without ever studying about the real people in their neighborhoods. They learn about police officers, fire fighters, and mail carriers, all of whom may live outside their immediate neighborhood. Often, children and their families do not consider these to be "helpers" at all but outsiders who control their communities. Students may learn about doctors and lawyers and businesspeople but may never have met one of them in their neighborhood. Yet the owner of the corner "bodega," the local factory worker, or community service staff are rarely mentioned as "community helpers."

When studying the "four food groups," children learn to make up fictitious breakfasts to satisfy their teachers' questions, for to admit to having eaten bread and butter and coffee or cold noodles for breakfast is to admit that they are doing something wrong, at least in the eyes of the school. Similarly, a teacher may have to struggle to find relevant ways to describe the lives of Dutch children to her class, whereas the heritage and background of the children in his or her own room may never be discussed. Or there may be the incongruous situation of Mexican American, Puerto Rican, and other Latin American children who are fluent in Spanish being forced to learn "Castilian Spanish" because their teachers have accepted the premise that it is more "correct." Children learn early in their academic experience that what goes on in school is frequently irrelevant to their lives and reflects a different, often imposed, reality.

If we define curriculum as the organized environment for learning in a classroom and school, we see that it is never neutral but represents what is thought to be important and necessary knowledge by those who are dominant in a society. Given the vast array of knowledge available, only a tiny fraction of it finds its way into textbooks and teachers' guides. Decisions about what is most important for students to learn are generally made by those furthest from the lives of students. These decisions let students know whether the knowledge they or their communities value is accorded prestige within the formal curriculum. For example, students reprimanded for speaking Black English (or what is increasingly being called *African American Language*, or *AAL*) pick up a powerful message about the language variety that has prestige and power in our society. Curriculum thus serves as one primary means of social control. Students learn quite forcefully that what is afforded status at home is often negated in school. Yet curriculum is often taught as if it were the whole, unvarnished, and uncontested truth.

The curriculum is also often "watered down" by teachers who, in their belief that such accommodations will better meet the needs of diverse learners, fall into the trap of expecting less of some children. It is probably true that this practice comes from a legacy of responding in what seems to be an equitable way. Yet although all children can benefit from high expectations and a challenging curriculum, some students are invariably presented with diluted, undemanding, and boring educational programs. Moll's research on classroom analysis of successful Latino students revealed that their teachers were "social mediators," that is, that they arranged, changed, improved, or modified the curriculum to teach at the highest level possible. The teachers assumed that their students were capable of doing high-level work and that it was their responsibility to provide a challenging, innovative, and intellectually rigorous curriculum. This may explain why these students, although speaking little English and from working-class or poor families, were achieving at or above grade level on standardized measures of academic achievement. As one of the teachers said, watering down the curriculum would be "degrading and disrespectful to the children."[17]

Textbooks, an important component of the curriculum in most schools, also reinforce the dominance of the European American perspective and sustain stereotypes of any group perceived to be outside the mainstream. This finding is not new. A 1949 comprehensive analysis of 300 textbooks revealed that many of them perpetuated negative stereotypes of "minority" groups.[18] This result has been found time and again in more recent years. A 1980 study by the Council on Interracial Books for Children found that the history, perspectives, and life-styles of people of color are omitted from most history books, and a 1985 study by the same group questioned the ability of U.S. history texts to develop an awareness of social justice.[19] Although in recent years some progress has been made in publishing books that are more representative, much more needs to be done. As late as 1991, an extensive study by Sleeter and Grant found the textbook situation to be surprisingly similar to previous research. In examining the treatment of various groups across the major subject areas in textbooks currently used in grades 1 through 8, they found the following:

- Whites still consistently dominate textbooks, although their margin of dominance varies.

- Whites still receive the most attention and dominate the story line and lists of accomplishments in most textbooks.

- Women and people of color are shown in a much more limited range of roles than are White males.

- Textbooks contain very little about contemporary race relations or the issues that most concern people of color and women.

- Textbooks continue to convey an image of harmony among different groups and contentment with the status quo.

All in all, they found that although textbooks now include more people of color and women, they continue to legitimize the status of White males. In addition, although the culture and adaptation of other groups continue to be seen as a problem, European American culture is not.[20]

A similar situation has been found in most children's literature, which tends to omit or stereotype the lives and experiences of African American, Mexican American, Puerto Rican, Asian, American Indian, and other groups.[21] Even when newer and more inclusive literature is available, it is not clear if schools include it in their reading and library offerings.

Research on the inappropriateness of the school curriculum to the lives of children demonstrates that it alienates many students. Grant and Sleeter, for example, found that even in a culturally diverse junior high school, what was taught by the great majority of teachers was the European American, middle-class experience that is taught in most schools. Even on special occasions such as Black History Month, teachers did not seriously address diversity in spite of the fact that they all verbalized great support and sympathy for such events. They tended to see multicultural education as lessons about getting along or about different cultures. The result was that the students' own natural interest in their racial and cultural diversity was seen as irrelevant in the curriculum. The researchers concluded that if the students, based on their home experiences, thought that cultural diversity was valuable, they learned in school that it was not as valuable as the dominant culture.[22]

This is an important lesson many children learn in school, even though it is not part of the expressed curriculum. The extensive research by Anyon in schools in four different settings reinforces the importance of the "hidden curriculum" for children from different social classes.[23] For example, in the working-class schools she researched, work was defined as following the steps of a procedure; these were generally mechanical and emphasized rote learning and drill. At the other extreme, at the "executive elite school" work was characterized as developing one's analytical, intellectual powers. In all cases, the work that these children did in school was tacitly preparing them for their future work in society. The differing curricula and pedagogy at each setting emphasized different cognitive and behavioral skills. That is, children's school experiences differed qualitatively by social class. Thus, in discussing curriculum, we are concerned not only with the "expressed" or written curriculum but also with the hidden and not-so-hidden messages implicit in it.

Children who are not in the dominant group have a hard time finding themselves or their communities in the books they read or the curriculum to which they are exposed. When they do see themselves, it is often through the distorted lens of the dominant group. American Indian children read about themselves as "savages," who were bereft of culture until the Europeans arrived; African Americans read sanitized versions of slavery; Mexican Americans read of the "Westward expansion," with no indication that their ancestors were already living on the land onto which Europeans were expanding; and working-class children learn virtually nothing of their history except perhaps that the struggle for the eight-hour workday was a long one. Little wonder, then, that school curricula and real life are often at polar extremes.

The way the class day is structured, particularly in secondary schools, also militates against success in school. The fact that classes are usually divided into 50-minute blocks of time is based on the dubious assumption that meaningful teaching and learning can take place only within such blocks of time. Eisner has defined this as the "structurally defined character" of schools and claims that it is one of the major problematic features of high schools.[24] Such a division of the school day may be particularly troublesome for students in the middle grades between elementary and high school. A study of middle schools found that those most likely to be successful were organized more like elementary schools than secondary schools.[25] These are described as "developmentally appropriate" schools; that is, they are more apt to respond to the particular needs of children of middle school age, who often need more, not less, attention and care. Features of these schools include smaller "home groups" of children, who remain together for the entire day, and a smaller number of teachers, who coordinate the curriculum.

A related issue is the division of knowledge into separate and discrete "subject matter" such as math, science, social studies, and language. Although such organization may be necessary to the extent that it attempts to make learning and teaching more manageable, it is also arbitrary and artificial and gives students the impression that reality is indeed divided up in this way. Students learn to see the world as disconnected bits of information that belong in preordained compartments. This problem is further complicated by the fact that few high schools offer interdisciplinary classes. Not only are teachers not given the time to work on cooperative ventures but also little credibility and respect are given to such courses, often deemed "soft" and not academically rigorous since they do not form part of what is defined as the "core curriculum."

The division of knowledge in this way may also reflect a European American world view. Not all peoples separate knowledge in this way. Churchill, an American Indian scholar, makes a cogent case for the fact that what we have in most schools, particularly colleges and universities, is what he calls "White Studies."[26] Not only is the content of our schools that of the Euro-American, Western experience, but so is the very framework by which knowledge is presented. In this conception, for example, philosophy and religion are different "subject areas," which would not be how most American Indians might conceive of the very same knowledge. The world view of some ethnic groups is missing from most schools, a further disjuncture between what some children learn at home and what they learn at school.

PEDAGOGY

The observation that schools are uninteresting and tedious places where little learning takes place and where most students are not challenged to learn is hardly new. It is particularly true of secondary schools, where subject matter dominates pedagogy and classes are too often driven by standardized tests as gatekeepers to promotion and/or accreditation. In his extensive research on secondary schools, Goodlad found that textbooks were used too frequently and mechanistically, whereas other materials were used infrequently if at all; that teaching methods varied little from the traditional "chalk and talk" methodology common 100 years ago; and that routine and rote learning were favored over creativity and critical thinking.[27] Other studies have found that what makes school boring for children is not so much the content of education as the process.[28]

Pedagogy does not simply mean, however, the techniques or strategies that teachers use to make learning more fun or interesting, although these are important dimensions. Pedagogy also refers to how teachers perceive the nature of learning and what they do to create conditions that motivate students to learn and to become critical thinkers. Most classrooms, for example, reflect the perception that learning can best take place in a competitive and highly charged atmosphere. Techniques that stress individual achievement and extrinsic motivation are most visible. Ability grouping, testing of all kinds, contests, and rote learning are the result. Although learning in such classrooms may indeed be "fun" or interesting, students learn other important lessons as well: that learning is memorization, that reciting what teachers want to know is what education is all about, and that critical thinking has no place in the classroom. It is important to have an expanded repertoire of teaching skills and methods, but this in itself will not change how and what students learn in school.

There are many reasons for the stagnation of pedagogy. One concerns the content "to be covered." Especially at the middle and high school levels, there is great pressure on teachers to finish the course of study at all costs. Rather than helping teachers focus on creative means of presenting content, this pressure forces them to rush through the course with sometimes dizzying speed, without focusing in any depth on the important concepts or principles of the subject matter. Teachers' pedagogy is likewise influenced by their own school experiences and by unexamined assumptions of what schools are supposed to be and do. An intriguing study by Britzman concluded that certain myths teachers carry with them (the teacher as expert, as self-made, and as all-powerful in the classroom) help perpetuate authoritarian practices in the schools.[29] The role of the teacher as supreme authority is unchallenged because it reflects teachers' own experiences as students, as student-teachers, and finally, as teachers.

Teachers' pedagogy is also influenced by their own lack of knowledge of the diversity of their students and information about how this diversity may affect learning. Because most teacher education programs still function within a framework that is exclusively Eurocentric, few teachers are prepared for different cultures, languages, lifestyles, and values in their classrooms. The result is the attempt by many teachers to treat all students in the same way, thus reinforcing the unchallenged assumption that "equal means the same." The same methods and approaches perceived as appropriate for students from mainstream backgrounds, whether or not they were ever effective, are used for all students.

PHYSICAL STRUCTURE

The physical structure of schools also gets in the way of educational equity. It is not unusual in poor urban areas to find schools with police officers standing guard. In some, students are frisked before entering. Teachers sometimes feel afraid unless they lock their classrooms. In many schools, desks are nailed to the ground, halls and classrooms are airless and poorly lit, and shattered glass can be found in courtyards where young children play. Add the lack of relevant and culturally appropriate pictures, posters, and other instructional materials as well as the lifeless and institutional colors of green and gray on the walls, and we are left with environments that are scarcely inviting centers of learning.

Many times, of course, schools are made uninviting and fortresslike places by school officials who are trying to protect them against vandalism and theft. Students from these very schools are often the ones who do the damage. It is important that we understand the role of boredom and rage in institutions that show little regard for students. Whether understood as resistance or adolescent rebelliousness, this kind of destructiveness represents a clear message that some schools are incompatible with students' emotional and physical needs. The Carnegie Council on Adolescent Development, in a report on the middle grades, concluded that there is a volatile mismatch between the organization and curriculum of middle-grade schools and the intellectual, emotional, and social needs of young adolescents.[30]

The resemblance of some schools to factories or prisons has been mentioned more than once.[31] This is not true of all schools, of course. In general, the further away from urban, inner-city schools or poor rural schools, the less institutional-looking the school. Suburban schools or those in wealthy towns, for example, tend to look strikingly different from those that serve the poor. Not only do they usually have more space, bigger classrooms, and more light, but they also have more material supplies and are in general in better physical condition, partly because the level of financing for the education of poor students is lower than for children in more affluent districts.[32] But it also concerns the expectations educators have of the capabilities of the students in their schools. If students are perceived to be "deficient," the educational environment will reflect a no-nonsense, back-to-basics, drill orientation. However, if they are perceived as intelligent and motivated young people with an interest in the world around them, the educational environment will tend to reflect an intellectually stimulating and academically challenging orientation.

The major problem with the physical environment of many schools is that it provides a stark contrast to the stated purposes of teaching and learning. When schools are not cared for, when they become fortresses rather than an integral part of the community they serve, and when they are "holding places" instead of learning environments, the contradiction between goals and realities is a vivid one. This chasm between ideal and practice is not lost on the students.

DISCIPLINARY POLICIES

Disciplinary policies often discriminate against particular students, especially in middle and secondary schools, where they may be at odds with the developmental level of students and where they are imposed rather than negotiated. Research that supports this hypothesis is compelling. Using longitudinal data from the national *High School and Beyond* study, Wehlage and Rutter found that certain conditions in the schools themselves can *predict* the dropping-out behavior of students.[33] Conditions that encourage students to leave include disciplinary policies that are perceived as unfair and ineffective. Consequently, there is a serious problem with what Wehlage and Rutter call the "holding power" of school for some students. They conclude that it is the *combination* of certain student characteristics and certain school conditions that are responsible for the decision to drop out. Other research has found that dropouts are more likely to come from schools with disproportionately high rates of suspensions and expulsions.[34] The connection between total school environment and dropout rates has been found to be quite strong in three areas. Research by Bryk and Thum found that an *orderly environment, a committed and caring faculty,* and *an emphasis on academic pursuits* contribute to lower dropout rates.[35]

Further aggravating the problem of disciplinary policies, interpretations of student behavior may be culturally or class biased. For example, students in poor schools who insist on wearing highly prized leather jackets in class may be doing so out of a well-founded fear that they may be stolen if left in the closet. African American students who keep a pick in their hair may not be doing so out of rebelliousness but simply for style. And Latino children who cast their eyes downward when being scolded are not being defiant but simply behaving out of respect for their teachers, as they were taught at home. A lack of awareness of these cultural and social factors leads time and again to misinterpretations and faulty conclusions.

One of the major problems is the vague terms used in suspensions. In Boston, for example, it was found that a disproportionate number of students suspended for being "disruptive" in class are Black. In addition, students of color in general are suspended far more often for the kind of offenses cited above than their majority peers.[36] Once again, students who experience the least success in school are those who bear the brunt of rigid school policies.

LIMITED ROLE OF STUDENTS

That many students are alienated, uninvolved, and discouraged by school is abundantly clear. This fact is most striking, of course, in dropout rates. A national study found that one of the main characteristics of dropouts is alienation from school life.[37] Students who drop out are usually uninvolved and passive participants in the school experience.

Schools are not usually organized to encourage student involvement. Although students are nominally represented in the governance structure of many schools, this representation is often window dressing, which has little to do with the actual running of the school. Rather than being designed to prepare students for democratic life, most schools are more like benign dictatorships in which all decisions are made for them, albeit in "their best interests."[38] They are more often organized around issues of control than of collaboration or consultation.

Even more serious is the fact that students are often uninvolved in their own learning. That is, what they learn is decided, designed, and executed by others. Often, it is not the teacher or even the school that determines the content but some mythical "downtown" or state agency. Everybody in the school is thus disempowered; frustration and alienation are the result. Students' voices are not heard, and frequently neither are those of teachers.

In the classroom itself, even the pedagogy is conceived of as a one-way street. It is what Freire calls "banking" education, that is, a process by which teachers "deposit" knowledge into students, who are seen as empty receptacles. It is education for powerlessness. In a characterization of what happens in most schools, Freire contrasts the expected role of the teacher with that of the student:

(a) the teacher teaches and the students are taught;
(b) the teacher knows everything and the students know nothing;
(c) the teacher thinks and the students are thought about;
(d) the teacher talks and the students listen—meekly;
(e) the teacher disciplines and the students are disciplined;
(f) the teacher chooses and enforces his choice, and the students comply;
(g) the teacher acts and the students have the illusion of acting through the action of the teacher;
(h) the teacher chooses the program content, and the students (who were not consulted) adapt to it;
(i) the teacher confuses the authority of knowledge with his own professional authority, which he sets in opposition to the freedom of the students;
(j) the teacher is the subject of the learning process, while the pupils are mere objects.[39]

What impact does involvement of students have on their school experiences and achievement? Although there has been little research on this issue, Cummins has reviewed a number of programs that have as one of their goals the empowerment of students. His conclusion is that students who are empowered to develop a positive cultural identity through interactions with their teachers experience a sense of control over their own lives and develop the confidence and motivation to succeed academically.[40] The same has been found by García and others.[41] In investigating the characteristics of instructional features that have shown promise with language minority students, they found that effective classrooms are characterized by, among other things, student collaboration in almost all academic activity. That is, when students are involved in directing their own learning in some way, they learn more effectively. In contrast, in a study of a comprehensive public high school in New York City, Fine found that "undesirable talk," that is, anything having to do with topics that might be perceived as dangerous in the classroom, is systematically silenced.[42] The result, especially with low-income and devalued students, was that they were further alienated from their educational experience because their heritage, home backgrounds, and lived experiences were excluded from school talk.

LIMITED ROLE OF TEACHERS

The limited role that teachers play in the life of the school is another structural problem. Traditionally not encouraged to become involved in decision-making processes in the schools, teachers in some ways were becoming even more alienated in the climate of "reform" that characterized the 1980s. The standardized test is fast replacing teacher creativity as the basis for the curriculum. Even more problematic is the fact that disempowered teachers who show little critical thought can hardly be expected to help students become empowered and critical thinkers. Another study by Fine demonstrates this tendency.[43] She found that teacher disempowerment correlates highly with disparaging attitudes toward students; that is, the more powerless teachers feel, the more negative they feel toward their students as well. In contrast, teachers who feel that they have autonomy in their classrooms and with their curriculum generally also have high expectations of their students.[44]

New structures such as teacher-led schools, weekly released time, or job sharing may help make teachers more active players in the schools, but this is only one aspect of the structural problem. Such changes should be seen as part of a general restructuring of schools which affects the curriculum, the tracking of students, and parent and community involvement and engagement.

LIMITED PARENT AND COMMUNITY INVOLVEMENT

The research is quite clear on the effectiveness of parent and community involvement: In programs with a strong component of parent involvement, students are consistently better achievers than in otherwise identical programs with less parent involvement. In addition, students in schools that maintain frequent contact with their communities outperform those in other schools. These positive effects persist well beyond the short term. For example, children of color and from low-income families who participated in preschool programs with high levels of parent involvement were still outperforming their peers when they reached senior high school.[45]

Nevertheless, what is meant by parent involvement is not always clear. Although it is true that parent involvement through activities such as attendance at parent-teacher conferences, participation in parent-teacher associations (PTA), and influence over their child's selection of courses predict student achievement, such parent involvement is becoming more and more scarce.[46] In a society increasingly characterized by either one-parent families or two-parent families in which both work outside the home, traditional kinds of parent involvement become more problematic. PTA meetings held during the day, parent-teacher conferences during school hours, and the ubiquitous cake sale are becoming remnants of the past. Most parents nowadays, regardless of cultural or economic background, find it difficult to attend meetings or otherwise to be involved in the governance of the school.

In addition, parents from linguistically and culturally diverse communities and from working-class neighborhoods frequently have a hard time with other forms of parent involvement that are expected by the school such as homework assistance, reading to children, and so on. These should not be taken as indications of noninvolvement or apathy, although they frequently are. For example, a research study by Epstein and Dauber on teacher attitudes and parent involvement in inner-city schools found that teachers generally feel that parents are not involved with the school or that they want to be.[47] Nevertheless, a survey of the parents in the very same school found that although the parents reported little involvement at the school itself because most worked full time, they were emphatic about wanting the schools and teachers of their children to advise them about how to help their children at home. Analysis of the data also confirmed that parents do indeed get more involved when the schools give them some direction.

That parent involvement, in whatever form it takes, affects student achievement should come as no surprise if we understand it as one way in which community values, life-styles, and realities can affect the school. In an institution so often far removed from its community, the entry of parents into the school also means that their language and culture and the expectations they have for their children become a part of the dialogue and of the tension, made explicit, that exists between school and home.

SUMMARY

Schools are governed by a great number of structures, which are often contrary to the needs of students and to the values of their communities and even to the expressed purpose of schooling in providing equal educational opportunity for all students. This review of the impact of structural factors in schools demonstrates that they often have a negative influence on the learning and achievement of a great number of students. In effect, structures within schools reflect and maintain the status quo and the stratification of society. These include such policies and practices as tracking; testing; limited and ethnocentric curricula; the physical structure of schools; discipline; and the lack of student, parent, and staff engagement.

Although these structural factors help us understand how schools effectively limit access to learning to a great number of students, they alone cannot explain lack of achievement. It is important to consider characteristics that students bring to school as further contributing to the mismatch of schools with the students whom they serve. These topics will be considered in the next chapters.

TO THINK ABOUT

1. Observe a number of similar classrooms that differ only in their tracking policies; that is, some are tracked and others are not. What do you see as the differences in these classrooms? Be specific, citing student engagement with work, expectations of student achievement, level of academic difficulty, and teacher-student and student-student relationships.

2. The nature versus nurture argument in explaining intelligence has been raging for many years. Some people believe that intelligence is primarily dependent on one's genetic background, whereas others believe that the environment plays a more important role. Take a position one way or the other and defend it.

3. Think about the curriculum in classrooms in which you have been a student. How have your experiences and cultures and those of your classmates been included? If they have not, what do you think has been the effect on you and others? If you could speak to some of your former teachers, what would you tell them about this topic?

4. Get some evaluation checklists for textbooks at your library. Review and evaluate the textbooks used in a particular classroom in your local school. Do they discriminate against students of any group? How? Give specific examples, based on the checklists you have used.

5. In your observations of a classroom, indicate the kind of pedagogical strategies used by the teacher. Are all students engaged in learning? Who are not? What might help engage them?

6. The physical structure of schools has been criticized for not being an appropriate environment for learning. Design a school for either the elementary or secondary level that might meet this requirement. State the primary objectives you would have for this school.

7. The limited roles of both students and teachers have been cited as a fundamental problem of schools. Specifically, the criticism has been that because schools do not provide opportunities for either teachers or students to exercise critical thinking or leadership, they subvert the very purpose of education as preparation for democratic participation. Think of how schools might provide more opportunities for both teachers and students to be more fully engaged.

NOTES

1. Ray Rist, "Student Social Class and Teacher Expectations: The Self-Fulfilling Prophecy in Ghetto Education," in *Challenging the Myths: The Schools, the Blacks, and the Poor,* Reprint Series #5. (Cambridge, MA: Harvard Educational Review, 1971).

2. John Goodlad, *A Place Called School* (New York: McGraw-Hill, 1984).

3. *Locked In/Locked Out: Tracking and Placement Practices in Boston Public Schools* (Boston: Massachusetts Advocacy Center, March 1990).

4. James Collins, "Using Cohesion Analysis to Understand Access to Knowledge," in *Literacy and Schooling,* ed. David Bloome (Norwood, NJ: Ablex, 1987).

5. Jomills H. Braddock, II, *Tracking: Implications for Student Race-Ethnic Subgroups,* Report No. 1. (Baltimore: Johns Hopkins University, Center for Research on Effective Schooling for Disadvantaged Students, February 1990).

6. Helen Gouldner, *Teachers' Pets, Troublemakers, and Nobodies: Black Children in Elementary Schools* (Westport, CT: Greenwood Press, 1978).

7. Jeannie Oakes, *Keeping Track: How Schools Structure Inequality* (New Haven, CT: Yale University Press, 1985).

8. Robert Slavin, in a best-evidence synthesis analysis of the effects of ability grouping in elementary schools, has concluded that it is largely ineffective. See *Ability Grouping and Student*

Achievement in Elementary Schools: A Best-Evidence Synthesis (Baltimore: Johns Hopkins University, Center for Effective Elementary Schools, 1986). In hearings across the nation, the National Coalition of Advocates for Students found that even in desegregated schools, tracking and sorting policies resulted in upper-level courses that were almost exclusively White and lower-level courses that were almost exclusively Black. See *Barriers to Excellence: Our Children at Risk* (Boston: National Coalition of Advocates for Students, 1985). See also the latest report by the Massachusetts Advocacy Center, which reports extensively on the research related to tracking (*Locked In/Locked Out*) and Anthony S. Bryk and Yeow Meng Thum, "The Effects of High School Organization on Dropping Out: An Exploratory Investigation," *American Educational Research Journal,* 26, 3 (Fall 1989), 353–383.

 9. Seymour Sarason, *The Culture of the School and the Problem of Change,* 2nd ed. (Boston: Allyn & Bacon, 1982).

10. Research by Kathleen Wilcox in two first-grade classrooms, one in a working-class community and the other in a wealthy community, analyzed features of teacher behavior to determine whether children from different social classes are given equal opportunity to learn skills and attitudes appropriate to a wide variety of work roles, or if instead they are socialized to fit the existing hierarchy of work roles. She found the latter to be primarily the case, although it certainly was not done intentionally or consciously by the teachers. For example, in the working-class school, external control was the overriding control mechanism used by the teacher, whereas internal authority was the one most used in the wealthy school. In addition, the children at the wealthy school received many more positive messages about their future than the children at the working-class school. Their teacher often said such things as "You'll be a good scientist," or referred to them as "artists" and "authors." See "Differential Socialization in the Classroom: Implications for Equal Opportunity," in *Doing the Ethnography of Schooling: Educational Anthropology in Action,* ed. George Spindler (New York: Holt, Rinehart & Winston, 1982). See also the research by Jean Anyon, "Social Class and School Knowledge," *Curriculum Inquiry,* 11, 1 (1981), 3–41; Joel Spring, *The Sorting Machine Revisited: National Educational Policy Since 1945* (White Plains, NY: Longman, 1989).

11. Kenneth K. Sirotnik and Jeannie Oakes, "Critical Inquiry for School Renewal: Liberating Theory and Practice," in *Critical Perspectives on the Organization and Improvement of Schooling,* ed. Kenneth K. Sirotnik and Jeannie Oakes (Boston: Kluwer-Nijhoff, 1986), p.70.

12. See a review of IQ testing in Stephan Jay Gould, *The Mismeasure of Man,* and Leon J. Kamin, *The Science and Politics of I.Q.* (New York: Erlbaum, 1974).

13. Lewis Terman, *The Measurement of Intelligence* (Boston: Houghton Mifflin, 1916); cited by Stanley Sue and Robert Chin, "The Mental Health of Chinese-American Children," in *The Psychosocial Development of Minority Group Children,* ed. Gloria Johnson Powell (New York: Brunner/Mazel Publishers, 1983).

14. See ibid. See also other reviews of the connection between IQ testing and eugenics in Gould, *The Mismeasure of Man;* Kamin, *The Science and Politics of I.Q.;* Eligio Padilla and Gail E. Wyatt, "The Effects of Intelligence and Achievement Testing on Minority Group Children" in *The Psychosocial Development of Minority Group Children,* ed. Gloria Johnson Powell (New York: Brunner/Mazel Publishers, 1983).

15. Noe Medina and Monty Neill, *Fallout from the Testing Explosion* (Cambridge, MA: Fair Test, June 1988).

16. See, for example, Donna Deyhle, "Learning Failure: Tests as Gatekeepers and the Culturally Different Child," in *Success or Failure? Learning and the Language Minority Student,* ed. Henry T. Trueba (Cambridge, MA: Newbury House, 1987); D. Monty Neill, and Noe J. Medina, "Standardized Testing: Harmful to Educational Health," *Phi Delta Kappan,* May 1989, pp. 688–697.

17. Luis C. Moll, "Some Key Issues in Teaching Latino Students," *Language Arts*, 65, 5 (September 1988), 467.
18. Study by the American Council on Education in 1949; cited by Gordon Allport, *The Nature of Prejudice* (Reading, MA: Addison-Wesley, 1954), p. 202.
19. *Guidelines for Selecting Bias-Free Textbooks and Storybooks* (New York: Council on Interracial Books for Children, 1980); "U.S. History Textbooks: Help or Hindrance to Social Justice?" *Bulletin of the Council on Interracial Books for Children*, 15, 5 (1984), 3–8.
20. Christine E. Sleeter and Carl A. Grant, "Race, Class, Gender and Disability in Current Textbooks," *The Politics of the Textbook*, ed. Michael W. Apple and Linda K. Christian-Smith (New York: Routledge & Chapman Hall, 1991).
21. See, for example, Rudine Sims, *Shadow and Substance: Afro-American Experience in Contemporary Children's Fiction* (Urbana, IL: National Council of Teachers of English, 1982); Sonia Nieto, "Self-Affirmation or Self-Destruction: The Image of Puerto Ricans in Children's Literature Written in English," in *Images and Identities: The Puerto Rican in Two World Contexts*, ed. Asela Rodríguez de Laguna (New Brunswick, NJ: Transaction Books, 1987); Hap Gilliland, "Selecting Reading Material for Indian Students," in *Teaching the Indian Child: A Bilingual/Multicultural Approach*, ed. Jon Reyhner (Billings: Eastern Montana College, 1986); Violet Harris, ed., *Teaching Multicultural Literature in Grades K–8* (Norwood, MA: Christopher-Gordon, 1992).
22. Carl A. Grant and Christine E. Sleeter, *After the School Bell Rings* (Philadelphia: Falmer Press, 1986).
23. Jean Anyon, "Social Class and the Hidden Curriculum of Work," *Journal of Education*, 162, I (Winter 1980), 67–92.
24. Elliot W. Eisner, "The Ecology of School Improvement," *Educational Leadership*, 45, 5 (February 1988), 24–29.
25. Joan Lipsitz, *Successful Schools for Young Adolescents* (New Brunswick, NJ: Transaction Books, 1984).
26. Ward Churchill, "White Studies: The Intellectual Imperialism of Contemporary U.S. Education," *Integrated Education*, 19, 1–2 (January 1982), 51–57.
27. Goodlad, *A Place Called School*.
28. See, for example, the study by Edwin Farrell, George Peguero, Rasheed Lindsey, and Ronald White, "Giving Voice to High School Students: Pressure and Boredom, 'Ya Know What I'm Sayin'?" *American Education Research Journal*, 25, 4 (Winter 1988), 489–502; Robert B. Everhart, *Reading, Writing, and Resistance: Adolescents and Labor in a Junior High School* (Boston: Routledge & Kegan Paul, 1983).
29. Deborah P. Britzman, "Cultural Myths in the Making of a Teacher: Biography and Social Structure in Teacher Education," *Harvard Education Review*, 56, 4 (November, 1986), 442–456.
30. Carnegie Council on Adolescent Development, *Turning Points: Preparing American Youth for the Twenty-First Century* (Washington, DC: Task Force for the Education of Young Adolescents, 1989).
31. David B. Tyack, *The One Best System: A History of American Urban Education* (Cambridge, MA: Harvard University Press, 1974); Michael B. Katz, *Class, Bureaucracy, and the Schools: The Illusion of Educational Change in America* (New York: Praeger, 1975); Linda M. McNeil, *Contradiction of Control: School Structure and School Knowledge* (New York: Methuen/Routledge & Kegan Paul, 1986).
32. *Barriers to Excellence*.
33. Gary G. Wehlage and Robert A. Rutter, "Dropping Out: How Much Do Schools Contribute to the Problem?" in *School Dropouts: Patterns and Policies*, ed. Gary Natriello (New York: Teachers College Press, Columbia University, 1986).

34. Lawrence G. Felice, "Black Student Dropout Behavior: Disengagement from School Rejection and Racial Discrimination," *Journal of Negro Education,* 50 (1981), 415–424.
35. Anthony S. Bryk and Yeow Meng Thum, "The Effects of High School Organization on Dropping Out: An Exploratory Investigation," *American Educational Research Journal,* 26, 3 (Fall 1989), 353–383.
36. *Barriers to Excellence.*
37. Ruth B. Ekstrom, Margaret E. Goertz, Judith M. Pollock, and Donald A. Rock, "Who Drops Out of High School and Why? Findings from a National Study," in *School Dropouts: Patterns and Policies,* ed. Gary Natriello (New York: Teachers College Press, Columbia University, 1986).
38. See, for example, Everhart, *Reading, Writing, and Resistance.*
39. Paulo Freire, *Pedagogy of the Oppressed* (New York: Seabury Press, 1970), p. 59.
40. Cummins, *Empowering Minority Students* (Sacramento: California Association for Bilingual Education, 1989), p. 4.
41. In research that explored classrooms effective with language minority students, García, Flores, Moll, and Prieto found that teachers who felt they had the autonomy to create or change the curriculum were also highly committed to the educational success of all their students. See Eugene García, "Attributes of Effective Schools for Language Minority Students," *Education and Urban Society,* 20, 4 (August 1988), 387–398.
42. Michelle Fine, "Silencing in Public Schools," *Language Arts,* 64, 2 (February 1987), 157–174.
43. Michelle Fine, "Why Urban Adolescents Drop Into and Out of Public High School," in *School Dropouts: Patterns and Policies,* ed. Gary Natriello (New York: Teachers College Press, Columbia University, 1986).
44. García, "Attributes of Effective Schools."
45. Anne T. Henderson, *The Evidence Continues to Grow: Parent Involvement Improves Student Achievement* (Columbia, MD: National Coalition of Citizens in Education, 1987); see also *Parent and Community Involvement: Information Is a Key to Dropout Prevention* (Austin: Texas Education Agency, Fall 1989).
46. D. L. Stevenson and D. P. Baker, "The Family-School Relation and the Child's School Performance," *Child Development,* 58, 5 (October 1987), 1348–1357.
47. Joyce L. Epstein and Susan L. Dauber, *Teacher Attitudes and Practices of Parent Involvement in Inner-City Elementary and Middle Schools,* Report 33. (Baltimore: Center for Research on Elementary and Middle Schools, Johns Hopkins University, March 1989).

Avi Abramson:

"I didn't know what to expect 'cause it was such a different curriculum."[1]

Talbot is a small, quiet, and aging working-class town. Located in eastern Massachusetts a few miles from the busy metropolis of Boston, its total area is a mere 1.6 square miles, and it has a population of approximately 20,000 people. With the exception of salt marshes and surplus federal installations, there is little additional vacant land.

One gets a sense of the community's aging by looking at its housing: More than half of the dwellings are at least 50 years old, partly because of the nature of the population. In recent years, the number of youths has been declining, with younger adults and families moving to more prosperous settings. The older residents are remaining, continuing to live in homes that have long since lost their newness and modern veneer. Both public and parochial school enrollment has been dwindling over the past several years. From 1975 to 1986 there was a particularly dramatic decline: Student enrollment plummeted from 4,128 to 2,163. One of the three elementary schools has recently been turned into condominiums. There is one high school in town, Talbot High School, with approximately 700 students.

A great many ethnic groups, primarily European and Catholic in origin, make up the population. The percentage of people of color is quite low, only a handful of families. Talbot is home to many Italians and Irish as well as to smaller concentrations of other European American immigrants. The number of Jewish families is very small, although there was a thriving community here just a generation ago. As evidence, there are two synagogues in town, one known as the "big synagogue" and the other as the "small synagogue." Many Jewish families have moved to other communities, and the remaining Jews are mostly senior citizens, particularly those who are observant and go to temple. There, according to Avi Abramson, the subject of this case study, there are many who are close to 85 years of age. At the high school there are no more than ten Jewish students in all.

Avi Abramson has lived in Talbot almost all his life, except for a year when his family moved to North Carolina. He went to first and second grade in public school, before going to a Jewish day school until eighth grade. He is now 16 years old and a senior at Talbot High School. Avi was not always a successful student and had a hard time adjusting to public school when he first started. Planning on going to college next year, he has given some thought to becoming either a history teacher or a graphic designer. Since both parents have been teachers and drawing is one of his hobbies, these choices are not surprising. Currently he is studying English, basic trigonometry, marine science, and psychology. He has already finished all the requirements for his favorite subject, history.

Avi lives on the water tower hillside of this quaint, old town in a quiet neighborhood of single and multifamily homes. During the Christmas season, his house can be easily spotted: It is the only one on the street without Christmas lights. He describes his town as peaceful, and he enjoys living here. Avi and his family have developed good relationships with their neighbors, whom he describes with fondness ("Everybody looks out for each other," he says). Nevertheless, he clearly longs to live in a community where he is not perceived as being so "different."

Avi lives with his mother and brother, who is ten years his elder. His older sister is married and lives in New York City with her husband and two children. Avi's father came from Israel originally, met his Jewish American wife in the United States, and stayed here to live. He died six years ago after a long illness. Although he was ten when his father died, Avi remembers little about him, probably because he was sick for so long. Before his illness, he was a much-loved teacher in various Hebrew schools. Avi's mother was also a Hebrew teacher, and although she loved teaching, there is not much call for Hebrew teachers in the area nowadays. Recently, she began studying computers to prepare for a new career.

There is a warm glow of familiarity and old, comfortable furniture in Avi's home. The house is filled with the aroma of latkes (potato pancakes) during the Hanukkah season and of many other Jewish foods at others times of the year. Books and artifacts are everywhere, reflecting the family's respect for continuity and history. Avi is a typical American teenager in many ways. He has a girlfriend and enjoys frequent telephone conversations with his friends. His bedroom is crammed with posters, comic books, encyclopedias, track team gear, woodworking projects, Star Trek memorabilia, drawing pads full of his own comics, and underneath it all, bunk beds.

Avi is also different from many other American youths. His serious, wise dimension is evident in the profound care, respect, and love that he has for his culture and religion. Few young people of any religion would dedicate every Saturday, as he does, to leading the last elderly remnants of his community in their Sabbath prayers at the small synagogue (what one might call a "role model in reverse"). He enjoys speaking Hebrew, loves the Jewish holidays, and devotes a great deal of time to religious and cultural activities. He is an energetic and serious young man who enjoys school as well as sports and other hobbies. Nevertheless, Avi is not what one would call a "nerd." Although he is serious about his studies, he has not always excelled in school and does not spend an inordinate amount of time studying.

Three basic themes were revealed through Avi's interviews. One is his sense of responsibility—to himself, his family, and his community—as well as persistence in fulfilling this responsibility. This trait is especially evident in the seriousness with which he treats his culture and religion. The joy and pain of maintaining them is another theme frequently mentioned by Avi. The role of positive pressure, from peers, family, and through activities such as track, is the third.

INDEPENDENT RESPONSIBILITY AND PERSISTENCE

I usually do my homework on my own and study for my tests on my own. That way, I can just do it on my own. I won't be able to have people around me to help me all the time, so I might as well learn how to do it myself.

If you don't go to school, then you can't learn about life, or you can't learn about things that you need to progress your life—go on with your life . . . so you could have a life.

I think that anybody that goes to school tries, at least. Accomplishes something. . . . I guess it goes back to what I said before. . . . It helps you with your life. 'Cause if you don't go to school, you probably won't get a good job someplace.

What am I getting out of school? I'm learning to be with people. . . . Learning to work with people. . . . Learning how to get through situations with people and with work that you have to do, and learning things that you . . . would say earlier, "I would never know that," or "I would never hear about that again." Then you would hear about it again.

I admire a lot of people 'cause I look at people and I see all kinds of things in them, in all kinds of people. . . . I admire my mother. 'Cause she's been through a lot and she's held on. . . . I admire people in school that in freshman and sophomore years just goofed off and did nothing and now they can be in Level One and really . . . prove themselves. . . . I admire people who can get off drugs. People like that. Nobody I knew, I just admire people who can do that.

I got the willpower. I don't give up so easy on some things. Some things I give up, though. But if I really want something, I usually try to work as hard to get it.

[To be successful, you have to] work hard and have confidence in yourself.

I'm currently working, or helping out, in Temple Solomon. With their services. . . . A lot of people here too, they come to temple but . . . some of them don't understand exactly what they're doing. They come and if there weren't certain people here, they wouldn't know what to do and they wouldn't come at all, probably. . . . So, I guess one of the reasons why I probably do what I'm doing is well, I enjoy it 'cause I enjoy doing the services. I enjoy being that kind of leader. To help them.

I guess it would be part from the way, as a smaller child, I was going to temple every Saturday. . . . When I was little, of course, I didn't follow along, but I just listened to them every time and I got the tune and everything. And it wasn't as hard for me. It wasn't hard for me at all to learn the service for my Bar Mitzvah 'cause I already knew half of it in my head. . . . Yeah, it's fun, it is.

I'm fairly religious. I mean, I work in a temple on Saturdays, so I keep myself orthodox. . . . I try to keep the law, you know, for Shabbos [Yiddish for "Sabbath"], 'cause I'm reading the Torah [holiest book for Jews] so it would be nice if the person who's reading at least . . . if you're reading the law, then you might as well follow it. . . . Set an example, in a way. Try to. . . . Again, I don't know how much of a role model I can be to 85-year-olds [*laughs sadly*].

THE PRICE OF MAINTAINING LANGUAGE AND CULTURE

There were more [Jews] years ago. Yeah, and now everybody has aged and all the young ones are gone and left. So, there's not too many young ones coming up, 'cause there's not too many families—young families. . . . The average age is probably 50s.

I'm the only, really, person that I guess follows the laws. So I wouldn't go out on a Friday night or something like that. . . . Right now, most people know that I don't usually come out on a Friday night. . . . But when I started high school, people used to say sometimes, "Ya coming out tonight?" I'm like, "No, I can't." . . . In a way, it brought me away from those people. . . . I mean, I have different responsibilities than most people.

If I miss track and say, 'cause it's not exactly the holiday, it's the day before and I have to go home and prepare, most people won't understand. "What do you mean, you have to prepare?" or "I thought the holiday was tomorrow?"

Most other religions don't have so many holidays during the year. So there's not that much preparation that they have to do, I guess. [*How would he feel if he lived in a place where everybody was Jewish?*] Have a good feeling every day, 'cause everybody knows there's a holiday. . . . It would be fun, 'cause I mean, it wouldn't be boring on Shabbos 'cause when you can't do, not really do anything, there's always somebody around. . . . That's why I go to [Jewish] camp, too.

There's not too many other Jewish children around [here]. I'm sure there's some families. I know there are a few families that live in Talbot. But they aren't religious or they . . . just don't have time to send their children to temple.

We just had Simchat Torah here the other day. . . . It was really pathetic. I mean, on Thursday night, there were 4 little kids there and there were less than 20 people all together. . . . And then, Friday morning, there was 11 men at the big shul [temple] and there were 10 at the little shul.

When I have kids, I want to bring them up in a Jewish community. And from the looks of it here, there might be a Jewish community. I mean, there is one now, but it's dwindling away, or starting to rebuild itself. But it will probably take a while before it actually becomes a large Jewish community again, when people start coming and bringing their children to the temple and actually doing something. . . .

And I'd like to be in a place myself, even if I'm not married, I'd like to be in a place where I could walk to the temple on Saturday, or I could just go down the street and I won't have to travel so far to where I could get some good kosher meat. Or things like that. Some place where I can always, where there's always something to do. You don't have to travel too far.

If the other people that are out there, if the reason that they don't come is also probably 'cause their parents. . . . 'Cause I remember, I was just speaking to a friend of mine last week who's Jewish and I said to him . . . "When was the last time you were in Temple? I'm just curious." I was just joking around with him, of course. And, he was like, "Yeah, I haven't been there in a while, you know. It's pretty sad. My parents don't follow anything, so I don't," he basically said.

A couple of years ago, I had some anti-Semitic things happen. . . . But that was cleared up. I mean, it wasn't cleared up, but they, I don't know. . . . There's a few kids in school that I still know are anti-Semites. Basically Jew haters. . . .

I was in a woods class, and there was another boy in there, my age, and he was in my grade. He's also Jewish and he used to come to the temple sometimes and went to Hebrew school. But then, of course, he started hanging around with the wrong people and some of these people were in my class, and I guess they were . . . making fun of him. And a few of them started making swastikas out of wood. . . . So I saw one and I said to some kid, "What are you doing?" and the kid said to me, "Don't worry. It's not for you. It's for him." And I said to him, "What?!" And he walked away. And after a while, they started bugging me about it and they started saying remarks and things and. . . . Finally, it got to a point where I had them thrown out of class. . . . 'Cause I just decided to speak up. . . .

And there was one kid that I didn't have thrown out because I didn't think he was as harmful as they were. But it turned out, as the year went on, I had a little incident with him, too.

It was one of the last days of school, and I was wearing shorts, and it was hot out, you know. . . . And I came into the class and I said to myself, "This is it. If he says something to me today, I'm gonna go hit him." So I walked in there and I was just walking around and he started bugging me again, so I did the same thing. I just went up to him and I pushed him and he must've been 300 pounds. . . . And I just started pushing him and I said, "Come on, let's go already. I'm sick of you. . . ." I don't remember exactly what happened, but I know I got pulled away. . . . And he walked by me again and he goes, "You ready for the second holocaust?"

And then I think I had him thrown out. . . . Yeah, you see, I went up to the teacher and I said to her, "I'm either gonna leave the class or they leave."

It was funny 'cause one of the kids I got thrown out actually wasn't that harmful. . . . I don't know, he was just like a little follower on the side. And it turns out last year, I was on track team and he decided to do track and I became friends with him. And I got to know him, and . . . apparently his grandfather had converted to Judaism before he died. . . . This year, I'm pretty good friends with him and every time I'm talking to him, he's always mentioning Judaism. . . . And he's very interested in Judaism and he told me that he would like to convert himself. . . . He just asked me last week if he could come to the temple.

He understands a lot now. . . . So, I mean, he was hanging around with the wrong. . . . They didn't care. I mean, they weren't doing anything in the class, anyways. They were just sitting around. . . . Yeah, druggies basically.

[*When asked if he felt his teachers understand his culture, Avi responds*] Yeah, When I tell them I'm gonna be out of school for the holidays and they say, "Okay, don't worry. Make up, don't worry." They know about Rosh Hashana and Yom Kippur [major Jewish holidays], but they don't know about Succot. There's the first day and the last day. After Yom Kippur I say I'm gonna be out these other days and they go, "Oh, I thought the holidays were over with," and I go, "No, there's a few more." But they're nice about it, anyway. I mean, sometimes, once in a while, someone gets a little frustrated. You know, if I come in the next day after a holiday and I'm not ready for the test 'cause I couldn't write or do anything to study for it, but I make up my work in pretty good time. And I don't usually have any trouble. . . .

I knew who was [Jewish at school]. . . . I knew them from early age. Some of those kids used to go to the temple, to the junior congregation on Saturdays. But . . . I don't really know 'cause, for example, a history teacher I had in ninth grade—I didn't know he was Jewish. Last year somebody told me he was Jewish. . . . I mean, I don't know why I just didn't want to believe he was Jewish. I mean, he never really mentioned anything to me or said anything about being Jewish or whatever.

[*When asked how he celebrates holidays with his family, Avi answers, laughing*] With pride and tradition! . . . I usually have to stay around here 'cause I work in the temple. . . . But if we can, we invite somebody over for the seder [Passover dinner]. . . . It's nice to have people over for the holidays. It makes the holiday more enjoyable.

I like the taste of chicken on a Friday night. That I've waited for all week long. It's just not the same on Wednesday night. . . . You can't even smell it the same. It's different. I like deli stuff: corned beef, a nice sandwich, a little pickle, you know. . . . I like kugel [pudding] too. . . . All the Jewish food's good. . . . On like Shavuoth or Pesach or Succot, we usually get special fruits, like the new spring fruits, the first fruits of the harvest.

[Pesach, or Passover] is my favorite holiday. . . . I love the preparation for it. I don't like it after the third day because there's no more seders and there's nothing left to do except for waiting it out. I mean, it wouldn't be so bad. . . . You see, if I have to go to school, I have to go to school in the middle. But if I didn't have to go to school, then

I could sit home and kind of enjoy it. But I have to go to school, and I just say it's not the same when you see other food that you can't eat. I mean, it would be a whole different feeling if you saw so many other people eating matzoh or whatever.

When I went to day school, it was nice to have people who were Jewish around you. . . . I mean, it made you understand. I mean, it was a Hebrew day school so you obviously did things that involved the religion. . . . So, it gave you a good background, is what they did.

There wasn't anybody in my town that went to the school I went to, so like, I had friends here but like when I had a holiday, no one would understand. "Why can't you come out?" You know, "Why can't you come out on a Friday night?" . . . I still get asked that same question today [*chuckles*]. . . . People know today that when I say it's a holiday, I can't come out, can't do anything.

When I came in the ninth grade, it was hard 'cause I didn't hardly know anybody, and I didn't know what to expect 'cause it was such a different curriculum. . . . I didn't know anybody, like I said, and you just walked around, you know, tried to speak to people, see who you could make friends with, who was right to make friends with.

I have a few [non-Jewish] friends around here. . . . I think this year I'm just starting to become better friends with them 'cause everybody's matured more and they're starting to go their different ways. . . . They're starting to realize that [*smiles*] they've gone wrong all these years. . . . I mean, it's our last year in high school, so I guess we're all just becoming better friends now, 'cause we're not gonna see each other again.

THE ROLE OF POSITIVE PRESSURE

[Good grades] give you confidence, show you what you're doing. . . . And keep on going.

I haven't done really bad in a while. . . . I mean occasionally, I'll do bad on a test or something, but I'll just bring it back up after. 'Cause I'll feel bad after. "Ugh, I really did bad. I should have done really well." And I just try and do it better the next time. . . . Let myself slip a little bit and then I'll go back. I'll take a break and go on.

If they [parents] see you're . . . having good grades, hopefully they'll trust you more and they won't nag you about this and that, and know you can function on your own.

Growing up at an early age, [my parents taught me] like what was right and wrong and the basics of Judaism.

One summer, my mother was teaching me Hebrew. My mother actually taught, sat me down and actually taught me.

She's fair. . . . She doesn't keep me bound, keep me in. You know, "Stay here; don't go anywhere. You can't go out if you have to." She trusts me. . . . Most of the time, I can see why she wouldn't want me to do something.

Most [teachers] are understanding. I mean, if you don't know how to do something, you can always just go ask them. And ask them again and again and again.

[*He singles out one particular teacher, a math teacher who he had in ninth grade*] 'Cause I never really did good in math till ninth grade and I had him. And he showed me that it wasn't so bad, and after that I've been doing pretty good in math and I enjoy it.

There's some teachers that understand the kids better than other teachers. . . . They teach from the point of view of the kid. They don't just come out and say, "All right, do this, blah, blah, blah." I mean, in a way, they like, sometimes joke around with the kid. They try to act like the student. . . . They're not so *one-tone voice.*

[A bad teacher is] one who just, for example, some student was doing really bad on his tests, test after test after test. The teacher would just correct them and that's it. Wouldn't say anything to the student. . . . I mean, you can't expect a teacher to come up to that kid every day or whatever. I mean, the teacher will say, "You know, I'm here after school. Come and get help. . . ." Instead of just walking in, writing on the board, erasing, and leaving.

[My classes are] challenging in some cases, but it's fun.

I try to run [track] as often as I can. I mean, during the season you kinda have to run every day just to keep in shape. But I like to run anyways, 'cause when you run you think about everything and just . . . it gives you time, in a way, [to] relax, and just get your mind in a different place. . . . It takes up most of my time, 'cause after that, you know you're tired. Come home from school, just go do your homework, whatever. And speak to your friends on the phone that are far away.

I do a lot of drawing. I've been drawing for years, just sometimes it's nothing special. Sometimes it's just doodling or drawing strange designs or things like that. But I enjoy it. It relaxes me to sit down, flip on my radio, anything I want to listen to and just draw away. . . . It just puts you away from the rest of the world.

During the week, you know, I come home late, it's after track . . . tired, don't usually go out and do something. And on the weekends, I like to relax. . . . [Shul on Saturday] tires me out for the rest of the day. . . .

I take a Hebrew course there [Hebrew College on Sunday] and I'm taking some other course . . . about the first Jews that came to America.

Some of my friends have an influence on me, too, to do well in school. . . . My friends from camp . . . I mean, they all do pretty good in school and we're all close friends. . . ,

Whenever one of us gets in, if we ever got into some sort of trouble, we'd bail each other out of it. . . . Because, well, I mean, we all trust each other, basically. . . . We keep in touch a lot. . . . We'll always be friends.

I run up my phone bill talking to them 'cause they're all out of state. . . . [Mother] tells me to write letters [*laughs*]. But sometimes it's hard 'cause sometimes, in a way, I live off my friends. . . . They're like a type of energy . . . like a power source.

COMMENTARY

When asked to describe himself, Avi said he was "fun-loving and religious," two adjectives that would not ordinarily be juxtaposed in this way. Yet, curiously, his description is an apt one. He is both deeply involved in his culture, as is apparent from his serious and responsible attitudes and the dedication he gives to his work at the synagogue, and a gregarious and playful teenager who enjoys camp, sports, and practical jokes. A little digging may reveal how Avi has been able to develop these seemingly divergent qualities.

Avi is the youngest of three children, and the older two are quite a bit older. Because of his father's illness, Avi's mother has been his major role model. It was she who taught him the need to be responsible. He grew up watching her care for his ill father and then adjust to the loneliness and demands of widowhood. Being responsible, in his family's context, meant being a good student and taking school seriously. This is evident in Avi's desire to be independent, taking the responsibility for making up work after holidays or bringing up his grades after a slip. It is equally evident in his persistence and self-confidence. His admiration for those who have the strength to overcome adversity, whether it be drugs or failing grades, is a further indication of his belief in sheer willpower to triumph.

Because both of his parents were teachers, and given the immensely important role of scholarship within religious education in the Jewish culture, it is no surprise that Avi has done well in school.[2] What is surprising, however, is the enormous commitment he has developed to his religious community in the "small synagogue." Throughout the interviews, this commitment was vividly apparent. Avi speaks Hebrew and works hard at it. He relishes Friday night Shabbos at home and services in the temple on Saturday. He studies the Torah and is open about the love he feels for his culture and religion.

Yet the price Avi is paying for maintaining his language and culture is often a steep one. Clearly, he has often thought about the dilemmas of being a minority in another culture. The mismatch of his culture with that of the school is evident in many ways, including interactions with teachers, the curriculum, and other structural factors. For example, Avi has accepted the fact that most of his teachers and classmates do not pronounce his name correctly. He appreciates that most of them try to be understanding about such things as holidays, although they often do not understand what holiday observance means within his particular religious context. His days off are always at odds with those of the other students. The curriculum is also at odds with his lived experience.

Other problems he talks about focus on his social life and the lack of friends in this community. For a teenager, having to make the decision to stay home on Friday evening with family or going out with friends can be a painful one. Incidents of anti-Semitism in school are even more painful reminders that being different from the majority can still be dangerous in our society.[3] The decisiveness with which he handled this particular situation reveals his great confidence and demonstrates how he takes control of his life (by "having them taken out of the class") and it is also sadly indicative of his own stereotypes and class biases about those he calls "druggies," a group Avi seems to consider worthless.

Given some of the painful consequences of remaining unassimilated, it is not surprising that Avi has thought about moving from Talbot when he has his own family. Right now, he maintains his Jewish culture and religion by going to temple, Hebrew college, and Jewish summer camp.

Most of his friends live out of town, and even out of the state. What he most looks forward to are their phone calls and visits. He has made some non-Jewish friends at school this year and alludes to the rejection he has felt in the past by joking about the fact that they're "starting to realize that they've gone wrong all these years. . . ." And although he may smile as he says it, there is more sadness than joy in the words. Avi does not even enjoy the solidarity of the few Jewish teachers in school, who he believes are trying to hide their Jewishness.

Combined with all of this pain is the joy of his culture and religion. It is obvious that they help to ground him. He relishes being "that kind of leader" within his community. It is ironic that he refers to his service in the temple as "work," given the prohibition of work on the Sabbath for observant Jews. Yet this too is an indication of the seriousness with which he takes his responsibilities. As a 16-year-old, he feels the burden of keeping his community alive, even if it means being a "role model for 85-year-olds." He loves his language, his holidays, being with his family, and being religious. Family traditions such as chicken on Friday evening and preparing for Pesach are some of his favorite things.

Straddling two worlds as he does, Avi is constantly confronted with the need to accommodate to the outside world. This is not a new challenge but one historically faced by most immigrants. As so well expressed by Brumberg, "In the immigrant world, learning to live simultaneously in two worlds may have been required for successful adaptation."[4] Brumberg was referring, of course, to the huge Eastern European Jewish immigration that numbered over 1.5 million between 1881 and 1914.[5] What is new in Avi's case, however, is the fact that this balancing act is increasingly taking place with those who have been here for more than one generation, not simply with new arrivals.

Positive pressures to be successful in school are apparent in several areas of Avi's life: high expectations at home; pressure from friends at camp, school, and Hebrew school; and the positive reinforcement that he gets from involvement in sports. Although his mother is not involved in school in any significant way, and in fact never has been, Avi knows that she has great hopes for him. The mere fact that she is a teacher herself has influenced him. Avi describes both parents as "very educated, hard working, dedicated," all adjectives that could be used to describe him as well.

At school, Avi's teachers also have high expectations for him. Given his academic seriousness, it is probably easy for his teachers to overlook his religious observance since they know that he will make up his missing work in no time. In addition, the perception that all Jewish children are good students, what has often been called a "positive stereotype," has placed an undue burden on many youths. Very similar to the "model minority" myth surrounding the academic achievement of Asian students, this stereotype may result in holding Jewish students as a point of reference for all other "minorities" and influencing teachers to have sometimes unrealistic expectations for all their Jewish students. Thus, other groups are blamed for not living up to the standards of another group. Additionally, just like the "model minority" myth, the consequences of this so-called positive stereotype are negative in that they treat a whole class of students in the same way without allowing for individual differences. Although the historic and important context of education in Jewish history has of course influenced the educational experiences of Jews in the United States, perceiving the Jewish community as monolithic is unfair to individual students as well as to the entire group.[6]

Avi is very involved in track. He specializes in distance and currently participates in three seasons—cross-country, indoor, and spring track, keeping him busy most of the school year. Two years ago, his team won the championship. Involvement in this activity has been the one way that Avi has been able to develop friendships outside of his culture. Because the team focuses on common goals, it is a positive environment in which to develop solidarity with others who are different from oneself. In addition, because involvement in sports is often regarded very positively by other students, track has given Avi a "hook" with which to relate to others in the school.

Finally, Avi's Jewish friends are, in his eloquent phrase, "a type of energy . . . like a power source." They put a positive pressure on him through their own academic success and their involvement with the religion and culture. The fact that peers can have this kind of influence on young people is often overlooked by schools and parents. Yet it is the very raison d'être of such institutions as Portuguese American schools, Hebrew camps, Saturday culture schools in the Chinese community, and so on.

Avi Abramson, a strong and confident young man, is maintaining a difficult balancing act between complete assimilation into the mainstream of U.S. life and holding onto his language and culture. This is not an easy task, even for seasoned adults. The fact that Jewish culture is often completely intertwined with religion and tradition, rather than with nationality as in other groups, makes this balancing act even more arduous. Although our society claims to be secular, clearly it is not. Rather, it is a frankly Christian nation, as can be seen in the abundance of Christian symbols and artifacts, from the daily prayer in Congress to the crêches that adorn small towns in New England, where Avi comes from, at Christmas. Added to this fact is the weight of centuries of oppression, minority status, and marginality to which Jews have been confined. Even in societies where they have been assimilated, Jews have often been victimized and treated as scapegoats.[7] Given this long history of oppression, Jews throughout the world have had to think long and hard about the degree of accommodating to host societies and maintaining their cultural traditions. The results have ranged all the way from becoming completely assimilated and losing all traces of their roots to remaining within religious and cultural enclaves removed from any but the most basic and necessary exchanges with non-Jews.

Pressure toward assimilation and the accommodations made to it are only one reflection of the diversity in the Jewish community. Jews differ in religiosity, tradition, political viewpoints, language, and social class, among others. The religious tenets in Judaism itself, that is, Orthodox, Reform, and Conservative elements, reflect this diversity. In addition, some Jews who are not religious at all, secular Jews, are still profoundly Jewish. Some Jews speak Hebrew, others speak Yiddish, and still others speak neither. Jews differ in their viewpoints on relations with the Arab world and on Zionism itself.

The Jewish community in the United States has often been portrayed in a unidimensional manner. Gross stereotypes depict Jews as wealthy merchants who control the banking industry and the media, landlords, moneylenders, and chiselers. The phrase *Jew down,* meaning to bargain downward, is a reflection of this racist stereotype. Yet although Jews as a group have a higher average income than other groups, they also have higher education levels. Rather than wealthy, most Jews in the United States are solidly middle class in income and profession. There is also a substantial number of Jews living in poverty.[8]

Avi is trying to be both an American and a Jew. For him, this means not giving in to assimilationist forces while also accommodating those parts of his life to U.S. society that will not compromise his values. He is trying to resist some elements of what Cortés calls "the societal curriculum," that is, all of the forces outside the home and the school that affect our values and behavior.[9] Going against the tide of assimilation is not an easy choice. Nevertheless, it is one that Avi, consciously or not, has made. With the help of his family, friends, and religious community, and with the support of his non-Jewish community, he may just be able to do it.

TO THINK ABOUT

1. What, in your view, keeps Avi Abramson so involved in his synagogue?
2. Do you think Avi's school life would be different if he were not on the track team? How?
3. Since the United States officially sanctions "separation of church and state," is it possible for teachers to affirm Avi's culture and background without bringing religion into the school? Think about some ways this can be done. If you do not believe it can be done, list some of the ways that the separation of church and state is violated by schools. What is the alternative to this practice?
4. Friends are, in Avi's words, "like a power source." How can teachers use this power source to good advantage? Think of some strategies through which this can be done.
5. It is obvious that Avi has little respect for those he calls "the druggies." Why should this be so? If you were a teacher in his school, what might you do about this problem?

NOTES

1. I appreciate Diane Sweet's work in locating and interviewing Avi and in providing extensive background information for this case study.
2. Seymour B. Sarason, "Jewishness, Blackishness and the Nature-Nurture Controversy," in *Psychology and Social Action: Selected Papers* (New York: Praeger, 1982).
3. For an analysis of this discrimination, see J. Feagin, *Racial and Ethnic Relations* (Englewood Cliffs, NJ: Prentice Hall, 1978).
4. Stephan F. Brumberg, *Going to America, Going to School: The Jewish Immigrant Public School Encounter in Turn-of-the-Century New York City* (New York: Praeger, 1986).
5. Ibid.
6. For a documentation of this historic context, see ibid.
7. See Meyer Weinberg's extensive history of anti-Semitism in 12 countries, *Because They Were Jews: A History of Anti-Semitism* (Westport, CT: Greenwood Press, 1986); Chapter 12 deals with the United States. See also David A. Gerber, ed., *Anti-Semitism in American History* (Urbana: University of Illinois Press, 1986).
8. Data from a 1984 study, for example, revealed that more than a quarter of Jewish families in the greater Philadelphia area lived in poverty. Similar conditions no doubt exist in other large urban areas. See Federation of Jewish Agencies of Greater Philadelphia, as cited in *Teaching Strategies for Ethnic Studies,* ed. James A. Banks (Boston: Allyn & Bacon, 1991).
9. Carlos E. Cortés, "The Societal Curriculum: Implications for Multiethnic Education," in *Education in the 80's: Multiethnic Education,* ed. James A. Banks (Washington, DC: National Education Association, 1981).

Fern Sherman:

"If there's something in the history book that's wrong, I should tell them that it is wrong."[1]

Springdale, a small city in Iowa, is surrounded by farm country. With a population of close to 50,000, the city is a haven from the problems of more populated midwestern cities yet affords the advantages of a large university and other cultural activities. Springdale is not very ethnically diverse. Most of its residents of European American background identify themselves as "American," with no ethnic classification. Many have been here for several generations. The African American community numbers just over 1,000, and there are fewer than 800 Latinos. There are slightly more than 3,000 Asians, the largest non-European American group. The number of Native Americans in the entire city is miniscule, totaling only about 60.

Fern Sherman is 14 years old and an eighth-grader in the middle school in town. With Chippewa, Ponca, Norwegian, German, and English heritage, Fern identifies herself as a Native American. She and her sisters are registered as both Turtle Mountain Chippewa and Northern Ponca, an Indian Nation that has recently been reinstated (it was "terminated," meaning no longer recognized by the federal government, in 1966). Tribal affiliation designations are so complex and bureaucratic that Fern and her sisters have been classified as 237/512, or slightly over half Indian. This kind of identification is arbitrary and clearly a social construct, having little to do with self-identification.

It is important to remember that the Indian community is extremely heterogeneous. With well over a million Indians, such diversity is bound to exist. Over 400 Nations are recognized by the federal government, of which over 200 have a land base or reservation. There are others that are not officially recognized. About two-thirds of all Indians now live away from reservations in other communities, primarily in urban areas. Although a growing number of Indians speak only English, currently over 200 languages are spoken and many are still vigorously maintained. For example, over 70 percent of Navajo children enter school speaking Navajo as their native language. Several Indian Nations have declared their languages to be official, designating English as a "foreign language."[2] Indians are also very diverse in cultural traditions and characteristics, physical appearance, religion, and lifestyle. In spite of these vast differences, a pan-Indian identity has been emerging in the past generation, probably because of several factors: many values shared by most Native peoples; the need to develop greater political strength; and the intermarriage among Native groups, as is the case in Fern's family.[3]

Fern says she is the only Native American in her entire school, although this was not always the case. Before moving to Springdale, she attended a tribal reservation school for kindergarten and first grade and later a public school where there were a large number of Indian students. In that particular school, there were some Indian teachers, an Indian Club, an Indian education program with special tutors, and other support services. In both settings, Fern and her sisters felt comfortable and accepted, which is not always so now.

Fern lives with her father, two sisters, and young nephew, although at present both sisters are away. Her father is a professor of political science at the local university, and her mother, who lives in another city, is a truck driver. Her parents have been separated for years, and Fern and her sisters rarely see their mother, who has taken little responsibility for their upbringing and education. Fern has two other sisters who live with their mother. Instrumental in raising her nephew, Daryl, now two years old, Fern knows firsthand what raising a child is like and wants to delay having children of her own for a long time. As she says, "I want to get my life started and on the go before I have a family."

Fern's sisters, Juanita and Rose, are 16 and 17 years old. They are all actually step-sisters, sharing the same mother. In spite of the fact that he is not their biological father, Mr. Sherman has taken responsibility for raising Juanita and Rose as well as his own daughter. Both of the older girls have a history of alcohol and drug abuse. Rose is in an out-of-state treatment center and is expected to move back home in a few months. Juanita is currently living at an alcohol and drug abuse residential center. According to her father, she began drinking a number of years ago because "she just never fit in." She was isolated and alone at school and sought support for this feeling of alienation through alcohol.

Drug abuse and alcoholism are tearing many Indian communities apart. Mr. Sherman's ex-wife and three daughters have all been affected. The girls' mother has been in four treatment centers for drug and alcohol abuse and has served a prison term of over two years for offenses related to her addiction. Rose and Juanita continue to receive treatment. Even Fern, a successful student who loves school and is heavily involved in sports and other extracurricular activities, has not been spared: She has tried marijuana and alcohol, although she is clearly not addicted and has probably learned a painful lesson from her sisters. Juanita has been at the center for two months and is getting back on her feet again. For the first time in years, she is learning to like school.

Mr. Sherman has been instrumental in helping Juanita and Rose overcome their addiction. Because he has seen the results of drug and alcohol abuse and is convinced that they are linked to poor self-esteem based on missed opportunities and lack of success in school, he pushes his daughters to excel in school. Having lived through the nightmare of addiction with his family, he thinks about the role that schools should be playing. "Do we have to intervene in every Indian kid's life that goes into these school systems," he asks ruefully, "in such drastic manners?" Although he does not place the whole blame on teachers for his children's problems, he feels that there are too many misunderstandings in school that lead to failure. Getting a good education is an essential that he feels his children can ill afford to neglect. He is tireless in his pressure on them to study, get good grades, prepare for college, and so on. Fern is only in eighth grade, and although she is doing very well, her father is keeping his fingers crossed that she will continue to do so. His painful experiences with his other daughters have cautioned his optimism.

Becoming aware and proud of their heritage is the other message that Mr. Sherman gives his daughters. They do not speak a language other than English at home, but he sometimes teaches them words in Ponca. Although they think his pressure on them to succeed and to identify themselves as Native American is sometimes overwhelming, they clearly appreciate him for giving them strength in their culture and a determination to get ahead.

Fern and her family live in a middle-class neighborhood close to the university. It is a friendly and close-knit community but, like most suburbs, affords little recreation for youths. She and her family live in a block of condominiums. Although they are the only Native American family in the area, Fern describes her community as a "really nice neighborhood" and "one big happy family." She feels that her neighbors are always there to help one another out and that they are understanding and kind.

Saying that the middle school she attends is "kinda stuck on itself," Fern nevertheless acknowledges that it is a good school. She loves going to school. She is taking classes in science, math, English, home economics, art, physical education, and family and consumer science, her favorite subject because it includes experiences in child care. Her grades are very good, although they do not necessarily reflect her interests accurately: Her highest grade was in English, her least favorite subject, and her worst grade, C, was in her favorite subject, science. Fern is very active in school activities such as chorus, cooking club, and sports and in out-of-school activities such as dance.

Aware of the role of teachers' expectations on her achievement, Fern spoke about her reaction to different teachers and schools. Family pressures and responsibilities, her indomitable strength and ambition, and the isolation she feels as the only Native American student in her school are the other themes that highlight Fern's interviews.

THE ROLE OF TEACHERS' EXPECTATIONS

I'd rather go through school and get A's and B's than D's and F's. . . . In Springdale, I've noticed if you're getting D's and F's, they don't look up to you; they look down. And you're always the last on the list for special activities, you know?

Most of my friends were from the same culture or background [in former school in South Dakota] 'cause there are a lot of Native Americans there. And you weren't really treated different there. . . . You were all the same and you all got pushed the same and you were all helped the same. And one thing I've noticed in Springdale is they kind of teach 25 percent and they kinda leave 75 percent out. . . . [Teachers] really push us hard, but if we're getting bad grades, they don't help us as much. . . .

Being at the top of my class, always being noticed as a top person, grade-wise [made me feel good]. I mostly got straight A's and B's until I moved to Springdale. And I got like a C and D the first semester, in science and math here because they just push you to your limits. I mean, it's just incredible the way they think you're like "Incredible Woman" or something.

I don't like being pushed to my limit. I mean, I think you should have a little bit of leeway. . . . Like, this past week, I had three different reports due in three different classes. . . . I think they [teachers] should have at least a little bit of communication, not to give you three reports due in the same week.

I like going to math or like science to do different experiments. I've always liked science, but it's not really my best subject. I like American history because sometimes I'll know more than the teacher, just because my dad has taught me stuff.

I don't really like English . . . because I hate when they make you cut off at 400 words. . . . If you can't write what you're gonna write, why write it?

In science, if you don't understand something, and the science teacher doesn't get in until 8:00 and the bell rings at 8:10. . . . In ten minutes, you can't learn something. . . . Like if you don't have your assignment done, and you need help on it, you have ten minutes to go in, get help, get it done. Because if it's not done by class time, you'll have detention. . . . That really holds me back. Because if they're not gonna take time to teach you and you're the one that's taking time to come in and let them teach you. . . .

[*What she would do to make school more interesting*] More like involved activities in class, you know? . . . 'Cause like when you're sitting in class, and the teacher is lecturing, I usually feel like falling asleep, 'cause it's just blah. And in chorus, there's like this rap about history, you know? It's really fun. . . . More like making the whole class be involved, not making only the two smartest people up here do the whole work for the whole class.

FAMILY PRESSURE, EXPECTATIONS, AND RESPONSIBILITIES

I do it [try to succeed academically] for my dad, but I mostly do it for myself.

[My sisters] are always like, "Yeah, you're daddy's girl, just 'cause you get A's and B's." . . . It's how they put me down for what I'm doing, for how I'm succeeding.

He's always involved in what's happening in school, unlike most parents. . . . My dad is just always there [at school]. He's always been there, every school activity, I mean, unless our car breaks down. . . . I sure remember, we were having a musical and it was set up with like 300 kids. And our car had a flat tire. And so my dad put this air stuff in so he could get me to the musical [*laughing*]. And he went and got the tire fixed and he made the guy give him a ride back to school so he could see it! . . . He's always been involved, so I really don't know what it's like to not be involved.

He thinks [school] is heaven! . . . When he was young, he only got A's and B's. . . . C was an F to him. And I sometimes have to stop him and say, "Hey, I'm not you!" But I'm glad he's pushing me.

Just from my family breaking up so many times . . . I've learned to always stick with it. . . . I've learned really to stick with my family. I've always been told to love everybody the same in your family, but sometimes that's really hard for me because I've always been so close to Juanita. . . . So, I really feel that Juanita's my mom. . . . My dad's probably the first person I go to and Juanita's probably someone I can go to, you know, for "woman help."

My dad is more or less a brick wall that you can't get through [*laughing*]. He's really set, like you always get those stupid lectures: "Well, my dad did it this way. . . ." But, Dad, you're not your dad. I know I might grow up and treat my children a little bit the same way as my dad, but knowing how much it hurts me inside when he says, "Well, you know, I was a straight A student when I was little . . ." I'm not gonna do that to my kids because it just makes them want to fail more. . . . When you're mad at your parents, you try to find something to get them back with. And I think grades are a very good way to get them back with.

He's a kid at heart. He doesn't try to be "Macho Parent" or "Mercedes Man." He doesn't try to fit in with people. He's himself, and he's always been himself. And if people don't like the way he is, tough sherlock!

He's a one-of-a-kind dad. I'll always love him for what he is.

I've really not known [my Mother] that much. From just what my dad's told me and what I've seen, she is really hard to get along with. She's like very emotional. . . . She makes all these excuses, of "Yeah, my phone bill's really high, I'm sorry I can't call you." Well, if the stupid boyfriend's more important than calling her own daughter, you know, that's not my fault. She's always been mean, in my eyes, but nice when she's face to face with me.

I think I'm gifted to have a family like this. But I'm glad we're not a Leave-it-to-Beaver-Cleaver family. I've got friends that their families are perfect, no problems. But I'm sure there are problems inside the locked doors, but not really showing it. But in my family, if I'm angry, I'm going to go out and tell them. . . . I hate people who try to hide it. . . .

You know how counselors say ''dysfunctional'' and ''functional'' families? I think every family's dysfunctional, in their own way. I mean, every family is gonna have a fight about what they're gonna eat for supper, or who gets the family car tonight, or whatever.

[Dad] always tries to comfort me, telling me that he's always there for me. He can always arrange for me to talk to somebody if I'm hurting. But I try to explain to him that he's the only person I really need. . . . He's always been understanding. . . . [When things go bad], I talk to my dad.

THE ISOLATION OF BEING NATIVE AMERICAN

[Former community in South Dakota] was more like everybody was a family. . . . You would go to your backyard and have a banquet with the whole neighborhood, you know? It was like the whole town was one big family.

Sometimes I get sick of hearing about it [being Native American]. . . . I mean, like my dad just goes on and on, and finally, I just space out and pretend like I'm listening to him. . . . Because I've already heard all of it. . . . And he always tries to make me what I'm not, make me more Native American. And since I'm the only Native American in the Springdale school district almost, he tries to make me go to the principal and say, ''We need this.'' There's no use, because there's no other Native Americans to help me!

I'm really not noticed as a Native American until something. . . . Like the ITBS test. . . . The woman was giving us our codes. . . . She called ''Native Americans,'' and she goes, ''Well, I don't think there is any.'' And the whole auditorium goes, ''Fern!'' I think it's really neat. . . . I don't hide it. I express it.

[My teachers don't understand my culture] Like if I say, ''This isn't done in my culture. This isn't the way it's done. . . .'' Like talking about abortion in history or something. For Native Americans, abortion is just . . . like you should really put the mother in jail for it. Because . . . the baby is alive, just like we are. And that's the way I feel. And when they sit there and say, ''It's the mother's right to do it,'' well, I don't think, really, it's the mother's right because it's not the baby's fault the mother doesn't want it. And so, when I try to tell them, they just, ''Oh, well, we're out of time.'' They cut me off, and we've still got half an hour! And so that kinda makes me mad. . . .

If there's something in the history book that's wrong, my dad always taught me that if it's wrong, I should tell them that it is wrong. And the only time I ever do is if I know it's *exactly* wrong. Like we were reading about Native Americans and scalping. Well, the French are really the ones that made them do it so they could get money. And my teacher would not believe me. I finally just shut up because he just would not believe me. . . . Just my arguments with them, they just cut it off.

[Other people] are not going to understand me as much, if I start talking about spirituality. . . . But I don't feel like people put me down or put me up for being Indian. . . . I always get good praises from people, you know. ''I'm glad you're sticking in there, not being ashamed of being Native American.''

We do have different values. . . . We do have different needs and we do have different wants. I mean, I'm sure every family needs love. Love is a very, very top thing in our list of needs. . . . For White people, it's usually shelter over their heads. For Native Americans, usually number 1, family love.

It can be different. Like my family sits down and eats corn soup and fried dough. It would be different from "Well, my family goes out for pizza."

I don't know why . . . other Native Americans have dropped out of Springdale schools. Maybe it's because I just haven't been in high school yet. But I remember one time, my sister came home and she was just mad. They said that . . . "Geronimo was a stupid chief riding that stupid horse" and my sister got mad!

I've always been taught to be kind to elders, to always look up to them. And my dad's always taught me that everybody's really the same. I mean, there's no difference between Black and White. . . . But he's always taught me that everybody's the same. I don't care if they're rich or poor. . . . I mean, really everybody's the same to me, because we're all the same blood, you know? . . .

It really disgusts me when somebody with brown hair wants blond hair. I mean, it's what God wanted you to have, you know? . . . It just makes me sick. . . . It really never made sense to me.

IDENTIFYING AS SUCCESSFUL

I found school fun. . . . I liked to do homework. I got moved: I didn't go to kindergarten, I went straight from Head Start to first grade because I was too bored in the classes and I wouldn't do the work because I fought with the teachers and told them I already did it because I had done it the year before. And so my dad made them move me out because there was no use for me to stay back if I wasn't gonna learn anything new.

I like sports a lot, volleyball and basketball. . . . I like sports and I'm just glad they offer them 'cause some schools don't have enough funding. . . . But basketball is mostly my sport. . . . I compare it to stuff, like, when I can't get science, or like in sewing, I'll look at that machine and I'll say, "This is a basketball; I can overcome it. . . ."

One [of my friends], she's really understanding. If I have family problems, she's always there to talk to. We're really close. . . . We're like involved in the same sports, and we love basketball. All of them, I can always go to talk to . . . Natalie, I can always talk to. . . . I mean, she's like free counseling!

I've like always wanted to be president of the United States, but I figured that was too hard [*laughs*]. . . . I don't know, I kinda wanna be a fashion lawyer. . . .

I've always wanted to be president and I think it's just because like, I'll see so many mess-ups and . . . I don't know, just George Bush right now. . . . I was infatuated with Ronald Reagan the whole time he was in office. . . . And like I'd make posters for Dad and tell him, "Yeah, this is me." And I just like the idea of being head honcho!

[Reason for going to school is] to learn and make something out of yourself when you're older, so you're not just, I don't know, a person on welfare or something.

I sure remember the day I got my first B; I started crying. . . . Most of my friends, you know, get A's and B's, and everything. And it's not to impress them; it's to show them that I'm just as good, you know? It's mostly just for me, to make me know that I'm just as good as anybody else and that I can really do it.

I'm ambitious. I always want to get things done. Like say I'm running for copresident for the school, I want to get my campaign done ahead, not the day before.

I succeed in everything I do. If I don't get it right the first time, I always go back and try to do it again.

COMMENTARY

Fern Sherman is a successful American Indian student although the group's dropout rates are the highest of any other group. According to data from the *High School and Beyond* study, over 35 percent of high school Indian sophomores were dropouts.[4] This percentage is misleading, however, because many students drop out before even reaching high school, as early as elementary school.

The role of teachers' expectations of Indian students achievement is important. They have certainly had an impact on Fern's school achievement. Although she says that she does not like to be pushed, it is obvious that when teachers hold high expectations, she is able to live up to them. What most distresses her is teachers with low expectations or those who teach to only the high achievers ("the top 25 percent"). Fern believes that all students can learn if the instruction is meaningful to them. She is supported in this view by research that points out the negative effect of tracking on student achievement. A review of relevant data found that student literacy is strongly affected by high school curriculum track placements. That is, tracking *in and of itself,* over and above other factors, is responsible for many of the uneven outcomes in student achievement. Moreover, it has been found that Indian students are significantly overrepresented in remedial English and mathematics. The link between these two issues needs to be understood.[5]

Fern's father, who pushes academic achievement and ethnic pride and awareness, is clearly the major influence in her life. Having been a successful student himself, he knows the value of education. And as an American Indian, he is convinced that the only way to progress, both individually and for the community, is by having a good education. These are the messages Fern has been listening to since early childhood. They have had a profound impact on her. In terms of her schoolwork, she says that she tries to be successful for herself, her father, and her friends ("to show them that I'm just as good"). The need to excel on an individual basis is alien to most Indian cultures.[6] The individualistic notion of achievement simply does not work in most cases. In contrast, striving to excel for one's family, Nation, or community is a much better way of motivating children, which is why Fern's father stresses "making Grandmother proud." Providing an educational environment that emphasizes cooperative learning rather than individual competition is one important culturally appropriate strategy for schools to consider.[7]

Being the only Native American student in school is one of the key themes that came up repeatedly with Fern. At times, the pressure of being the only one is unbearable, especially when she feels that her father expects her to confront head-on every issue dealing with Native Americans. At other times, being the only one means being unique and special (e.g., she identified being singled out for this kind of interview as one of the benefits). Although some teachers, such as her English teacher, make accommodations in their content and structure, most others do not. When giving writing assignments about their families, her English teacher allows each student ample flexibility to discuss differences. And although she loves science, she feels that her teacher is not very helpful and probably the "least person for me to go talk to."

Being the only Native American in her school also means always being different. Although Fern is an extremely strong young woman, such pressure is inevitably difficult for adolescents going through the traumas of identification and peer acceptance. Her feeling that the Native American perspective is missing from school curricula is no doubt correct. Her perception that it is not welcome (e.g., in the discussion about abortion) may also be true but may simply be her reaction to feeling so different from her peers. We need to look at the history of the education of Indians to understand the legacy of resentment and suspicion with which some of them view the school.

Education has often been used to separate children physically, emotionally, and culturally from their families. A particularly graphic example of this practice is the 1895 *Annual Report* of the Indian commissioner to the secretary of the interior, in which the government's intent in educating Indian children was described as "to free the children from the language and habits of their untutored and oftentimes savage parents."[8] Such blatant expressions of racism would probably not be found today, but many of the patronizing attitudes stemming from this belief are still apparent. It is the disjuncture of culture from schooling that led one Indian superintendent of schools to say, "We need to educate a generation that can earn a living without paying the cost of cultural genocide."[9]

Being Native American, however, also brings with it benefits that Fern is quick to point out. She has a very strong sense of her culture and is proud of it. Although it may sometimes marginalize her, she has already assumed a mature understanding of what it means to be an Indian. It means accepting yourself for who you are. She says, for instance, that it sickens her to see people who want to dye their hair. This is a concrete example of the self-rejection of so many young people from culturally dominated groups. Fern is also beginning to enjoy the tangible expressions of her culture, from corn soup to powwows.

Unlike other young people her age, Fern is astute in understanding cultural differences. She has to be since she is usually the one who has had to accommodate to the majority. She is quite sophisticated in identifying differences between her ethnic group and the dominant culture. These are both concrete (differences in food, such as corn soup and fried dough) and intangible (such as Native American spirituality and her preference for some activities over others in school). When asked what she would like to see more of in schools, she is quite explicit: "more like involved activities, you know?" she says, capturing the general tendency of Indian students to do better in tests and activities requiring ability in observation, memory, and attention to detail than those emphasizing language and verbal expression.[10] The fact that Fern has a hard time in science as it is taught in her school is probably a manifestation of this tendency. National data corroborate her experience. According to the National Science Foundation, in 1986, only 15 percent of the 4,626,500 scientists in the country were women; of those, a tiny 0.4 percent were American Indians.[11] One researcher has pointed out that science projects that build on Indian cultures are a natural way of involving these students more in scientific pursuits. These include activities that emphasize investigating, discovering, experimenting, observing, defining, comparing, relating, inferring, classifying, and communicating.[12]

Fern sometimes sees exaggerated cultural differences between herself and others. For example, she maintains that for Whites, shelter is a number-one priority, whereas for Native Americans it is love. Such perceptions may be the result of the lack of dialogue in schools concerning differences. Always feeling as if she is on the outside, she may assume an oppositional culture even when such is not the case. It is doubtful, for example, that many European Americans would classify shelter as their number-one value.

Staying in school, studying hard, and being successful are important to Fern in spite of what she knows about the experiences of other Native American students. She identifies the dropout problem as a significant one and quite rightly asserts that perhaps she has not faced it because she has yet to go to high school. Her sister Juanita's experience is, sadly, not that unusual. In fact, dropout rates of Indian students tend to be higher in urban schools than in reservation schools. Three basic reasons have been proposed for this situation: discouragement on the part of students, insensitive teachers, and a lack of awareness of their students' culture.[13] Yet underachievement and illiteracy have not always been the norm. When schools are culturally sensitive and make sense to the students, the students tend to succeed. An interesting historical example is the fact that the Cherokees of Oklahoma, using an alphabet developed by Sequoyah, achieved an incredibly high literacy rate of 90 percent during the 1850s.[14] The fact that the culture and language were inextricably tied together probably explains this impressive accomplishment.

The connection among culture, language, and community can still be seen today. Fern's father's assertion that her former school was a better environment for learning is based on the support system that was in place for Indian students there. Even having Indian teachers, for example, has an impact on students' feelings of belonging and consequently on their achievement. One study found that Indian students who have Indian teachers do better on standardized achievement tests in reading and language arts.[15] Yet Indian teachers in the United States represent only 0.6 percent of all teachers in the profession, and this number is expected to decrease in the years ahead.[16]

American Indian children are faced with other difficult situations as well. Suicide is ten times more prevalent among reservation Indians than in the general population.[17] The rate of unemployment is extraordinarily high, and health care, particularly on reservations, is either absent or completely inadequate. Infant mortality is 11 percent above the national average, the incidence of tuberculosis is eight times higher, and there are widespread nutritional deficiencies. In addition, alcoholism may affect the lives and functioning of more than 60 percent of all children.[18] The poverty rate on reservations is generally agreed to be between 45 and 58 percent; some reservations report unemployment rates of 90 percent.[19] Struggling against these odds is an awesome responsibility; sometimes school, which is seen as irrelevant in any case, takes a back seat. Fern has developed a number of successful strategies to deal with these overwhelmingly negative barriers to success. She is, for instance, conspicuously ambitious. She wants to succeed in school and beyond and is quite certain that she will ("I succeed in everything I do," she says confidently). When asked who she most admires, she says President Bush, not the man, but rather "his power and success, and I just wish I could be as successful." This ambition spurs her on to do her best both in and out of school. In fact, when asked what she likes most about herself, she is quick to single out her ambition.

In raising her nephew; supporting her sister Juanita during this difficult time; adjusting to a school where she is clearly different from all her peers; and confronting the dual challenges of academic success and parental pressures, no matter how positive they may be, Fern Sherman has to contend with tremendous responsibilities at an early age. In spite of the obstacles, she has identified a goal: becoming president of the United States. Given her resoluteness and courage, she may make it.

TO THINK ABOUT

1. Fern's feeling of isolation in a city with so few American Indians affects her life in a great many ways. When have you been the only _____ (fill in the blank) in a particular setting? What impact did this have on you? Describe how you felt in school, at home, and in your community.

2. What is meant by the statement that tribal affiliation is a social construct? Who determines what a person is? How has that been done for some and not others in our society?

3. What are some of the pressures that can lead to alcohol and drug abuse for young people? What are specific situations in the Indian community that can exacerbate this problem? What can schools do to help alleviate it?

4. If you could talk with Fern about remaining a successful and confident student, what would you say?

5. What approaches might work to lower the dropout rate of Indian students? What can schools, communities, and families do together to help?

6. Work together with a small group of your colleagues and plan a science lesson in which you incorporate some of the Indian concepts mentioned by Ovando (see footnote 12). How might it differ from another science lesson? Would Indian students be the only ones to benefit from such lessons? Why or why not?

NOTES

1. I would like to thank Carlie Collins Tartakov for the extensive interviews with Fern Sherman, her sister Juanita, and their father. We especially appreciate the time, perspectives, and hope that Juanita conveyed to Carlie.
2. The Northern Ute Nation, for example, declared English a foreign language in 1984; see Jon Reyhner, "Native American Languages Act Becomes Law," in *NABE News*, 14, 3 (December 1, 1990); for data on the Indian population, see U.S. Bureau of the Census, *We, the First Americans* (Washington, DC: U.S. Government Printing Office, December 1988); Hap Gilliland, "The Need for an Adapted Curriculum," in *Teaching the Indian Child: A Bilingual/Multicultural Approach*, ed. Jon Reyhner (Billings: Eastern Montana College, 1986).
3. Fred Wise and Nancy Brown Miller, "The Mental Health of the American Indian Child," in *The Psychosocial Development of Minority Group Children*, ed. Gloria Johnson Powell (New York: Brunner/Mazel Publishers, 1983).
4. Samuel B. Peng, William B. Peters, and Andrew J. Kolstad, *High School and Beyond: A National Longitudinal Study for the 1980's: A Capsule Description of High School Students* (Washington, DC: U.S. Department of Education, Office of Educational Research and Improvement, 1981).
5. Jomills H. Braddock, II, *Tracking: Implications for Student Race-Ethnic Subgroups*, Report No. 1. (Baltimore: Johns Hopkins University, Center for Research on Effective Schooling for Disadvantaged Students, 1990).
6. See, for example, C. Barnhardt, " 'Tuning In': Athabaskan Teachers and Athabaskan Students," in *Cross-Cultural Issues in Alaskan Education*, Vol. 2, ed. R. Barnhardt (Fairbanks: University of Alaska, Center for Cross-Cultural Studies, 1982); Evelyn Lance Blanchard, "The Growth and Development of American Indian and Alaskan Native Children" and John Red Horse, "Indian Family Values and Experiences," in *The Psychosocial Development of Minority Group Children*, ed. Gloria Johnson Powell (New York: Brunner/Mazel Publishers, 1983); Frederick Erickson and Gerald Mohatt, "Cultural Organization of Indian Students," in *Doing the Ethnography of Schooling: Educational Anthropology in Action*, ed. George Spindler (New York: Holt, Rinehart & Winston, 1982); Susan Urmston Phillips, *The Invisible Culture: Communication in Classroom and Community on the Warm Springs Indian Reservation* (White Plains, NY: Longman, 1982).
7. Lee Little Soldier, "Cooperative Learning and the Native American Student," *Phi Delta Kappan*, October 1989, pp. 161–163.

8. As cited in Jon Reyhner, "Bilingual Education: Teaching the Native Language," in *Teaching the Indian Child: A Bilingual/Multicultural Approach*, ed. Jon Reyhner (Billings: Eastern Montana College, 1986), p. 39.

9. "Stuck in the Horizon: A Special Report on the Education of Native Americans," *Education Week*, August 2, 1989, pp. 1–16.

10. Gilliland, "Need for an Adapted Curriculum."

11. *Women and Minorities in Science and Engineering* (Washington, DC: National Science Foundation, 1988).

12. Carlos J. Ovando, "Teaching Science to the Native American Student," in *Teaching the Indian Child: A Bilingual/Multicultural Approach*, ed. Jon Reyhner (Billings: Eastern Montana College, 1986).

13. For a description of an investigation by representatives of the Indian community in Lansing, Michigan, see *Barriers to Excellence: Our Children at Risk* (Boston: National Coalition of Advocates for Students, 1985).

14. "Stuck in the Horizon."

15. Reyhner, "Bilingual Education."

16. Quality Education for Minorities Project, *Education That Works: An Action Plan for the Education of Minorities* (Cambridge, MA: Massachusetts Institute of Technology, January 1990).

17. Hap Gilliland, "Self-Concept and the Indian Student," in *Teaching the Indian Child: A Bilingual/Multicultural Approach*, ed. Jon Reyhner (Billings: Eastern Montana College, 1986).

18. "Stuck in the Horizon."

19. U.S. Bureau of the Census, *We, the First Americans.* See also "Stuck in the Horizon."

CHAPTER 5

Cultural Issues and Their Impact on Learning

OVERVIEW

Many teachers and schools, in an attempt to be color-blind, do not want to acknowledge cultural or racial differences. "I don't see Black or White," a teacher will say, "I see only *students.*" This statement assumes that to be color-blind is to be fair, impartial, and objective. It sounds fair and honest and ethical, but the opposite may actually be true. That is, to see differences, in this line of reasoning, is to see defects and inferiority. Thus, to be color-blind may result in *refusing to accept differences* and therefore accepting the dominant culture as the norm. It may result in denying the very identity of our students, thereby making them invisible. What seems on the surface to be impeccably fair may in reality be fundamentally unfair. Being color-blind can be positive if it means being *nondiscriminatory* in attitude and behavior. However, it is sometimes used as a way to deny differences that help make us who we are.

A good example was provided by the U.S. Supreme Court in the *Lau* decision of 1974.[1] The San Francisco School Department was sued on behalf of Chinese-speaking students who, parents and other advocates charged, were not being provided with an equal education. The school department, however, argued that they were indeed providing these students with an equal education because they received *exactly* the same teachers, instruction, and materials as all the other students. The U.S. Supreme Court, in a unanimous decision, ruled against the school department. They reasoned that giving these students the same instruction, teachers, and materials as English-speaking students flew in the face of equal educational opportunity because Chinese-speaking students could not benefit from instruction provided in English. The dictum "Equal is not the same" is useful here. It means that treating everyone in the same way will not necessarily lead to equality; rather, it may end up perpetuating the inequality that already exists. Learning to *affirm* differences rather than deny them is what a multicultural perspective is about.

What are the educational implications of "Equal is not the same"? First, it means *acknowledging the differences that children bring to school,* including their gender, race, ethnicity, language, and social class. Not acknowledging these differences often results in schools and teachers labeling children's behavior as deficient.

Second, it means *admitting the possibility that such differences may influence how students learn.* This should in no way devalue children's backgrounds or lower our expectations of them, yet this is precisely why so many educators have a hard time accepting "Equal is not the same." That is, they are reluctant to accept this philosophy because they may feel that in doing so, they must lower their expectations or water down the curriculum so that all children can learn. Yet neither of these practices should be seen as necessary.

Third, *accepting differences also means making provisions for them.* That is, students' cultural and linguistic backgrounds should be viewed as a strength on which educators can draw. Although this approach is based on the best of educational practice, that is, that individual differences must be taken into account in teaching, it is often overlooked for cultural and linguistic differences.

The purpose of this chapter is to explore cultural differences and the importance they may have in student learning. Rather than viewing cultural diversity as a burden, a problem, or even a challenge, it will be approached as a key factor that must be taken into account if we are serious about providing all students with educational equity. We will review a number of cultural differences among students, including learning and communication styles, and then consider some of the instructional and curricular changes that have been developed to help students succeed in school.

We are always on shaky ground when considering cultural differences. Although it is important to examine how culture may influence learning and therefore achievement in school, the danger lies in overgeneralizing its effects. Overgeneralizations can lead to gross stereotypes, which in turn may lead to erroneous conclusions about individual students' abilities and intelligence. It is important to emphasize that although culture is integral to the learning process, it affects every individual differently. It may be true that Appalachian people share a rich heritage that includes a strong sense of kinship, but this culture may not have the same effect on every child.[2] Given differences in social class, family structure, psychological and emotional differences, birth order, residence, and a host of individual distinctions, it would be folly to think that culture in and of itself accounts for all human differences. Culture is neither static nor deterministic. It gives us just one important way in which to understand some differences among student learning and thus can indicate appropriate strategies and modifications in curriculum. The assumption that culture is the primary determinant of academic achievement can be oversimplistic, dangerous, and counterproductive. Thus, the area of culture and cultural differences should be handled with great caution so that we as educators do not make assumptions about students because of the culture from which they come.

One of the reasons for insisting on the importance of cultural differences is that some people, primarily those from dominated and disenfranchised groups within society, have been taught that they *have no culture.* This is how a term such as *cultural deprivation,* which in reality means that some people do not share in the culture of the dominant group, came to mean that a group was deprived of culture *altogether.* This, of course, is nonsense. Everybody has a culture because everybody has the ability to create and re-create ideas and material goods and to affect their world in a variety of ways. Multicultural education is one way of counteracting the notion that culture is within the purview of only the privileged.

Before we can ask schools to change in order to teach all students, we need to understand the differences students bring with them to school. This chapter will consider how one primary difference, culture, may affect the learning of students. *Culture can be understood as the ever-changing values, traditions, social and political relationships, and worldview shared by a group of people bound together by a combination of factors that can include a common history, geographic location, language, social class, and/or religion.* Thus, it includes not only such tangibles as foods, holidays, dress, and artistic expression but also less tangible manifestations such as communication style, attitudes, values, and family relationships. These implicit features of culture are often more difficult to pinpoint, but doing so is necessary if we want to understand how learning may be affected.

Cultural differences in learning may be especially apparent in three areas: *learning styles, interactional or communication styles,* and *language differences.* Examples of the first two areas will be explored below. Language and language issues will be considered in the next chapter. Nevertheless, it should be understood that language is an indispensable component of culture and therefore interacts with it in numerous ways.

Much of the research reported here, and from which part of the conceptual framework for multicultural education is developed, is *ethnographic research,* that is, educational research based on anthropological constructs and including methods such as fieldwork, interviewing, and participant observation. According to McDermott, ethnography is "any rigorous attempt to account for people's behavior in terms of their relations with those around them in different situations."[3] This important area of research has had a profound effect on educational thinking, particularly in the last 20 years. According to Wilcox, because of its grounding in anthropology, ethnographic research helps us to understand education as *cultural transmission* (i.e., as a process through which the values and practices of particular cultures are fostered and developed) and schools as one arena of potential cultural conflict.[4] This research has numerous implications for policy and practice in schools. Results are being seen in some educational settings and will be reported here.

LEARNING STYLE

By learning style we mean the way in which individuals receive and process information.[5] Witkin, an early theorist in this field, suggested that people are either *field independent* or *field dependent* in their learning.[6] The former tend to learn best in situations that emphasize analytic tasks and with materials void of a social context. Individuals who favor this mode generally prefer to work alone and are self-motivated. Field-dependent learners, on the other hand, tend to learn best in highly social settings. For these learners, the context is of maximum importance. They are likely to do best with materials that have human, social content and in situations guided by a teacher and in cooperation with other learners.

Ramirez and Castañeda have applied Witkin's theory to ethnic groups and found some intriguing patterns.[7] For example, in research with children of various cultural backgrounds, they discovered that European American students tend to be the most field-independent learners. Mexican American, American Indian, and African American students, in contrast, tend to be closer to field *sensitive* (their substitution for *dependent*, which has negative connotations), with Mexican Americans closest to this pole.

A number of other research studies have explored the patterns of learning style among children of different ethnic groups. An early study by Stodolsky and Lesser affirmed the importance of ethnicity and culture on children's learning.[8] The patterns among various mental abilities in 6- and 7-year-old children of different social class and ethnic backgrounds were explored, specifically, Chinese, Jewish, Black, and Puerto Rican children of both poor and middle-class backgrounds. It was found that the *patterns* among the mental abilities were different for all ethnic groups and remained quite stable in spite of class background. For example, the mental ability patterns of both middle-class and poor Chinese children were strikingly similar. The researchers concluded that ethnicity must play a part in influencing these patterns and that it was more salient than social class.

Exactly how culture influences learning is not clear. Learning style research maintains that mothers' (or primary caregiver's) child-rearing practices are primarily responsible for the learning styles children develop.[9] The case is made that the values, attitudes, and behaviors taught at home are the basis for how children learn to learn. It is not clear, however, that it is as direct a process as this statement implies. There are vast differences among, for example, Mexican American learners: although a great many may indeed be classified as field sensitive, some will most certainly be field independent and many will be somewhere between the two. These differences may be due to social class, language spoken at home, number of years or generations in the United States, and simple individual differences. Among children from similar backgrounds or even from the same home, the differences are often striking. It is clear that child-rearing practices, although playing a part in determining a child's learning style, is by no means a sufficient explanation. Other factors are at work here as well, and some are frequently even more important.

Social class, for example, has been proposed as equally or more important than ethnicity in influencing learning style. *Social class* refers to membership within a particular social grouping, based on both economic variables and values. Thus, the working class may differ from the middle class not only in economic resources but also in particular values and practices. The reasoning behind the hypothesis that social class is more important an influence on learning style than is ethnicity is that the intellectual environment and socialization of children in the home may be due more to economic than to cultural resources. In a comprehensive review of related studies, Banks found in general that ethnicity seemed to have a greater influence on cognitive style than did social class. He also found that ethnic differences persist in spite of upward mobility.[10] This line of research points out the apparently strong and continuing link between culture and learning.

There are important implications for teaching and learning in this research. Ramirez and Castañeda, for example, believe that a major goal of what they call *culturally democratic* education should be *bicognitive development*.[11] That is, all children should be exposed to and become adept at *both styles* of learning, although they will probably still maintain their preferred style. The researchers recommend strategies for identifying the learning styles of students and the teaching styles of teachers as well as for teaching in a culturally democratic manner.

Two problems are inherent in this type of research. First, it tends to dichotomize learning. It is doubtful that a process as complex as learning can be characterized with only two poles. As many as 14 learning styles and 13 different learning style theories have been suggested. Some studies have focused on differences in visual or verbal emphasis, which can be related to holistic versus analytic thought processes.[12] All of these point out the difficulties inherent in developing learning classifications. Second, although helpful in identifying learning differences that may be related to ethnicity and culture, this research also runs the risk of oversimplification. Not all European Americans are field independent and not all American Indians are field sensitive, yet this is often the conclusion that educators reach. In addition, such research can be used as a rationale for poor or inequitable teaching. For example, in integrated classrooms in which Hispanic children were present, research by Ortiz revealed that they tended to receive a lower-quality education than others.[13]

Ironically, teachers used the "cooperative" attribute from the learning style literature to justify a number of clearly discriminatory pedagogical decisions: seldom granting Hispanic students solo performances in plays or leadership activities in other situations; placing them in activities they had not themselves chosen, whereas other children were allowed choices; and having them share books when there were not enough to go around, whereas the non-Hispanic students could have individual copies. Teachers rationalized that because they felt that Hispanics are field sensitive, they would be more likely to feel uncomfortable in the limelight or in leadership roles. They also reasoned that Hispanic children liked to share books because of their preference for working cooperatively. The teachers' negative, preconceived notions of children's ability were in this way reinforced by faulty interpretations of research. It is a good example of the truism that "a little knowledge is a dangerous thing."

Although not specifically related to cultural differences, Gardner's work on "multiple intelligences" has important implications for culturally compatible education.[14] According to this theory, each human being is capable of several relatively independent forms of information processing and each of these is a specific "intelligence": logical-mathematical, linguistic (the two most emphasized in school success), musical, spatial, bodily kinesthetic, interpersonal, and intrapersonal. Intelligence is defined here as the ability to solve problems or develop products that are valued in a particular cultural setting. The salience of what may be cultural differences in intelligence becomes apparent. Gardner's research has demonstrated that individuals differ in the specific profile of intelligences that they exhibit. These differences may in effect be due to what is valued in their culture. The importance of this research lies in the fact that because a broader range of abilities is considered, the talents and abilities of individuals previously considered inferior or unexceptional may be brought to the surface.

The implications of the theory of multiple intelligences for multicultural education may be significant because it goes beyond the limited definition of intelligence that is valued in the school. In opening up our understanding of intelligence, this theory permits schools and teachers to look at their students with a different perspective. The danger, as always, lies in extrapolating from individual cases to an entire group. Although it may be true, for example, that certain cultures are highly developed in bodily kinesthetic intelligence, we should not conclude that all its members will manifest this kind of intelligence equally. Nor should educators assume that individuals from this culture would be *primarily* or *only* intelligent bodily-kinesthetically, and therefore not able to manipulate language, for example.

COMMUNICATION STYLE

Other examples of cultural influences are found in interactional or communication styles. This area focuses on the way in which individuals interact with one another and the messages they may send, intentionally or not, in their communications. For example, Willet has suggested that the culturally shaped interaction patterns of language learners may influence the type of "language input" they receive, thus helping to explain their learning styles and developmental language output.[15] In her research, she found that two young children who were learning English, one Korean and one Brazilian, approached the task with very different strategies. In spite of these differences, both were successful language learners. It is important that such differences be acknowledged and understood by teachers to help them develop appropriate curriculum and instruction for all their students.

McDermott hypothesizes that for many culturally different children, school failure is best explained not by biological, psychological, or linguistic deprivation but by the cultural makeup of the classroom.[16] He labels schools in which African American children are taught by European American teachers as "pariah-host" communities and maintains that children and teachers in these environments produce communication breakdowns simply by being themselves, that is, by behaving in ways their subcultures see as "normal." The result of this cultural conflict is school failure. Thus, school failure is actually "achieved" because it is the product of miscommunication between teachers and students and a rational adaptation by students perceived as being in a "pariah" relationship to "host" schools. Unless changes are made in these environments, school failure is almost inevitable.

Cultural variables may be compatible or incompatible with the expectations and structures of schools. Tharp has suggested at least four: *social organization, sociolinguistics, cognition,* and *motivation.*[17] An example or two can be considered under the general rubric of communication style and will suffice to demonstrate their complex and fascinating interplay. Social organization, for instance, refers to the ways in which classrooms are organized. Tharp reviews a number of classroom organizations that have proven to be effective and concludes that the traditional U.S. whole-class organization, with "rank-and-file" seating and a teacher-leader who instructs or demonstrates, is not necessarily the best arrangement for all children. For example, Williams's ethnographic work in an inner-city school suggests that African American students are skillful at manipulating the dynamics of their classrooms. This is often interpreted as "acting out" or delinquent behavior, such as staging spontaneous "dramas" designed to tease and even to intimidate teachers. Rather than ignoring such skills, some teachers have reported using them successfully in front-of-the-class performances related to instructional goals.[18]

In the area of sociolinguistics, Tharp explains how short "wait times" tend to be disadvantageous to Indian students, who generally take longer to respond to teachers' questions because the culture of most American Indians tends to emphasize deliberate thought. The cultural expectation here is that one can make informed and appropriate choices only when considering all the possible ramifications and implications of a decision. This value of careful consideration of all aspects of a question may influence the classroom behavior of many American Indian students. Another example of sociolinguistics has to do with "rhythm." For example, African American mothers and their children often use a "contest" style of speech that approximates the call and response patterns found in Black music. Research suggests that using such rhythms in classroom instruction by teachers of African American students has had positive results.[19] Based on his extensive review of culturally compatible education, Tharp concludes that when schools change and are more attuned to children's cultures, the children's academic achievement invariably improves.

Cultural differences probably influence students in more ways than we can even imagine. A teacher of English as a second language (ESL), a young woman who was sincerely committed to and interested in her students' achievement, was nevertheless unaware of many aspects of their culture. The children, all Puerto Rican and recently arrived in the United States, used the communication style typical of their culture. For example, many Puerto Ricans use a nonverbal wrinkling of the nose to signify "what?" When this teacher would ask the children if they understood the lesson, some would invariably wrinkle their noses. Not understanding this gesture, the teacher simply went on with the lesson, assuming that their nose wrinkling had no significance. It was not until two years after first confronting this behavior, while attending a workshop on Puerto Rican gestures in which the work of Nine-Curt was reviewed, that she learned that nose-wrinkling among Puerto Ricans was a way of asking "What?" or "What do you mean?" or of saying "I don't understand."[20] From that point on, she understood that when they used this gesture, her students were asking for help or for further clarification.

In Alaska Native cultures, we find a similar example of nonverbal gestures: Raised eyebrows are often used to signify yes and a wrinkled nose means no. Because teachers might interpret these as rude nonresponses to their questions, there have been communication problems between Alaska Native students and their non-Alaska Native teachers. Many teachers tend to look for verbal rather than nonverbal responses.

Through ethnographic research, some of the ways teachers and students miscommunicate are becoming more visible. If such research helps teachers to design appropriate environments for all their students, it will prove to be extremely useful. The communication styles explored above are only the tip of the iceburg, but they help to point out the sometimes subtle ways that culture, if not understood, can actively get in the way of learning.

CULTURAL DISCONTINUITIES
AND SCHOOL ACHIEVEMENT

A review of the emerging research on culture-specific educational accommodations will be helpful in pinpointing cultural discontinuities particular to some groups. A number of researchers have focused on the differences between African American culture and that of the school. Gilbert and Gay have identified four areas of potential cultural conflict:[21] *learning style, interactional* or *relational style, communication style,* and *differing perceptions of involvement.* They suggest, for instance, that African American students devote a lot of energy to the "stage setting" that precedes the performance of a task. This may include a host of elaborate activities such as sharpening pencils, preparing paper, rearranging posture, and asking teachers to repeat instructions. Such activities are often interpreted by teachers as either wasting time or not paying attention.

In communication style, the researchers focus on the use of the spoken language among African Americans and the attendant "stylistic flair" valued in that community. In the schools, in contrast, what are most valued are precision and conciseness in the written language. The conflict in communication is thus a dual one: written versus oral language and direct versus dramatic use of language. Finally, Gilbert and Gay consider differing "perceptions of involvement." Whereas the schools generally define cognitive involvement as taking place only within a structured and orderly environment, African American students tend to be multimodal; that is, their involvement is cognitive, emotional, and physical all at the same time. Their behavior may be disconcerting to teachers who are unfamiliar with this style.

An intriguing study by Kathleen Bennett is informative here as well. Bennett found that even though a teacher was considered excellent by her principal and peers, she was not able to make a significant difference in the reading achievement of a group of Appalachian first-graders. There were several reasons for this lack, including a sharp dissonance between the expressed philosophy of the district and the actual reading program offered in the classroom and the ideology of stratification that permeated the entire reading program. In addition, the culture of the classroom was in stark contrast to the culture, natural language, and experiences of the children. There was thus a cultural incongruence between the children's backgrounds and the classroom and school they attended.[22]

Heath's research in the Piedmont Carolinas during the 1970s is another example.[23] In exploring the language of Black children at home and at school, she found that different ways of using language resulted in certain tensions between them and their mostly White teachers in the classroom. To repair this communication breakdown, teachers began to experiment with different ways of asking questions. The result was that teachers helped children bridge the gap between their home and school experiences and the children's language use in the classroom was enhanced.

A very different example might come from the experiences of a newly arrived Vietnamese immigrant to a U.S. school. Such a child might feel extremely off-balance and uncomfortable in a classroom environment in which teachers are informal and friendly, students are expected to ask questions and speak in front of the class, and group work is the order of the day.[24] The cultural discontinuity from a learning environment in which teachers are revered and have a formal relationship with their students and students are expected to learn individually and by listening and memorizing can be a dramatic one. Another example concerns Alaska Natives. Because going to high school often meant that students were physically separated from their parents in distant boarding schools, it was discovered that half of the boarding school students experienced school-related social and emotional problems. The dropout rate among Alaska Native students was very high, and although it remains high in some areas, it has been reduced dramatically in the rural schools in which secondary education has been returned to local communities.[25]

A further example is seen in research by Sindell.[26] He found that when they first enter school, Mistassini Cree children have to learn to act according to norms that contradict much of what they have learned at home. Some of the cultural expectations are almost polar opposites. For example, at home children are expected to be self-reliant, but at school they have to be dependent on the teacher; at home they learn to do tasks co-operatively, but at school they must compete; at home they learn to do practical tasks that are important for the welfare of their community, but at school they are expected to live in a world of play unrelated to their future participation in society. The result of these cultural discontinuities may be that children reject their parents' definition of appropriate behavior and serious intergenerational conflicts often develop. Although this is an extreme example of cultural incompatibility, because the children in this case actually leave their home environments to live at school, it is nevertheless representative of the kinds of miscommunication that can result when schools and homes have radically different values, objectives, and practices. The same, for example, has been found of Appalachian children. Although they do not leave home to attend boarding schools, they, too, are expected to be self-reliant at home and change to a dependent role in school.[27] These children often feel that they must choose between home and school and that choosing one over the other will make them unsuitable for life in the other setting.

An example from a field not related to schoolchildren can illustrate this communication breakdown dramatically. Based on several years of ethnographic research, Jordan described the participation of Maya midwives in government-sponsored training courses in the Yucatán region of Mexico. She found that these courses, for all their good intentions, generally failed; that is, although the midwives were exposed to years of training, their day-to-day practice did not change as a result, partly because of the culturally inappropriate teaching strategies employed in the government-sponsored courses. Specifically, Jordan mentions the teachers' imperialist view of the world and thus their dismissal of the local culture and its solutions. Official training sessions, in Jordan's words, "render midwives' praxis and discourse deficient and without import."[28] It is not too far-fetched to apply this description of cultural imperialism in the Yucatán in the way in which children's cultures and life-styles are devalued every day in U.S. classrooms. Although the settings are quite different, the process is unfortunately very familiar. The culture and language children bring to school are often disregarded and replaced.

Let us consider an additional example concerning American Indian children. Core Indian values of respect and value for the dignity of the individual, harmony, internal locus of control, and cooperation and sharing inevitably influence students' reactions to their educational experiences.[29] That a teacher's best intentions may be ineffective if students' cultural differences are neglected in curriculum and instruction is seen by Philips's ethnographic work on the Warm Springs Reservation among Indian schoolchildren.[30] Students performed poorly in classroom contexts that demanded individualized performance and emphasized competition. Their performance improved greatly when the context did not require students to perform in public and when cooperation was valued over competition. Cooperative learning, which is compatible with many of the values of Indian students, is an approach worth exploring. It may be helpful in other settings as well. That is, cultural compatibility is only one criterion for using particular strategies; another is exposing *all* children to a variety of ways of learning.

Culture is not simply what children bring to school, however. Teachers, too, have a culture and approach their teaching roles with their own experiences and philosophy about the nature of teaching and learning. The possibility that the teachers' culture may influence students' behavior and learning has been investigated by Hernández and

Santiago.[31] In analyzing teachers' disapproval behavior in third- and fourth-grade classrooms, they found that Latino teachers tended to use indirect forms in making their disapproval felt, including conditional tenses, appeals of a personal nature, and polite forms like *please* and *thank you.* Latino teachers were much more apt to use less brusque means than European American teachers to control student behavior. According to the researchers, all of these behaviors reflect the Puerto Rican value of *respeto,* a highly intense form of respect.

European American teachers, in contrast, tended to be more direct, terse, and to the point in their disapproving behaviors. In addition, they appealed more to individual control, whereas Latino teachers appealed more often to group control. These differences were apparent even though all of the classes were conducted in English and were ethnically mixed. Although the full effects of these differentiated behaviors are not known, Hernández and Santiago concluded that Latino children may interpret what they consider non-Latino behaviors in negative ways and may thus suffer from rejection in ways we may not fully understand. Research of this kind is important if we are to grasp how children from different cultural backgrounds respond to teachers' behaviors and what teachers can do to change the unconscious messages they may be sending to their students.

All of these examples demonstrate that the cultural incompatabilities of children with their teachers and schools are varied and complex. In spite of the importance that culture may have, however, it is important to remind ourselves that overgeneralizing about its effects may be dangerous. No one solution will bridge the gap between school and home cultures. In the next section, we will examine a number of programs that have designed environments specifically for one cultural group. We will then explore some of the problematic features of this approach.

CULTURE-SPECIFIC
EDUCATIONAL ACCOMMODATIONS

A number of examples of modifying instruction to be more culturally appropriate can reveal the reasoning behind this approach as well as some preliminary promising results. Described by Vogt and others, KEEP in Hawaii is a particularly striking example.[32] Cultural discontinuities in instruction were identified as a major problem in the poor academic achievement of Native Hawaiian children.[33] As a result, the Kamehameha Elementary Education Program, more popularly known as KEEP, was begun. A privately funded, multidisciplinary educational research effort, its purpose was to explore remedies for children's chronic academic underachievement by changing certain educational practices: from a phonics approach to one emphasizing comprehension; from individual work desks to work centers, with heterogeneous groups; and from high to more culturally appropriate praise, including indirect and group praise. The KEEP culturally compatible K–3 language arts program has met with great success, including significant gains in reading achievement.

The changes in instructional style more closely paralleled the children's cultural styles. The move from phonics to comprehension, for instance, allowed the students to contribute in a speech style called the "talk-story," which is a familiar linguistic event in the Hawaiian community. The other instructional changes were also compatible with Native Hawaiian culture, including a preference for cooperative work and group accomplishment.

The logic of KEEP has been used as the basis for the KEEP-Rough Rock Project, a collaborative project with the Rough Rock Demonstration School on the Navajo Reservation.[34] It is not simply a replica of KEEP, however. On the contrary, several of the features of KEEP had to be modified to be more culturally compatible with the Navajo culture. Thus, the instructional approaches in KEEP could not simply be transferred to any cultural setting. For example, it was found that Navajo children preferred working in same-sex groups, a preference that is culturally congruent. Therefore, same-sex groups became a feature of Rough Rock-KEEP. In addition, it became clear that Navajo children were more comfortable with holistic than linear thinking. This finding influenced the instructional choices that teachers made. The preference for holistic thinking among American Indians had been documented before, but this was probably the first time that a school had used these data as a basis for the comprehensive modification of their curriculum and pedagogy.[35]

Although promising, this line of research is also problematic. Few children go to culturally homogeneous schools; many schools are still largely segregated, but few are made up of only one ethnic group. Thus it is unrealistic to expect that completely culturally compatible instruction can be provided for all children. In addition, there are numerous examples of successful schools that do not provide any culturally defined instruction (possible explanations will be examined in the Chapter 7). Education that is *completely* culturally compatible is not necessarily a requisite for academic success. Other factors may be even more important in guaranteeing equal educational opportunity for all students. In addition, realistically speaking, such educational modifications are a possibility for only a small number of students in our society (this in completely segregated settings), and other means to achieve academic success should be explored.

In spite of these limitations, this research is helpful because it points out that *all* children can learn if appropriate modifications in instruction are made. Teachers intuitively and consistently make such modifications, both in their curriculum and in their instructional practices. Erickson and Mohatt, for example, reported on the social relationships in two classrooms of culturally similar Indian children, one taught by an Indian and the other by a non-Indian.[36] Although the classroom organizations differed substantially at the beginning of the year, both teachers had adapted their instructional practices by the end of the year in the direction of *greater cultural congruence*. The non-Indian teacher, for example, ended up by seating children in table groups, not individually in rows, and also began to spend more time on small-group lessons and tutoring than on whole-group lessons. This teacher used what Erickson and Mohatt call "teacher radar," and the result was cultural congruence, apparently arrived at intuitively.

Although this dramatic example focuses on one particular cultural group, changes in instruction and curriculum that reflect the *multicultural* character of schools are also possible. For example, most schools favor a highly competitive and individualistic instructional mode. In this kind of environment, dominant-culture children and males are more likely to succeed, whereas students from other cultural groups and females may be at a distinct disadvantage. By combining this style with a more cooperative mode, the learning and cultural styles of all children can be respected and valued. The lesson to be learned is that although all schools cannot become *culturally compatible,* they can nevertheless become *multiculturally sensitive.*

SUMMARY

This discussion has identified some of the ways in which cultural differences may affect students' learning. Relatively recent methodologies of ethnographic investigation have yielded important findings that can help teachers and schools recognize the possible impact of culture and some of the modifications they can make in interactional style, programmatic structures, and instructional strategies. Ethnography has been helpful in providing insights that can influence educational policy and practice.

In spite of their usefulness, however, culture-specific accommodations are limited by several factors. First, the multiplicity of student needs in most schools mitigates against culturally specific modifications. Schools can change their instructional strategies, for example, to be compatible with students from one ethnic group but these same strategies might be just the opposite of what students from other ethnic groups need. Yet most of our schools are multicultural, with students from a diversity of ethnic, social class, and linguistic backgrounds. Satisfying the needs of, say, Mexican American students at the expense of everyone else in the same school would be a replication in reverse of the policy common today in most schools: It would be a monocultural education, except that it would be based in this case on Mexican American rather than European American culture.

Another problem with making educational choices that are solely culturally compatible is that segregation is posited as the most effective solution to educational failure. Yet history has amply demonstrated that segregation does not work, especially for dominated groups in a society. "Separate but equal" is rarely that; on the contrary, it usually means that powerless groups are precisely those that end up with an inferior education because, for one, they receive the least material resources with which to educate their children. Although culturally compatible education has been shown to be dramatically effective in some cases, it is unworkable in many situations.

Finally, culturally compatible education can provide only a partial explanation for school success and failure because there are numerous cases of culturally diverse students who have been successfully educated in what by all accounts would be considered culturally incompatible settings. Yet these children have thrived. Other factors not related to cultural conflict must be involved as well. After we review the implications of linguistic diversity for multicultural education in the next chapter, we will explore in Part II a more comprehensive explanation of school success and failure by taking into account some of these factors.

TO THINK ABOUT

1. What are the advantages of being color-blind? What are the disadvantages?
2. Give some concrete examples of the saying "Equal is not the same," with reference to children.
3. Observe three different students in a classroom. How would you characterize their learning styles? How do they differ? Do you think these differences have something to do with their gender, race, ethnicity, or class? Why? What are the implications for teaching these children?

4. What strategies have helped you most as a learner? If you could talk to a former teacher, what would you tell him or her about making education more meaningful for you?

5. McDermott has used the term *pariah-host communities* to refer to schools in which teachers and students from substantially distinct cultures interact. Do you believe this is an appropriate term? Why or why not?

6. Tharp has suggested that the traditional "rank-and-file" seating of students with a teacher in front of the classroom is not an appropriate learning environment for a great number of students. What do you think? What are the implications for classroom organization? Suggest some alternatives to the traditional classroom organization that might give more students an equal chance to learn.

7. Review the research on Mistassini Cree children cited by Sindell. Given the contradictory messages between home and school received by the children, it is no surprise that they began to reject their parents' culture and way of life. What could the school have done to minimize the contradictions?

8. Think about a culturally pluralistic school that you are familiar with. What steps could be taken by the school to make it more *culturally compatible* with its student body? Consider changes in curriculum, organization, use of materials, and pedagogical strategies.

NOTES

1. *Lau* v. *Nichols*, 414 U.S. 563 (St. Paul, MN: West Publishing, 1974).
2. See Kathleen P. Bennett "Doing School in an Urban Appalachian First Grade," in *Empowerment Through Multicultural Education*, ed. Christine E. Sleeter (Albany: State University of New York Press, 1991).
3. R. P. McDermott, "Social Relations as Contexts for Learning in School," *Harvard Educational Review*, 47, 2 (May 1977), 198–213.
4. Kathleen Wilcox, "Ethnography as a Methodology and Its Application to the Study of Schooling: A Review," in *Doing the Ethnography of Schooling: Educational Anthropology in Action*, ed. George Spindler (New York: Holt, Rinehart & Winston, 1982).
5. For an excellent overview of different categories of learning styles and an analysis of each, see Christine I. Bennett, *Comprehensive Multicultural Education: Theory and Practice* (Boston: Allyn & Bacon, 1986).
6. Herman A. Witkin, *Psychological Differentiation* (New York: Wiley, 1962).
7. Manuel Ramirez and Alfred Castañeda, *Cultural Democracy, Bicognitive Development and Education* (New York: Academic Press, 1974).
8. Susan S. Stodolsky and Gerald Lesser, "Learning Patterns in the Disadvantaged," in *Challenging the Myths: The Schools, the Blacks, and the Poor*, Reprint Series #5. (Cambridge, MA: Harvard Educational Review, 1971).
9. Ramirez and Castañeda, *Cultural Democracy*.
10. James A. Banks, "Ethnicity, Class, Cognitive and Motivational Styles: Research and Teaching Implications," *Journal of Negro Education*, 57, 4 (1988), 452–466.
11. Ramirez and Castañeda, *Cultural Democracy*.
12. See critiques on this line of research by Courtney B. Cazden and Ellen L. Leggett, "Culturally Responsive Education: Recommendations for Achieving *Lau* Remedies," in *Culture and the Bilingual Classroom: Studies in Classroom Ethnography*, ed. Henry T. Trueba, G. P. Guthrie, and K. H. Au (Rowley, MA: Newbury House, 1981); Arturo Romero, "The Mexican-American Child: A Socioecological Approach to Research," in *The Psychosocial Development of Minority Group Children*, ed. Gloria Johnson Powell (New York: Brunner/Mazel Publishers,

1983). For a review of holistic versus analytic thought processes and implications for educational practice, see Roland G. Tharp, "Psychocultural Variables and Constants: Effects on Teaching and Learning in Schools," *American Psychologist,* 44, 2 (February 1989), 349–359. For a review of different learning style theories, see Lynn Curry, *Learning Styles in Secondary Schools: A Review of Instruments and Implications for Their Use* (Madison: National Center on Effective Secondary Schools, University of Wisconsin, 1990).

13. Flora Ida Ortiz, "Hispanic-American Children's Experiences in Classrooms: A Comparison Between Hispanic and Non-Hispanic Children," in *Class, Race and Gender in American Education,* ed. Lois Weis (Albany: State University of New York Press, 1988).

14. Howard Gardner, *Frames of Mind* (New York: Basic Books, 1983).

15. Jerri Willet, "Contrasting Acculturation Patterns of Two Non-English Speaking Preschoolers," in *Success or Failure? Learning and the Language Minority Student,* ed. Henry T. Trueba (Cambridge, MA: Newbury House, 1987).

16. Ray McDermott, "Achieving School Failure: An Anthropological Approach to Literacy and Social Stratification," in *Doing the Ethnography of Schooling: Educational Anthropology in Action,* ed. George Spindler (New York: Holt, Rinehart & Winston, 1982).

17. Tharp, "Psychocultural Variables and Constants."

18. Melvin D. Williams, "Observations in Pittsburgh Ghetto Schools," *Anthropology and Education Quarterly,* 12 (1981), 211–220.

19. Tharp, "Psychocultural Variables and Constants."

20. Carmen Nine-Curt, *Nonverbal Communication in Puerto Rico* (Cambridge, MA: Evaluation, Dissemination, and Assessment Center, 1977).

21. Shirl E. Gilbert and Geneva Gay, "Improving the Success in School of Poor Black Children," *Phi Delta Kappan,* October 1985, pp. 133–137. See also Janice E. Hale-Benson, *Black Children: Their Roots, Culture, and Learning Styles* (Baltimore: Johns Hopkins University Press, 1982); A. Wade Boykin, "The Triple Quandry in the Schooling of Afro-American Children," in *The School Achievement of Minority Children: New Perspectives,* ed. Ulric Neisser (Hillsdale, NJ: Erlbaum, 1986).

22. Kathleen P. Bennett, "Doing School in an Urban Appalachian First Grade," in *Empowerment Through Multicultural Education,* ed. Christine E. Sleeter (Albany: State University of New York Press, 1991).

23. Shirley Brice Heath, *Ways with Words* (New York: Cambridge University Press, 1983).

24. Tam Thi Dang Wei, *Vietnamese Refugee Students: A Handbook for School Personnel* (Cambridge, MA: National Assessment and Dissemination Center, 1980).

25. See Quality Education for Minorities Project, *Education That Works: An Action Plan for the Education of Minorities* (Cambridge, MA: Massachusetts Institute of Technology Press, 1990).

26. Peter Sindell, "Some Discontinuities in the Enculturation of Mistassini Cree Children," in *Doing the Ethnography of Schooling: Educational Anthropology in Action,* ed. George Spindler (New York: Holt, Rinehart & Winston, 1982).

27. See, for example, James S. Brown and Barry Schwarzweller, "The Appalachian Family," in *Appalachia: Its People, Heritage, and Problems,* ed. Frank S. Riddel (Dubuque, IA: Kendall/Hunt Publishing, 1974); William W. Philliber and Clyde B. McCoy, eds., *The Invisible Minority* (Lexington: University Press of Kentucky, 1981).

28. Brigitte Jordan, "Cosmopolitan Obstetrics: Some Insights from the Training of Traditional Midwives," *Social Science and Medicine,* 28, 9 (1989), 925–944.

29. See John Red Horse, "Indian Family Values and Experiences," and Fred Wise and Nancy Brown Miller, "The Mental Health of the American Indian Child," in *The Psychosocial Development of Minority Group Children,* ed. Gloria Johnson Powell (New York: Brunner/Mazel Publishers, 1983); Lee Little Soldier, "Cooperative Learning and the Native American Student," *Phi Delta Kappan,* October 1989, pp. 161–163; Susan Urmston Philips, *The Invisible*

Culture: Communication in Classroom and Community on the Warm Springs Indian Reservation (White Plains, NY: Longman, 1982).

30. Philips, *Invisible Culture.*
31. Shirley Munõz Hernández and Isaura Santiago Santiago, "Toward a Qualitative Analysis of Teacher Disapproval Behavior" in *Theory, Technology, and Public Policy on Bilingual Education,* ed. Raymond V. Padilla (Rosslyn, VA: National Clearinghouse for Bilingual Educaton, 1983).
32. See, for instance, Katherine H. Au, "Participant Structures in a Reading Lesson with Hawaiian Children," *Anthropology and Education Quarterly,* 11, 2 (1980), 91–115; Lynn A. Vogt, Cathie Jordan, and Roland G. Tharp, "Explaining School Failure, Producing School Success," *Anthropology and Education Quarterly,* 18, 4 (December 1987), 276–286.
33. Research by Gallimore, Boggs, and Jordan, cited in Vogt, Jordan, and Tharp, "Explaining School Failure."
34. Ibid.
35. See Ward Churchill, "White Studies: The Intellectual Imperialism of Contemporary U.S. Education," *Integrated Education,* 19, 1 and 2 (January 1982), 51–57; Little Soldier, "Cooperative Learning and the Native American Student"; Philips, *Invisible Culture.*
36. Frederick Erickson and Gerald Mohatt, "Cultural Organization of Participation Structures in Two Classrooms of Indian Students," in *Doing the Ethnography of Schooling: Educational Anthropology in Action,* ed. George Spindler (New York: Holt, Rinehart & Winston, 1982).

Marisol Martinez:
"I'm proud of myself and my culture, but I think I know what I should know."

Marisol Martinez was born and raised in the United States, living first in New York City and later in Milltown, a small industrial city in the Northeast. Both of her parents were born in Puerto Rico and have raised most of their eight children in this country. Marisol's first language was Spanish, but she learned English before going to school and therefore was never in a bilingual program. She is still fluent in both languages and uses both when talking with bilingual speakers. When addressing her parents, she speaks Spanish. In this language use, she is typical of Puerto Ricans: An astonishing 91 percent still speak Spanish at home, higher than any other group in the United States. An almost equal percentage speak English too, also higher than any other Latino group.[1]

Marisol lives in a city housing project. It is a small brick town house type of dwelling, two stories high, in the middle of a row of exact replicas along the length of a city block. There is a patch of ground in front of each and a larger one in back, which some families have enclosed for a small vegetable or flower garden in the spring and summer. The neighborhood is active and noisy with the sounds of children, music (both English rap and Spanish salsa), and traffic. The living room of the Martinez apartment is very small, crowded with furniture and many family pictures and religious figures on tables and walls. It, like the eat-in kitchen next to it, is clean and well kept. Upstairs are three bedrooms and a bath. Marisol lives here with one brother, three sisters, and her parents. Her older siblings are married or living on their own. She is 16 and the fifth-oldest of the children.

The Martinez family is very close-knit. The oldest daughter is 31, and Marisol's parents are older than those of most of Marisol's friends. Because of medical problems, neither her mother nor father work. Both seem to have a firm hold on their children and are quite involved with them, particularly their educational accomplishments. All of Marisol's older siblings have managed to graduate from high school, quite a feat in view of the dropout rate among Latinos, which has been estimated to be anywhere between 40 and 80 percent.[2] Both of her parents have graduated from high school, as have just under 60 percent of Puerto Rican adults in the United States.[3]

Over the past two decades, the demographics of the town where Marisol and her family live have changed dramatically. Nowhere is this more evident than in the schools, where the proportion of Puerto Ricans now ranges from 50 to 60 percent. African Americans make up a small percentage of the total, and the remainder of the students are European Americans, primarily Irish and French Canadians. In the city as a whole, however, Puerto Ricans make up just over a third of the population. The substantially higher percentage in the schools is due to several factors, including the larger family size in the Puerto Rican community and the considerable "White flight" that has taken place since the schools were desegregated a decade ago.

The change in demographics has also been felt in town politics. Puerto Ricans, both in the schools and in town in general, have been the object of discrimination and stereotypes. There are frequent newspaper articles and editorials about the rising crime rate, drug abuse, and the subsequent disintegration of the city from an overidealized past, all with not so subtle implications that Puerto Ricans are somehow responsible. Ironically, Milltown is a city of immigrants, and each new group has had to struggle with similar conditions of discrimination and rejection.

Marisol is a sophomore in the public comprehensive high school in the city. She is following an academic course of study and her grades are all A's and B's. She likes all her classes, especially biology and geometry and expects to go to college, although her future plans are still quite uncertain. Right now, she is fluctuating between the seemingly disparate goals of wanting to be a model and a nurse. If she does go to college, she will be the first in her family to do so.

Marisol's early school experiences, until fourth grade, occurred in New York City. She remembers being "very smart" in school and doing well there. However, because her family considered the neighborhood too "violent" for the children, they moved to Milltown, where they have lived for about ten years. This pattern of migration is not unusual for Puerto Ricans, who frequently first settle in New York and then move to other urban areas in the Northeast. The latest census figures indicate that there are approximately 2.5 million Puerto Ricans living in the United States, with over a million of these residing in New York.[4]

Puerto Rico has been a colony of the United States since 1898, which helps explain some of the differences between Puerto Rican migration and that of other immigrations.[5] Taken over by the United States as a result of the Spanish-American War in 1898, Puerto Rico now officially has "commonwealth" status, although some people maintain that this is a camouflage for what is in reality a colony.[6] After 1900, first U.S. absentee landlords and later large corporations dominated the economy, displacing small farmers and creating economic and political dependence for the island. Furthermore, because Puerto Ricans were made U.S. citizens in 1917 (some say, to coincide with the tremendous need in the armed forces during World War I, for which Puerto Rican men were recruited en masse), they do not need passports or special permission to migrate to the United States. Consequently, this migration has been one of the largest out-migrations, proportional to the population, in history. Over two-fifths of all Puerto Ricans now reside in the continental United States.[7] In addition, there is a great deal of "back and forth" migration, depending on the economic situation on the island or in the United States at any particular time. To explain the formidable economic dependence of the island, it is often said that "when the United States sneezes, Puerto Rico catches cold."

Although the economic situation of Marisol's family has not improved substantially after the move from New York, they feel safer in this small city. The attendant problems of urban living, including drug abuse and crime, however, are quite apparent here as well. There are frequent drug raids by police in this community and others throughout the city. The signs of incipient gang activity are also being seen. Nevertheless, there is in this city a "smalltown" atmosphere, which makes it more comfortable than large urban areas for many of its residents.

Marisol is shy but eager to discuss her experiences in school and at home. She seems to be very aware of her academic success as compared to the situation of many of her friends. It is both a source of pride and of pressure. Three major themes emerged from Marisol: wanting to "be someone"; a keen awareness of peer pressure and her attempts to deal with it; and a contradictory cultural identity, which ranged from pride to lack of awareness or even embarrassment. We will focus on each of these themes and relate them to Marisol's school experiences and family relationships.

"I WANT TO BE SOMEONE"

I wanted to be a good student. I wanted to be someone when I grew up. . . . . I wanted to have a future. I want to be someone, you know. Have work and be someone people can look up to, not be out in the streets doing nothing.

Like behaving myself and doing my work and paying attention. . . . I was [a good student] because I respected the teachers, and I did my work, and I behaved. . . . Well, I go to school to learn. If I know I'm trying and my grades are down, the point is I tried.

[*When asked to say what she would tell a new student in her school what it means to be successful*] I would say not a nerd, actually. I would just say that he has to keep up with the grades and the books and things like that, but then again, watch yourself in the school because if you're gonna stay quiet and be behaving, they're gonna take advantage of you, the bigger ones, you know, and the tougher ones. I would just say not take things.

I think I can make it, I think I wanna make it, I think I'm successful. . . . I'm still going to school, and I don't plan to drop out, and I'm still keeping on with everything, not like others that will quit and that have quit. . . . I don't think there's anything stopping me. I don't think there *should* be anything stopping me. If I know I can do it, I should just keep on trying. Of course, no one can stop me and there's nothing that can get in the way of me wanting to do what I want to do.

[*This steely determination to be successful in school is contrasted to the experiences of some of her friends. Many are "out in the street, trying to make it." One is in prison, others are home with babies, some are on drugs, some live on welfare. Their lives, as she puts it, are "down the drain." It is in fact, these very experiences that serve as the primary motivation for Marisol to do well in school.*]

I just think of that, you know. I wouldn't want to see myself like that. So that's what keeps me going.

[*Those of her friends who have stayed in school, however, are like her.*] They want to make it, just the way I want to make it. They *plan* to make it and they have faith in themselves. They want to go to college, the same way I want to. They don't want to be in the streets. They want to be someone too.

[My parents] want me to be someone, I guess. . . . They talk to me, you know. They're open with me and they tell me what's right for me and what's not right. I do things to please them. . . . They like school and they encourage you to keep going, you know. I think they're proud of us 'cause my sisters and brothers, they all have nice report cards; they never stood back, you know, and usually we do this for my mother. We like to see her the way she wants to be, you know, to see her happy.

I think if I believe in being something and if I believe that I want to do something, I think I should do my best in doing it. . . . I would take it on my own. I wouldn't go to teachers or counselors. I mean, I would talk to my friends about it, but I would take it on my own.

[*When thinking about what it takes to be successful later in her future, she displays an almost complete lack of concreteness.*] I don't know. . . . I guess never quit . . . and . . . have my hopes up. That's about it. I don't know. . . . I mean, keep up with what I'm doing now and just keep on going.

PEER PRESSURE AND BUILDING DEFENSES AGAINST IT

[Me and my family] talk about mainly things that are happening nowadays, such as drugs and teen pregnancy and, you know, things that are important to us. They really care about us and just tell us the rights from the wrongs. She prefers, and he prefers, us to be open to them, you know, and never keep things from them.

My parents are really beautiful people. They're peaceful, you know; they don't like problems. They like to share with other people. But one thing, if people come giving them problems, they will not stay shut, their temper will rise like this [*snaps her fingers*]. They're really nice people to get along with. . . . They understand us. They take time out to stay with us and talk to us, you know. Not too many parents do that. . . . I like living with these people and I like being with them.

[*When asked if she would change anything about them, she is quick to respond.*] Nope. Not a thing, absolutely nothing.

[At the Teen Clinic], we answer questions, for instance, students have. You know, they're free to ask us because we're students like them. We put up, like, the questions they might ask with the answers. We all get together and talk about topics and make fliers and give them out. . . . We also have like a "Dear Abby" sort of thing. . . . They do write letters and we do read them and we keep it up because I guess they enjoy it.

There's a lot of girls out there getting pregnant and dropping out of school. I don't want one of those girls to be me, you know? I just want to stay away, you know? And I want to advise the ones that are not pregnant as to why they shouldn't get pregnant at an early age and how to prevent from doing that. . . . I would like the kids such as myself to realize what's happening out in the streets and not to put everything to waste. . . . If they're really interested in going to school and having a nice future, I think they should read things and take time to think about it and learn about it. . . . I think there are students out there that need this information and would take time to read it and know more about it.

CULTURAL IDENTITY: PRIDE AND EMBARRASSMENT

I'm proud of it [being Puerto Rican]. I guess I speak Spanish whenever I can. . . . To me, it's important, you know, because I have to stand up for Puerto Ricans, to say like for the Whites probably it's more important for them too, just like the Blacks. . . .

I used to have a lot of problems with one of my teachers 'cause she didn't want us to talk Spanish in class and I thought that was like an insult to us, you know? Just telling us not to talk Spanish, 'cause they were Puerto Ricans and, you know, we're free to talk whatever we want. . . . I could never stay quiet and talk only English, 'cause sometimes, you know, words slip in Spanish. You know, I think they should understand that.

[*Although at first maintaining that there are no differences between Puerto Rican students and others (" 'cause you know you can't say that Puerto Ricans act one way and the Whites act the other"), she amends this statement by saying*] I know that Puerto Ricans are way, way badder than the Whites. . . . You know, the way they act and they fight. . . .

You know, but everybody's the same, everyone's human, and I don't know, I think they should understand everyone just the way they are.

I think they [teachers] should get to know you, and whatever they don't like about Puerto Ricans, or they feel uncomfortable with, you know, just talk to you about it, and you can teach *them* things that probably they're confused about and they don't understand. That way we can communicate better.

I don't think [having a class in Puerto Rican history] is important. . . . I'm proud of myself and my culture, but I think I know what I should know about the culture already, so I wouldn't take the course.

No, 'cause [teachers] would have to know about Black and White and Irish [too]. . . . I think they should treat us all the same, you know?

[*Marisol says that the person she most admires in the world is Joan Collins and "all them cute actresses." What about people in real life? People in her community? She answers in almost a shocked way.*] Admire them?! No! I admire my mother; that's it.

COMMENTARY

This case study of Marisol Martinez brings up several dilemmas facing a great many young people from dominated cultures. One of these is wanting to be successful while also trying to maintain one's culture. This strain is evident in Marisol's determination to "be someone," also a major theme in Suarez-Orozco's ethnographic study of Central American high school students.[8] The differences between Central American and Puerto Rican communities in the United States are substantial, including both historical and cultural contexts. Yet there is the same insistence on "making it," which challenges the assumption that it is only those who are "voluntary immigrants" (compared to Puerto Ricans, who would be considered "involuntary immigrants") who have this drive to succeed academically.

To "be somebody," Marisol has had to be a good student. When she talks about what it takes to be a good student, her focus is not so much on grades as on how she acts. Being respectful and obedient in school is very much within the framework of what many Latino parents consider a "good student."[9] To be *educado* in the Latino sense of the word means not only to be educated academically but also to be respectful, polite, and obedient. This multiple definition of *educado* has a profound effect on many Latino children, who learn that to be a good student also means to be quiet and reserved, a departure from what are considered to be important characteristics of intellectually curious children in other cultures.

Marisol is caught in the classic struggle between what her parents and teachers want her to strive for and what her peers, including some of her close friends, have experienced. This dilemma was described poignantly by Marisol on several occasions. However, she absolves the school of almost all responsibility. When she mentions it at all, it is to say that students may drop out because they simply do not like school. The fact that certain school policies and practices might disadvantage some students or even be a risk factor for dropping out is not considered by Marisol. She believes that youths must accept complete responsibility for their own success, that it is only their own determination that can help them get an education.

The role of family is evident in Marisol's determination and academic success. She says that her parents do not pay attention to grades as much as to their children's "trying." What makes them angry is lack of effort or good behavior from their children. They have taught their children to "want to be someone," and this concern is reflected in Marisol. Her parents are involved in their children's education in ways that might not be evident to the school but may in the long run be even more important in their children's academic success. However, when asked if her parents participate in school, she was quick to answer that they did not. That is, they do not visit the school or go to parent meetings or volunteer. Nevertheless, their influence seems to be a determining factor in the children's drive to do well in school.

Although Marisol has a dogged determination not to drop out and succumb to the many negative pressures around her, she is quite unclear about how to plan for her future. She receives little help from teachers or counselors, and her parents are unable to give her the kind of information she needs for choosing a college or even for the kinds of classes she should be taking to prepare for it. She also has no idea of how to go about fulfilling her dream of becoming a model. Even the choice of modeling as a possible profession indicates how she has accepted the limited role of women within society. Nursing, definitely a far second in her life choices, is only a backup if modeling fails. The fact that she does well in school, particularly in the sciences, is not enough to point her in the direction of a career as a physician.

Marisol has not seriously thought about which college she might attend or about what she needs to do to prepare for it. Given her seeming acceptance of the limited role of women as either objects of beauty or helpmates to men's careers, the school needs to play a role in opening the horizons of students such as Marisol. The kind of assistance teachers and schools provide for middle-class students in other settings is missing here, including nonsexist and nonracist career counseling, college admissions information, and advice on financial aid. Marisol has learned to rely on herself and does not expect this kind of help. The incongruence between her illusions for success and the vague notions she has of getting there is quite striking. She has learned that she has to "make it on her own," and this becomes one more indication of her strong-willed determination to succeed. Unfortunately, it is seldom enough.

Despite this vagueness, Marisol's strength and resoluteness to continue in school and to do well seem shatterproof. She has convinced herself, with the support of her close-knit family, that she can succeed and that she is worthy of it. However, the models she has around her, especially her peers, are not always positive, and she has had to develop strategies for dealing with difficult situations and temptations. Marisol, like other young people her age, is faced with the pressures of conforming to values and behaviors of other teenagers. In an urban setting, especially in a poor economic environment, these pressures are compounded.

Marisol's work at the Teen Clinic at the high school supports and affirms her desire to be a good student and to persist in her education. The rate of teenage pregnancy in this community is one of the highest in the state. In explaining why she has been so concerned about this issue, Marisol seems to imply that she sees her work at the clinic almost as a vaccine against pregnancy. She is not involved in any other school activities: She does not participate in sports and is not interested in the few clubs that are available. Fortunately, one outlet for her is the Teen Clinic, and she is immersed in its work.

Marisol is fighting a constant battle to "make it" in this society while maintaining her heritage. Yet she has also obviously picked up the message that she needs to abandon her heritage to be successful. These contradictory sentiments are evident in many of Marisol's beliefs.

Messages about cultural and linguistic differences and how they are valued or not valued in society are delivered not only or even primarily in school but also throughout the media and in the everyday life of a community. The attitudes young people develop about their culture and heritage and the decisions they come to about who they are cannot be separated from the social and political context in which they live. In this particular city, for example, there have been actual proposals to limit the number of Puerto Ricans coming into town, based on the argument that they are a drain on the welfare rolls. (It is instructive to note that the Puerto Rican population of the city increased by 227 percent from 1970 to 1980; a similar increase is expected in 1990. Given the estimated 20 percent unemployment rate among the Puerto Rican community, the proposal was positively received by some segments of the non-Puerto Rican population.) In addition, the "English only" furor found its way here when municipal workers were told they could not speak Spanish on the job. Some Puerto Rican residents have claimed to see signs reading "No Puerto Ricans" on apartments for rent. That these negative messages might have a profound impact on young people is not surprising. What is surprising is that young people retain any pride at all in their culture. Marisol is obviously caught in this dilemma.

To resolve it, she has only one argument to fall back on, that is, the traditional reasoning that *equal means same.* Because she cannot resolve the challenge posed by the pluralism of her school and society, Marisol repeats what she has learned throughout her education: that treating everyone the same is the fairest way. Thus she does not believe that a course in Puerto Rican history is necessary or even desirable. In spite of her limited knowledge of her own history, she seems reluctant to learn about it because somehow it would seem to be "special treatment." That European American students are accorded this kind of special treatment in the curriculum through courses on "world" (primarily European) history and American (primarily White) history has probably not occurred to her.

The fact that Marisol is uncertain about the distinction between cultural and individual differences and that she seems uncomfortable in talking about these things in anything but a superficial way is no doubt related to how these issues are treated in school. For example, Marisol has never learned anything in her classes about being Puerto Rican. In social studies classes, she remembers studying about Spain, "but not to the point of studying about Puerto Ricans." One of her homeroom teachers in junior high school, Mr. Perez, a Puerto Rican teacher of bilingual classes, stands out as the only one who ever bothered teaching his students anything about Puerto Rican history and culture. She remembers seeing reports that students in his classes had done on the bulletin boards, along with books and other exhibits that were available in his classroom. She was interested in many of the things he taught, and although he was never her teacher, she says she learned a lot from him simply by looking through the materials he had in the classroom. She used to feel, she says, "quite proud of myself" when she saw these things.

Marisol's tastes are all very "mainstream." That is, her favorite foods are seafood and pizza, she likes to cook lasagne, and her favorite music is hip hop and rap. She never mentioned Puerto Rican food, music, holidays, or famous people. She says that her parents listen to "old-fashioned" music, referring to Puerto Rican music, which she is very clear about not liking ("Nope, I want them to hear me: NO.") There is nothing, at least in her stated tastes, that would distinguish her as Puerto Rican.

Yet Marisol is so obviously Puerto Rican in intangible but fundamentally more important ways: her deep feelings for her family, respect for parents, and maintaining important traditions such as staying with family rather than with friends on important holidays. She is also respectful, *humilde* (humble), and soft-spoken but also very strong. The last characteristic is evident, for example, in her uncompromising determination to maintain her native language. At home, she is often spontaneously affectionate, rushing over to her mother to hug her tightly and kiss her. She also has a larger share of the family responsibilities than a great many young people from other cultural backgrounds. This is what is referred to in Hispanic culture as *capacidad,* or a combination of maturity, a sense of responsibility, and capability. It is a trait that is very valued in the culture and that parents work hard to inculcate, particularly in their daughters.[10]

Thus, in spite of the veneer of U.S. cultural traits she displays, Marisol is also very much a product of Puerto Rican culture, at least as it is manifested in the United States. The traits of her native culture that she maintains can be compared to the "deep structure" of language. Marisol, and many like her, have created a new culture, one that has elements of the native culture, albeit not as apparent as those of the new culture, which fit over it like a cloak.

Both the peer culture and the demands of living in a community where her ethnic group in not admired, but rather disparaged, have an effect on Marisol. In addition, her definition of success, being a model or even a nurse (rather than a physician), is evidence that she has internalized the sexist and limiting roles of women in our society. Nevertheless, her strong family network has helped Marisol counteract some of these negative effects by providing models, at least within the family, that Marisol admires deeply. This admiration has unfortunately not spread to others in the community.

On the one hand, Marisol has learned the lessons of this assimilationist society very well. On the other, she is hard at work at holding onto what is clearly important for her: a culture and language that the people who she most loves speak and maintain. The dilemma is a real one for this bright young woman who "wants to be someone."

TO THINK ABOUT

1. What do you think is responsible for Marisol's success in school?

2. Why is it so important for Marisol to "be someone"?

3. Why does Marisol say that "Puerto Ricans are way, way badder than Whites"?

4. How is the issue of "positive role models" resolved for Marisol? How does Joan Collins fit into the picture?

5. Why do you believe that Marisol is divided about wanting to be a model or a nurse? What has influenced this decision? If you were her school counselor, what would you say to her?

NOTES

1. As cited in Clara E. Rodriguez, *Puerto Ricans: Born in the U.S.A.* (Boston: Unwin Hyman, 1989).

2. See, for example, *Racial and Ethnic Dropout Rates in New York City: A Summary Report* (New York: ASPIRA, 1983); Ray Valdivieso and Cary Davis, *U.S. Hispanics: Challenging Issues for the 1990s* (Washington, DC: Population Trends and Public Policy, December 1988); *The Education of Hispanics: Status and Implications* Washington, DC: National Council of La Raza, 1987; the report of the National Commission of Secondary Education for Hispanics, *"Make Something Happen": Hispanics and Urban School Reform*, 2 vols. (Washington, DC: Hispanic Policy Development Project, 1984).

3. According to the National Council of La Raza, cited above, over 17 percent of Latinos 25 years and over are illiterate. In addition, data indicate that only 58 percent of Hispanics 25–34 are high school graduates, compared with 88 percent of the general population; see Bureau of the Census, *Condition of Hispanics in America Today* (Washington, DC: U.S. Department of Commerce, 1983).

4. Bureau of the Census, *Condition of Hispanics.* It is probable that this is an undercount. In August 1980, the bureau was sued by several plaintiffs, including New York City, for an undercounting. See Rodriguez, *Puerto Ricans.*

5. The term *migration* is used to refer to movement within one political sphere, *immigration* within two.

6. The Decolonization Committee of the United Nations has termed Puerto Rico a colony and has consistently called on the United States to hand over sovereignty to the island. See Rodriguez, *Puerto Ricans.*

7. Whereas the 1985 population of Puerto Ricans in the United States was 2.562 million, that of the island was 3.270 million; ibid.

8. Marcelo M. Suarez-Orozco, "'Becoming Somebody': Central American Immigrants in U.S. Inner-City Schools," *Anthropology and Education Quarterly*, 18, 4 (December 1987), 287–299.

9. See, for example, Joseph O. Prewitt-Díaz, "Home-School Discrepancies and the Puerto Rican Student," *Bilingual Journal*, 5, 2 (Winter 1980), 9–12; Herbert Grossman, *Educating Hispanic Students: Cultural Implications for Classroom Instruction, Classroom Management, Counseling, and Assessment* (Springfield, IL: C. C Thomas, 1984); Catherine E. Walsh, *Pedagogy and the Struggle for Voice: Issues of Language, Power, and Schooling for Puerto Ricans* (New York: Bergin & Garvey, 1991); and the ethnography of a bilingual school by Richard L. Warren, "Schooling, Biculturalism, and Ethnic Identity: A Case Study," in *Doing the Ethnography of Schooling: Educational Anthropology in Action*, ed. George Spindler (New York: Holt, Rinehart & Winston, 1982). See also three helpful chapters in *The Psychosocial Development of Minority Group Children*, ed. Gloria Johnson Powell (New York: Brunner/Mazel Publishers, 1983): Daniel Mejia, "The Development of Mexican-American Children"; William A. Vega, Richard L. Hough, and Annelisa Romero, "Family Life Patterns of Mexican-Americans"; and Emelicia Mizio, "The Impact of Macro Systems on Puerto Rican Families."

10. For a fuller description of *capacidad*, see Vega, Hough, and Romero, "Family Life Patterns," and Mizio, "Impact of Macro Systems." See also the description of Mexican American students at home by Nancy Commins, "Language and Affect: Bilingual Students at Home and at School," *Language Arts*, 66, 1 (January 1989), 29–43.

James Karam:
"I'd like to be considered Lebanese."[1]

James Karam is 16, a junior in high school. His dark eyes are serious but animated when he speaks. He thinks he has a big nose and jokes that it is one of the characteristics of being Lebanese. Poised between childhood and adulthood, James is that pleasing combination of practical, responsible, wise adult and refreshing, spirited, eager kid. No doubt his maturity is due in part to his role as the "responsible" male in the household. His mother and father are separated and he is the oldest of three children, a position he generally enjoys, although he admits it can get trying at times.

James is Lebanese Christian, or Maronite. His father was born and raised in the United States. He met James's mother while visiting Lebanon and brought her here as his bride. She has been in this country for almost 20 years and is fluent in English. Although his parents are separated, it is clear that both are close to their children and continue to take an active part in their upbringing and education.

The Lebanese community in the United States is little known to the general population. It is, in this sense, an "invisible minority," about which more will be said later. There are scattered communities of Lebanese throughout the United States, with large concentrations in several cities, including Springfield, Massachusetts. In a participant-observer study of the Arab community in this city over two decades ago, it was reported that the first Arab settlers arrived in the 1890s from Lebanon. Most were laborers and worked in the city's factories, on the railroad, or in peddling businesses. They were both Christian and Muslim Lebanese, and there was generally little animosity between them. On the contrary, there was a genuine sense of solidarity and cohesiveness in the entire community.[2]

James went to a Catholic school from kindergarten until third grade but has been in public school ever since. Although he was held back in third grade because his family moved out of the state and he lost a good deal of school time (this still bothers him a lot), James is a very successful student and has given much thought to his plans after high school. He works at keeping his grades high so that he can get into a good college and is pretty certain that he wants to be a mechanical engineer. His real dream, however, is to become a professional bike racer. This is his first love. Even if he were to do this, he wants a college education. Education is very important to James, as it is to his family. It has been speculated that the Arab American community in the United States is strongly committed to education because so many of the first generation had to drop out of school to care for their families. Consequently, it has become a prime value for their children.[3]

Springfield is a mid-size metropolitan city. It is culturally, racially, and economically diverse. James attends one of the high schools in the city, which he describes as almost "a little college," and he likes all his classes. His classmates represent many of the cultures and languages of the world, and the school system has been intent on incorporating this cultural diversity into the curriculum in many ways, some more successful than others. They have a number of bilingual programs for the Spanish-speaking, Portuguese, Russian, Vietnamese, and Khmer communities). Some other activities, such as cultural festivals and international fairs, although a promising start, are initial and somewhat superficial attempts at acknowledging the rich cultural diversity in the city.

James is fluent in both English and Arabic. Although he has never studied it formally in school, Arabic is important to him and he means to maintain it. The Maronite Church in the city, first called the Church of St. Peter and Paul, was established in 1905 and has had an important influence in encouraging the use of Arabic and the maintenance of other cultural values in the community. In fact, the Rev. Saab, who was the pastor for over 50 years, made the following statement, indicative of the church's role as a whole, during his investiture as monsignore: "I did not want them to forget their Lebanese heritage because this is a wonderful thing."[4] Given the tenor of the times, in which assimilation was seen as a great value, the Lebanese community was clearly bucking the tide. This is apparent even today in the large percentage of second and even third generation Lebanese in Springfield, both Christian and Muslim, who still speak Arabic. In the case of the Maronites, the church's role was not merely providing a place for worship; rather, it served, and continues to do so, as a haven for cultural pride and maintenance.

In other ways, however, the Arab American community has undergone great changes and has acculturated to the U.S. mainstream. In Springfield, for instance, it was found that Arabic surnames are almost nonexistent, and most family names have been Anglicized. In fact, were it not for the influence of the church and to a lesser extent other social and religious organizations and clubs, assimilation might have proceeded much more rapidly. The class structure has changed as well. The Lebanese community in the city started out as working class and is now primarily middle class. The Arab community in the first decades of the century was similar to many other immigrant communities. It was characterized by large families (an average of ten children), overcrowded flats, congested sidewalks and doorsteps, and dirty and unpaved streets. Now about 77 percent of the Arabs in Springfield own their own homes and live in middle-class communities.[5]

This is true of James and his family as well. He, his mother, 14-year-old brother, and 9-year-old sister live in a quiet residential neighborhood in the city. His community is much more homogeneous than the city itself, primarily European American. He says the difference between his neighborhood and the city proper is that there are lots of trees ("Believe me, I know! I have to rake the leaves every year"). He enjoys living here and would probably want to live in a community just like it when he has his own family.

James's perception of himself as a good student, as "smart," is an important theme, which will be explored further. In addition, his role as "apprentice" will be discussed. The most important theme to emerge, however, is the invisibility of James's culture, which will be considered first.

THE INVISIBLE MINORITY

[*About Mr. Miller, an elementary school teacher*] I just liked him. . . . He started calling me "Gonzo" 'cause I had a big nose. He called me "Klinger"; he said 'cause Klinger's Lebanese. You know, the guy on "M.A.S.H." . . . And then everybody called me Klinger from then on. . . . I liked it, kind of . . . everybody laughing at me. Yeah, it doesn't bother me. I don't care if somebody talks about my nose.

We had a foreign language month in school. They had posters and signs and everything. Spanish, French, Spain, Italy—they had all these signs and posters and pictures and stuff all over the school. . . . There's Chinese; they had Japanese; they had Korea. They had lots of stuff.

[*However, they did not have Arabic. When asked why, he answers quietly*] I don't know.

They made this cookbook of all these different recipes from all over the world. And I would've brought in some Lebanese recipes if somebody'd let me know. And I didn't hear about it until the week before they started selling them. . . . They had some Greek. They had everything, just about. . . . I asked one of the teachers to look at it and there was nothing Lebanese in there.

[*There was also a multicultural festival in his school. Flags from countries all over the world were hung. There was no flag from Lebanon.*] But there's like there's Poland, there was Czechoslovakia, there was Spain, there was Mexico, there was France. There was a lot of different flags. I didn't see Lebanon, though.

I don't know. I guess there's not that many Lebanese people in . . . I don't know; you don't hear really that much. . . . Well, you hear it in the news a lot, but I mean, I don't know, there's not a lot of Lebanese kids in our school. There's about eight or nine at the most.

I don't mind, 'cause I mean, I don't know, just, I don't mind it. . . . It's not really important. It *is* important for me. It would be important for me to see a Lebanese flag. . . . But you know, it's nothing I would like enforce or like, say something about. . . . If anybody ever asked me about it, I'd probably say, "Yeah, there should be one." You know, if any of the teachers ever asked me, but I don't know.

Some people call me, you know, 'cause I'm Lebanese, so people say, "Look out for the terrorist! Don't mess with him or he'll blow up your house!" or some stuff like that.

But they're just joking around, though . . . I don't think anybody's serious 'cause I wouldn't blow up anybody's house—and they know that. . . . I don't care. It doesn't matter what people say. . . . I just want everybody to know that, you know, it's not true.

ON BEING A GOOD STUDENT

I'm probably the smartest kid in my class. . . . It's just like, usually I can get really into the work and stuff. But everybody else, you know, even the people that do their homework and assignments and stuff, they just do it and pass it in. You know, I like to get involved in it and *learn* it.

If you don't get involved with it, even if you do get, if you get perfect scores and stuff . . . it's not gonna like really sink in. You'll probably forget it. . . . You can memorize the words you know, on a test. . . . But you know, if you memorize them, it's not going to do you any good. You have to *learn* them, you know?

I want to make sure that I get my college education. I want to make sure of that. Even if I do get into the career that I specialize in in college, I still want to get a college education.

[*James decided to go to summer school to bring up an English grade.*] I think it's just because I didn't try. . . . I thought it was too easy so I didn't try. . . . I don't think [Mom] liked that too much. . . . I said, "Mom, I wanna go to summer school, you know, just to bring up my grade." So she paid for it.

In a lot of the things that I do, I usually do good. . . . I don't like it when I don't finish something or when I do real bad. It makes me want to do better. . . . If I ever get a bad grade on a test, it makes me want to do better next time.

I have a counselor, but she's never in. She's always out with some kind of sickness or something. She helps figuring out my schedule and stuff like that. . . . I don't really talk to my counselor, you know, as personal talks and stuff like that.

Some teachers are just . . . they don't really care. They just teach the stuff. "Here," write a couple of things on the board, "see, that's how you do it." "Go ahead, page 25." You know, some teachers are just like that.

Maybe it's not that they don't care. It's just that they don't put enough effort into it, maybe . . . I don't know.

I like going over it with the class, and you know, letting . . . everybody know your questions. And you know, there could be someone sitting in the back of the class that has the same question you have. Might as well bring it out.

[*James describes his favorite teacher, his geometry teacher, and her role in the Helping Hand Club at school.*] The people send her letters and brochures and stuff. And, you know, she says, "This is a good idea." You know, she brings it up at the meeting. And we say, "O.K." and then figure out. . . . She's like the head of it. She's the one that's really thoughtful and helpful.

[Teachers should] make the classes more interesting. . . . Like not just sit there and say, "Do this and do this and do this." You know, just like explain everything, write things on the board.

I'd love to be an engineer, but my real dream is to be a bike racer. . . . Yeah, it's my love. I love it.

When things go bad, I go ride my bike. . . . That's what I did, in the middle of the night. . . . The faster I ride, the harder I pushed, the more it hurt. It made me keep my mind off [things].

APPRENTICESHIP WITHIN THE FAMILY

[*James is fluent in both Arabic and English. He speaks, he says, "a mixture of both."*] Sometimes it's just like, some words come out Arabic and some words come out English. . . . Whichever expresses what I want to say the best, I guess, at the time.

[My parents] basically taught me to be good to people. You know, I've never really been mean to anybody. I don't like fighting. My mother taught me that, mostly.

We go to a lot of Lebanese parties and, you know, gatherings and stuff. . . . We go to Catholic-Lebanese [Maronite] church every week. . . . I always want to go to church. . . . Most of my friends don't go to church. . . . A lot of them do but most of them don't.

My mother's really proud to be Lebanese, and so am I. . . . First thing I'd say is I'm Lebanese. . . . I'm just proud to be Lebanese. If somebody asked me, "What are you?" . . . everybody else would answer, "I'm American," but I say, "I'm Lebanese" and I feel proud of it.

Even though somebody might have the last name like LeMond or something, he's considered American. But you know, LeMond is a French name, so his culture must be French. His background is French. But, you know, they're considered Americans. But I'd like to be considered Lebanese.

My mother's really old-fashioned. "You gotta be in early." "You gotta be in bed at a certain time." That kind of stuff. . . . I guess it'll pay off. When I'm older, I'll realize that she was right, I guess. But right now, I wish I could stay out like a little later. . . . I don't mind it, 'cause I don't think I'm really missing much. . . . There must be a reason why.

I know a lot of kids that can stay out and, you know, they go out till 12:00, 1:00 in the morning. They don't come back home and their mothers don't even ask them, you know, where they've been or whatever. [My parents are] really loving and caring. . . . I wouldn't want to be a part of any other family, put it that way.

COMMENTARY

James's experiences in school have reinforced the fact that Arab Americans are an invisible minority in the United States. This fact became clear not only through discussions with him but also through a review of the literature. Whereas much has been written about numerous other ethnic groups in the United States, even those fewer in number, very little is available about Arab Americans, their culture, school experiences, or learning styles. Few curricula address this group, and no ethnographic accounts focusing on Arab American children in schools could be found. Compared to most other groups, for whom volumes of information are available (although not necessarily understood or used appropriately), Arab Americans represent in this sense a unique case of invisibility.

The reasons for this invisibility are probably varied. For one, the majority of Arabs did not come in a mass influx as the result of famine, political or religious persecution, or war, as have other refugees. Although many have indeed come under these circumstances in the recent past, their numbers have not been conspicuous. Consequently, their immigration to this country has been a relatively quiet one, given scant attention by the media. In addition, their problems of adjustment, although no doubt difficult, have not caught the public imagination as have those of other immigrants. Theirs has been an apparently smooth transition. Likewise, their children have not faced massive failure in the schools, as is true with other groups. For this reason, they have not been the target of study or research as others have. Finally, they are not generally a racially visible minority, as in the case with Asians, Caribbeans, or most Latinos. They are thus much more apt to "blend in" with the European American population, even if they choose to maintain their cultural heritage.

Nonetheless, this lack of information is astonishing in light of the number and diversity of Arabs in the United States. The simple fact that Lebanon and the Middle East are involved in a devastating conflict and are always in the news is reason enough for more information about Arab Americans. Yet this is not the case. Beyond the conflict, however, the reality of the approximately 150 million Arabs, with their unique histories and cultures, deserves some mention on its own merit.

Representing different religions, socioeconomic classes, and national origins, the Arab community is one of the most heterogeneous in the United States. It is also one of the most misunderstood, shrouded in mystery and consequently in stereotypes. The popular images of Arabs as rich sheiks, religious zealots, or terrorists are gross stereotypes that do little to stir pride in Lebanese and other Arab Americans. Yet this is sometimes the only "information" the general public has. These are also the images that James and other Arab American children have to struggle against every day. In a poignant account of how this kind of stereotyping affected his own children when they decided not to use their ethnic clothes for a multiethnic festival at school, James Zogby, a Lebanese American, concluded, "Confusion and perhaps fear made them resist any display of pride. What for other students was the joy of ethnicity had become for my Arab-American children the pain of ethnicity."[6] He also cites the results of a 1981 public opinion survey on the issue. They are startling: Many respondents described Arabs as barbaric, treacherous, rich, and cruel to women. Very few positive images were cited.[7]

James's experiences echo this situation. He has either been made invisible or his culture has been referred to in only negative ways. Because Mr. Miller, the teacher who called him "Gonzo" joked in the same way with many of the other students, and because he allowed them to "make fun" of him too, James liked this attention. It made him feel special and meant that his background was at least being acknowledged. However, James mentioned many ways in which his culture was not acknowledged.

The stereotypes about his background have, in spite of what he says, probably taken their toll on James. Although he is quite active in school activities, he does not want to belong to student government. "I hate politics," he says. His distaste for it is understandable.

James is conscious of being a good student. He is extremely confident about his academic success. This perception of being a successful student is important to him. He is proud, for example, of being persistent, a quality that he believes is his best characteristic. But it goes beyond just thinking of himself as a good student; he demonstrates persistence through his actions as well. For example, in sophomore year all his grades were A's and B's, except for a D+ in English. On his own, he made the decision to attend summer school. His mother supported him in this decision, and he did very well.

When he began his junior year, after summer school, James broke his foot while playing sports. It required surgery and he was on crutches for several weeks. Because he had missed two weeks of school, he stayed after school every day for a number of weeks, making up labs and quizzes and other assignments. He was struggling with both schoolwork and crutches, but his attitude was a positive one. "I can't wait to be done with all my makeup work," he said, with a touch of frustration. He got through it, though, as with everything else that he has to do.

James's family has had a great deal to do with this perception of the importance of education and the need to persevere. Although his family is not typical of the majority of recent immigrants to the United States, who are overwhelmingly Asian and Hispanic, they nevertheless share some fundamental characteristics. For example, faith in the rewards of education is common among immigrant families. A national report found that 70 percent of those interviewed wanted their children to go to college. In addition, these parents often made great sacrifices to help their children succeed in school.[8] James appreciates this effort and explains that his mother is not involved in school, at least not in going to parent meetings and such. "My mother's really busy; she's always working," he explains, seeming to understand that this is in fact how she is involved.

Perhaps because of his persistence and because he is so self-motivated, or perhaps because the services in his school are not adequate, James has not counted on anybody at school to help him plan for the future. Although he is intent on going to a good college, it is unclear where he will get the advice he needs to make proper decisions about this important goal.

James's favorite teacher in high school is his geometry teacher, the one who "takes the time" and goes over everything in class. She is also the faculty advisor for the Helping Hand Club, a group that is involved in community service in the school and neighborhood. James is quite involved in this group, which helps raise funds for individuals in need and for charitable organizations. "I like doing that kind of stuff," he says, "helping out."

He is involved in other activities as well, and these seem to give him the energy and motivation he needs to keep up with schoolwork. He plays soccer and baseball and is on the swim team. He becomes most enthusiastic, however, when talking about his favorite activity, biking. This sport seems to give James great support. He was in a biking accident last year and still has not been able to have his heavily damaged bicycle repaired. He is thinking of organizing a biking team and has contemplated seeking financial support from neighborhood shop owners. Biking has given him the opportunity to learn about many things: that "practice makes perfect," leadership skills, how it feels to have a setback and not let it be a permanent loss, how to use a hobby to help relieve stress, and how to develop interpersonal skills. Not only is biking a physical challenge, but it is an important motivation as well. James's room is filled with biking magazines. The person who he most admires is Greg LeMond, the only U.S. racer who has ever won the Tour de France and the world championship. "I want to be just like him," he says. He is even talking about preparing for the 1992 Olympics.

Like all families, James's parents teach him the values and behaviors that they believe are most important for his survival and success. In the case of a family culturally different from the mainstream, this role becomes even more crucial. Teaching children their culture can be called an "apprenticeship." It is a role that is particularly evident among immigrant families who are attempting, often against great odds, to keep their native culture alive.

For dominant culture families, this apprenticeship is usually an unconscious one, for their children are surrounded by and submerged in the culture every day. They hear the dominant language, see dominant culture behaviors, and take part in all the trappings of what is to them "the" culture. For immigrant families, or even for third- or fourth-generation families who have chosen to maintain some of their native culture, the task of their children's apprenticeship is appreciably more difficult. The language they speak at home is not echoed in the general population; their values, traditions, and holidays are often at odds with those of the dominant culture; even the foods they eat or the music they listen to are not reflected in the dominant culture. Their culture is in many ways simply unacknowledged. These families are engaged in a sophisticated and often impossibly difficult balancing act of cultural adaptation without complete assimilation.

James's family, although certainly not immune from the difficulties inherent in this role, seems to be quite successful at this balancing act. For instance, James has a strong and healthy self-image, not only as a student but also as a Lebanese. The house is filled with Lebanese artifacts, and James displays them proudly. In addition, in his room there is a Lebanese pennant prominently displayed, and his bike racing helmet has a Lebanese flag on it. James has never been to Lebanon but definitely plans on going in the future, "when this war is over." He also says that he and his family talk about the situation in Lebanon. James loves Lebanese food, some of which he has even learned how to cook. The only thing he seems to dislike, in fact, is Lebanese music, which he considers "boring."

Being a part of a family out of the mainstream is not without its problems, however, particularly for adolescents. For James, it means having different rules than his friends, for example, in the demand that he attend church regularly. The church provides a particularly strong link with his culture. As long as he can remember, he has been going to church every Sunday. He never misses, and in fact still goes to catechism. He is the oldest in the class because everybody else his age feels too old to continue. He still enjoys going.

He does not feel, however, that this practice makes him particularly different from other youths. For the most part, James feels comfortable in two worlds. His apprenticeship has been a largely successful one. He is proud of his culture; he is bilingual; he is not generally embarrassed or ashamed about appearing "different." In addition, he considers his family to be "the average American family" in some ways. He would probably consider himself to be an "all-American kid." He likes to do what he calls "normal teenager stuff."

James Karam has been successful in forging his family, culture, language, hobbies, church, friends, and schoolwork into a unique amalgam, which has resulted in a strong self-image and a way of confronting a society not always comfortable with or tolerant of the kind of diversity he represents. This achievement has not made him immune, however, to being an ethnic minority and to the different and painful issues that arise because of it. The price James has had to pay for being from an invisible culture has no doubt been a steep one. He has learned, for example, to hide hurt feelings when his culture is disparaged and to treat everything "as a joke." He has learned to be quiet, preferring to accept invisibility rather than risk further alienation or rejection. He has also learned not to demand that his culture be acknowledged. Nevertheless, the uncompromising strength of his family, the support he gets from his extracurricular activities, and the enduring faith he has in himself can help to make the difference between surviving the tension or succumbing to it.

TO THINK ABOUT

1. What other invisible minorities are you aware of? Why would you classify this group in this way?
2. Why is James reluctant to bring up his feeling of exclusion in activities in the school?
3. How would you characterize the role that biking has played in James's life?
4. What advice do you think James would give new teachers about being successful teachers? Why?
5. If a teacher knew about James's apprenticeship within the family, how might he or she use this information?

NOTES

1. I want to thank Diane Sweet for the interviews with James as well as for transcripts and other extensive information she was able to find on the Arab American community.
2. Naseer H. Aruri, "The Arab-American Community of Springfield, Massachusetts," in *The Arab-Americans: Studies in Assimilation*, ed. Elaine C. Hagopian and An Paden (Wilmette, IL: Medina University Press International, 1969).
3. Ibid.
4. Ibid.
5. Ibid.
6. James J. Zogby, "When Stereotypes Threaten Pride," *NEA Today*, October 1982, p. 12.
7. Zogby refers to the results of a poll published in the Spring 1981 issue of *Middle East Journal*.
8. *New Voices: Immigrant Students in U.S. Public Schools* (Boston: National Coalition of Advocates for Students, 1988).

Hoang Vinh:

"They just understand something outside, but they cannot understand something inside our hearts."[1]

Hoang Vinh's hands move in quick gestures as he tries to illustrate what he has to say, almost as if wishing that they would speak for him.[2] Vinh is very conscious of not knowing enough English to express himself and keeps apologizing that "my English is not good." Nevertheless, his English skills are quite advanced for someone who has been here for such a short time.

Vinh is 18 years old. He was born in the Xuan Loc province of Dong Nai about 80 kilometers from Saigon. He came from Vietnam three years ago and lives with his uncle, two sisters, and two brothers in a mid-size town in New England. They first lived in Virginia but moved here a year and a half ago. Vinh and his family live in a humble and immaculately clean house in a residential neighborhood in this pleasant, mostly middle-class college town. Signs of the family's Catholicism are evident in the statues of Jesus and the Virgin Mary in the living room. Everybody in the family has chores, and they all contribute to keeping the house clean and making the meals. In addition, the older ones make sure that the younger children keep in touch with their Vietnamese language and culture: They have weekly sessions in which they write to their parents; they allow only Vietnamese to be spoken at home; and they cook Vietnamese food, something that even the youngest is learning to do. When they receive letters from their parents, they sit down to read them together. In addition, their uncle reinforces literacy by telling them many stories. Vinh also plays what he calls "music from my Vietnam," to which they all listen.[3]

Because Vinh's father was in the military before 1975 and worked for the U.S. government, he was seen as an American sympathizer and educational opportunities for his family were limited after the war. Vinh and his brothers and sisters were sent to the United States by their parents, who could not leave Vietnam but wanted their children to have the opportunity for a better education and a more secure future. Vinh and his family came in what has been called the "second wave" of immigration from Indochina;[4] that is, they came after the huge exodus in 1975. Although Vinh and his family came directly from Vietnam, most of the second wave immigrants have not come directly from Indochina but rather from refugee camps in Thailand, Malaysia, and elsewhere. This second wave has generally been characterized by greater heterogeneity in social class and ethnicity, less formal education, fewer marketable skills, and poorer health than previous immigrants.

Vinh's uncle works in town and supports all the children. He takes his role of "surrogate father" very seriously and tries to help the children in whatever way he can. He discusses many things with them, and Vinh mentions with gratitude the lengthy conversations they have. Mostly, he wants to make sure that all the children benefit from their education, and he constantly motivates them to do better.

Vinh's older brother makes dried flower arrangements in the basement and sells them in town. In the summers, Vinh works to contribute to his family here and in Vietnam, but during the school year he is not allowed to work because he has to focus on his studies ("I just go to school, and after school, I go home to study," he explains). He uses the money he makes in the summer to support his family "because we are very poor." They rarely go to the movies and spend little on themselves.

Vinh will be starting his senior year in high school. Because the number of Vietnamese speakers in the schools he has attended has never been high, Vinh has not been in a bilingual program. Although he does quite well in school, he enjoys the opportunity to speak his native language and would have profited from a bilingual education. He is currently in an

ESL class at the high school with a small number of other Vietnamese as well as other students whose first language is not English. Some teachers encourage him and his Vietnamese classmates to speak Vietnamese during the ESL class so that their understanding of the content of the curriculum improves. But other teachers discourage the use of their native language. All his other classes are in the "mainstream program" for college-bound students and include physics, calculus, French, music, and law. His favorite subject is history because, he says, he wants to learn about this country. He is also interested in psychology.

Homework and studying take up many hours of Vinh's time. He places great value on what he calls "becoming educated people." His parents and uncle constantly stress the importance of an education and place great demands on Vinh and his brothers and sisters. He also enjoys playing volleyball and badminton and being with his friends in the gym. He does not enjoy staying home because he loves school. Although he is a good student and wants desperately to go to college, at this late date he has yet to receive any information concerning different colleges, how to apply, how to receive financial aid, and admission requirements. He does not want to bother anyone in asking for this information. Added to his reluctance to ask for assistance is the economic barrier he sees to a college education. Because he wants to make certain that his brothers and sisters are well cared for, housed, and fed, he may have to work full time after graduating from high school.

Vinh is very concerned about becoming a good student. His explanation of what this means will be explored further below. Three other themes that surface are the stringent demands he places on himself, confusion and ignorance about other groups, and the strength he derives from his culture and family.

ON BECOMING "EDUCATED PEOPLE"

In Vietnam, we go to school because we want to become educated people. But in the United States, most people, they say, "Oh, we go to school because we want to get a good job." But my idea, I don't think so. I say, if we go to school, we want a good job *also*, but we want to become a good person.

[In Vietnam] we go to school, we have to remember *every single word*. . . . We don't have textbooks, so my teacher write on the blackboard. So we have to copy and go home. . . . So, they say, "You have to remember all the things, like all the words. . . ." But in the United States, they don't need for you remember all the words. They just need you to *understand*. . . . But two different school systems. They have different things. I think in my Vietnamese school, they are good. But I also think the United States school system is good. They're not the same. . . . They are good, but good in different ways.

When I go to school [in Vietnam], sometimes I don't know how to do something so I ask my teacher. She can spend *all the time* to help me, anything I want. So, they are very nice. . . . My teacher, she was very nice. When I asked her everything, she would answer me, teach me something. That's why I remember. . . . But some of my teachers, they always punished me.

[Grades] are not important to me. Important to me is education. . . . I [am] not concerned about them [test scores] very much. I just need enough for me to go to college. . . . Sometimes, I never care about [grades]. I just know I do my exam very good. But I don't need to know I got A or B. I have to learn more and more.

Sometimes, I got C but I learned very much, I learned a lot, and I feel very sorry, "Why I got only C?" But sometimes, if I got B, that's enough, I don't need A.

Some people, they got a good education. They go to school, they got master's, they got doctorate, but they're just helping *themselves*. So that's not good. . . . If I got a good education, I get a good job, not helping only myself. I like to help other people. . . . I want to help other people who don't have money, who don't have a house. . . . The first thing is money. If people live without money, they cannot do nothing. So even if I want to help other people, I have to get a good job. I have the money, so that way I can help them.

In class, sometimes we [students] speak Vietnamese because we don't know the words in English. . . . Our English is not good, so that's why we have to speak Vietnamese.

In school, if we get good and better and better, we have to work in groups. Like if we want to discuss something, we have to work in groups, like four people. And we discuss some projects, like that. And different people have different ideas, so after that we choose some best idea. I like work in groups.

Sometimes, the English teachers, they don't understand about us. Because something we not do good, like my English is not good. And she say, "Oh, your English is great!" But that's the way the American culture is. But my culture is not like that. . . . If my English is not good, she has to say, "Your English is not good. So you have to go home and study." And she tell me what to study and how to study to get better. But some Americans, you know, they don't understand about myself. So they just say, "Oh! You're doing a good job! You're doing great! Everything is great!" Teachers talk like that, but my culture is different. . . . They say, "You have to do better. . . ." So, sometimes when I do something not good, and my teachers say, "Oh, you did great!" I don't like it. . . . I want the truth better.

Some teachers, they never concerned to the students. So, they just do something that they have to do. But they don't really do something to help the people, the students. Some teachers, they just go inside and go to the blackboard. . . . They don't care. So that I don't like. . . .

I have a good teacher, Ms. Brown She's very sensitive. She understands the students, year to year, year after year. . . . She understands a lot. So when I had her class, we discussed some things very interesting about America. And sometimes she tells us about something very interesting about another culture. But Ms. Mitchell, she just knows how to teach for the children, like ten years old or younger. So some people don't like her. Like me, I don't like her. I like to discuss something. Not just how to write "A"; "You have to write like this." So I don't like that. . . . She wants me to write perfectly. So that is not a good way because we learn another language. Because when we learn another language, we learn to discuss, we learn to understand the word's *meaning*, not about how to *write* the word.

I want to go to college, of course. Right now, I don't know what will happen for the future. . . . If I think of my future, I have to learn more about psychology. If I have a family, I want a perfect family, not really perfect, but I want a very good family. So that's why I study psychology. . . . When I grow up, I get married, I have children, so I have to let them go to school, I have good education to teach them. So, Vietnamese want their children to grow up and be polite and go to school, just like I am right now. . . . I just want they will be a good person.

I don't care much about money. So, I just want to have a normal job that I can take care of myself and my family. So that's enough. I don't want to climb up compared to other people, because, you know, different people have different ideas about how to live. So I don't think money is important to me. I just need enough money for my life.

DEMANDING STANDARDS

I'm not really good, but I'm trying.

In Vietnam, I am a good student. But at the United States, my English is not good sometimes. I cannot say very nice things to some Americans, because my English is not perfect.

Sometimes the people, they don't think I'm polite because they don't understand my English exactly. . . . I always say my English is not good, because all the people, they can speak better than me. So, I say, "Why some people, they came here the same year with me, but they can learn better?" So I have to try.

When I lived in Vietnam, so I go to school and I got very good credit [grades], but right now because my English is not good, sometimes I feel very sorry for myself.

[My uncle] never told me, "Oh, you do good," or "Oh, you do bad." Because every time I go home, I give him my report card, like from C to A, he don't say nothing. He say, "Next time, you should do better." If I got A, O.K., he just say, "Oh, next time, do better than A!" . . . He doesn't need anything from me. But he wants me to be a good person, and helpful for my life. So he wants me to go to school so someday I have a good job and so I don't need from him anymore.

He encourages me. He talks about why you have to learn and what important things you will do in the future if you learn. . . . I like him to be involved about my school. . . . I like him to be concerned about my credits [grades].

Some people need help, but some people don't. Like me, sometime I need help. I want to know how to. . . . apply for college and what will I do to get into college. So that is my problem.

I have a counselor, but I never talk to him. Because I don't want them to be concerned about myself because they have a lot of people to talk with. So, sometimes, I just go home and I talk with my brother and my uncle.

If I need my counselor every time I got trouble, I'm not going to solve that problem. . . . So, I want to do it by myself. I have to sit down and think, "Why did the trouble start? And how can we solve the problem?" . . . Sometimes, I say, I don't want them to [be] concerned with my problem.

Most American people are very helpful. But because I don't want them to spend time about myself, to help me, so that's why I don't come to them. One other time, I talked with my uncle. He can tell me whatever I want. But my English is not good, so that's why I don't want to talk with American people.

I may need my counselor's help. When I go to college, I have to understand the college system and how to go get into college. . . . The first thing I have to know is the college system, and what's the difference between this school and other schools, and how they compare. . . . I already know how to make applications and how to meet counselors, and how to take a test also.

Sometimes I do better than other people, but I still think it's not good. Because if you learn, you can be more than that. So that's why I keep learning. Because I think, everything you can do, you learn. If you don't learn, you can't do nothing.

Right now, I cannot say [anything good] about myself because if I talk about myself, it's not right. Another person who lives with me, like my brother, he can say something about me better than what I say about myself. . . . Nobody can understand themselves better than other people.

I don't know [if I'm successful now] because that belongs to the future. . . . I mean successful for myself that I have a good family; I have a good job; I have respect from other people.

LACK OF INTERETHNIC AWARENESS AND UNDERSTANDING

[*Vinh talks about his experience of having gone to a predominately Black school in Virginia. The students, he says, "were very dirty," smoked a lot, and played their music very loud. When asked why he thought this was so, he said*] I think that depend on the culture. . . . I don't understand much about Black culture. . . .

But not all Black people. Some people very good. . . . Most Black people in [this town], they talk very nice. . . . Like in my country, some people very good and some people very bad.

I am very different from other people who are the same age. Some people who are the same age, they like to go dancing, they like to smoke, they want to have more fun. But not me. . . . Because right now, all the girls, they like more fun [things] than sit down and think about psychology, think about family. . . . I think it's very difficult to find [a girlfriend] right now. . . . If I find a girlfriend who [does] not agree with any of my ideas, it would not be a good girlfriend. . . . I don't need very much like me, but some. . . . we would have a little in common. . . . It is not about their color or their language, but their character. I like their character better.

I think it's an important point, because if you understand another language or another culture, it's very good for you. So I keep learning, other cultures, other languages, other customs. . . .

I have Chinese, I have Japanese, I have American, I have Cambodian [friends]. Every kind of people. Because I care about character, not about color.

STRENGTH FROM CULTURE AND FAMILY

Sometimes I think about [marrying] a Vietnamese girl, because my son or my daughter, in the future, they will speak Vietnamese. So, if I have an American girlfriend, my children cannot speak Vietnamese. Because I saw other families who have an American wife or an American husband, their children cannot speak Vietnamese. It is very hard to learn a language. . . . In the United States, they have TV, they have radio, every kind of thing, we have to do English. So, that why I don't think my children can learn Vietnamese.

When I sleep, I like to think a little bit about my country. And I feel very good. I always think about my fathers [parents] . . . my family . . . what gifts they get me before, how they were with me when I was young. . . . Those are very good things to remember and to try to repeat again.

I've been here for three years, but the first two years I didn't learn anything. I got sick, mental. I got mental. Because when I came to the United States, I missed my fathers [parents], my family, and my friends, and my Vietnam.

So, everytime I go to sleep, I cannot sleep, I don't want to eat anything. So I become sick.

I am a very sad person. Sometimes, I just want to be alone to think about myself. I feel sorry about what I do wrong with someone. Whatever I do wrong in the past, I just think and I feel sorry for myself.

I never have a good time. I go to the mall, but I don't feel good. . . . I just sit there, I don't know what to do.

Before I got mental, okay, I feel very good about myself, like I am smart, I learn a lot of things. . . . But after I got mental, I don't get any enjoyment. . . . I'm not smart anymore.

After I got mental, I don't enjoy anything. Before that, I enjoy lots. Like I listen to music, I go to school and talk to my friends. . . . But now I don't feel I enjoy anything. Just talk with my friends, that's enough, that's my enjoyment.

My culture is my country. We love my country; we love our people; we love the way the Vietnamese, like they talk very nice and they are very polite to all the people.

For Vietnamese, [culture] is very important. . . . I think my country is a great country. The people is very courageous. They never scared to do anything. . . . If we want to get something, we have to get it. Vietnamese culture is like that. . . . We work hard, and we get something we want.

If I have children, I have to teach them from [when] they grow up to when they get older. So, when they get older, I don't have to teach them, but they listen to me. Because that's education, not only myself, but all Vietnamese, from a long time ago to now. That's the custom. So that's why I like my customs and my culture.

Every culture . . . they have good things and they have bad things. And my culture is the same. But sometimes they're different because they come from different countries. . . . America is so different. . . .

[My teachers] understand something, just not all Vietnamese culture. Like they just understand something *outside*. . . . But they cannot understand something inside our hearts.

[Teachers should] understand the students. Like Ms. Mitchell, she just say, "Oh, you have to do it this way, you have to do that way." But some people, they came from different countries. They have different ideas, so they might think about school in different ways. So maybe she has to know why they think in that way. . . . Because different cultures, they have different meanings about education. So she has to learn about that culture.

I think they just *think* that they understand our culture. . . . But it is very hard to tell them, because that's our feelings.

When I came to United States, I heard English, so I say, "Oh, very funny sound." Very strange to me. But I think they feel the same like when we speak Vietnamese. So they hear and they say, "What a strange language." Some people like to listen. But some people don't like to listen. So, if I talk with Americans, I never talk Vietnamese.

Some teachers don't understand about the language. So sometimes, my language, they say it sounds funny. And sometimes, all the languages sound funny. Sometimes, she [teacher] doesn't let us speak Vietnamese, or some people speak Cambodian. Sometimes, she already knows some Spanish, so she lets Spanish speak. But because she doesn't know about Vietnamese language, so she doesn't let Vietnamese speak. . . .

[Teachers] have to know about our culture. And they have to help the people learn whatever they want. From the second language, it is very difficult for me and for other people.

I want to learn something good from my culture and something good from American culture. And I want to take both cultures and select something good . . . you know. . . . If we live in the United States, we have to learn something about new people.

[To keep reading and writing Vietnamese] is very important. . . . So, I like to learn English, but I like to learn my language too. Because different languages, they have different things, special. [My younger sisters] are very good. They don't need my help. They already know. They write to my parents and they keep reading Vietnamese books. . . . Sometimes they forget to pronounce the words, but I help them. . . .

At home, we eat Vietnamese food. . . . The important thing is rice. Everybody eats rice, and vegetables, and meat. They make different kinds of food. . . . The way I grew up, I had to learn, I had to know it. By looking at other people—when my mother cooked, and I just see it, and so I know it.

Right now, I like to listen to my music and I like to listen to American music. . . . And I like to listen to other music from other countries.

We tell them [parents] about what we do at school and what we do at home and how nice the people around us, and what we will do better in the future to make them happy. Something not good, we don't write. . . .

They miss us and they want ourselves to live together. . . . They teach me how to live without them.

COMMENTARY

Hoang Vinh's experiences in the United States closely parallel those of other Southeast Asian refugees in some respects, but they are quite different in others. His case study gives us many lessons about teachers' expectations, demands on Asian students, and the pain of cultural clash and language loss. Vinh is emphatic about wanting to become "educated people," which he explains as wanting to know about other people and about the world and to be able to get along with and help others. By "educated people," he refers not only to academics but also to behaviors not always related to studies. Grades are not as important as doing "the best you can." He is very clear about the differences between being "educated" in the Vietnamese sense and in the United States. There is not only a semantic difference here but a cultural one as well. His explanation is a good example of what many Asians believe is one of the main differences between U.S. and Asian cultures: Although U.S. culture is rich materially, it often lacks the spirituality so important in most Asian cultures.[5]

Certainly this attitude was developed in Vinh early in life. He was brought up in a strict home where he learned what it meant to be responsible and hard-working. He had many chores to do and was not allowed to play soccer with his friends until his room was clean and he had finished everything. He was expected to go to school and then to study for many hours afterward. In school, he remembers his teachers as being very "difficult." They expected him to be well behaved and polite, to come to school with clean hands, and to study.

It is important to point out that the Vietnamese and other Indochinese immigrants have a substantially higher level of education than previous immigrants. The proportion of Vietnamese immigrants with high school degrees, for instance, is 64 percent.[6] This high literacy rate has to affect their schooling in this country as well. For example, a national study found that Southeast Asians in U.S. schools typically spend more than three hours a night on homework, far more than any other group, including all native-born groups.[7] Literacy and educational activities are part of the home as well as the school. The effects of his family background and his early school experiences are evident in Vinh's attitudes toward school and in his study habits.

Although Vinh remembers his teachers in Vietnam with some fear because they were strict and demanding, he also recalls them with nostalgia. He seems to long for the kind of extra attention and help that they used to provide. He particularly remembers that they spent a great deal of time with each child, until all the children had learned. Vinh notices differences in the educational system in the United States. Some of these are positive, others negative. He appreciates, for example, being allowed to use his language in class and the individual help he receives from teachers. However, Vinh also thinks it is necessary for teachers to explain *why* the subject they teach is important. But mostly he talks about how he loves working in groups. He particularly mentions one ESL teacher, his favorite teacher, who often has the students working in groups, talking to one another, and coming up with their own solutions and answers. Most of the themes they discuss are related to their lives here, their culture, and their adaptation.

Much of the literature about the traditional learning styles of most Vietnamese students stresses their passivity and reliance on rote memorization, but Vinh's case dramatizes how important it is to interpret such literature cautiously.[8] For one, there is a great diversity among all Asian groups and even within groups. His predilection for group work, for example, may demonstrate how the *form* of education is not as important as the *content*. That is, group work in this case is the *means* used to facilitate dialogue, so important in learning a second language and in learning in general. But the content is what may be the crucial factor here because it is based on the students' own experiences and engages them so completely in their own education.

Vinh also talks about things that are *not* helpful. He does not like what he considers "being treated like a child," with boring and repetitive seat work or work that has to be copied from the board with no follow-up. He can also see through the "false praise" that teachers give him and his fellow students, praise that is meant to motivate but has the opposite effect. He is too polite to call it patronizing behavior, but that is how he feels about it.

Lest we get the impression that all Vietnamese students are as concerned as Vinh with educational success, he is quick to point out that one of his best friends, Duy, is "very lazy." He does all his homework, but only at school and in a haphazard way. Although Duy is very smart and has a "very good character," he does not care about learning in the same way as Vinh. He has long hair and spends many hours listening to music or thinking about girls. Duy likes to be "cool" and tries to think in what Vinh calls "an American way." Unlike Vinh, he has a job after school and likes to spend his money at the mall.

Both Duy and Vinh, in different ways, shatter the "model minority" stereotype. According to this image, all Asian students excel in school, have few adjustment problems, and need little help. This stereotype is widely resented by many Asians. It is, according to Suzuki, "inaccurate, misleading, and a gross overgeneralization."[9] He points out that although many have attained a measure of success, a larger proportion of Asian and Pacific Americans are poor than are not in the general population. In addition, the model minority myth is often used as a standard against which all other minority groups are measured, thus helping to pit one group against the other. This is what Schaefer calls "praising the victim."[10] This kind of comparison may lead to the interethnic hostilities common in schools and occurring with more frequency in communities as well. In addition, this myth helps to discredit the very legitimate demands for social justice of other, more vocal groups. The "model minority myth" also overlooks the great diversity among Asian Americans, a diversity apparent in ethnicity, class, language, and reasons for being in the United States as well as history here.[11] It may place severe demands on students by teachers who have unreasonable expectations of their academic abilities. Furthermore, the myth is used to assuage the guilt of some cities and towns that do little to help Asians and Pacific Americans with social problems of adaptation since it perpetuates the belief that these communities "take care of their own" and do not need any help.

Vinh is extremely hard on himself. Much of this self-assessment is tied to his English. This use of the English language as a standard by which to measure his intelligence is not unusual among immigrant students, who often feel frustrated and angry by how long it may take them to learn the language. It is another example of blaming themselves for perceived shortcomings. Another, probably healthier way of expressing this frustration was cited by a national report on immigrant and refugee students, who quoted a Laotian student as saying, "I know that despite the English language, I am a very intelligent girl."[12] Although he obviously excels in school, Vinh does not consider himself to be a successful student. He often compares his success in Vietnam with his struggles as a student now.

However, Vinh is extremely self-reliant. Although this trait is understandable, given the high value placed on humility by his culture as well as his experiences as an immigrant, it also means that he has not learned how to use some of the services available to him as a student.[13] The other side of his being hard on himself is that he is undemanding of others. For example, although he is certain he wants to go to college, he has not received, nor has he sought, help with making the important decisions that will help him get there. The help he has received, he says, is advice from teachers on studying hard and being a good student, advice that echoes and reinforces that of his family. Although he goes to what is considered an excellent public school with an adequate number of counselors and good student services, he has not taken advantage of them. He does not want to bother other people or to have them worry about him.

The tremendous traumas refugees suffer when leaving their country and facing the challenges of a new society are well known. One of the results is the incidence of mental health problems, which has increased dramatically. These are often caused by guilt, depression, alienation, and loneliness and are sometimes aggravated by the hostility and discrimination immigrants face. In addition, Western ways of treating such problems are often at odds with the refugee's culture.[14] In Vinh's case, the problem was excacerbated because he came without his parents. Given the pivotal role of the family in Vietnamese culture, particularly the importance of parents and elders in general, Vinh was bound to suffer mental distress.[15] In addition, at the improbable age of 15, he had the formidable task of relocating his family and acting as one of the "elders" in dealing with a new society. The strength and security he had previously derived from his family and the comfort of a known language and culture were abruptly removed. The result was almost inevitable. He became sick. He talks about this period of missing his family and "my Vietnam" with great melancholy. Vinh has had a difficult time adjusting and is still suffering from what seems to have been a chronic depression.

The role of his culture and family are still paramount. His grounding in the culture has provided important support. For instance, the pride he has in his culture is obviously great. However, it is not acknowledged by the school. Although he appreciates his school and his teachers, Vinh does not feel that they know very much about his culture. Vinh makes few demands on others but he does feel that it is important for teachers to learn about his culture and be sensitive to the difficulty of learning a second language when you are older. He compares his situation to that of his younger sister, who was 8 when she started to learn English and at 11 is now fluent.

Adjusting to his new country has posed many challenges for Vinh: learning a new language and writing system; becoming familiar with a new and very different culture; and grieving the loss of parents who, although still living, are no longer with him. In such cases, even an apparent adjustment may be deceiving. For example, a study of a group of Cambodian refugee children found that as they became more successful at modeling their behavior to be more like that of U.S. children, their emotional adjustment worsened. In addition, the feeling of being different from other children increased with time in this country.[16] Thus, the problems of adolescence are aggravated by immigrant and minority status. Young people like Vinh have a double and sometimes triple burden compared to other youths. Continuing to rely on his culture is one way in which Vinh is trying to achieve this difficult adjustment.

In addition, newcomers must learn to live in a country that is extremely pluralistic, at times uncomfortably so. The result can be confusion and uncertainty about other cultures outside the mainstream. Immigrants are quick to pick up messages about what are the "valued" and "devalued" cultures in the society in general. Their preconceived notions about racial superiority and inferiority may also play into this dynamic. The lack of awareness and knowledge of other cultures and their experiences in the United States excacerbates the situation further. Given no guidance by schools, either through appropriate curricula or other means, new students are left on their own to interpret the actions of others. Moreover, immigrants are often the target of racist attitudes and even violence by other students.

All of these complex factors help explain how some of the attitudes brought by immigrants and later nurtured by prevailing racist attitudes and behaviors in society are played out in schools and communities. Vinh is no exception. His experience with African American children is an example. He explains that on several occasions he was jumped and robbed. Being a newcomer to this country, he was perplexed and frustrated about these behaviors and came to his own conclusion about why they occurred. In spite of some of these negative experiences, he made friends with some of the students in that school ("Some of them is very cool and very nice").

Vinh sees a difference between the Black students from that first school and those in the mostly middle-class town in which he now lives. He resorts to saying, "There are good and bad in every group," a cliché often used to soften the impact of gross stereotypes. Vinh is obviously grappling with the issue and tries very hard to accept all people for "their character" rather than for the color of their skin or the language they speak. Schools must often take the major responsibility in helping children confront these difficult issues. Yet this is often not the case. Given our changing demographics and the impact of the large influx of immigrants, this issue of rivalry and negative relationships among different groups of immigrants and native-born students is likely to be felt more and more.

Vinh's relationship with his uncle supports and affirms his commitment to school and education. In his case, culture and education are inextricably tied together. Although his uncle rarely goes to school, Vinh considers him to be very involved in his schooling: He checks his report card, encourages him to do better, makes sure that his friends are all appropriate and "polite," and in general oversees his life so that Vinh remains on the right track. "Because he love us, that's why he involved," he says, although he is quick to add that his uncle rarely attends school meetings or visits the school. His uncle is "very smart," he says, but is intimidated by not speaking English well and by unfamiliar and impersonal bureaucracies. Traditional respect for teachers along with these structural barriers erected by the school discourage many such guardians from attending school meetings and otherwise being involved in school matters. In this way, Vinh's uncle is similar to many Asian parents who demonstrate their concern for their children's education at home rather than at school.[17]

Hoang Vinh is obviously on a long and difficult road to adaptation, not only in cultural and linguistic terms but also, and probably not coincidentally, in terms of his mental health. Many of his issues are based on the traumas he has had to endure as an immigrant. Whether his school is able to deal effectively in helping him solve these problems is certain to have an impact on his future.

TO THINK ABOUT

1. How does Vinh's definition of "educated people" differ from yours? Why?
2. Vinh seems to resent false praise by some of his teachers. Some students, however, seek this kind of praise. What are the implications for teaching in culturally diverse schools?
3. What does Vinh mean when he says, "I'm not really good, but I'm trying"?
4. Vinh has trouble in asking his teachers and counselors for help. Knowing this, what can schools do to help students like Vinh?
5. After reading Vinh's case, what do you think of the conventional wisdom surrounding the "model minority"?
6. Given the interethnic experiences Vinh has had and the perceptions he has developed about other cultures, what can schools do to help students from different ethnic and racial groups understand one another better?
7. Because Vinh has never been in schools with high numbers of Vietnamese students, he has not been able to participate in a bilingual program. Do you think this is an advantage or a disadvantage? Why?

NOTES

1. I am grateful to Haydée Font for the interviews and transcripts for this case study.
2. The Vietnamese use family names first, given names second. The given name is used for identification. In this case, Vinh is the given name and Hoang is the family name. According to *A Manual for Indochinese Refugee Education, 1976–1977*, whereas a male in U.S. society named John Jones would be known formally as Mr. Jones and informally as John, in Vietnam, Hoang Vinh would be known both formally and informally as Mr. Vinh or Vinh (Arlington, VA: National Indochinese Clearinghouse, Center for Applied Linguistics, 1976).
3. This is hardly unusual. An astonishing 80 percent of parents interviewed believed it was important for their children to retain their native language and culture while at the same time wanting them to learn English. *New Voices: Immigrant Students in U.S. Public Schools* (Boston: National Coalition of Advocates for Students, 1988).
4. It is interesting to note that over 50 percent of the current population of Asian and Pacific Americans are recent immigrants. See, for example, Bob Suzuki, "The Education of Asian and

Pacific Americans: An Introductory Overview,'' and Vuong G. Thuy, "The Indochinese in America: Who Are They and How Are They Doing?'' in *The Education of Asian and Pacific Americans: Historical Perspectives and Prescriptions for the Future*, ed. Don T. Nakanishi and Marsha Hirano-Nakanishi (Phoenix, AZ.: Oryx Press, 1983); Ronald Takaki, *Strangers from a Different Shore: A History of Asian Americans* (New York: Penguin Books, 1987).

5. John Young, and John Lum, *Asian Bilingual Education Teacher Handbook* (Cambridge, MA: Evaluation, Dissemination, and Assessment Center, 1982). In addition, Tam says, "A very rich man without a good education is not highly regarded by the Vietnamese." Tam Thi Dang Wei, *Vietnamese Refugee Students: A Handbook for School Personnel* (Cambridge, MA: National Assessment and Dissemination Center, 1980).

6. *New Voices.*

7. Ibid.

8. See, for example, Young and Lum, *Asian Bilingual Education Teacher Handbook*, and Tam, *Vietnamese Refugee Students*. However, Suzuki critiques the stereotype of the Asian student as quiet, hard-working, and docile because "it tends to reinforce conformity and stifle creativity." Thus, because they do not develop the ability to express themselves verbally, they are often channeled in disproportionate numbers to the scientific and technical fields. See "Education of Asian and Pacific Americans."

9. Suzuki, "Education of Asian and Pacific Americans"; see also Takaki, *Strangers from a Different Shore*.

10. Richard T. Schaefer, *Racial and Ethnic Groups*, 3rd ed. (Glenview, IL: Scott, Foresman, 1988).

11. See Diane Divoky, "The Model Minority Goes to School," *Phi Delta Kappan*, November 1988, pp. 219–222.

12. *New Voices.*

13. Tam, *Vietnamese Refugee Students*.

14. See, for example, Vuong, "The Indochinese in America"; *New Voices*.

15. Tam, *Vietnamese Refugee Students*.

16. The study, by the Metropolitan Indochinese Children and Adolescent Service, was done in 1985 and reported in *New Voices*.

17. Suzuki, "Education of Asian and Pacific Americans."

CHAPTER 6

Linguistic Diversity
in Multicultural Classrooms

OVERVIEW

Language is inextricably linked to culture. It is a primary means by which people express their cultural values and the lens through which they view the world. Yet it is often overlooked when referring to cultural differences. The language that children bring to school inevitably affects how and what they learn. Because of the close link between language and culture, it is important to understand that it is an essential component of multicultural education. Nevertheless, some of the most comprehensive approaches to multicultural education, while including race, class, and gender concerns, have failed to include language issues in their conceptual framework.[1]

Part of the reason for the exclusion of language issues is related to the lack of relevant terms in general use. Terms that describe discrimination based on race, gender, and class, among others, are part of our general vocabulary. *Racism, sexism, ethnocentrism, anti-Semitism, classism*, and so on are widely understood by the general public. Until recently, no such term existed for language discrimination, although this does not mean that language discrimination as such did not exist. Skutnabb-Kangas, by coining the term *linguicism* to refer to discrimination based specifically on language, has helped to place it under the same general umbrella as the other terms.[2]

The purpose of this chapter is to investigate the impact of linguistic differences on student achievement. Specifically, we will explore bilingual education as a way to approach language differences in a positive and empowering manner. Before doing so, we will discuss some of the ways in which language differences have been viewed in classrooms.

The stripping away of students' native language and culture is often done for what teachers and schools believe are good reasons. One study of the repression of Spanish in Texas, for instance, found that schools often make a direct link between the students' English assimilation and their economic and social mobility. Thus, students who speak a language other than English are frequently viewed as "handicapped." It was found that

Spanish was repressed in school in what teachers believed were the best interests of students. Teachers felt that continuing to speak Spanish was a way of persisting in being "foreign" and in effect refusing to be "American." Although 90 percent of the students were U.S. citizens, their status as "outsiders" was maintained, at least in the eyes of teachers, if they persisted in speaking Spanish.[3] The influence this devaluation of native language in the school may have cannot be dismissed.

LINGUISTIC DIVERSITY AND IMPACT
ON LEARNING

In spite of the enormous impact that language has on children's schooling, it is important to emphasize that lack of English skills *alone* cannot explain the poor academic achievement of students. It is tempting to fall back on this explanation and thus count on simple solutions like English "sink or swim" programs to solve the problem. Cuban students, for example, have been found to have the *highest* educational level of all Latinos, yet they are the most likely to speak Spanish at home.[4] They are also more likely to come from middle-class backgrounds than any other Latino children. One study focusing on the relationship between Spanish-language background and achievement among first-, second-, and third-generation Mexican American high school students concluded that contrary to the conventional wisdom, Spanish is *not* an impediment to student achievement. Another large-scale study of Latino high school sophomores and seniors found that those who were highly proficient in Spanish actually performed *better* on achievement tests and had higher educational aspirations than those who were not. In spite of such findings, the fact that students speak Spanish is treated by many teachers as a social problem.[5] There is also evidence that teachers interact more negatively with students who do not speak English than with those who do.[6] If this is the case, the language dominance of students is not really the issue; rather, *the way in which teachers and schools view their language may be even more crucial to student achievement.*

Speaking a language other than English is not in and of itself a handicap. On the contrary, it can be a great asset to learning, as will be documented later. How language and language use are perceived by the schools and whether modifications in the curriculum are made as a result are important factors to keep in mind. The fact that English speakers rarely have the opportunity to enter bilingual education programs reinforces the inferior status of these programs. Bilingualism, at least in the case of dominated groups, is generally viewed as a burden, although it is seen as an asset among middle-class and wealthy students. It is not unusual to find in the same high school the seemingly incongruous situation of an entire group of students having their native language wiped out while another group of students struggles to learn a foreign language. Issues of social class may have an even greater effect than language on academic performance.

EXPLORING LINGUISTIC DIVERSITY
THROUGH BILINGUAL EDUCATION

Because bilingual education has been a consistent and controversial educational concern in the United States since the 1960s, it will be examined as one of the fundamental ways in which language differences are handled in the schools. This is not meant to downplay the importance of other language differences. *Black English*, the vernacular spoken by a great many African American children, increasingly being called *African American Language*, is one such language difference. It affects the educational experiences of a large number of students because they must cope with the burden of the negative stigma attached to the language they speak at the same time they learn a different variant of the language when they enter school.[7] Nor is the discussion of bilingual education meant to diminish the difficult and traumatic experiences that students from *low incidence populations* have in our schools. This term refers to students who speak a particular language for which there may not be sufficient speakers to entitle them legally to a bilingual program. Such is often the case with Asian, Southeast Asian, and some European languages. In this situation, the most common programmatic practice is some kind of ESL approach.

We will focus on bilingual education because it represents an intriguing case study of the policies and practices that have evolved over the years to deal with language differences in our schools. In addition, bilingual education needs to be understood as a fundamental part of multicultural education. The purpose of this section is to review the need for bilingual education, its history and program models, and its connection with multicultural education.

BILINGUAL EDUCATION: THE NEED GROWS

The number of students who are classified as having *limited English proficiency* in the United States is growing dramatically. This term refers to students whose lack of facility in the English language may have negative consequences for their academic achievement in monolingual English classrooms. One report estimates that there are currently between 1.2 million and 1.7 million such students.[8] Even more dramatic is the expectation that by the year 2020, the number of children speaking a primary language other than English will be almost 6 million.[9] Asian children are supplanting those from Spanish-speaking countries as the leading group entering the country, doubling the number of Asian children already in the United States.[10] These changes are part of a larger immigrant trend in the United States, which in the last two decades has been among the largest in our history. The reasons for this new trend are varied, from a rise in the number of refugees from countries where the United States has been involved in aggression (as in Central America and Southeast Asia) to a loosening of immigration restrictions for some parts of the world. Legal immigration alone between 1980 and 1990 will probably have equaled that of 1900 to 1910. The largest numbers of new immigrants are now from Asia and Latin America, a marked departure from previous times, when they were overwhelmingly from Europe.[11]

All of these changes in the demographics of the United States have profound implications for education. Yet most students who need and could benefit from bilingual programs are not currently receiving them. Only about 15 percent of students needing special language services are in federally funded bilingual programs; only about one-third are receiving *any* language assistance at all. In addition, the percentage of students in bilingual programs has actually declined in some places since 1980, precisely when they are most needed.[12] The reasons for this decline are varied, from the fact that many states do not have bilingual education statutes to poor enforcement of those state and federal mandates that do exist. Finding qualified personnel has been another major problem, and the fact that fewer bilingual people are entering the teaching profession makes the problem even more serious.

DEFINITIONS AND PROGRAM MODELS

Bilingual education is generally defined as an educational program that involves the use of two languages of instruction at some point in a student's school career. This definition is broad enough to include the many program variations that are classified as bilingual education. For example, a child who speaks a language other than English, say Vietnamese, may receive instruction in content areas in Vietnamese while at the same time learning English as a second language. The culture associated with the primary language of instruction is generally part of the curriculum, as is that of the second language. The approach is sometimes called *bilingual/bicultural education* and is based on the premise that the language and culture children bring to school are assets that must be used in their education. Thus there is an emphasis on students' native culture, including their history and traditions, within the curriculum. The bicultural aspect of bilingual education is unfortunately neglected or downplayed in some programs. For example, the materials used in some programs, that is, textbooks, curricula, and so on, are simple translations into other languages of the English-language materials used in monolingual classrooms. This practice helps to defeat the purpose of bilingual/bicultural education, which is to use students' prior knowledge for new learning.

There are numerous interpretations of bilingual education in the schools, ranging all the way from ESL to developmental bilingual education. Some of these will be briefly described, although it should be pointed out that there is not always agreement on what these program options are.[13]

Although *English as a second language (ESL)* is sometimes viewed as a kind of bilingual education, it is not generally considered to be bilingual education in and of itself because the child's native language is not used in instruction. Sometimes ESL classrooms have aides who speak the children's language and help in translating or explaining concepts, but this alone does not make them bilingual classrooms. The ESL approach, if not part of a bilingual program, simply focuses on teaching language skills in English so that children can learn their content in English. While they are learning English, these students may be languishing in their other subject areas because they do not understand the language of instruction. Education, for them, usually consists only of learning English until they can function in the regular English-language environment.

It must be emphasized that a primary objective of bilingual education is to have students become proficient and literate in the English language. As such, ESL is an integral and necessary component of all bilingual programs. That is, ESL goes hand in hand with native-language instruction in content areas. Rather than seeing these as separate areas of the curriculum, successful bilingual programs use students' talents, including their knowledge and literacy in another language, to help them learn new skills. In this way, student learning is reinforced in two languages.[14]

Probably the most common model of bilingual education in the United States is the *transitional bilingual education* approach. In this approach, students receive their content area instruction in their native language while learning English as a second language. As soon as they are thought to be ready to benefit from the monolingual English-language curriculum, they are "exited" out of the program. The rationale behind this model is that native-language services should serve only as a transition to English. Therefore, there is a limit on the time a student may be in a bilingual program, usually three years. This limit was established in 1971 by Massachusetts, the first state to mandate bilingual education, and has served as a model for subsequent states. The number of states that mandate bilingual education has fluctuated over the years, depending on the political climate in different states at different times.[15] The primary objective of a transitional program is to teach students English as quickly as possible so that they can continue their education in a monolingual English classroom.

Another approach is called *maintenance bilingual education*, a more comprehensive and long-term model. As in the transitional approach, students receive content area instruction in their native language while learning English as a second language. The difference is that there is generally no limit set on the time students can be in the program. The reasoning here is that a child's native language is worth maintaining because it is an asset in its own right and therefore an appropriate channel for continued learning. That children literate in their native language will be more successful students than those whose language is ignored, denied, or replaced has been documented repeatedly.[16] This approach builds on their literacy and extends it to a second language as well. The objective is for the children to become fluent in both languages by using them both for instruction. Students may, in theory, remain in a maintenance bilingual program throughout their education. The longer they remain in the program, the more functionally bilingual they become and, therefore, the more balanced is the curriculum to which they are exposed. That is, they can potentially receive equal amounts of instruction in English and in their native language.

In recent years, the term *developmental bilingual education* has been substituted for the more politically charged term *maintenance*, as the latter has become associated in the minds of some opponents of bilingual education with separatism. Some opponents have raised the specter of terrorism and even civil war as possible results of bilingual education. This has been the case generally with right-wing groups or other organizations waging the battle for "English only."[17]

The positive effects of maintenance bilingual education have been highlighted by Warren in an ethnographic study of one such program. He found that although the curriculum in the program was what he called "culturally Anglo," it was nevertheless highly successful because it had an important mediating role in the students' achievement. Although the school's curriculum was not totally Mexican American or Latino, the continuing importance of bilingual competency for the students was assumed by all staff. For example, students could express their needs in the language that was most meaningful to them at every grade level. In this way, the maintenance model affirmed the equal worth of the ethnicity and language of the students.[18]

Two-way bilingual education is a program model for integrating students whose native language is English with those for whom English is a second language. The purpose of this approach is to develop bilingualism in both. Therefore, all students learn content in their native language while they learn the other language as a second language. Let us take the example of a Spanish-English bilingual program. English-speaking children would learn Spanish as a second language, and those who speak Spanish as their native language would learn English (ESL). They would each learn content in their stronger language, but they would be integrated for some academic work. The more fluent students become in their second language, the more time they are integrated for instruction. This approach also lends itself quite well to cooperative learning and peer tutoring since all the students have important skills to share with one another. There is generally no time limit to this approach, although some two-way programs are part of existing transitional programs and therefore have the same entrance and exit criteria, at least for the students who do not speak English.

Finally, *immersion bilingual education* represents quite a different approach to learning a second language. In these programs, students are generally immersed in their second language for a year or two before their native language is introduced as a medium of instruction. By their fifth or sixth year of schooling, they may be receiving equal amounts of instruction in their two languages, or they may continue to receive the lion's share in their second language. Immersion has been found to be quite effective with middle-class students whose language is the dominant language of the society. Thus, in Canada, English-speaking students have been quite successful learning in French.[19] Unfortunately, the success of this kind of program has been used by opponents of bilingual education as the basis for suggesting *submersion bilingual education* for linguistic minority students in the United States. It has been suggested that linguistic minority students be placed in a totally English-language environment in order for them to learn English as quickly as possible and thus benefit from their schooling. The fallacy of this kind of thinking will be reviewed later as we investigate the results of research in bilingual education. To understand the context for this kind of thinking, however, it is important to explore first the history of bilingual education in the United States.

THE HISTORY AND POLITICS
OF BILINGUAL EDUCATION

Bilingual education is not new. It is as old as the United States and can probably be traced as well to the many Indian Nations before the arrival of the Europeans. Castellanos has said that the history of bilingual education is also the history of the United States; he is probably not far from the mark.[20] That is, the cycle of policies and practices related to languages and language use in society in general and schools in particular reflects the many ways in which the United States has attempted to resolve the issue of language diversity. These have ranged all the way from "sink or swim" policies (i.e., immersing language minority students in English-only classrooms to fend on their own), through the imposition of English as the sole medium of instruction, to allowing and even encouraging German-English bilingual schools in the last century. By 1900, for example, it was estimated that over 200,000 children were being taught in German in public elementary schools, with smaller numbers being taught in Polish, Italian, Norwegian, Spanish, French, Czech, Dutch, and other languages.[21]

Where bilingual education is concerned, everyone from parents to presidents has gotten into the fray. Theodore Roosevelt, very much a spokesperson for the restrictive language policies at the beginning of the century, which were a response to the huge influx of primarily East European immigrants to the United States, stated; "We have room for but one language here, and that is the English language; for we intend to see that the crucible turns our people out as Americans, of American nationality, and not as dwellers in a polyglot boardinghouse; and we have room for but one sole loyalty, and that is loyalty to the American people."[22] Roosevelt's views were widely shared by many people who felt threatened by the new wave of immigrants. The language policies of the time, particularly those restricting instruction in a language other than English, reflect these concerns.

The issue of language use and patriotic loyalty have often been bound together, especially in the teaching of German after World War I.[23] It remains true today, particularly with regard to Spanish. The fact that bilingual education has as one of its fundamental goals the learning of English is often overlooked. Note, for example, the words of a more recent president. Ronald Reagan, responding to a reporter's question about support for bilingual education, stated, "It is absolutely wrong and against American concept to have a bilingual education program that is now openly, admittedly dedicated to preserving their native language and never getting them adequate in English so they can go out into the job market."[24] The "English-only" movement of the past decade is a reflection of this feeling.[25]

The zigzag of support and rejection of languages other than English demonstrates the schizophrenia with which language diversity has been viewed in the United States. The latest cycle of support for bilingual education, albeit at times lukewarm, began with the passage of the Elementary and Secondary Education Act of 1968. Even in times of support, bilingual education has always been controversial and the target of much antagonism. Why this should be so is no mystery. First, the use of languages other than English has generally been perceived in our society as a threat to national unity. This view has at times resulted in counterproductive policies that inhibit the learning of foreign languages as well as the understanding of other peoples. That our society continues to be ignorant of other languages and cultures is self-evident; that it is now jeopardized by this monolingualism and monoculturalism in a world becoming increasingly interdependent is becoming more and more apparent. Second, bilingual education has been perceived as a threat because it questions the very basis of much of our educational system. The fact that it has been successful at all thus becomes problematic. That is, successful bilingual programs have demonstrated that students *can* learn in their native language while *also* learning English *and* achieving academically. This achievement contradicts the conservative agenda of the 1980s, which called for a return to a largely European American curriculum and pedagogy. Successful bilingual education threatens to explode the myth of the "basics" if the basics means only valuing a Eurocentric curriculum and the English language.

This brings us to one of the most salient aspects of bilingual education. Bilingual education is now, has always been, and will no doubt continue to be a fundamentally *political* issue. It is concerned with the relative power or lack of power of various groups in our society. This assertion is not at all meant to detract from the sound pedagogical basis of bilingual education or from its primarily positive results. However, in spite of these results, bilingual education continues to be controversial. By representing the class and ethnic group interests of traditionally disempowered groups, bilingual education has been characterized by great controversy and debate. The issue is not whether or not it works but the real possibility that it might. Bilingual education is a political issue because both its proponents and opponents have long recognized its potential for empowering these traditionally powerless groups. The closer such programs come to using students' language and culture in a liberating way, the more they are criticized. For example, maintenance programs tend to be much more controversial than transitional programs; ESL programs, with no bilingual assistance, are viewed as less problematic than either. Understanding the political nature of bilingual education, and of multicultural education in general, is essential if we are to develop effective programs geared toward meeting the needs of all our students. Both the political nature of bilingual education and its research results have to be kept in mind.

RESULTS OF BILINGUAL EDUCATION: WHAT WORKS AND WHY?

Bilingual education has been characterized by major achievements in providing equal educational opportunity to students whose native language is not English. Nevertheless, opponents to bilingual education in the United States have attempted to use the success of immersion programs in Canada as a rationale for such programs in this country. However, the issues are quite different. First, most bilingual programs in the United States serve children of economically oppressed communities. Second, the native language of the majority of these students is what is called a *marked* language, that is, a language not highly valued by the society at large. This situation is in stark contrast to the use of standard English in a primarily English-speaking country. Finally, an immersion program in this country would not mean placing limited English-proficient students in all-English classrooms. On the contrary, such a program would place native English-speaking students in another language setting until the second or third year of their schooling. Even the researchers associated with Canada's immersion program have cautioned against using it as a model with language minority students in the United States.[26] The immersion model, if applied to language minority students, would properly be called *submersion*.

There is a dizzying array of program alternatives in bilingual education, each claiming to be more successful than the others. In general, most research has found that bilingual programs, either transitional or maintenance in approach, are effective not only in teaching students content area knowledge in their native language but also in teaching them English. This has proven time and again to be the case in research analyses and specific program reviews.[27] Even more important, however, bilingual programs may have secondary effects such as motivating students to remain in school rather than dropping out, making school more meaningful, and in general making the school experience more enjoyable.[28] According to Hakuta, the most significant effect of bilingual education may not be that it promotes bilingualism, which he claims it does not, but rather that it "gives some measure of official public status to the political struggle of language minorities, primarily Hispanics."[29] Official public status may have a positive effect on the achievement of students.

A related phenomenon may be that bilingual education reinforces important relationships among students and their family members, allowing them to engage in more communication than would be the case if they were instructed solely in English and lost their native language. In a prize-winning essay on the importance of bilingual education, a seventh-grade Navajo student wrote, "The ability to communicate in two languages is an advantage because I can talk and understand my elders." He explains, "Being bilingual is also important for maintaining the native tongue. Without this, our language will die out. This cannot happen because it is the basis of our culture."[30] A nationwide survey of over 1,000 families for whom English is a second language echoes these findings. Researchers found evidence of serious disruptions of family relations when young children learn English in school and lose their native language. Attempts to get three- and four-year-old preschoolers into programs in which they are taught English before kindergarten are linguistically and culturally unsound and may have negative consequences on language, social, and intellectual development.[31]

The fact is that bilingual education is generally more effective than other programs such as ESL alone, not only in learning content through the native language but also in learning English. This apparently contradictory finding can be understood if one considers that students in bilingual programs are given continued education in content areas *along with* structured instruction in English. In addition, they are building on a previous literacy. This becomes what Lambert has called an *additive* rather than a *subtractive* form of bilingual education.[32] This may not be the case in other programs, even in ESL programs, which may concentrate on English grammar, phonics, and other language features out of context with the way in which the real, day-to-day language is used.

Even in programs in which English is not used, results often show dramatic gains in students' achievement. This achievement helps prepare them for the academic demands of school, no matter what language is used. Campos and Keatinge, for example, found that Hispanic children enrolled in a Spanish-only preschool program developed more skills that would prepare them for school than comparable children in a bilingual preschool program whose main objective was to develop English proficiency.[33]

The claim that immersion programs are appropriate for language minority students has not been borne out. Although a small number of studies find that immersion is effective in teaching English skills, a large-scale comparative evaluation of immersion and bilingual education programs by Ramirez concluded that students in bilingual programs do as well or better than those in immersion programs, even in their English-language performance.[34] Ironically, the more native-language instruction students received, the more likely they were to be reclassified as proficient in English. Even if the primary purpose of instruction is to learn English (a debatable position), immersion programs do not seem to work as well. In contrast, the positive effects of bilingual education, from lowering dropout rates to literacy development, have been found time and again.[35]

The Ramirez study, as well as others, provides yet another rationale for late-exit models of bilingual education, that is, programs in which students remain until they have developed adequate proficiency for high-level academic work. By continuing to use students' native language in substantive ways, late-exit programs encourage them to maintain close relationships with family members, particularly linguistic interactions, thus helping students' in their schoolwork and emotional needs at the same time. In addition, late-exit models tend to encourage parental involvement to a greater degree than early-exit models because parents feel more comfortable in settings where their native language is used.

BILINGUAL EDUCATION AND EQUAL EDUCATIONAL OPPORTUNITY

There is an important relationship between bilingual education and equity. Bilingual education has frequently been addressed as simply an issue of language, but it goes much deeper than this. Bilingual education is a civil rights issue because it is the only guarantee that children who do not speak English will be provided education in a language they understand. Without it, millions of children may be doomed to educational underachievement and limited occupational choices in the future.

The U.S. Supreme Court has recognized the relationship of language and equal educational opportunity. In 1969, plaintiffs representing 1,800 Chinese-speaking students sued the San Francisco Unified School District for failing to provide students who did not speak English with an equal chance to learn. They lost their case but in 1974 had taken it all the way to the Supreme Court. In the landmark *Lau* v. *Nichols* case, the Court ruled unanimously that the civil rights of students who did not understand the language of instruction were indeed being violated. Based on Title VI of the Civil Rights Act, the Court stated, in part,

> There is no equality of treatment merely by providing students with the same facilities, textbooks, teachers, and curriculum; for students who do not understand English are effectively foreclosed from any meaningful education. Basic skills are at the very core of what these public schools teach. Imposition of a requirement that, before a child can effectively participate in the educational program he must already have acquired those basic skills is to make a mockery of public education.[36]

Although the decision did not impose any particular remedy, its results were immediate and extensive. By 1975, the Office for Civil Rights and the Department of Health, Education, and Welfare issued a document called "The *Lau* Remedies," which has served as the basis for determining whether or not school systems throughout the country are in compliance with the findings of *Lau*. In effect, the document provides guidance in identifying, assessing the language abilities, and providing appropriate programs for students with a limited proficiency in English. Bilingual programs are the common remedy of most school systems.

The Equal Educational Opportunities Act (EEOA) of 1974 has also been instrumental in protecting the language rights of students for whom English is not a native language. This law interprets the failure of any educational agency to "take appropriate action to overcome language barriers that impede equal participation by its students in its instructional programs" as a denial of equal educational opportunity.[37] A number of federal cases have resulted in a strong interpretation of this statute. In both *Lau* and the EEOA, bilingual education has emerged as a key strategy to counteract the language discrimination faced by many students in our schools.

Linguicism, or discrimination based on language use, has been fairly widespread.[38] Entire communities have been denied the use of their native language, not only for instruction or in schools but also in social communication of all kinds. Throughout our history, the language rights of substantial numbers of people have been denied, from prohibiting enslaved Africans from speaking their languages to the imposition of recent "English only" laws in a growing number of states.[39] Landry has charged that the government, in favoring one language over all others, is in effect violating the language rights of everybody whose primary language is not English. Through its massive support for only one language, particularly in schools, he maintains that the government is failing to protect other language rights. He says that at least Native American languages, Spanish, and French can be considered native to the United States and are therefore entitled to special consideration in light of the Helsinki agreement, in which national minority rights are protected. He makes this claim because in the case of these particular languages, territory was incorporated into the United States without the consent of the people involved.[40]

Even if one does not go so far as Landry in defense of language rights, it can be said that bilingual education services represent one important guarantee of a fundamental right. As such, a bilingual education is an equitable education for over a million students in our schools. Just as racial integration has been considered an important civil right for those who were segregated and doomed to an inferior education, bilingual education is understood by language minority communities as an equally important civil right. Thus bilingual education is an essential, although often overlooked, part of multicultural education. Skutnabb-Kangas has proposed what she calls "The Declaration of Children's Linguistic Human Rights," a proposal that puts linguistic rights on the same level as other human rights and includes the right to identify positively with one's mother tongue, to learn it, and to choose when to use it.[41] For language majority children, these rights are self-evident, but not for those who speak a language with a negative stigma. Because language and culture are so intertwined, and because both bilingual and multicultural approaches attempt to involve and empower students, particularly the most disenfranchised, it is essential that their natural links be understood.

PROBLEMS AND ISSUES

Although bilingual education represents an important advance over monolingual education, there are a number of problems with proposing it as the only alternative. One is that it is often perceived as a panacea for all the educational problems of language minority students. Yet even with a bilingual education, many children are likely to face educational failure, which is true of multicultural education in general as well. No approach or program can cure all the problems, educational and otherwise, facing our young people if it does not also address the fundamental issues of discrimination and stratification in schools and society. Only a comprehensively conceptualized approach can hope to achieve success for most students. Simply substituting one language for another, or books in Spanish with Dick and Jane in brownface, will not guarantee success for language minority students. Expecting too much of even good programs is counterproductive because in the absence of quick results, the children are again blamed for their failure.

Cummins's work on student empowerment through bilingual programs is based on this important premise. In fact, he claims that the crucial element in reversing students' school failure is not the language of instruction but rather the extent to which teachers and schools attempt to reverse the institutionalized racism of society as a whole. Although this statement is not meant to downplay the great benefits of native language instruction, unless bilingual education becomes "anti-racist education," according to Cummins, "it may serve only to provide a veneer of change that in reality perpetuates discriminatory educational structures."[42]

One of the implications for teachers is to consider how modifications can be made in their instruction and curriculum to help students achieve. Effective pedagogy is not simply teaching subject areas in another language but rather finding ways to use the language, culture, and experiences of students in their education. Therefore, the traditional environments, strategies, and policies of many bilingual programs—in which straight rows of desks, ditto sheets, and silence are viewed as signs of "real learning," whereas questioning, talking, and other signs of active participation are viewed as either disrespectful or culturally inappropriate—need to be challenged. Montero-Sieburth's ethnography of a bilingual teacher faces this challenge squarely.[43] The bilingual teacher with whom she worked turned her classes into "problem-posing forums," where the issues that the students faced on a daily basis became the curriculum.

A further problem has to do with the definition of success of most bilingual programs. Bilingual programs, particularly those with a transitional focus, are meant to "self-destruct" within a limited time. Success in these programs is measured by the rapidity with which they mainstream students. That being the case, their very existence is based on a "compensatory education" philosophy and departs very little from the "deficit" theories reviewed in Chapter 3. Students who enter school knowing little or no English are regarded as needing compensation. Their knowledge of another language is not considered an asset but at best a crutch to use until they master the "real" language of schooling. This is at best a patronizing and at worst a racist position.

Given this perspective, it is little wonder that many parents do not want their children in bilingual programs or that these programs are often isolated and ghettoized in the schools. This message is not lost on students either. In an ethnographic study of four bilingual students, Nancy Commins found that some children are reluctant to speak Spanish because it is perceived to be the language of the "dumb kids."[44] Thus, children may unconsciously jeopardize their own language development by dropping Spanish, a language that benefits their academic achievement by allowing them to use higher-level cognitive skills than with their English, which they do not speak as well. Commins concludes, "Both the overt hostility expressed by some towards Spanish and the implicit message sent by the supremacy of English in the environment reinforced the students' perceptions, internalized over many years, that the use of Spanish in school was unacceptable. . . ."[45]

There are other problems with this self-destruct aspect of bilingual education. For example, these programs are in perpetual limbo because the number of students of limited English proficiency may vary from year to year. The program, perceived as unstable, may be granted low priority in the school. This practice places an unnecessary burden on bilingual teachers, who are in a precarious situation because it is their job to "exit" students out of their program. These teachers, sometimes from the same linguistic and cultural background of the students they teach, bring an important element of diversity into the school. But because they are often isolated and marginalized in the schools, they tend to have little interaction with other staff.

In spite of the "quick exit" philosophy of most bilingual programs, much of the research has documented that students generally need a minimum of five to seven years to develop the level of English proficiency needed to succeed academically in school.[46] With most programs permitting students to remain a maximum of only three to four years, only partially positive results can be expected. The research evidence is in direct contrast to program implementation, although many programs are successful nevertheless.

Equally troublesome for some school districts is that they have numerous language groups in their student population. That is, they may have small numbers of students representing a great many languages. Providing a bilingual program for each of these small groups would not only be impractical but also impossible. Research by Trueba has suggested that even when bilingual education is not possible, instruction can still be tailored to children's "cultural knowledge and experiences," for example, placing students in learning environments that promote success, identifying their learning strengths and modifying instructional strategies to match, and developing a group of teachers who become colleagues and effective supporters of innovative approaches.[47] Such options may become necessary in dealing with low-incidence groups.

Another problematic feature of bilingual education concerns its need to separate students. Bilingual education has been characterized by some as tracking because students are separated from their peers for instruction. Although the reasons for this separation are legitimate and based on sound research and pedagogy, tracking as a practice flies in the face of equal educational opportunity. These issues need to be sorted out carefully. Landry has suggested that whereas discrimination in race, class, gender, and disability tends to be resolved by *integration*, the opposite is true for bilingual education. That is, bilingual education demands the opportunity to *separate* students, at least for part of their education.[48] This makes it a particularly thorny issue in a democratic society. Add the research evidence suggesting that students should remain in bilingual classrooms until they develop sufficient academic competency in English, and we would be left with some students in segregated settings for the major part of their schooling.

Although this dilemma seems particularly disturbing in a multicultural philosophy, there are ways in which the needs of limited English-proficient and mainstream students can be served at the same time. Within every bilingual program, there are opportunities for integrating students for nonacademic work. Students in the bilingual program can take art, physical education, and other nonacademic classes with their English-speaking peers. In addition, bilingual programs can be integrated into the school rather than separated in a wing of the building, so that teachers from both bilingual and nonbilingual classrooms are encouraged to collaborate on projects.

Two-way bilingual programs provide another opportunity for integration. Few programs have attempted to incorporate both language majority and language minority students in one setting, although the results have generally been quite positive when they have been documented. Collier, for example, in a preliminary follow-up study of one two-way program, found that both the English-speaking and Spanish-speaking students, now in early adulthood, had benefited substantially from their involvement in such a program.[49] They were all still bilingual, years after leaving the program. Even their worldviews and career choices were being influenced directly by their positive experiences in a cross-cultural and bilingual setting. For example, many of the English-speaking graduates of the program were very involved in Spanish-speaking communities in the United States. A great many of the former students had become advocates of multilingual and multicultural education. In addition, most were in college, in spite of the fact that at least the Latinos in the program were from primarily poor and working-class backgrounds and therefore greatly exceeded the average educational expectations for their group. Finally, that English-speaking students had to undergo the difficult process of learning a second language tended to make them more sensitive to the situation of their Spanish-speaking peers and to cultural differences in general.

Other approaches to resolving the integration/segregation dilemma of bilingual education have been explored,[50] for example, setting aside times for joint instruction and setting up bilingual options in desegregation plans and magnet schools. The fact remains, however, that much remains to be done in this regard. Although the programmatic imperatives of separating students for literacy development must be respected, ways to make bilingual education a central concern for all schools have to be found.

SUMMARY

There are numerous ways in which linguistic differences may affect students' learning. Language differences per se are not necessarily barriers to learning, but the history of linguicism in our society has resulted in making them so. Language policies and practices in the United States have ranged from a grudging acceptance of language diversity to outright hostility. We have seen the positive impact that recognizing and affirming students' languages can have on their learning. We have also pointed out some of the issues and concerns that arise when students are separated for instruction, as is often the case with bilingual education.

Bilingual education is certainly not the only approach for dealing with linguistically diverse students. The claim that it can completely reverse the history of failure of linguistic minority students is both unrealistic and naive. Nevertheless, bilingual education still represents the best and most effective program for most students for whom English is a second language. The fact that it alone cannot change the achievement of students is an indication of the complexity of factors that affect learning. Following the case studies, Part II will explore a more comprehensive explanation of school success and failure by taking into account some of these factors.

TO THINK ABOUT

1. Do some research on the "English-only" movement. Can it be considered an example of *linguicism*? Why or why not?
2. Why has the bilingual education debate always been so controversial? Why has it been less controversial at some times than at others? What does this say about the purposes of education?
3. Review the program models of bilingual education as presented in the chapter. Which one is most appropriate in a culturally diverse school? In a school with a primarily Vietnamese student body? In a school with a primarily English-speaking student body? Why?

4. The argument that "My folks made it without bilingual education; why give other folks special treatment?" has often been made, particularly by descendants of European American immigrants. Is this a compelling argument? Why or why not?

5. One of the strongest arguments against bilingual education is that it is in conflict with the goals of equal educational opportunity because students have to be segregated to receive bilingual services. Is this a valid argument? Defend your position based on the research you have read.

6. Some people are offended when the term *English as a Second Language* is used. They believe that English should be the *first* language of everybody who lives in the United States. Why do people react in this way? What would you say to someone who said this?

NOTES

1. An excellent example of a comprehensive and progressive approach to understanding multi-cultural education can be found in Christine E. Sleeter and Carl A. Grant, "A Rationale for Integrating Race, Gender, and Social Class," in *Class, Race, and Gender in American Education*, ed. Lois Weis (New York: State University of New York Press, 1988). Even here, however, language differences are not included as a separate category. Gollnick and Chin, however, have included linguistic diversity as a separate issue in their conceptualization of multicultural education; see Donna M. Gollnick and Philip C. Chin, *Multicultural Education in a Pluralistic Society*, 3rd ed. (New York: Maxwell Macmillan International Publishing, 1990).

2. By *linguicism* she means "*ideologies and structures which are used to legitimate, effectuate and reproduce an unequal division of power and resources (both material and non-material) between groups which are defined on the basis of language. . . .*" See Tove Skutnabb-Kangas, "Multilingualism and the Education of Minority Children," in *Minority Education: From Shame to Struggle*," ed. Tove Skutnabb-Kangas and Jim Cummins (Clevedon, Eng.: Multilingual Matters, 1988), p. 13.

3. Aída Hurtado and Raúl Rodriguez, "Language as a Social Problem: The Repression of Spanish in South Texas," *Journal of Multilingual and Multicultural Development*, 10, 5 (1989), 401–419.

4. Ray Valdivieso and Cary Davis, *U.S. Hispanics: Challenging Issues for the 1990s* (Washington, DC: Population Trends and Public Policy, December 1988).

5. See the studies by Raymond Buriel and Desdemona Cardoza, "Sociocultural Correlates of Achievement Among Three Generations of Mexican American High School Seniors," *American Educational Research Journal*, 25, 2 (1988), 177–192; Francois Nielson and Roberto M. Fernandez, *Hispanic Students in American High Schools: Background Characteristics and Achievement* (Washington, DC: National Opinion Research Center, National Center for Education Statistics, 1981).

6. U.S. General Accounting Office, *Bilingual Education: A New Look at the Research Evidence* (Washington, DC: U.S. Government Printing Office, March 1987).

7. See Selase W. Williams, "Classroom Use of African American Language: Educational Tool or Social Weapon?" in *Empowerment Through Multicultural Education*, Christine E. Sleeter, ed. (Albany NY: State University of New York Press, 1991).

8. Laurence Steinberg, Patricia Lin Blinde, and Kenyon S. Chan, "Dropping Out Among Language Minority Youth," *Review of Educational Research*, 54, 1 (Spring 1984), 113–132.

9. Gary Natriello, Edward L. McDill, and Aaron M. Pallas, *Schooling Disadvantaged Children: Racing Against Catastrophe* (New York: Teachers College Press, 1990).

10. Dorothy Waggoner, "Foreign-Born Children in the U.S. in the Eighties," *NABE Journal*, Fall 1987, pp. 23–49.

11. Cited in John B. Kellogg, "Forces of Change," *Phi Delta Kappan*, November 1988, pp. 199–204.

12. See Sonia Nieto, "Excellence and Equity: The Case for Bilingual Education," *Bulletin of the Council on Interracial Books for Children*," 17, 3 and 4 (1986); *Barriers to Excellence: Our Children at Risk* (Boston: National Coalition of Advocates for Students, 1985); *Federal Education Funding: The Cost of Excellence* (Washington, DC: National Education Association, 1990); *Hispanic Education: A Statistical Portrait* (Washington, DC: National Council of La Raza, 1990).

13. For an excellent description and analysis of the many program models and their implications, see Carlos J. Ovando and Virginia P. Collier, *Bilingual and ESL Classrooms: Teaching in Multicultural Contexts* (New York: McGraw-Hill, 1985).

14. For examples of how children's literacy in their native language is used as the basis for further learning, see Jim Cummins, "The Role of Primary Language Development in Promoting Educational Success for Language Minority Students," in Office of Bilingual Bicultural Education, *Schooling and Language Minority Students: A Theoretical Framework* (Sacramento: Evaluation, Dissemination, and Assessment Center, California State University, 1981); see also Carole Edelsky, "Bilingual Children's Writing: Fact and Fiction," in *Richness in Writing: Empowering ESL Students*, ed. Donna M. Johnson and Duane H. Roen (White Plains, NY: Longman, 1989).

15. The National Clearinghouse for Bilingual Education, Washington, DC, has current data on bilingual programs throughout the country.

16. See Shirley Brice Heath, "Questioning at Home and at School: A Comparative Study," in *Doing the Ethnography of Schooling: Educational Anthropology in Action*, ed. George Spindler (New York: Holt, Rinehart & Winston, 1982); Francois Nielsen and Roberto M. Fernández, *Hispanic Students in American High Schools: Background Characteristics and Achievement* (Washington, DC: National Opinion Research Center, National Center for Education Statistics, 1981); Virginia P. Collier, "How Long? A Synthesis of Research on Academic Achievement in a Second Language," *TESOL Quarterly*, 23, 3 (September 1989), 509–531; Ruben G. Rumbaut and Kenji Ima, *The Adaptation of Southeast Asian Refugee Youth: A Comparative Study*, Final Report. (San Diego: Office of Refugee Resettlement, September 1987).

17. *On Creating a Hispanic America: A Nation Within a Nation?* (Washington DC: Council on Inter-American Security, 1986).

18. Richard L. Warren, "Schooling, Biculturalism, and Ethnic Identity: A Case Study," in *Doing the Ethnography of Schooling: Educational Anthropology in Action*, ed. George Spindler (New York: Holt, Rinehart & Winston, 1982).

19. See, for example, Jim Cummins, "Linguistic Interdependence and the Educational Development of Bilingual Children," *Review of Educational Research*, 49 (Spring 1979), 222–251; Merrill Swain, "Bilingual Education for the English-Speaking Canadian," in *Georgetown University Round Table on Languages and Linguistics 1978: International Dimensions of Bilingual Education*, ed. J. Alatis (Washington, DC: Georgetown University Press, 1978).

20. Diego Castellanos, *The Best of Two Worlds* (Trenton: New Jersey State Department of Education, 1983).

21. Ibid.; see also Gary S. Keller and Karen S. van Hooft, "A Chronology of Bilingualism and Bilingual Education in the United States," in *Bilingual Education for Hispanic Students in the United States*, ed. Joshua Fishman and Gary Keller (New York: Teachers College Press, 1982); Charles Leslie Glenn, Jr., *The Myth of the Common School* (Amherst: University of Massachusetts Press, 1988); David Tyack, *The One Best System: A History of American Urban Education* (Cambridge, MA: Harvard University Press, 1974).

22. As cited by Stephan F. Brumberg, *Going to America, Going to School: The Jewish Immigrant Public School Encounter in Turn-of-the-Century New York City* (New York: Praeger, 1986), p. 7.

23. For a review of some of these policies, see Kenji Hakuta, *Mirror of Language: The Debate on Bilingualism* (New York: Basic Books, 1985).

24. *New York Times*, March 3, 1981.

25. For a review of the "English only" movement, see *English Plus: Issues in Bilingual Education,*" a special issue of *The Annals of the American Academy of Political and Social Science,* ed. Courtney B. Cazden and Catherine E. Snow, 508 (March 1990); Harvey A. Daniels, *Not Only English: Affirming America's Multilingual Heritage* (Urbana, IL: National Council of Teachers of English, 1990).

26. See, for example, W. E. Lambert, "The Two Faces of Bilingual Education," *Focus*, No. 3 (Rosslyn, VA: National Clearinghouse for Bilingual Education, 1980); "An Overview of Issues in Immersion Education," in *Studies on Immersion Education: A Collection for U.S. Educators* (Sacramento: California State Department of Education, 1984); G. R. Tucker, "Implications for U.S. Bilingual Education: Evidence from Canadian Research," *Focus*, No. 2 (Rosslyn VA: National Clearinghouse for Bilingual Education, 1980).

27. See, for example, Kenji Hakuta, *Bilingualism and Bilingual Education: A Research Perspective*, No. 1 (Washington, DC: National Clearinghouse for Bilingual Education, Spring 1990); A. C. Willig, "A Meta-Analysis of Selected Studies on the Effectiveness of Bilingual Education," *Review of Educational Research*, 55 (1985), 269–317; James Crawford, *Bilingual Education: History, Politics, Theory, and Practice* (Trenton, NJ: Crane Publishing, 1988); Cummins, "Role of Primary Language."

28. See Christina Bratt Paulston, *Bilingual Education: Theories and Issues* (Rowley, MA: Newbury House, 1980); *Locked In/Locked Out: Tracking and Placement Practices in Boston Public Schools* (Boston: Massachusetts Advocacy Center, March 1990).

29. Hakuta, *Mirror of Language*.

30. Aaron Jones, "Why Being Bilingual Is Important to Me and My Family," award-winning essay reported in *NABE News*, February 1, 1991, p. 13.

31. This research was reported in "The NABE No-Cost Study on Families," *NABE News*, February 1, 1991, p. 7.

32. For research on additive and subtractive bilingualism, see W. E. Lambert, "Culture and Language as Factors in Learning and Education," in *Education of Immigrant Students*, ed. A. Wolfgang (Toronto: OISE, 1975); Collier, "How Long?"

33. J. Campos and R. Keatinge, "The Carpinteria Language Minority Student Experience: From Theory, to Practice, to Success," in *Minority Education: From Shame to Struggle*, ed. Tove Skutnabb-Kangas and Jim Cummins (Clevedon, Eng.: Multilingual Matters, 1988).

34. For a study on the effectiveness of immersion, see "Adequate Motivation and Bilingual Education," *Southwest Journal of Linguistics*, 9, 2 (1990). The results of the large-scale study were first reported by Jim Crawford, "Immersion Method Is Faring Poorly in Bilingual Study," *Education Week*, 5 (April 23, 1986), pp. 1, 10; and later by Julie A. Miller, "Native-Language Instruction Found to Aid LEP's," *NABE News*, 14, 3 (December 1, 1990). Although its results were withheld from the general public for a long time, the report was finally officially released in March 1991; see J. David Ramirez, *Final Report: Longitudinal Study of Structured English Immersion Strategy, Early-Exit and Late-Exit Transitional Bilingual Education Programs for Language Minority Children* (Washington, DC: Office of Bilingual Education, 1991). This massive study of 4,000 students of limited English proficiency was proposed and funded by the Reagan administration, which was openly hostile to bilingual education.

35. The Massachusetts Advocacy Center, for instance, has found that bilingual education in Boston appears to act as a "buffer" against dropping out. See *Locked In/Locked Out*.

36. *Lau v. Nichols*, 414 U.S. 563 (1974).

37. Equal Educational Opportunities Act of 1974, 20 U.S.C. 1703 (f).

38. See Meyer Weinberg, *A Chance to Learn: A History of Race and Education in the U.S.* (Cambridge: Cambridge University Press, 1977); Cummins, "Linguistic Interdependence"; Hurtado and Rodriguez, "Language as a Social Problem"; Deirdre F. Jordan, "Rights and Claims of Indigenous People," in *Minority Education: From Shame to Struggle*, ed. Tove Skutnabb-Kangas and Jim Cummins (Clevedon, Eng.: Multilingual Matters, 1988); Hakuta, *Mirror of Language*.

39. According to U.S. English, a national organization founded in 1983 "to preserve our national unity by protecting our common language—English" (from their promotional brochure), there are currently 17 states with official English-only laws. See "U.S. English—A Common Language Benefits Our Nation and All Its People" (Washington, DC: U.S. English, n.d.).

40. Walter J. Landry, "Future *Lau* Regulations: Conflict Between Language Rights and Racial Nondiscrimination," in *Theory, Technology, and Public Policy on Bilingual Education*, ed. Raymond V. Padilla (Rosslyn, VA: National Clearinghouse for Bilingual Education, 1983).

41. Skutnabb-Kangas, "Multilingualism and the Education of Minority Children."

42. Cummins, *Empowering Minority Students*, p. 51.

43. Martha Montero-Sieburth, "*Echar Pa'lante*, Moving Onward: The Dilemmas and Strategies of a Bilingual Teacher," *Anthropology and Education Quarterly*, 18, 3 (September 1987), 180–189.

44. Nancy L. Commins, "Language and Affect: Bilingual Students at Home and at School," *Language Arts*, 66, 1 (January 1989), 29–43.

45. Ibid., p. 38.

46. Cummins, "The Role of Primary Language Development in Promoting Educational Success"; see also the research synthesis by Collier, "How Long?" for an excellent review of pertinent studies.

47. Henry T. Trueba, "Instructional Effectiveness: English-Only for Speakers of Other Languages? *Education and Urban Society*, 20, 4 (August 1988), 341–362.

48. Landry, "Future *Lau* Regulations."

49. Virginia P. Collier, "Academic Achievement, Attitudes, and Occupations Among Graduates of Two-Way Bilingual Classes," paper presented at the annual meeting of the American Educational Research Association, San Francisco, March 1989.

50. Tony Baez, "Desegregation and Bilingual Education: Legal and Pedagogical Imperatives," *Bulletin of the Council on Interracial Books for Children*," 17, 3 and 4 (1986).

Manuel Gomes
"It's kind of scary at first, especially if you don't know the language."[1]

The first thing you notice about Manuel Gomes is that he is constantly on the move, as if the engine has started and he is ready to shift to fourth without moving through the other gears. Of slight stature and with a somewhat rumpled look, Manuel has an infectious and lively sense of humor and a generally positive attitude about life. Manuel is 19 years old and will be graduating from high school this year.

In many urban high schools, 19 is no longer a late age to graduate, although the average age used to be lower. Many immigrant students graduate quite late. According to a national study, immigrant and refugee students are more likely to be retained in-grade, inappropriately placed in special education, and at risk of being placed in low academic tracks on the basis of language barriers or slow academic progress. That Manuel has graduated is noteworthy, for the same study reports that the dropout rate for foreign-born students is close to 70 percent.[2]

Manuel came to Boston with his family from the Cape Verde Islands when he was 11 years old. Even before its independence from Portugal in 1975, Cape Verde had a huge out-migration of its population. Official documents estimate that close to 180,000 Cape Verdeans emigrated voluntarily between 1970 and 1973, some 20,000 to the United States alone. The process of emigration had begun with the arrival of North American whaling boats from New England in the late seventeenth century. By the end of the nineteenth century, there was already a sizable Cape Verdean community in Massachusetts. Currently, well over twice as many Cape Verdeans reside abroad than live at home. The 325,000 who live in the United States (about equal to the number who reside on the islands) is the largest Cape Verdean community outside of Cape Verde.[3]

Having suffered from more than 400 years of colonial neglect under Portugal, Cape Verde, an archipelago of ten large and several smaller islands off the West Coast of Africa, was left in poor economic and social condition. For example, the literacy rate in 1981 was 14 percent, a testament to the few educational opportunities available to the majority of the people. Since independence, the situation has improved remarkably, and the literacy rate in 1987 was over 57 percent.[4] Although the official language of the islands is Portuguese, the lingua franca is Crioulo, an Afro-Portuguese creole.

Most Cape Verdeans live in the New England states, especially Rhode Island and Massachusetts. Manuel's family, like most, came to the United States for economic reasons. Although formerly farmers in Cape Verde, they quickly settled into the urban scene. His father found a job cleaning offices downtown at night. His mother stayed home to take care of the many children. They settled in Boston, which has a large Cape Verdean community, and currently live in a three-decker home with apartments that are used by other members of the large family. The neighborhood was once a working-class Irish community and is now multiracial, with a big Catholic church close by and Vietnamese and Cape Verdean restaurants up the street. The older homes, the din on the street, and the crowding all add to the sense of an aging but still struggling urban community.

Manuel is the youngest of 11 children and the first in his family to graduate from high school. He was in a bilingual program for several years after arriving in Boston. The language of instruction in the program was Crioulo. The State Assembly of Massachusetts passed legislation in 1977 distinguishing Crioulo as a language separate from Portuguese and required that Crioulo-speaking students be placed in separate programs from those for Portuguese-speaking students.[5] The result was a scramble to locate Crioulo-speaking teachers and aides and to develop appropriate materials since few or none had existed previously. The rationale behind placing Cape Verdean students in a separate program, notwithstanding the administrative problems it may have created, was a sound pedagogical one: Students should be taught in the language they speak and understand, not in their second or third language.

Another result of separating the program was that a strong sense of community among teachers, students, and parents developed. Some of the teachers and other staff in the program, for example, are quite involved in the life of the community, and thus the separation that often exists between school and home, especially for immigrant children, was lessened. Manuel's participation in the bilingual program proved to be decisive in his education because it allowed a less traumatic transition to the English language and U.S. culture. Nevertheless, he constantly refers to how hard it has been to "fit in," both in school and in society in general.

Boston, like most big cities in the United States, is a highly diverse metropolitan area. It is not unusual to walk from street to street and hear languages from all over the world, smell the foods of different continents, and hear the music of a wide variety of cultures. In spite of this diversity and perhaps in part because of it, the city is not without its tensions, including diverse economic vested interests and interethnic hostility. These tensions are evident in many arenas, including the schools. The attendant problems of court-ordered desegregation, with a long and tumultuous history in the city, are still apparent. The city's schools, for example, have experienced a vast decrease in the percentage of White and middle-class students since desegregation began. In addition, whereas the public schools of Boston were once highly regarded, they have lost much of their prestige in the last two decades.

Manuel's plans for the future are sketchy, but right now he is working in a downtown hotel and would like to use the accounting skills he learned in high school to find a job at a bank. His positive experience in a theater class as a sophomore, along with his great enthusiasm and expressiveness, make him want to continue in the acting field, perhaps doing commercials. He has begun making inquiries about this possibility. He has also talked of continuing his education and may register in a community college in the near future.

Manuel is excited and proud of graduating from high school but reflects on how difficult it has been to achieve. This is the major theme that characterizes Manuel's experiences, both as a student and as an immigrant to this society. The important roles that he and members of his family have played for one another is another key issue. Finally, the mediating role of bilingual education has probably been pivotal in his success as a student. Each of these themes will be explored further.

THE PAIN AND FEAR OF IMMIGRATION

We have a different way of living in Cape Verde than in America. Our culture is totally different, so we have to start a different way of living in America. . . . It's kind of confusing when you come to America, you know.

I liked going to school in Cape Verde, you know, 'cause you know everybody and you have all your friends there. . . .

In our country, we treat people different. There's no crime. You don't have to worry about people jumping you, taking your money. Or walking at night by yourself. There's no fear for that, you know. . . . In Cape Verde, you don't have to worry about something happening to your child or you don't have to worry about using drugs.

My father and mother used to work on plantations. We used to grow potatoes; we used to grow corn; we used to grow beans and stuff like that. . . . We had a lot of land. Every season, we farmed. . . . We had cows. Me and my brother used to feed the cows and take them to walk and give them water to drink and stuff like that. We used to sell our milk to rich folks and I used to deliver there. It was kinda fun. These rich people, every time I'd go there, they'd feed me, which I liked very much [*laughs*]. They used to give me cake and stuff like that, cookies. I liked that. . . .

We'd have a lot of crops and we'd give some away to poor people, those that don't have any. . . . We had a lot of friends and stuff like that.

When we came to America, it was totally different. . . .

In Cape Verde, they have this rumor that it's easier to make a living up here. So everybody wants to come up here. They have this rumor that once you get here, you find money all around you, you know. So, when you're like coming up here, they make a big commotion out of it. "Oh, you're going to America, rich country," and stuff like that. So they think once you come here, you got it made . . . you're rich. People in our country actually think that *we're* rich here, that we are filthy rich, that money surrounds us, we eat money!

I was disappointed in a lot of ways, especially with the crime, especially with the kids. They don't respect each other, they don't respect their parents. It's very different here. It's very tough.

I was afraid. I had people jumping me a few times, trying to take my wallet and stuff like that. . . . It's a scary situation.

It didn't really bother me, but like what got to me, is if they try to start a fight with you, you go to tell like a teacher, they couldn't do nothing about it. That's what got to me, you know.

It was a few students. I know this kid, this big Black kid, he tried to fight me like three times. Then I had a brother that was going to the same middle school so he had a fight with my brother, my big brother. After that, it calmed down a little bit, you know.

Kids might try to stab you if you probably step on them. . . . That happened to me once. I stepped on this kid's sneaker once and he tried to fight me. He said, "What you doing?" I said that I'm sorry and he said, "That's not enough," and he tried to punch me. He didn't, but he was very furious.

You gotta get used to it. That's why a lot of Cape Verdean kids, when they get here, they change. They become violent, like some of the kids in America. So, it's sad. It's very hard for the parents. The parents are not used to that and it's happening a lot with parents in our neighborhood. It's happening to our family. I have a cousin and his mother tried to commit suicide because her son was dealing drugs and hanging with the wrong crowd, with all these hoods. . . . The son almost died because someone beat him up so bad. And it's sad, you know.

They try to be strict about it, you know. But with kids, they try to copy kids that were born here. They try to be like them. They try to go out and do the stuff that *they're* doing. It's like teen pressure, you know. So, it's very hard, you know. You want to fit in. You like to fit in with the crowd.

If you hang with the wrong crowd, you're going to be in big trouble. You just change, change—and you're going to be a person that you don't want to be. . . . You'll probably end up in jail.

I been here eight years and I never hang with the wrong crowd. I've never used drugs in my life. I've never *smelled* cigarettes. So, I really hate when I see other kids doing it. It's sad when you see especially your friends doing it . . . So I had to say, "Go away. I don't want that life." . . . So I had to separate from them.

I had a hard time finding friends that wasn't doing that stuff like they were doing. . . . It's very hard if you hate what your friends are doing.

Start learning the language was hard for me. And then start making friends, because you gotta start making new friends. . . . When American students see you, it's kinda hard [to] get along with them when you have a different culture, a different way of dressing and stuff like that. So kids really look at you and laugh, you know, at the beginning.

It was difficult like when you see a girl at school that you like. It's kind of difficult to express yourself and tell her the way you feel about her, you know. When you don't even know the language, it's kind of hard. I had a hard time.

I was kind of afraid of school, you know, 'cause it's different when you're learning the language. . . . It's kind of scary at first, especially if you don't know the language and like if you don't have friends there. . . .

Some people are slow to learn the language and some just catch it up easy. It wasn't easy for me. It's kinda hard for me, like the pronunciation of the words and stuff like that. Like in Portuguese and in English, they're different. It's kinda hard, you know.

I don't think I want to be an American citizen. . . . To tell you the truth, I don't like America at all. . . . I like it but I don't like the life-styles. It's different from my point of view. What I'm thinking of doing is work in America for ten years and go back to my country because America's a violent country. It's dangerous with crime, with drugs.

ROLE REVERSALS WITHIN THE FAMILY

I took [my father] to the hospital. Then I found out that he had cancer. I didn't wanna tell him. The doctor told me that he had cancer. I didn't wanna tell him because he hates to get sick and he hates to die! He hates to die. If you tell him he's gonna die, he'll kill you before he dies!

This happened when I was in school so I was missing school a lot. . . . He was really sick, you know.

I was the only one that was able to understand the language and stuff like that. . . . It actually got to the point that *I* had to tell him. It was like sad when I had to tell him because it's very hard to tell him that he had cancer. . . .

I was worried. And I had to explain to the whole family. And the doctor, I had to translate for him and stuff like that, tell him what's going on. And I had to tell the whole family that he was sick and stuff like that. It was really hard for me, you know.

Because they don't speak English, I have to go places with them to translate and stuff like that. So I'm usually busy. . . . We have a big family, you know. I have to help them out.

If I felt like I had support from my family, if they only knew the language. . . . If they were educated, I could make it big, you see what I'm saying? . . . I would've had a better opportunity, a better chance.

I'm very happy about [graduating]. It means a lot to me. It means that I did something that I'm very proud. It feels good, you know. And I'd really like to continue in my education, because you know, I'm the first one. And I want to be successful with my life.

I just wanted to help them, you know. I wanted to be the one to help them, you know? They didn't support me, but I wanted to support them.

My mother's proud of me. My father is too. . . .

It was tough for me when I found out that my father had cancer because, you know, I really wanted to graduate. I just want to show him that I can be somebody, you know? I actually did this, try to graduate from high school, for *him*, you know? I just try to do this for him.

BILINGUAL EDUCATION AS LINGUISTIC AND CULTURAL MEDIATOR

A Cape Verdean person is usually, he looks like he's a nice person, educated, you know. Not all of them, but like 70 percent of Cape Verdeans, they look educated. . . . They're not violent. . . . You can tell someone is Cape Verdean . . . if he starts pointing at you. That's a sign that he's Cape Verdean automatic. If he starts staring at you, he's Cape Verdean.

We have problems when we look at American people. They might think we are talking about them and stuff like that. So we have to change that behavior. We have to get used to not pointing at people and not looking at them very much, because American people are not used to people staring at them. . . .

What we do in our country, we *observe* people. It don't mean nothing to us Cape Verdeans. It's just normal. But if we do it to an American person, it makes that American person nervous, I guess, and he would ask you, "What are you looking at?" or "Why are you looking at me?" and start questioning and probably start trouble with you.

It's normal to us. That's why other people got to understand that not everybody has the same culture; not everybody is the same. So some people don't understand.

Like a Spanish [Hispanic] person, what he usually do, they use their body in a different way. . . . With Spanish, what they do, they point with their lips. They go [*demonstrates puckering of the lips*]. So, that's different. Other cultures, they might use their head; they might use their eyebrows.

It's good to understand other people's culture from different countries. America is made up of different countries and we all should know a little bit about each one's cultures.

I think [teachers] could help students, try to influence them, that they can do whatever they want to do, that they can be whatever they want to be, that they got opportunities out there. . . . Most schools don't encourage kids to be all they can be.

What they need to do is try to know the student before they influence him. If you don't know a student, there's no way to influence him. If you don't know his background, there's no way you are going to get in touch with him. There's no way you're going to influence him if you don't know where he's been.

You cannot forget about [your culture], you know. It's part of you. You can't forget something like that. . . . You gotta know who you are. You cannot deny your country and say, "I'm an American; I'm not Cape Verdean."

That's something that a lot of kids do when they come to America. They change their names. Say you're Carlos, they say, "I'm Carl." . . . They wanna be American; they're not Cape Verdean. . . . That's wrong. They're fooling themselves.

I identify myself as Cape Verdean. I'm Cape Verdean. I cannot be an American because I'm not an American. That's it.

[*When asked to describe himself as a student, Manuel answers, with his ever-present sense of humor, "I'm not a genius!" He goes on to say, however*] I know that I can do whatever I want to do in life. Whatever I want to do, I know I could make it. I believe that strongly.

COMMENTARY

Manuel's voice is eloquent in expressing the concerns he has had as an immigrant and a student, concerns related to his academic success and his motivation for graduating and possibly continuing his education.

Behind the sometimes forced enthusiasm he displays, Manuel's voice is also tinged with sadness at what might have been. His expression changes when discussing his early experiences in Cape Verde. In spite of the obviously difficult circumstances of going to school, where he was in a crowded, one-room schoolhouse with many other students of all ages and where corporal punishment was a common practice—which made going to school "scary"—Manuel seems to have idealized his experiences there. The harsh life seems to have been forgotten over the years, although Manuel does admit that he did not like farming. Nonetheless, life in Cape Verde was, at least when he reflects on it now, easier and more familiar. Manuel often contrasts the crime and violence in the United States with a now idealized and bucolic childhood in Cape Verde. He also compares child-rearing styles, the respect children learn and show adults, and the priority on making "quick money" in this society with other values in Cape Verde.

Manual describes, with obvious pain, what it was like being perceived as "different" by his peers. For example, other kids would call him names ("foreign and stuff like that") and ridicule him ("it really gets to a student when other students make fun"). The situation changed after he reached high school, but those first years are indelibly etched in his memory.

The distress caused by immigration is many-faceted. Not only do immigrants leave behind a country that is loved and an existence that is, if not comfortable, at least familiar, but they also leave a language and culture that can never find full expression in their adopted country. In addition, they are coming into a situation that in spite of the many rich possibilities it may offer, is frightening and new. Manuel is ambivalent about his experience in this country. He does not yet have U.S. citizenship and he is not sure that he wants it.

Several of the painful incidents described by Manuel focus on interethnic rivalries and violence. This situation is a guarded secret, especially at many middle schools and senior high schools. School officials, perhaps fearful of being labeled racists, are reluctant to confront the prejudicial behaviors and actions of one group of students toward another, whether they involve conflicts between Black and White students or between different students of color. Yet the issue is a real one and is becoming more apparent all the time. Racial stereotypes and epithets are quite commonplace and evident in the most seemingly sensitive students; for example, Manuel's comment about a "big Black kid," a term often used when referring to African American youths, reinforces the negative stereotype of Blacks as frightening and violent.

In hearings across the country, the National Coalition of Advocates for Students (NCAS) uncovered racial tension between newcomers and native-born students and among immigrant groups themselves. Incidents included name-calling, mimicking, actual fights, and gang activity. Parents and children alike frequently reported being afraid of the crime and violence in the schools. The NCAS attributed such tensions primarily to the lack of comprehensive multicultural education. In addition, they found that immigrant students were frequently at the very bottom of the ranking order in high schools.[6]

Another issue is the role reversal many immigrant children experience with their parents as a result of their parents' lack of English fluency. Manuel carries out a pivotal role in his family, being the "public face" that interacts with the greater community. Thus he is the one to deal with "the system," whether schools, clinics, or other agencies in the community. Manuel's role of translator was especially vivid when his father developed cancer a couple of years ago. Because his parents speak little English, Manuel was placed in the extraordinary position of being the one to tell him that he had cancer! He was very much affected by this experience, especially as the cancer was considered terminal. Manuel's words express the great apprehension he felt in telling his father the news. Moreover, after he told his father he had cancer, he also had to tell him that he needed an operation. This was tremendously difficult to do, given his father's memories of the seriousness of surgery in Cape Verde, where it was used only as a last resort and where, according to Manuel, chances of recovery were slim. Although his father seems to have recovered from the cancer, against all the odds, the experience left Manuel quite shaken. His grades also suffered during that period.

This important but often draining responsibility in his family is familiar to others in Manuel's situation but not always known by teachers and schools. According to the NCAS report, the role of "interpreter and arbiter" is carried out by approximately half of all immigrant students, often resulting in the transfer of authority and status from parents to children, which, in turn can lead to further conflicts at home. In addition, it often takes students away from school to attend to family business.[7] Teachers not accustomed to this kind of adult responsibility often interpret students' absences and lateness as a sign that their parents do not care about education or that the students are irresponsible. Frequently, just the opposite is true. That is, it is precisely the most responsible young people who are kept home to attend to important family concerns. In addition, the judgment that parents do not care about the education of their children is based on the assumption that schooling is the most important factor in their lives. For families struggling to survive in a hostile environment, this assumption is often erroneous.

This does not mean that parents are oblivious to the benefits of education but rather that they need support in attending to their basic needs. Here is where the school, as an advocate of children and their families, can come in, by helping to locate needed services or helping parents devise ways to attend to family needs while not keeping their children home.

Whereas the role of family arbiter has obviously made Manuel mature beyond his years, the other side of the coin is that he has had to count on himself for many things. Because his family is not fluent in English, they have been unable to give him the help he needs in school. They rarely went to school, for example. Parent involvement in schools in most countries is minimal. The feeling is that once students are in school, it is the school's responsibility to educate them. The parents, in essence, hand over their children to the school in the hope that the school will educate them. Once again, however, to jump to the conclusion that these parents do not care about education is to miss the mark. Rather, most economically oppressed parents see the role of education as extremely important and stress this to their children constantly. Using this belief as the basis for involving parents in their children's education can lead to very positive results, as has been proven in a number of projects.[8]

That the bilingual program acted as a linguistic and cultural mediator is evident in many of Manuel's comments. For example, he is extremely perceptive about culture and its manifestations. This is an issue that comes up repeatedly in bilingual programs, in which culture and language become the very focus of the educational experience. The description of how his Latino classmates use their lips to point rather than their fingers demonstrates Manuel's great sensitivity and sophistication in this area. Few teachers, even those who work with children from different cultures, pick up these sometimes subtle cues.

Manuel has also been able to maintain the cultural meanings attached to particular terms, as seen in his use of the term *educated* to describe Cape Verdeans. Manuel is referring to the connotation for the word used by various ethnic groups such as Portuguese speakers, including Cape Verdeans, and Hispanics. That is, besides referring to being schooled, it also means someone who is respectful and polite; when used with children, it has the added meaning of being obedient.

By the time he got to high school, Manuel had learned enough English to be able to speak up. The bilingual program at the high school was a "safe environment" for him and other Cape Verdean students. It is a rather large program, much more so than the one at the middle school, and most of the teachers and some of the other staff are Cape Verdean as well. Cape Verdean students in the city have a strong identification with this high school and look forward to attending. There is also a close-knit sense of community within the program. In fact, it has always been one of the more constructive and distinguishing characteristics of this particular urban school.

Manuel's bilingual program was a positive one for a number of other reasons as well. For example, the staff is quite involved with and connected to the community. Cape Verdean students are usually looked on very positively by all staff members, who consider them well behaved and more serious than other students in the school. The generally high expectations teachers may have of them may have an impact on their achievement. Ogbu's theory of "voluntary" and "involuntary" immigrant status seems to hold some validity in this case.[9] Nevertheless, in recent years, problems similar to those experienced by U.S.-born students are surfacing in Manuel's school and community. For example, some Cape Verdean staff members in his high school are becoming increasingly concerned with the rising rate of teen pregnancy and intergenerational conflicts in the community. Whether they will affect the academic achievement of the Cape Verdean students in the school remains to be seen, but it is an issue about which the staff seems to be concerned.

Manuel speaks fondly of his experiences with the teachers and students in the program. He says that it was "more comfortable" for him there. The program also helped mediate his experiences in the rest of the school and in his community in general. For example, he remembers the theater workshop that he took as a sophomore. Although it was not part of the bilingual program and all the skits were in English, it focused on similar issues. He still recalls with great enthusiasm a monologue he did about a student going to a new school. He could identify with him because it was so reminiscent of his own experiences. The theater class always had a mixture of students of diverse backgrounds and language skills, so it was a place to deal with communication and interpersonal skills in an active way. The performances allow students to use a lot of different skills and draw on their experiences for content.

The bilingual program was able to help Manuel retain his language and culture and, with it, his ties to his family and community. It has given him something to hold onto. Even this kind of program, however, is not enough if it is not part of a larger whole that affirms the diversity of all within it. It, and other bilingual programs like it, become tiny islands in a sea of homogeneity and pressure to conform.

The tension is well expressed by Manuel when he pits being Cape Verdean against being American. The possibility that he could be *both* Cape Verdean and American is not perceived as an option. That is, if he identifies with being American, he is abandoning his culture and country; if he chooses to remain Cape Verdean, his possibilities in this society are limited. These are hard choices for young people to make and are part of the pain of living in a culture that has a rigid definition of "American."

It is obvious that Manuel has not fully come to terms with his experience in the United States. He has had a difficult time with "fitting in" but is also uncompromising about keeping his culture and language. This tension is not unusual for students who have gone through the pain of uprooting. The transition is always a difficult one and may take many years. How much he can assimilate, how far he wants to go in adjusting, how much he feels ambivalent or disappointed about his opportunities here are issues for Manuel to resolve. The pain that this balancing act has caused is evident in his conflict over his future in this country.

One of the ways he has chosen to deal with ambivalence is by joining and becoming very active in a fundamentalist Christian church. As Manuel so eloquently expressed it, "That's the place I belong to. I fit there. I felt that God had moved there. Jesus got hold of me. He said, 'Calm down.' "

A number of issues were apparently influential in leading Manuel to this particular church. For example, it was about the time that his father developed cancer and Manuel was immersed in his role as "the man of the family." It was also around the time that he decided to drop some of his friends (as he said, "It's very hard if you hate what your friends are doing"). In looking for something to keep him on track, as the bilingual program and other cultural supports had done previously, he looked toward the community. Although Manuel had been raised a Catholic, the local Catholic church was completely unappealing to him. This, too, became an issue of "fitting in." It was apparent that the Catholic church had made few accommodations to its newest members, many of whom were immigrants who spoke little or no English. His new church, however, seems to have made some accommodations to welcome Cape Verdeans, and Manuel finally feels he has found a place to fit in.

Manuel has had the good sense, throughout his life in the United States, to follow the sound advice of kin and to seek the kind of support that would help him succeed. He has overcome many barriers and has now graduated from high school, a tremendous accomplishment when seen in the social and historical context in which he lives. That he has emerged with a few scars is not surprising. Insecurity about his life in the United States, what his future holds for him, how to resolve the issues to identity and "fitting in" are all problems that he must continue to cope with. Manuel is now at a crossroads. Given his resolve, one clearly has the feeling that he will succeed in life as he has in school.

TO THINK ABOUT

1. Explain some of the ways in which Manuel's experience as an immigrant have been frightening and painful.
2. Why has Manuel idealized his former life on the Cape Verde Islands?
3. What accounts for Manuel's highly developed sensitivity to cultural differences?

4. Given Manuel's many absences from school during his father's illness, it is probable that school authorities and teachers assumed that his family was wrong in keeping him home to attend to family business. What do you think? What could the school have done to accommodate his family's needs?

5. Why is it important for Manuel to graduate ''for'' his father?

6. In what ways do you think the bilingual program acted as a *linguistic* and *cultural mediator* for Manuel?

7. Do you understand why Manuel feels reluctant to identify as ''American''? How would you approach this issue if he were one of your students?

NOTES

1. I am grateful to Carol Shea for the interviews and transcriptions and for many valuable insights for the development of this case study.
2. *New Voices: Immigrant Students in U.S. Public Schools* (Boston: National Coalition of Advocates for Students, 1988).
3. Colm Foy, *Cape Verde: Politics, Economics, and Society* (London: Pinter Publications, 1988).
4. Ibid.; also Office of Bilingual Bicultural Education, *A Handbook for Teaching Portuguese-Speaking Students* (Sacramento: California State Department of Education, 1983).
5. Office of Bilingual Bicultural Education, *Handbook for Teaching Portuguese-Speaking Students*.
6. *New Voices*.
7. Ibid.
8. See, for example, discussions of the following parent involvement projects in *Minority Education: From Shame to Struggle*, ed. Tove Skutnabb-Kangas and Jim Cummins (Clevedon, Eng.: Multilingual Matters, 1988): Alma Flor Ada, ''The Pajaro Valley Experience: Working with Spanish-Speaking Parents to Develop Children's Reading and Writing Skills Through the Use of Children's Literature''; Ian Curtis, ''Parents, Schools, and Racism: Bilingual Education in a Northern California Town''; S. Jim Campos and H. Robert Keatinge, ''The Carpinteria Language Minority Student Experience: From Theory, to Practice, to Success.''
9. John U. Ogbu, ''Variability in Minority School Performance: A Problem in Search of an Explanation,'' *Anthropology and Education Quarterly*, 18, 4 (December 1987), 312–334.

Yolanda Piedra:

"Once you get the hang of it, you'll start getting practice with people and teachers, no matter if you talk English or Spanish."[1]

Yolanda Piedra did not learn English until she was 7, but at 13 she is equally comfortable in both Spanish and English. Born in Mexico, Yolanda came to California after having completed kindergarten and part of first grade. In this, she and her family are typical of the immigration wave of the 1970s and 1980s. During this time, 28 percent of all newcomers to the United States settled in California, far more than in any other state. In addition, an average 27 percent of all immigrants admitted during these two decades have come from Mexico.[2] In fact, California's Hispanic population is expected to increase by 109 percent to 9.5 million, between 1980 and 2000.[3] By 1989, 10 percent of all school-age children in the United States were Hispanic, and most of these were Mexican American.[4]

Yolanda lives in a mid-size, low- to middle-income city in southern California. The primarily one-family houses, most of which are rented, hide the poverty and difficult conditions in which many of the residents live. Yolanda lives in an economically oppressed, largely Mexican and Chicano community, although there are also smaller numbers of White and Black residents in the city.[5] Until a few years ago, this was a primarily rural area, and farm work is one of the main reasons that Mexicans first came here. Gangs were unknown just a few years ago, but they are now a growing problem. Spreading from the Los Angeles area, gangs are involving more and more young people, especially boys, who sometimes join as young as 13 years of age. The need to deal with the growing gang activity is recognized by residents as their major problem.

Yolanda's parents are separated and she lives with her mother, 12-year-old brother, and 3-year-old sister (both of whom she describes as "wild"). Her brother is what she calls a "troublemaker," frequently getting involved in problems at school. He is beginning to get into trouble in the community as well, which may be a sign that further problems, particularly gang activity, will follow. Her father lives in Mexico, and she rarely sees him. Her mother works in a candy factory. From what Yolanda says, her mother is quite strict with the children, limiting their social interactions and expecting them all to take on family obligations. She is a single parent struggling to survive with her three children in what can best be described as adverse conditions. Her constant message to all of them concerns the importance of getting an education. Yolanda and her family speak mostly Spanish at home, although sometimes they speak English to help her mother "practice."

In spite of the fact that she spoke no English and that the transition to a new school and society was a difficult one, Yolanda recalls mostly positive experiences during her elementary school years. She was in a bilingual program when first entering school and is now in the general education program. Currently an eighth-grader in a primarily Mexican American junior high school, Yolanda is by all accounts a successful student. She is enthusiastic about school and becomes noticeably enlivened when talking about learning and wanting to "make my mind work," as she says. She uses English, her second language, in beautifully expressive ways, making unusual and descriptive constructions, probably influenced by her bilingualism. Yolanda consistently gets high grades in most of her subjects. Her favorite class is physical education and her least favorite is English, although she manages to get A in it as well. Although quite young, Yolanda has narrowed down her future aspirations to two (one not at all consistent with her scholastic success but very much related to the limiting societal expectations based on gender): She would like to be either a computer programmer or a flight attendant.

Yolanda's city contains one of the largest elementary school districts in California. About 60 percent of the students are Hispanic, Whites making up the majority of the remainder; the Black community is small but growing. Her junior high school is situated in what is acknowledged to be a tough barrio and is beset with the same kinds of problems of most inner-city schools: gang activity, drugs, and unmet family needs that may interfere with learning. Yet in both her elementary and junior high schools, there is a feeling of community support. The school is successful with quite a number of its students, but it also faces a great many problems. The school's success may be due in part to the fact that many of the staff are attuned to what is going on in the community. Most teachers seem genuinely concerned about their students. This concern is reflected, for example, in the great number of workshops on issues ranging from gangs to cultural diversity. The Spanish class recently given for staff had a full enrollment, including some high-level administrators.

The number of Latino professionals, however, is very low, although an effort is being made to recruit more; recently, a Latino psychologist was hired. There is also a Latino community liaison, and the principal has an open-door policy for staff, students, and parents, which helps to create a feeling of engagement and support. The staffs in both of the schools Yolanda has attended have made conscious efforts to include and affirm aspects of Mexican culture and experience in the curriculum and in extracurricular activities. Yolanda's positive feelings about her school experiences are in part a reflection of the environments these schools have tried to create.

One of the youngest students to be involved in this project, Yolanda Piedra is nevertheless a very mature young woman who is quite certain about many things: the importance of communication; the benefits of being Mexican and speaking Spanish; and the necessity of surrounding oneself with support from teachers, family, and peers.

COMMUNICATION

My mom . . . takes really good care of me. . . . She talks to me [about] problems and everything. . . . My mom says that they want me to go to school. That way, I won't be stuck with a job like them. They want me to go on, try my best to get something I want and not be bored . . . to get a job that I like and feel proud of it.

She wants everything kind of like good, perfect, not perfect, but kind of like the best I could do.

I feel proud of myself when I see a [good] grade. And like I see a C, I'm gonna have to put this grade up. And I try my best. . . . When I get a C, my mom doesn't do anything to me 'cause she knows I try my best. . . . Well, she tells me how to work it out.

[*Although her mother is not involved in school activities, Yolanda makes it clear that when it is important, her mother is there.*] First of all, 'cause she understands English, but she's just embarrassed, shy to talk. . . . And 'cause she's always busy.

Like when it's something important for me, like, "Mom, I'm gonna do this, I want you to be there," she'll be there no matter what.

[*In fact, Yolanda prefers not to have her mother too involved or to have her visit school too frequently.*] If she takes too much care of me when I'm at home, now at school I'll be dead!

[When I'm older, I want to] take my mom places and just be with my mom all the time.

I'd say [to teachers], "Get along more with the kids that are not really into themselves. . . . Have more communication with them." . . . I would get along with the students. 'Cause you learn a lot from the students. That's what a lot of teachers tell me. They learn more from their students than from where they go study. . . . I would help people get along with each other. 'Cause actually what they do around here, is that they see them doing trouble and everything, what they really are is suspending them. . . . They're really pushing them to do it again.

SURROUNDING ONESELF WITH SUCCESS

Actually, there's one friend of mine . . . she's been with me since first grade until eighth grade, right now. And she's always been with me, in bad or good things, all the time. She's always telling me, "Keep on going and your dreams are gonna come true."

Actually, when I got here, I didn't want to stay here, 'cause I didn't like the school. And after a little while, in third grade, I started getting the hint of it and everything and I tried real hard in it. . . .

I really got along with the teachers a lot. . . . Actually, 'cause I had some teachers, and they were always calling my mom, like I did a great job. Or they would start talking to me, or they kinda like pulled me up some grades, or moved me to other classes, or took me somewhere. And they were always congratulating me.

[*What Yolanda remembers most about her early school experiences are the Cinco de Mayo festivities.*[6]] That's my favorite month, 'cause I like dancing. And over there, in [elementary school] they had these kinds of dances, and I was always in it. . . . It's kind of like a celebration.

Sometimes you get all tangled up with the grades or school or the teachers, 'cause you don't understand them. But you have to get along with them and you have to work for it.

So, actually, I feel good about it because I like working, making my mind work

[*Yolanda was recently selected Student of the Month. Her picture is prominently displayed in the main hall of the school.*] They take her [student of the month] out, and they call her up, and they take her to dinner with the principal. They give her a certificate and they get her picture over there.

I'm in a folkloric dance. [Teachers] say, "Oh, Yolanda, this is coming up. Do you want to go? I know you dance. . . ."

They brought a show last time, about air and jets. . . . And some lady was working around there. . . . The vice-principal came up to me: "That's a good chance for you, 'cause I know you talk Spanish and English. . . ."

They just really get along with me. They tell what their lives are . . . and they compare them with mine. We really get along with each other. . . . Actually, it's fun around here if you really get into learning.

My social studies class is kind of like really hard for me. But some of the things, I don't know, I find really interesting. . . . I like learning. I like really getting my mind working for that.

[My English teacher] doesn't get along with any of us. She just does the things and sits down.

Materials [in classes] are too low. I mean, they have enough materials and everything, but I mean . . . the kind of problems they have. . . . They're too low. . . . We are
supposed to be doing higher things. And like they take us too slow, see, step by step. And
that's why everybody takes it as a joke.

[Education] It's good for you. . . . It's like when you eat. It's like if you don't eat
in a whole day, you feel weird. You have to eat. That's the same thing for me.

THE BENEFITS OF BEING MEXICAN

I feel proud of myself. I see some other kids that they say, like they'd say they're Co-
lombian or something. They try to make themselves look cool in front of everybody. I
just say what I am and I feel proud of myself. . . . I don't feel bad like if they say, "Ooh,
she's Mexican" or anything. . . . It's like you get along with everything; you're Spanish
and English, and you understand both. . . . Once you get the hang of it, you'll start getting practice with people and teachers . . . no matter if you talk English or Spanish.

For me, it's good. For other people, some other guys and girls, don't think it's nice;
it's like, "Oh, man, I should've been born here instead of being over there." Not me,
it's O.K. for me being born over there 'cause I feel proud of myself. I feel proud of
my culture.

COMMENTARY

The importance of communication emerges as a central theme. Whether discussing family,
school, or friends, Yolanda sees communication as crucial for success. Although she says
she used to have problems with her mother, they now get along very well. Given the primacy
of the family in Mexican and Mexican American culture, this consistent communication has
had a positive influence.[7] Yolanda sees it as one aspect of her mother's care. She and her
mom "communicate," she says, because they talk to one another about many things, including "girl stuff."

Grades provide another issue for Yolanda and her mother to communicate about. They
are important, but only in the sense that they motivate her to work harder. "You feel some
of your body falling off when you see F's around your grades," she says dramatically.

Yolanda's mother is typical of other Mexican parents in her desire to have her children
succeed in school. She talks to them about the importance of school and supports their
accomplishments, but she may be unclear about how else to help them succeed. Delgado-
Gaitán worked with several Mexican and Mexican American parents to determine their "folk
theory of success," or what they perceived success meant in the U.S. context. She found
that their theory of success was based on their low status in this society as well as their
desire to prevent their children from experiencing the same kind of oppression they had
known. Even more significant, however, in every case but one, these parents were unaware
of what was needed for their children to succeed. They knew that their children needed to
learn English, an objective they all supported, but the only other concrete advice they could
give their children was to listen to their teachers and do everything they said.[8]

Given the great emphasis in middle-class families on developing the kinds of attitudes
and behaviors that lead to academic success, families such as Yolanda's are at a distinct

disadvantage. Yolanda's mother has been very successful at imparting certain values and goals to her children. The fact remains, however, that European American, middle-class parents, given their own experiences and exposure to the schools, are much more aware of those activities that lead to academic success than are poor and working-class parents from linguistic and cultural backgrounds different from the mainstream. Although Yolanda's mother has been able to give her great motivation and discipline, she has been unable to give her the actual tools or engage her in some of the activities she may need for further success in school. Imbedded in this situation are implications of the responsibility of the schools to assist such parents. The interaction and support between home and school in supporting the messages and activities each values become important for ensuring the success of all students. Yet in spite of some parents' inability to prepare their children for learning academic skills, communication is at the very least a necessary and important first step. Yolanda seems to understand and appreciate this fact.

Communication in school is equally important. Yolanda thinks carefully about the advice she would give teachers about providing a better education for their students. She would tell teachers to try to understand their students, especially those who hang out in the street, "like people that dress kind of like weird, if you know what I mean."

Gender expectations and the traditional roles assigned to women in her culture as well as the mainstream culture have left their imprint on Yolanda in ways that can be considered both limiting and affirming. She is adamant, for instance, about not wanting to get married. This may represent a liberating decision, given her analysis of marriage. (" 'cause I've been having so many experiences by my family"). However, she has tentatively selected at least one prospective career (flight attendant) that reinforces women's role as servers. Interestingly, she herself describes attendants as "kind of maids." She is still quite young and these plans are likely to change, particularly given Yolanda's great determination and strength of character. In any event, she describes her future as "working, being happy, having fun and freedom," and knowing she is doing the best she can.

A particularly important way for young people to succeed is to surround themselves with people and an environment that supports their success. It can almost be described as a cloak for success, fencing out the negative influences and corraling the positive ones. Yolanda has done so in several ways. For example, she talks about her best friend, the one who "helped me grow up," as the most important person in keeping her motivated. Contrary to conventional wisdom, most adolescents have internalized the values held by the adults who surround them. In looking for friends, therefore, they seek those who voice the same values. Several major reports have found far more congruence than conflict between the worldviews of parents and their teenage children.[9]

Although the junior high school environment makes her feel both "comfortable and afraid," time and again Yolanda mentioned teachers as the pivotal factor in helping her succeed in school. Teachers who "care" have made the difference. Yolanda's articulation of this factor reinforces what national commissions have been reporting for some time.[10] Teachers' caring makes a difference, for example, when children first enter a new school. Yolanda remembers the trauma of moving to California as a first-grader. It was tremendously difficult adjusting to a new culture, community, and school, although she has always been a good student. Yolanda's positive perceptions about learning are bound to the kind of environment that has been established in the school. The culture of her school, for example, emphasizes learning. She is enthusiastic about learning, and this eagerness is especially reserved for her challenging classes.

Whereas Yolanda is quick to ascribe her success to teachers, she has also given some thought to what might be holding her back. She cites "problems at home" and not having her father around as two barriers. At school, she believes that teachers create barriers, too.

For Yolanda, success consists of not only doing well in classes but also enjoying and getting something from them. She criticizes attitudes or practices she feels detract from a positive learning environment. One of these is the low expectations teachers have of some students (materials are "too low.") And although Yolanda herself has benefited from policies that reward some students (Student of the Month, for example), it is worth examining whether practices that foster competition are always beneficial. Clearly, the school is searching for ways to motivate and reward students for their hard work, but falling back on the old standbys that stress competition and exclusion may simply make any attainment unreachable for the majority of students.

Yolanda wants teachers to know about their students' families. She also wants them to understand that unlike some of the stereotypes about Mexican American students, "they try real hard, that's one thing I know." Yet in spite of the criticisms she has of her school and some teachers, Yolanda clearly loves learning. The metaphor of "education as nutrition" is a good example ("It's good for you. . . . It's like when you eat").

Tied to her positive feeling as a student is an equally positive self-concept. Yolanda is quite certain that being Mexican is a good thing. Her culture is important to her. She compares herself to other Mexican American children who deny their background, and it is clear that she feels sorry for them. Her attitude about the benefits of being Mexican can probably be traced to several sources. One is her family, which reinforces cultural pride in the home. Even when this is consciously done, however, it is often not sufficient to counteract many of the negative messages young people pick up about their devalued status in the society in which they live. Frequently, it is the school that makes the difference in whether students accept or reject their culture, as seen in research by Iadicola with sixth-grade Hispanic students in selected schools in California. He examined the relationship between power differences and curriculum factors in schools to explore the "symbolic violence" suffered by the students. "Symbolic violence," as used by Bourdieu, refers to the maintenance of power relations of the dominant society in the school.[11] It is evident in such concrete factors as the presence or absence of specific people, topics, or perspectives in the curriculum or through the power differences among students, staff, and parents. In the curriculum, for example, how "knowledge" is defined, who are portrayed as "makers of history," which heroes are acknowledged and celebrated, and so on determine whether groups of people are either valued or devalued in that environment.

Specifically, according to Iadicola, "symbolic violence is performed through curricular choices and pedagogical techniques which impose within the school the power relations of the larger society."[12] Such a process has succeeded when dominated groups learn to view their own culture as unworthy and to consider themselves to be "culturally deprived." They begin to identify not with their own group but with the dominant group. Iadicola found that the higher the level of Anglo dominance in the school, the higher the level of symbolic violence as measured by Hispanic students' attitudes toward their own group. In contrast, the higher the level of Hispanic presence in the curriculum, the higher the level of ethnic salience in self-identification.[13] The school is crucial in giving students information, both formally and informally, about what knowledge is of most worth. As a consequence of this information, at least partially, students develop either pride or shame in their background.

The fact that she began her early schooling in Mexico, where her culture was affirmed and valued, cannot be dismissed as a contributing factor in Yolanda's sense of worthiness and pride. Matute-Bianchi, for example, in an ethnographic study in California, found that many of the Mexican American students who were doing well in school were born in Mexico.[14] Nevertheless, the role of Yolanda's first elementary school and of her current school in accepting and reflecting at least some aspects of Mexican culture is a contributing factor. The fact that the culture of Hispanic students is at the very least acknowledged in the educational environment seems to have made a difference in how Yolanda and some of her peers react to their ethnicity.

Yolanda Piedra has several more years of schooling to complete. She is a fortunate young woman in the sense that both her elementary and her junior high school have been quite affirming of her culture and language. It is unclear whether the high school she attends will be the same. Nonetheless, she has gotten a good start in a number of ways. First, she knows what it is to be a successful student. Her "track record" may be enough to keep her going in the same path. Second, in spite of many messages in the larger society to the contrary, she has learned the benefits of being Mexican. It is doubtful that she will lose this sense of self in the years to come. And third, Yolanda has learned to enjoy learning, to make "her mind work." At this point, probably nothing can take away that now ingrained zeal for education.

TO THINK ABOUT

1. Many of Yolanda's teachers are resolved to provide a productive and positive environment for her and the other students in her school. Besides the examples given, think of other ways in which that kind of environment could be achieved in this particular school.

2. Yolanda says that when kids are suspended from school, it is "pushing them to do it again." What does she mean? What are the implications for school disciplinary policies?

3. When Yolanda says of her English teacher that "She just does the things and sits down," what does she mean? Why doesn't Yolanda like her?

4. Yolanda has criticized materials in her classes for "being too low." Why do you think she says this? What kinds of practices can schools develop to counteract this perception?

5. Yolanda has been selected Student of the Month for being successful in school. Some would criticize this practice because it alienates and excludes a large number of students; others believe that it helps to motivate good students. What do you think? Why? What other approaches might you recommend?

6. Pride in her culture, her language, and herself in general is obvious in Yolanda. How do you think she developed it?

7. Yolanda's decision to be either a computer programmer or a flight attendant sounds like a contradiction. What factors do you think influenced Yolanda in making this decision? What can schools do to help students make good decisions about their future?

NOTES

1. I am grateful to Mac Morante for the interviews and background information for this case study.

2. *New Voices: Immigrant Students in U.S. Public Schools* (Boston: National Coalition of Advocates for Students, 1988).

3. Carlos E. Cortés, "The Education of Language Minority Students: A Contextual Interaction Model," in *Beyond Language: Social and Cultural Factors in Schooling Language Minority Students* (Los Angeles: Office of Bilingual Education, California State Department of Education, Evaluation, Dissemination, and Assessment Center, 1986).

4. Amy Stuart Wells, *Hispanic Education in America: Separate and Unequal.* ERIC Clearinghouse on Urban Education (New York: Teachers College, Columbia University, 1989).

5. The terms *Mexican, Mexican American,* and *Chicano* are all used here, depending on the context. For example, Yolanda identifies herself as "Mexicana" or Mexican. Other students may use the term *Mexican American* or *Chicano.* These distinctions usually depend on place of birth, upbringing, social class, language used at home, and other factors. For a more detailed discussion of some of these important distinctions, see Concha Delgado-Gaitán, "Parent Perceptions of School: Supportive Environments for Children," in *Success or Failure? Learning and the Language Minority Student,* ed. Henry T. Trueba (Cambridge, MA: Newbury House, 1987).

6. Cinco de mayo is the celebration of Mexican independence from France. On May 5, 1862, French forces that had invaded Mexico were defeated at Puebla. It is one of the most important Mexican holidays and is celebrated in many schools with Mexican American students.

7. See, for example, Daniel Mejia, "The Development of Mexican-American Children"; William A. Vega, Richard L. Hough, and Annelisa Romero, "Family Life Patterns of Mexican-Americans"; and Frank J. Trankina, "Clinical Issues and Techniques in Working with Hispanic Children and Their Families," in *The Psychosocial Development of Minority Group Children,* ed. Gloria Johnson Powell (New York: Brunner/Mazel Publishers, 1983).

8. Delgado-Gaitán, "Parent Perceptions of School."

9. See, for example, Francis A. Ianni, *The Search for Structure: A Report on American Youth Today* (New York: Free Press, 1989); S. Shirley Feldman and Glen R. Elliott, *At the Threshold: The Developing Adolescent* (Cambridge, MA: Harvard University Press, forthcoming).

10. This is also one of the findings of the hearings reported in *Barriers to Excellence: Our Children at Risk* (Boston: National Coalition of Advocates for Students, 1985), and of the report by the National Commission on Secondary Education for Hispanics, *"Make Something Happen":* *Hispanics and Urban School Reform* (Washington, DC: Hispanic Policy Development Project, 1984).

11. See Pierre Bourdieu, *Outline of Theory and Practice* (Cambridge: Cambridge University Press, 1977).

12. Peter Iadicola, "Schooling and Symbolic Violence: The Effect of Power Differences and Curriculum Factors on Hispanic Students' Attitudes Toward Their Own Ethnicity," *Hispanic Journal of Behavioral Sciences,* 5, 1 (1983), 21–43.

13. Ibid.

14. María E. Matute-Bianchi, "Ethnic Identities and Patterns of School Success and Failure Among Mexican-Descent and Japanese-American Students in a California High School: An Ethnographic Analysis," *American Journal of Education,* 95, 1 (1986), 233–255.

Implications of Diversity for Teaching and Learning in a Multicultural Society

OVERVIEW

The stories of the students whose voices you have heard in the preceding pages are compelling examples of strength and resilience, of the capacity to do well and succeed in spite of sometimes overwhelming odds. They have much to teach us about education in a multicultural society. As Yolanda so perceptively said, teachers "learn more from their students than from where they go study." The purpose of this section is to analyze their experiences in a broad conceptual framework of multicultural education and review some of the lessons these young people have to teach us by placing their stories in the socio-political context of our society.

Given the small number of students whose experiences we have presented, a caveat is in order. These young people are not meant to stand for all other students of their ethnic, racial, or economic backgrounds. Each of their stories is unique. As case studies, they provide vivid portraits of the lives and experiences of *particular* students. They are examples of the complex interplay of relationships within families, communities, and schools that define students' struggle for identity and survival. Therefore, overarching claims for the education of *all* students in U.S. society cannot be made. However, it should also be said that these case studies can be extremely helpful in identifying some experiences and viewpoints of students who have been successful in our schools. In spite of the small number of students interviewed, they represent a wide cross section of those enrolled in U.S. schools. These case studies can thus help illuminate some key issues about culture and power relationships and schooling for success in a multicultural society. Furthermore, because the stories of these students have been placed in the particular sociopolitical context of their families, schools, and communities, it is hoped that readers will find useful information for learning about students in similar circumstances. Finally, students, although rarely consulted, are eloquent in expressing their own needs, interests, and concerns. It is in this spirit that their stories and hopes are presented here.

Part II will begin with an analysis of the many factors that can influence school achievement. The purpose of Chapter 7 is to critique some current theories and develop a more comprehensive view for understanding student learning. In Chapter 8, a definition of multicultural education will be proposed, using the following seven characteristics: *antiracist* and *antidiscriminatory*; *basic education*; *important for all students*; *pervasive*; *education for social justice*; a *process*; and *critical pedagogy*. This definition takes into account the structural, political, cultural, and linguistic factors that were presented in Part I and sets the stage for exploring the general themes that emerged from the case studies. The aim of Chapter 9 is to highlight those factors and experiences that students in the case studies perceive to have been important to their academic success. Some of these cut across the school experiences of many youths in spite of great differences in their communities, cultures, and families. This exploration will describe how young people, in their own words, define academic success; what factors they believe have helped them; and what barriers in their schools, families, or communities have held them back. The purpose of this exploration is to discover what teachers and schools can do to provide successful academic environments for all their students.

Chapter 10 will explore educational environments that foster high-quality education for all students. Specifically, it will focus on three major areas: maintaining and affirming pride in culture; providing support for students beyond the curriculum; and developing environments in schools that help foster success. In Chapter 11, the role of multicultural education as an essential component in the process of affirming diversity will be analyzed. The seven characteristics used to define multicultural education will then be considered in a model ranging from *tolerance* to *affirmation, solidarity, and critique*. Specific issues regarding the role of teachers, schools, and communities in affirming the diversity of their students will also be investigated. Finally, Chapter 12 provides some concrete examples of multicultural education based on the structural, cultural, and linguistic issues considered in Part I and challenges readers to develop their own. The purpose of this chapter is to provide a space for teachers to reflect creatively and critically on their own pedagogy in classrooms and schools.

CHAPTER 7

Toward an Understanding of School Achievement

OVERVIEW

The simple dichotomy traditionally used to explain the school failure of students, particularly those from culturally diverse and poor backgrounds, was presented in the previous chapters and can be summarized as follows: School failure is either the fault of the students themselves, who are genetically inferior, or of the social characteristics of their communities, which suffer from economic and cultural disadvantages and thus are not able to provide their children with the necessary preparation.[1] Alternative explanations are that school failure is caused by the structure of schools, which are static, classist, and racist and represent the interests of the dominant classes; or by cultural incongruencies between the home and the school.[2]

The first of these explanations has been widely discredited as both ethnocentric and not founded on scientific fact. William Ryan, for example, turned the argument of "cultural deprivation" on its head by claiming that it represented a strategy of "blaming the victim." In a book that had a great impact in challenging the theory of cultural inferiority, he stated,

> We are dealing, it would seem, not so much with culturally deprived children as with culturally depriving schools. And the task to be accomplished is not to revise, amend, and repair deficient children, but to alter and transform the atmosphere and operations of the schools to which we commit these children.[3]

Thus although the viewpoint of cultural inferiority held great sway, particularly during the 1960s and was responsible for much of our social and educational policy, the popularity of these deficit theories has waned during the past three decades as newer and more comprehensive explanations for school underachievement have taken root. Nevertheless, the genetic and cultural inferiority arguments have left a legacy that is still apparent, as we saw, for example, in the way that bilingual education continues to be conceptualized as a ''compensatory'' program. The rationale for ''compensatory'' programs is very much an argument of the 1960s: that children from ''deprived homes'' need to be compensated for their deprivation, be it genetic, cultural, or linguistic, and brought up to the norm represented by the mainstream.

The alternative arguments, that is, that underachievement is caused by school structures because they reproduce a system that is racist and classist and/or by cultural incompatibilities between the home and the school, have advanced the thinking in this area considerably. They provide a more cogent analysis of academic failure by placing schools in a political and social context. However, these analyses, too, are not wholly satisfactory because they can fall into mechanistic explanations of dynamic processes. They may assume a simple cause-effect relationship among complex factors. Such theories fail to explain why some ethnic groups have generally succeeded in school in spite of striking cultural incompatibilities or why some schools in poor communities are extraordinarily successful in spite of tremendous odds.

In this chapter we will review a number of theories to explore the complexity of factors that may affect school achievement. We will then consider how these factors, acting in tandem, may influence the academic success or failure of students. Using this discussion as a basis, the next chapter will propose multicultural education as an alternative educational philosophy that can help provide equal educational opportunity for all students.

DEFICIT THEORIES REVISITED

The theories of genetic inferiority and ''cultural deprivation'' popularized during the 1960s have left their mark, particularly on the schooling of poor children and children of color. These theories are not only classist and racist but also simply inadequate in explaining the failure of so many students. Although the social, cultural, and economic impact of their communities are often important factors in helping to explain the academic failure of some students, in themselves they are simply not enough. Furthermore, these factors are usually not subject to change by the school. That is, schools cannot change the poverty of so many students. The challenge is to find ways to teach them effectively in spite of the poverty or other disabling conditions in which they live.

The characteristics students bring with them to school, including their race, ethnicity, social class, and language, also often have a direct impact on their success or failure in school. Nevertheless, it is essential to stress that it is not simply that there is a *causal* effect between these characteristics and school failure. Instead, it is the school's perception of students' language, culture, and class as *inadequate* and *negative,* and the subsequent devalued status of these characteristics in the academic environment, that helps to explain school failure.

That the behaviors of middle-class parents of any race or ethnic group tend to be different from those of poor parents is amply documented. Parents living in poverty may be either unaware of the benefits of what middle-class parents know by experience or unable to provide certain activities for their children. Middle-class parents, for example, tend to engage in school-like prereading activities much more regularly than do working-

class parents.[4] Other activities in which middle-class parents and their children participate are deemed essential to educational success: going to the library on a consistent
basis, attending museums and other cultural centers, and providing a host of other experiences that the school and society have labeled "enriching."

That these may in fact be enriching is not in question; the problem resides in the fact
that the activities of poor families, some of which may be just as enriching, are not classified in the same way. For example, many poor families travel either to their original
home or to other parts of the country from where they originally came. Children often
spend summers "down South" or in Jamaica or Mexico, for example. These activities
are not generally considered enriching, at least not for poor people. What children learn
on these trips is frequently ignored by the school in spite of its potentially enriching character. The strengths that students bring to school, including knowledge of languages other
than English and a host of other cultural experiences and insights, are usually not considered an adequate basis for the curriculum and subsequently for their education. Such
strengths, whether related to students' experiences with their families or to interactional
differences in communication in the home, can be an important source of success when
used appropriately in the schools.

Students' ability to develop literacy and other academic skills as traditionally defined
by schools is an important and necessary aspect of academic success. If defined only in
this way, however, academic success is dysfunctional because it encourages students to
lose part of their culture in the process. Students' abilities to use the skills, talents, and
experiences learned at home and community to further their learning must also be included in a definition of academic success.

Heath's work with a poor Black community that she called "Trackton" is a compelling example. She found that the kinds of questioning rituals in which parents and
other adults engaged with children were not preparing the children adequately for school
activities.[5] In observing the middle-class teachers of these children at home, she found
that their questions, both to their own children and to their students, were qualitatively
different from the kinds of questions to which the Trackton children were accustomed.
Teachers' questions, for example, concerned pulling attributes of things out of context. In
contrast, in their homes the Trackton children were asked questions about whole events
or objects as well as about their uses, causes, and effects. Thus, there was often no
"right" answer. Rather, their answers usually involved telling a story or describing a situation. The result of the different kinds of questions asked in the different contexts was
a perplexing lack of communication in the school: Normally communicative students
were often silent and unresponsive to teachers' questions, and teachers frequently assumed that their students were deficient in language or simply unintelligent.

There was nothing *wrong* with the questions asked by families in Trackton; they
were simply different from those asked in school, and therefore they put the children at
a disadvantage for school success. Teachers, for example, often asked questions requiring
attributes to be pulled out of context and named (to identify size, shape, or color, for
example). Questions asked by parents often required children to make analogical com-
parisons and understand complex metaphors. These questions were often linguistically
complex and required a sophisticated use of language on the part of the children. An
interesting example given by Heath was the case of a grandmother who, pointing to a
brown crayon that her grandson was using, asked, "Ain't that [color] like your pants?"

a question requiring an analogy. She then turned to the researcher and explained, "We don't talk to our chil'un like you folks do; we don't ask 'em 'bout colors, names, 'n things."[6]

When teachers became aware of the differences in questioning rituals, they studied the kinds of questions asked by adults in Trackton. They found that some of them could be called "probing questions" and began using them in their lessons. The results were dramatic: Children became active and enthusiastic participants in these lessons, a far cry from their previous passive behavior. Teachers were then able to use these questions as a basis for asking more traditional "school" questions, to which children should also become accustomed if they are to be successful in school.

This felicitous example of learning to use the culture of students in their education contradicts the scenario of failure in many schools, where parents are expected to provide help in ways in which they may not be able. The fact that economically oppressed parents may be primarily concerned with survival on a daily basis and, in any event, may be unaware of how to give their children concrete support in such areas as homework should also be taken into account. Yet this lack of support in itself does not necessarily produce school failure. Edmonds's work on effective schools, for example, found that some highly effective schools had little parent involvement.[7] Likewise, in her research with academically successful Punjabi students, Gibson reported that their parents were not only uninvolved in their schools but most had never even visited the schools.[8]

This does not mean that parents were uninvolved in their children's education but rather that they were not involved in typically expected ways. Their support of education, the discipline they imposed, and their faith in the rewards of education were all crucial in their children's success. Although traditional parent participation has proven to be successful in many cases, whether in homework assistance or through parent organizations, it is simply not a sufficient explanation for school success. No single factor can explain academic achievement or the lack of it. Only the analysis of a combination of factors can help us understand how school success is achieved.

Blaming parents or children for these perceived deficiencies also begs the question, for in the final analysis it is the responsibility of schools to use the knowledge and experiences that children bring to school as the basis for their education. Somehow, schools feel that they must start out with poor children or children of color as if they were a tabula rasa. In effect, this means tearing down the building blocks the children already have in order to start from a middle-class foundation. School-related skills may indeed be necessary for academic success, but there is no reason why they cannot be built on the foundation that children already have, be it linguistic, cultural, or experiential. The fact that some children come to school with a rich oral tradition is a case in point. Perhaps their parents never read stories to them but instead *tell* them stories. This experience can either be dismissed by schools as unimportant or used as the basis for academic success.

The role of schools is to educate *all* students from all families, not only the most academically gifted students from advantaged, mainstream, English-speaking, European American families. Since schools can do nothing to change a student's social class or home background, it makes sense to focus on what they can change: themselves. Nevertheless, we also need to understand the power of what has been called the *cultural capital* of dominant groups. According to Bourdieu, cultural capital can exist in three forms: dispositions of the mind and body; cultural goods, such as pictures, books, and other material objects; and educational qualifications. In all three forms, transmission of cultural capital is "no doubt the best hidden form of hereditary transmission of capital."[9] That is, some values, tastes, languages, dialects, and cultures have more status, and these are invariably associated with the dominant group. The power of cultural capital cannot be ignored; to do so would be both naïve and romantic. This point has been well stated by Giroux:

> To argue that working-class language practices are just as rule-governed as standard English usage and practice may be true, but to suggest at the same time that *all* cultures are equal is to forget that subordinate groups are often denied access to the power, knowledge, and resources that allow them to lead self-determined existences.[10]

Power, knowledge, and resources are inevitably located in the norms of dominant cultures and languages. Thus, to imply that working-class students and those from dominated groups need not learn the cultural forms of the dominant group is effectively to disempower the very same students who are most unsuccessful in schools. A self-determined culture is often the result of learning through an alien and imposed one.

ECONOMIC AND SOCIAL REPRODUCTION REVISITED

The argument that schools reproduce the economic and social relations of society and therefore tend to serve the interests of the dominant classes, articulated first during the 1970s by such scholars as Bowles and Gintis, Spring, and Apple, also moved the debate about school failure to new arenas.[11] This theory placed schools squarely in a political framework. The role of the schools was explained as keeping the poor in their place by teaching them the proper attitudes and behaviors for becoming good workers, and of keeping the dominant classes in power by teaching their children the skills of management and control that would presumably prepare them to manage and control the working class. Schools therefore reproduced the status quo and not only reflected but actually maintained structural inequalities based on class, race, and gender.

According to these theorists, this function of the schools is apparent in everything from their physical structure to their curriculum and instruction. For example, the schools of the poor are generally factorylike fortresses that operate with an abundance of bells and other controlling mechanisms, whereas the schools of the wealthy are much more "open" physically and allow for more autonomy and creative thinking on the part of students. In addition, relations between students and teachers in poor communities reflect a dominant-dominated relationship much more so than in middle-class or wealthy communities. The curriculum also differs: More sophisticated and challenging knowledge is taught in wealthy schools, whereas the "basics" and rote memorization are relegated to poor schools. Therefore, the "sorting" function of the schools, to use a term coined by Spring, results in an almost perfect replication of the stratification of society.

This thinking revolutionized the debate on the purposes and outcomes of schools and placed the success or failure of students in a new light. The benign, stated purpose of schooling to serve as an "equalizer" began to be questioned more seriously than ever, especially when it became clear that schools had in fact historically been engaged in the service of a dominant class to control not only the lives but even the ideas of dominated groups. School failure became a perfectly understandable byproduct of this control. For example, that 70 percent of students in urban schools were dropping out was understood not as a *coincidence* but actually as an *intended* outcome of the educational system. In other words, these students were intentionally channeled by the schools to be either fodder for war or a reserve uneducated labor force. They were doing just exactly what they were expected to do: They were succeeding at school failure.

The arguments of the social reproduction theorists were compelling and have had a tremendous impact on educational thinking since the 1970s. Nevertheless, by concentrating on the labor market purpose of schooling, they tended to fall into a somewhat mechanistic explanation of school success or failure. School life, according to this analysis, is almost completely subordinated to the needs of the economy, thereby leaving little room for understanding the role that students and their communities have in influencing school policies and practices. Put in its most simplistic form, this analysis assumes that schooling is simply imposed from above and accepted from below.

These theories have been criticized on a number of levels. For example, school structures are sometimes simplistically perceived as corresponding directly with class structure. Yet because schools are complex and sometimes contradictory institutions, the relationship is not always this neat or apparent. An ethnographic study by Wilcox in which teacher behavior was analyzed in two classes, one in a working-class school and the other in a school with students from professional, executive-level families, did not find such a neat correspondence. Although she did find that both schools had a sorting role and that it was indeed based on the class structure of the schools, she also found that contrary to her expectations, the teacher in the upper-middle-class school had *tighter* discipline and control than the one in the working-class school.[12] Given the expectations that schools in working-class neighborhoods prepare young people for their role as uncritical workers, this finding was surprising. Nevertheless, Wilcox did find that external control proved to be the overriding control mechanism used in the working-class school, whereas internal control was called on in the upper-middle-class school. Sophisticated analyses such as these are necessary if we are to go beyond simple expectations of schools based only on their economic functions.

Another problem with the theories of social and cultural reproduction of the schools is that the lengthy struggles over schooling in which many communities have been involved, including integrated schools, bilingual education, multicultural education, and access to education for females, are not taken into account. If education were simply imposed from above, these reforms would never have found their way, even imperfectly, into the school. Some of these theorists have modified their thinking to reflect that schools are in fact a product of such conflicts. The purposes of the dominant class are not perfectly reflected in the schools but are resisted and modified by the recipients of schooling.[13]

These theories help us understand that academic failure and success are not unintended outcomes but rather quite logical results of differentiated schooling. They help remove the complete burden of failure from students, their families, and communities to the society at large, and they therefore provide a *macroanalytic*, or societal, understanding of schooling. Nevertheless, social reproduction theories and even more comprehensive structuralist theories generally fail to take cultural and psychological issues into account. They are therefore incomplete.

CULTURAL INCOMPATIBILITIES REVISITED

Another explanation for school failure is that it is caused by cultural incompatibilities; that is, the school culture and home culture are often at odds. Because they have different objectives, values, and practices, the result is a "cultural clash" which produces school failure. It therefore becomes necessary to consider the differing experiences, values, skills, expectations, and life-styles with which children enter school and how these differences, in being more or less consistent with the school environment, affect student achievement. The more consistent the home and school cultures are, the reasoning goes, the more successful will the student be, in general terms. The opposite is also true: The more students' experiences, skills, and values differ from the school setting, the more failure they will experience.

This explanation makes a great deal of sense and in fact goes a long way in explaining school failure more convincingly than simple deficit theories. The fact that some students may learn more effectively in cooperative than in competitive settings is not a problem per se. What makes it a problem is that schools persist in providing only competitive environments. Given this reality, cultural differences begin to function as a risk factor. This reasoning turns around the popular conception of "children at risk," so that the risk comes not from within the child but rather through school policies and practices.

Likewise, the fact that some students enter school without speaking English is not in and of itself a satisfactory explanation for why they fail in school. Rather, the interpretation given to this condition and the value or lack of value given to the child's language are what matter. For example, whereas in some schools a student might be identified as *non-English-speaking*, in another school that same child might be called *Khmer-speaking* The difference is not simply a semantic one, for in the first case the child is assumed to be *missing* language, whereas in the second case, the child is assumed to possess language already. Since language ability is the primary ingredient for school success, how schools and teachers perceive children's language is significant.

Nevertheless, the cultural mismatch theory, although more comprehensive than the cultural or genetic deficit theories and certainly without their implicit racist and classist overtones, is still not a sufficient explanation for why some students succeed and others fail. For example, Gibson's ethnographic research has documented that although culturally very different from their peers, Punjabi students have been quite successful in school.[14] Their grades and high school graduation rates have equaled or surpassed those of their classmates, in spite of what may be considered severe handicaps: Their families are primarily farm laborers and factory workers and many are illiterate and speak little or no English; they have had to become fluent in English in nonbilingual settings, and very few have received any special assistance; and they have been subjected to discrimination by both peers and teachers. In addition, their home values and those practiced by the school are in sharp contrast to one another. Given their situation, their cultural background should indeed predispose them to school failure; that this is not the case leads us to other explanations. Gibson's research is related to and corroborates Ogbu's work, to which we will now turn.

THE IMMIGRANT EXPERIENCE VERSUS THE "MINORITY" EXPERIENCE

Ogbu explains that it is important to look not only at a group's cultural background but also at its situation in the host society and its perceptions of opportunities available in that society.[15] Immigrants tend to see the United States as a land of opportunity, where one gets ahead through education and hard work. According to this view, even a relative new-comer with few skills and little education can succeed economically. Their children can experience even more success if they work hard in school and apply themselves. The fact that they may have to undergo great sacrifices, including racism, economic hardships, and working at several menial jobs at the same time, is understood and accepted.

In the case of the Punjabis, their reference point is not the United States but their country of origin, where there were few employment and educational opportunities and sometimes even more discrimination than in the United States. In the case of those com-ing from war-torn countries, where they may have lived in refugee camps and even faced death, living in an urban ghetto and engaging in backbreaking work are not considered insurmountable challenges or severe hardships. Given their new situation, immigrants such as the Punjabis are happy to make great sacrifices for what they are certain will be a return on their investment. They are, in Gibson's words, "willing to play the school game by the rules of the dominant group."[16] Similar findings have been reported by Suarez-Orozco.[17] He documents the extraordinary success of Central Americans, who go to the same schools and live in the same communities as Mexican Americans, who on the contrary are for the most part consistently unsuccessful in the schools.

Ogbu's work in explaining differences in the school experiences of what he calls *castelike* or *involuntary* minorities (those incorporated into a society against their will) and *immigrant* minorities is instructive.[18] He claims that the major problem in the aca-demic performance of children from castelike minorities is not that they possess a dif-ferent language, culture, or cognitive or communication style. Rather, the problem lies in the nature of the history, subjugation, and exploitation that they have experienced *to-gether with* their own responses to their treatment. Castelike minorities in the United States (African Americans, Mexican Americans, Native Americans, and Puerto Ricans) perceive schooling as providing *unequal* returns. In these communities, the children do not see older people getting jobs, wages, and other societal benefits commensurate with their level of education; the adults tend to be overqualified and overeducated for their jobs. These perceptions are not incorrect.[19]

In addition, given the long history of discrimination and racism in the schools, these children and their families are often leery of the education offered by them. Children in these communities have routinely been subjected to what Cummins calls "identity eradication."[20] Their culture and language have been systematically, although not nec-essarily intentionally, stripped away as one of the conditions for school success. Ironi-cally, not only have they experienced school failure but also the schools have been at least partially successful in stripping away their language and culture. These negative experiences result in communities' *perception* that equal educational opportunity and the "folk theories" of getting ahead in the United States are a myth. The "folk theories," however, are accepted by immigrants because they have not had this long history of discrimination, at least in this country, and thus their perceptions are quite different.

It is not unusual for students from castelike minorities to engage in what Ogbu calls "cultural inversion," that is, to resist acquiring and demonstrating the culture and the cognitive styles that are identified with the dominant group. These behaviors are considered "Uncle Tom-ish" and include being studious and hardworking at school, speaking standard English, listening to "White" music, going to museums, getting good grades, and so on. Even extremely bright students from these groups may try just to "get by." Students from castelike minorities who engage in behaviors that conform to the mainstream culture are frequently ostracized by their peers. They must cope, in the words of Fordham and Ogbu, "with the burden of acting White."[21] There is little benefit, in terms of peer relationships, in being successful students. Frequently, those who excel in school feel both internal ambivalence and external pressures not to manifest such behaviors and attitudes. Ogbu claims that successful students who *are* accepted by their peers are either also very successful in sports or have found another way to hide their academic achievement.

Ogbu states that parents from castelike minorities, themselves involuntary immigrants with a long history of discrimination and negative experiences at school, may subconsciously mirror these same attitudes, thus adding to their children's ambivalent attitudes about education and success. Many times, students emphasize those cultural behaviors that *differentiate* them from the majority and are in opposition to them, including language, speech forms, and other behaviors that help to characterize their group but are contrary to those promoted by the schools. The further they are from appearing to be "brainiacs," the further they are from "acting White." Similar findings have been reported by McDermott, who cites the results of sociometric tests in an urban elementary school that placed *nonreaders* at the very center of all peer group activities.[22] Reading success was obviously interpreted by these children as running counter to developing leadership skills. To become a reader meant to lose esteem among one's peer group.

RESISTANCE THEORY

Ogbu's theory of school failure adds an important dimension in explaining why students from some groups in general succeed and those from other groups in general fail. It too is incomplete, however, because in virtually dismissing the "cultural mismatch" position, it fails to account for such successes as the KEEP program (see the discussion of this program in Chapter 5) and similar attempts at developing learning environments that are congruent with the culture of students. Erickson, among others, attempts to develop a synthesis between these two positions.[23] He argues that the cultural mismatch theory can become too culturally determinist. The "perceived labor market" argument of Ogbu and others, in contrast, can become too economically determinist. Erickson explains the school failure of involuntary minorities by using both of these explanations within the framework of *resistance theory*, as articulated by Apple, Giroux, McLaren, and others.[24]

According to resistance theory, *not learning* what schools teach can be interpreted as a form of political resistance. Erickson maintains that whereas cultural differences may cause some initial school failures and misunderstandings, it is only when they become entrenched over time that *not learning*, a consistent pattern of refusing to learn, becomes the outcome of schooling. Resistance theory is helpful because it attempts to explain the complex relationship of disempowered communities and their schools. Students and their families are not only victims of the educational system but also actors. They learn to react to schools in ways that make perfect sense, given the reality of the schools, although some of these coping strategies may in the long run be self-defeating and counterproductive.

There are numerous examples of students' refusal to learn as a sign of resistance. Misbehavior, vandalism, and poor relationships with teachers are all examples, albeit unconscious, of students' resistance. In the research by Anyon in working-class schools, for example, she found that this is the dominant theme characterizing the relationship of students and teachers. Resistance could be seen in students' attitudes toward schoolwork, their lack of attention, and their general misbehavior. It was apparent in virtually all interactions between teachers and students.[25]

The most extreme form of refusing education is dropping out. An ethnographic study by Fine of dropouts in a large urban school found two major reasons for students' decisions to leave: a political stance of resistance and disappointment with the "promise of education."[26] Many students were articulate in their resistance to school; even some of those who stayed were unsure what benefits they would derive from their education. Felice, in investigating the high dropout rate of African American students in an urban high school, found that many left school because they found the "educational exchange" for staying in school to be tenuous.[27] Given the small chance of getting a job commensurate with their education, they felt that putting up with racial discrimination and low teachers' expectations were simply not worth the trouble. The idea that education leads to social mobility was just not consistent with these students' perceptions or experiences. Interestingly, Felice found that the measured IQ of the dropouts was significantly *higher* than that of those remaining; difficulty of schoolwork was not even mentioned as a reason for dropping out. Many dropouts felt that their decision was an intelligent one, given the circumstances.

A MORE COMPREHENSIVE VIEW

No simple explanation accounts for student achievement or failure. A number of explanations have failed to consider the *context* of schooling, that is, the social, cultural, and political situation in which the students' education takes place. Cortés, in an attempt to confront the problem of these decontextualized explanations, forged a *contextual interaction model* based on two previous models. It takes into consideration the effect that school and nonschool factors have on the school's context and process. These nonschool factors include

1. educational input factors (including educators and their expectations, skills, and attitudes, fiscal resources, school policies and educational theories and assumptions)
2. student qualities (including proficiency in one or more languages, skills, knowledge, self-image, goals, and motivation)
3. instructional elements (including curriculum, materials, strategies, school services, and parent involvement).[28]

The interaction among these three factors and the affect of societal forces on them helps us understand school achievement; all of these issues, taken together, go further in explaining why some students succeed and others fail. Cultural mismatch alone does not explain it; neither does students' and families' oppositional relationships to schools. Even the persistence of racism and discrimination, structural factors within schools, or the role that schools play in reproducing existing societal inequities do not in and of themselves explain school failure. Cummins's argument that underachievement is the result of particular kinds of interactions between teachers and students and their families helps complete the explanation.[29] Changing these interactions can help change student achievement as well.

We can take these ideas further and argue that how students and communities *perceive* and *react to* schools is an additional important consideration. These perceptions and reactions can be both group-based, as described by Ogbu, or individual. Individual or family reactions have probably not been given enough consideration. Although not meant to romanticize the success of a minority of students in environments in which a great majority fail (the Horatio Alger-type stories of educational success), it is important nevertheless to learn from these examples and to try to understand how these students can succeed in spite of some negative environments. In addition, by looking at success rather than failure, we move away from a deterministic explanation for school achievement. Not all African American students, even those from economically oppressed communities, fail; some do not see school success as "acting White." In addition, not all voluntary immigrants are successful in school, and neither are all Asians. For instance, according to one study, one-quarter of all dropouts from New York City schools are Asian.[30] Unless we look at individual cases as well as at entire groups, we fall into rather facile but not always accurate explanations of failure. These can lead to stereotypes and inappropriate educational expectations.

Clark's research with African American families in three inner-city Chicago neighborhoods helps us understand why some students succeed and others do not.[31] His conclusion, based on extensive interviews with numerous families, was that children's social and academic behavior cannot be solely explained by characteristics of family units, including single-parent families. That is, coming from a single-parent family is not necessarily a handicap if other conditions exist in the home to help motivate students for academic success. He found that parents of high achievers, even in single-parent homes, tend to employ what he calls a "sponsored independence" technique of child rearing, which includes large amounts of parental involvement and interest in the children's home activities; a consistent monitoring of their time; and frequent joint activities involving studying, reading, and other literacy activities. Research by Steinberg and others reinforces these findings.[32] They found that students perform better in school when they are raised in homes characterized by supportive but demanding parents who are involved in their schooling and who expect their children to achieve. Like Clark, they found that social class was far less important in explaining this achievement than they had previously assumed.

It is tempting to use such research to fall back on blaming families for their children's failure. After all, if some parents engage in such activities, which obviously motivate children for success, why cannot all families do the same? The purpose of reviewing this research, however, is not to place sole responsibility for students' success on their families but rather to make the case that all students and families are *differently affected* by the schools and by other societal institutions and conditions. Without including this important consideration, we are left with only megastructural or cultural explanations that limit our understanding of very complex processes. In effect, if only structural factors are to blame, we are left with no hope for the school success of great numbers of students. These students become understood as simple pawns who are acted on by the schools. The role that parents, families, and communities can play in students' school achievement, given a deterministic understanding of this phenomenon, would be minimal.

There are other examples of students who succeed in spite of evidence, both structural and cultural, that would lead to a contrary expectation. Particular learning environments, for example, seem at first glance to be totally inappropriate for some children. The so-called "Catholic school effect" is a good example in this regard. Nothing could seem more culturally incompatible for African American and Latino students than a Catholic school: Bilingual programs are often unavailable, the classes are generally overcrowded, and formal environments that stress individual excellence over cooperation are usually the order of the day. Nevertheless, they have been successful environments for many Latino and African American children, even those from poor communities. The literature suggests that Catholic schooling seems to result in higher achievement regardless of students' social class.[33] Recent studies, however, point to the fact that Catholic schools, because of restricted resources, tend to offer *all* students a less differentiated curriculum, less tracking, and more academic classes.[34] What may at first glance appear to be incongruous in terms of cultural compatibility is thus explained as a result of school structures that imply similarly high expectations for most students.

The same kind of success is evident among African American students in Black Muslim schools, which tend to be quite demanding and highly disciplined. In both these cases, the promise of a rigorous education, together with parents' admonitions to their children on the monetary and other sacrifices they are making to provide this education, may be enough to mediate what in other ways might be perceived as totally inappropriate environments for these children, at least in cultural terms. Another explanation might be that in some cases these schools develop strategies and perspectives that are in active opposition to and defense against the outside society. This factor might also help explain the success of the Amish, categorized by McDermott as "closed" communities, with their schools.[35]

Finally, there are sometimes baffling examples of school failure that defy easy categorization but must also be taken into account. Fernández and Shu, for example, analyzed the *High School and Beyond* data and found that Hispanic students dropped out at significantly higher rates than other students.[36] Although this finding is nothing new, there were higher dropout rates even when these students had higher grades than others, were in the academic rather than the "general" track, were not from poor families, did not have parents with less schooling, and did not have problems with their teachers. The researchers concluded that schools have not been successful in retaining even Hispanic students who show *no* risk factors. Most of the research on dropping out of school simply cannot explain why these students leave school. The only possible clue came from the finding that a great many Hispanic students, both dropouts and others, expressed significantly more negative feelings about their schools than other students in the national sample. This research reinforces the importance of placing students and their school experiences in the broader context of their communities and the larger society in which they live.

That students can achieve in spite of tremendous structural and cultural obstacles has been proven time and again. Based on research spanning more than a decade, from the 1970s to the 1980s, in ten diverse communities throughout the United States, Ianni concluded that it is possible, although certainly not easy, for adolescents from economically poor backgrounds to succeed in school. But he also concluded that such success requires a constellation of factors, including exceptional intrinsic motivation on the part of the student, a family that values and encourages educational achievement, and teachers and schools dedicated to success.[37] This conclusion was evident in our case studies. However, the burden that it places on poor students is inequitable, given the meager resources they may have at their disposal. Given these burdens, it is unrealistic at best and unethical at worst to expect all students to be academically successful, particularly those most severely and negatively affected by poverty, discrimination, and other social characteristics that may prepare them poorly for school.

This discussion leads us to the conclusion that school achievement can be understood and explained only as a multiplicity of sometimes competing and always changing factors: the school's tendency to replicate society and its inequities, cultural and language incompatibilities, the limiting and bureaucratic structures of schools, and the political relationship of ethnic groups to society and the schools. Nevertheless, it is tricky business to seek causal explanations of school success and failure. Although these factors may be important in understanding school success or failure, they rarely operate in simple or neat ways. Nevertheless, all of these factors taken together help us understand in a more comprehensive way the wholesale school failure of many students. Structural inequality and cultural incompatibility may be major causes of school failure, but they work *differently* on different communities, families, and individuals. How these factors are mediated within the school and home settings and their complex *interplay* probably are ultimately responsible for either the success or failure of students in schools. This is in effect the sociopolitical context of multicultural education and forms the basis for the conceptual framework that has been developed here.

SUMMARY

In this chapter, we have explored a number of theories to understand the factors that influence school failure and success. The deficit theories popularized in the 1960s were responsible for much of our educational policy during that time and beyond. These theories assumed that children from culturally diverse families or poor neighborhoods were either genetically or culturally inferior to culturally dominant children from the middle class.

An alternative explanation developed during the 1970s was that schools were responsible for school failure because they reproduced the economic and social relations of society and therefore replicated structural inequality. During this time, the cultural mismatch theory was also developed. According to this theory, schools are unsuccessful with a substantial number of students because there is a mismatch between their home cultures and the culture of the school. The argument by Ogbu and others that there is an important distinction between castelike minorities and immigrant minorities was also developed during the 1970s. This theory argues that cultural differences alone cannot explain the differential school achievement of distinct "minority" groups.

Finally, resistance theory has helped us understand that students and their families are frequently engaged in some form of resistance to the education to which they are exposed. Resistance may be either passive or active and may have consequences that are counterproductive to the interests of these very students.

I have attempted to develop a comprehensive view of school achievement by providing an analysis of each of these theories. It is clear that no one theory of achievement entirely explains why some students succeed and others fail in school. It is necessary to understand school achievement as *contextual* and as an *interactive, personal, cultural, political,* and *societal* process in which all of these factors affect one another in sometimes competing and contradictory ways. This sociopolitical, contextual framework will form the basis for the definition of multicultural education that will be presented in the following chapter.

TO THINK ABOUT

1. What does Ryan mean by "culturally depriving schools"? Give some examples.
2. Consider some of the culturally enriching activities of your students. How can they be used by teachers to create more culturally appropriate classrooms?
3. It has been claimed that our public schools perform the important role of "sorting" students according to their social class. Think about your own experiences and observations and give some examples of this "sorting" function.
4. How accurate do you think Ogbu's classification of *voluntary* and *involuntary immigrants* is? Consider the advantages as well as the disadvantages of this theory.
5. Think about schools and classrooms you are familiar with. Have you noticed *student resistance*? How? Give specific examples.
6. You and a group of your colleagues have to determine why a particular student has been doing poorly in your classes. What are the factors that you decide to look at?

NOTES

1. For full expositions of these arguments, see, for example, Carl Bereiter and S. Englemann, *Teaching Disadvantaged Children in the Preschool* (Englewood Cliffs, NJ: Prentice Hall, 1966); Arthur R. Jensen, "How Much Can We Boost IQ and Scholastic Achievement?" *Harvard Educational Review,* 39 (1969), 1–123; Frank Reissman, *The Culturally Deprived Child* (New York: Harper & Row, 1962); John U. Ogbu's review of Jensen's theories in "The Consequences of the American Caste System" in *The School Achievement of Minority Children: New Perspectives,* ed. Ulric Neisser (Hillsdale, NJ: Erlbaum, 1986); see also the review of "deficit theories" by Herbert Ginsburg, "The Myth of the Deprived Child: New Thoughts on Poor Children," in the same volume.

2. See Samuel Bowles and Herbert Gintis, *Schooling in Capitalist America: Educational Reform and the Contradictions of Economic Life* (New York: Basic Books, 1976); Joel Spring, *The Rise and Fall of the Corporate State* (Boston: Beacon Press, 1972); Michael W. Apple, *Ideology and Curriculum* (London: Routledge & Kegan Paul, 1979).

3. William Ryan, *Blaming the Victim* (New York: Vintage Books, 1972), p. 61.

4. See the research cited by Ann L. Brown, Annemarie Sullivan Palincsar, and Linda Purcell, "Poor Readers: Teach, Don't Label" in *The School Achievement of Minority Children: New Perspectives*, ed. Ulric Neisser (Hillsdale, NJ: Erlbaum, 1986).

5. Shirley Brice Heath, "Questioning at Home and at School: A Comparative Study," in *Doing the Ethnography of Schooling: Educational Anthropology in Action*, ed. George Spindler (New York: Holt, Rinehart & Winston, 1982).

6. Ibid., p. 117.

7. Ron Edmonds, "Characteristics of Effective Schools," in *The School Achievement of Minority Children: New Perspectives*, ed. Ulric Neisser (Hillsdale, NJ: Erlbaum, 1986).

8. Margaret A. Gibson, "The School Performance of Immigrant Minorities: A Comparative View," *Anthropology and Education Quarterly*, 18, 4 (December 1987), 262–275.

9. Pierre Bourdieu, "The Forms of Capital," in *Handbook of Theory and Research for the Sociology of Education*, ed. John G. Richardson (New York: Greenwood Press, 1986), p. 246.

10. Henry A. Giroux, *Theory and Resistance in Education: A Pedagogy for the Opposition* (South Hadley, MA: Bergin & Garvey, 1983), p. 229.

11. See Spring, *Rise and Fall of the Corporate State*; Bowles and Gintis, *Schooling in Capitalist America*; Apple, *Ideology and Curriculum*.

12. Kathleen Wilcox, "Differential Socialization in the Classroom: Implications for Equal Opportunity," in *Doing the Ethnography of Schooling: Educational Anthropology in Action*, ed. George Spindler (New York: Holt, Rinehart & Winston, 1982).

13. Michael W. Apple, *Teachers and Texts: A Political Economy of Class and Gender Relations in Education* (Boston: Routledge & Kegan Paul, 1986). See also Cameron McCarthy and Michael W. Apple, "Race, Class and Gender in American Educational Research: Toward a Nonsynchronous Parallelist Position," in *Class, Race and Gender in American Education*, ed. Lois Weis (Albany: State University of New York Press, 1988); Michael W. Apple and Lois Weis, eds., *Ideology and Practice in Schooling* (Philadelphia: Temple University Press, 1983); Henry A. Giroux, "Theories of Reproduction and Resistance in the New Sociology of Education: A Critical Analysis," *Harvard Educational Review*, 53 (1983), 257–293.

14. Gibson, "School Performance of Immigrant Minorities."

15. John U. Ogbu, "The Consequences of the American Caste System," in *The School Achievement of Minority Children: New Perspectives*, ed. Ulric Neisser (Hillsdale, NJ: Erlbaum, 1986).

16. Gibson, "School Performance of Immigrant Minorities."

17. Marcelo M. Suarez-Orozco, " 'Becoming Somebody': Central American Immigrants in the U.S.," *Anthropology and Education Quarterly*, 18, 4 (December 1987), 287–299.

18. Ogbu, "Consequences of the American Caste System."

19. It has been documented that European American males with a high school degree earn more in general than do African American males with a college degree. For example, in 1982, White men with four years of *high school* earned a median income of $17,583, whereas Black men with four years of *college* earned a median income of $16,532. U.S. Bureau of the Census, *Current Population Survey: Consumer Income Series* (Washington, DC: U.S. Department of Commerce, 1982), p. 60.

20. Jim Cummins, *Empowering Minority Students* (Sacramento: California Association for Bilingual Education, 1989).

21. Signithia Fordham, and John U. Ogbu, "Black Students' School Success: Coping with the 'Burden of Acting White,' " *Urban Review*, 18, 3 (1986), 176–206.

22. Ray P. McDermott, "The Cultural Context of Learning to Read," in *Papers in Applied Linguistics: Linguistics and Reading,* Series 1, ed. Stanley F. Wanat (Arlington, VA.: Center for Applied Linguistics, 1977).

23. Frederick Erickson, "Transformation and School Success: The Politics and Culture of Educational Achievement," *Anthropology and Education Quarterly,* 18, 4 (December 1987), 335–356. See also McCarthy and Apple, "Race, Class and Gender."

24. See Giroux, *Theory and Resistance in Education*; Michael Apple, *Education and Power* (London: Routledge & Kegan Paul, 1982); Tove Skutnabb-Kangas and Jim Cummins, eds., *Minority Education: From Shame to Struggle* (Clevedon, Eng.: Multilingual Matters, 1988).

25. Jean Anyon, "Social Class and School Knowledge," *Curriculum Inquiry,* 11, 1 (1981), 3–41.

26. Michelle Fine, "Why Urban Adolescents Drop Into and Out of Public High School," in *School Dropouts: Patterns and Politics,* ed. Gary Natriello (New York: Teachers College Press, Columbia University, 1986).

27. Lawrence G. Felice, "Black Student Dropout Behavior: Disengagement from School Rejection and Racial Discrimination," *Journal of Negro Education,* 50 (1981), 415–424.

28. This model integrates Cortés's "societal curriculum model"—see "The Societal Curriculum: Implications for Multiethnic Education," in *Education in the 80's: Multiethnic Education,* ed. James A. Banks (Washington, DC: National Education Association, 1981—with the "interaction model" developed by the Bilingual Education Office of the California Department of Education. Carlos E. Cortés, "The Education of Language Minority Students: A Contextual Interaction Model," in *Beyond Language: Social and Cultural Factors in Schooling Language Minority Students* (Los Angeles: Office of Bilingual Education, California State Department of Education, Evaluation, Dissemination, and Assessment Center, 1986).

29. Cummins, *Empowering Minority Students.*

30. Reported by Diane Divoky, "The Model Minority Goes to School," *Phi Delta Kappan,* November 1988, pp. 219–222.

31. Reginald Clark, *Family Life and School Achievement: Why Poor Black Children Succeed or Fail* (Chicago: University of Chicago Press, 1983).

32. Lawrence Steinberg, B. Bradford Brown, Mary Cider, Nancy Kaczmarek, and Cary Lazzaro, *Noninstructional Influences on High School Student Achievement: The Contributions of Parents, Peers, Extracurricular Activities, and Part-Time Work* (Madison: University of Wisconsin, Wisconsin Center for Educational Research, National Center for Effective Secondary Schools, September 1988).

33. See, for example, research by Andrew M. Greeley, *Catholic High Schools and Minority Students* (New Brunswick, NJ: Transaction Books, 1982); James Coleman, Thomas Hoffer, and Sally Kilgore, *High School Achievement: Public, Catholic and Private Schools Compared* (New York: Basic Books, 1982).

34. Recent research has uncovered this relationship. See V. E. Lee, and A. S. Bryk, "Curriculum Tracking as Mediating the Social Distribution of High School Achievement," *Sociology of Education,* 61 (1988), 78–94.

35. Ray P. McDermott, "Social Relations as Contexts for Learning in School," *Harvard Educational Review,* 47, 2 (May 1977), 198–213.

36. Ricardo R. Fernández and Gangjian Shu, "School Dropouts: New Approaches to an Enduring Problem," *Education and Urban Society,* 20, 4 (August 1988), 363–386.

37. Francis A. Ianni, *The Search for Structure: A Report on American Youth Today* (New York: Free Press, 1989).

CHAPTER **8**

Multicultural Education
and School Reform

OVERVIEW

When multicultural education is mentioned, many people first think of lessons in human relations, units about ethnic holidays, education in inner-city schools, or multicultural food festivals. The potential for substantive change in schools is diminished when we consider multicultural education in only this sense; when broadly conceptualized, it can have a great impact on the four areas of potential school conflict that have already been discussed: racism and discrimination, structural factors within schools that limit learning, the impact of culture on learning, and language diversity. This chapter will focus on how multicultural education addresses each of these areas.

Multicultural education is not being proposed as a panacea for all educational ills. It will not cure underachievement, remove boring and irrelevant curriculum, or stop vandalism. It will not automatically motivate parents to participate in schools, reinvigorate tired and dissatisfied teachers, or guarantee a lower dropout rate. Schools are part of our communities and as such reflect the stratification and social inequities of the larger society. As long as this is the case, no school program, no matter how broadly conceptualized, can change things completely. Furthermore, in our complex and highly bureaucratic school systems, no approach can yield instant and positive results for all students.

Given these caveats, we can nevertheless say that multicultural education, conceptualized as broad-based school reform, can offer hope for change. By focusing on the major factors contributing to school failure and underachievement, a broadly conceptualized multicultural education permits educators to explore alternatives to a system that leads to failure for too many of its students. Such an explanation can lead to the creation of richer and more productive learning environments, diverse instructional strategies, and a more profound awareness of the role culture and language can play in education. In this way, educational success for all students can be a realistic goal rather than an impossible ideal. Multicultural education in a sociopolitical context becomes both richer and more complex than simple lessons on getting along or units on ethnic festivals.

The purpose of this chapter is to propose a definition of multicultural education based on the conceptual framework developed in the previous chapters. Then the seven primary characteristics included in the definition of multicultural education will be analyzed. These characteristics underscore the role that multicultural education can play in reforming schools and in providing an equal and excellent education for all students. They address the factors contributing to school achievement discussed in previous chapters.

A DEFINITION OF MULTICULTURAL EDUCATION

Multicultural education in a sociopolitical context can be defined as follows:

> Multicultural education is a process of comprehensive school reform and basic education for all students. It challenges and rejects racism and other forms of discrimination in schools and society and accepts and affirms the pluralism (ethnic, racial, linguistic, religious, economic, and gender, among others) that students, their communities, and teachers represent. Multicultural education permeates the curriculum and instructional strategies used in schools, as well as the interactions among teachers, students and parents, and the very way that schools conceptualize the nature of teaching and learning. Because it uses critical pedagogy as its underlying philosophy and focuses on knowledge, reflection, and action (praxis) as the basis for social change, multicultural education furthers the democratic principles of social justice.

The seven basic characteristics of multicultural education are as follows:

Multicultural education is *antiracist education*.

Multicultural education is *basic education*.

Multicultural education is *important for* all *students*.

Multicultural education is *pervasive*.

Multicultural education is *education for social justice*.

Multicultural education is a *process*.

Multicultural education is *critical pedagogy*.

Each of these components will be described in more detail in the following pages.

Multicultural Education Is Antiracist Education

Antiracism, and antidiscrimination in general, is at the very core of a multicultural perspective. This is especially important to keep in mind when we consider that only the most superficial aspects of multicultural education are apparent in many schools, even those that espouse a multicultural philosophy. Celebrations of ethnic festivals are as far as it goes in some places. In others, sincere attempts to decorate bulletin boards or purchase materials with what is thought to be a multicultural perspective end up perpetuating the worst kind of stereotypes. And even where there are serious attempts to develop a truly pluralistic environment, it is not unusual to find incongruencies, such as the fact that the children of color are overwhelmingly visible in the lowest academic tracks and invisible in the highest. All of these are examples of multicultural education *without* an explicitly antiracist perspective.

It is important to stress multicultural education as antiracist because many people may believe that a multicultural program *automatically* takes care of racism. This is unfortunately not always true. According to Weinberg,

> Most multicultural materials deal wholly with the cultural distinctiveness of various groups and little more. Almost never is there any sustained attention to the ugly realities of systematic discrimination against the same group that also happens to utilize quaint clothing, fascinating toys, delightful fairy tales, and delicious food. Responding to racist attacks and defamation is *also* part of the culture of the group under study.[1]

Being antiracist and antidiscriminatory thus means paying attention to all the areas in which some students may be favored over others: the curriculum, choice of materials, sorting policies, and teachers' interactions and relationships with the students and their communities.

To be more inclusive and balanced, multicultural curriculum must by definition be antiracist. Teaching does not become more honest and critical simply by becoming more inclusive, but this is nevertheless an important first step in ensuring that students have access to a wide variety of viewpoints. Although the beautiful and heroic aspects of our history should be taught, so must the ugly and exclusionary. Rather than viewing the world through rose-colored glasses, antiracist multicultural education forces both teachers and students to take a long, hard look at everything as it was and and is, which also means considering the effects and interconnections among events, people, and things.

For example, the Reading Teacher in *Death at an Early Age* is afraid to confront the curriculum in this way. In wanting to present the cotton gin in isolation, as simply another invention, she is aware that to teach it as part of a system of slavery and exploitation would open up too many questions and perhaps too much real understanding on the part of the students ("I don't want these children to have to think back on this years later on and to have to remember that we were the ones who told them they were Negro," she reasons).[2] This is an example of what Fine calls the "fear of naming," which is part of the system of silencing in public schools. To name it might make it happen, or so the thinking goes. Thus, teachers refuse to engage their students in discussions about racism because it might "demoralize" them.[3] The Reading Teacher, afraid to name *Negro* was afraid also that her students might begin to reflect on what it meant to be Black in this society. Too dangerous a topic, it was best left untouched.

Related to the fear of naming is the insistence of schools on sanitizing the curriculum, or what Kozol calls "tailoring" important men and women for school use. Schools manage to take our most exciting and memorable heroes and completely bleed the life and spirit out of them. Because it is dangerous to teach a history that he describes as "studded with so many bold, and revolutionary, and subversive, and exhilarating men and women," Kozol maintains that schools instead drain these heroes of their passions, glaze them over with an implausible veneer, place them on lofty pedestals, and then tell "incredibly dull stories" about them.[4] For example, in trying to make Martin Luther King, Jr. palatable to the mainstream, schools have made him a milquetoast. The only thing most children know about him is that he kept having a dream. Bulletin boards are full of ethereal pictures of Dr. King surrounded by clouds. If children get to read or hear any of his speeches at all, it is his "I Have a Dream" speech. Rare indeed are the allusions to his early and consistent opposition to the Vietnam War; his strong criticism of unbridled capitalism; and the connections he made, near the end of his life, among racism, capitalism, and war. Martin Luther King, a man full of passion and life, becomes lifeless. He becomes a "safe hero."

Most of the heroes we present to our children are either those who are in the mainstream or those who have become safe by the process of "tailoring." Others who have fought for social justice are often downplayed, maligned, or simply ignored. For example, although John Brown's actions in defense of the liberation of enslaved people are considered noble by many, in our history books he is presented, if at all, as somewhat of a crazed idealist. Nat Turner is another example. The slave revolt that he led deserves an important place in our history, if only to acknowledge that people fought against their oppression and were not simply passive or victimized by it. Yet his name is usually overlooked, and Abraham Lincoln is presented as the "great emancipator." Nat Turner is not safe; Abraham Lincoln is.

To be antiracist also means to work affirmatively to combat racism. It means making antiracism and antidiscrimination an explicit part of the curriculum and teaching young people skills in confronting racism. It also means that students must not be isolated, alienated, or punished for naming it when they see it. If developing productive and critical citizens for a democratic society is one of the important goals of public education, antiracist behaviors are helping to meet that objective.

Racism is often not mentioned in school (it is bad, a dirty word) and therefore not dealt with. Unfortunately, many teachers think that simply having lessons in getting along or celebrating Human Relations Week will make students nonracist or nondiscriminatory in general. It is impossible to be unaffected by racism, sexism, linguicism, ageism, anti-Semitism, classism, and ethnocentrism in a society characterized by all of them. To expect schools to be an oasis of sensitivity and understanding in the midst of this stratification is unrealistic. Therefore, part of the mission of the school becomes creating the space and encouragement that legitimizes talk about racism and discrimination and makes it a source of dialogue in the schools. Part of this task includes learning the missing or fragmented parts of our history.

Multicultural education is also antiracist because it exposes the racist and discriminatory practices in schools discussed in the previous chapters. A school truly committed to a multicultural philosophy will closely examine its policies and the attitudes and behaviors of its staff to determine how these might be discriminating against some students. How teachers react to their students, whether native language use is permitted in the school, how sorting takes place, and the way in which classroom organization might hurt some students and help others are questions to be considered. In addition, individual teachers will reflect on their own attitudes and practices in the classroom and how they are influenced by their background as well as by their ignorance of students' backgrounds. Although such soul-searching is often difficult, it is a necessary step in becoming a teacher committed to an antiracist multicultural philosophy.

Nevertheless, being antiracist does not mean flailing out in guilt or remorse. One of the reasons that schools are reluctant to deal with racism and discrimination is because they are uncomfortable. They often place people in the role of either the victimizer or the victimized. An initial and quite understandable reaction of European American teachers and students is to feel guilty. Such a reaction, however, although probably serving an initial useful purpose, needs to be understood as only one step in the process of becoming multiculturally literate and empowered. If it remains at this level, guilt only immobilizes. Teachers and students need to move beyond the guilt stage to one of energy and confidence, where they take action rather than hide behind feelings of remorse.

The primary victims of racism and discrimination are those who suffer its immediate consequences, but racism and discrimination are destructive and demeaning to everybody. By keeping this in mind, it is easier for all teachers and students to confront it. Although everybody is not "guilty" of racism and discrimination, we are all responsible for it. Given this perspective, students and teachers can focus on discrimination as something everybody has a responsibility to confront. For example, in discussing slavery in the United States, it is important to present it not simply as slave owners against enslaved Africans. There were many and diverse roles among a great variety of people during this period: enslaved Africans and free Africans, slave owners and poor White farmers, Black abolitionists and White abolitionists, White and Black feminists who fought for both abolition and women's liberation, and so on. Each of these perspectives should be taught so that children, regardless of ethnic background or gender, see themselves in history in ways that are neither degrading nor guilt-provoking. The incident of the only Black child in a classroom who was asked by his teacher to draw himself as a character during the Civil War is a poignant example. This child drew a horse, preferring to see himself as an animal rather than as a slave. The deep sense of pain and emptiness that this child felt can only be surmised. Providing alternative roles for our students is therefore another aspect of an antiracist multicultural perspective.

Multicultural Education Is Basic Education

Given the recurring concern for the "basics" in education, it is absolutely essential that multicultural education be understood as *basic* education. Multicultural literacy is as indispensable for living in today's world as are reading, writing, arithmetic, and computer literacy. When multicultural education is unrelated to the core curriculum, it is perceived as unimportant to basic education.

One of the major stumbling blocks to implementing a broadly conceptualized multicultural education is the ossification of the "canon" in our schools. The canon, as used in contemporary U.S. education, assumes that the knowledge that is most worthy is already in place. According to this rather narrow view, the basics have in effect already been defined. Knowledge, in this context, is inevitably European, male, and upper class in origin and conception, especially in the arts and social sciences. Open up almost any literature anthology used in the high schools and you will find a list of European and

European American authors, almost exclusively male, sometimes with a smattering of women and people of color for "balance." In art history, courses rarely leave France, Italy, and sometimes England in considering the "great" artists. What is called "classical" music is classical only in Europe, not in Africa, Asia, or Latin America. This same enthnocentrism is found in our history books, which place Europeans and European Americans as the actors and all others as the recipients, bystanders, or bit players of history.

It is unrealistic, for a number of reasons, to expect a perfectly "equal treatment" in the curriculum. A "force-fit,"which tries to equalize the number of African Americans, women, Jewish Americans, and so on in the curriculum, is not what multicultural education is all about. The point is that those who *have* been present in our history, arts, literature, and science should be made visible. A great many groups have in effect been denied access in the actual making of history. Their participation has therefore not been equal, at least if we consider history in the traditional sense of great movers and shakers, monarchs and despots, and makers of war and peace. Nevertheless, the participation of these groups, even within this somewhat narrow view of history, has been appreciable. It therefore deserves to be included.

However, we are not talking here simply of the "contributions" approach to history, literature, and the arts. Such an approach may consider some small contributions from usually excluded groups and can easily become patronizing because it looks for contributions to a preconceived canon. Rather, the way in which generally excluded groups have made history and affected the arts, literature, geography, science, and philosophy *on their own terms* is what is missing.

The "canon" is unrealistic and incomplete because history is never so one-sided as it appears in most of our schools' curricula. What is needed is the expansion of what we define as "basic" by opening up the curriculum to a variety of perspectives and experiences. The problem that a canon tries to address is a real one: Modern-day knowledge is so dispersed and compartmentalized that our young people learn very little that is common. There is no *core* to the knowledge to which they are exposed.[5] However, proposing a static list of terms, almost exclusively with European and European American referrants, does little to expand our common culture.

The alternative to multicultural education is *monocultural education*. It is an education reflective of only one reality and biased toward the dominant group. Monocultural education is the order of the day in most of our schools. What students learn represents only a fraction of what is available knowledge. Those who decide what is most important generally reflect the dominant view and make choices that are of necessity influenced by their own background, education, and experiences. Because the viewpoint of so many is left out, monocultural education is at best a partial education. It deprives all students of the diversity that is part of our world.

No school can consider that it is doing a proper or complete job unless its students develop multicultural literacy. What such a conception might mean in practice would no doubt differ from school to school. At the very least, however, we would expect all students to be fluent in a language other than their own; aware of the literature and arts of many different peoples; and conversant with the history and geography not only of the United States but also of African, Asian, Latin American and European countries. Through such an education, we would expect our students to develop the social skills to understand and empathize with a wide diversity of people. Nothing can be more basic than this.

Multicultural Education Is Important for *All* Students

There is a widespread perception that multicultural education is only for students of color or for urban students or for so-called "disadvantaged" students. This belief is probably based on the roots of multicultural education, which grew out of the Civil Rights and equal education movements of the 1960s. The primary objective of multicultural education was defined as addressing the needs of those students who had historically been most neglected or miseducated by the schools, primarily students of color. In trying to strike more of a balance, it was felt that attention should be paid to developing curriculum and materials that reflect the reality of these students' history, culture, and experience and that this curriculum should be destined particularly for inner-city schools populated primarily by children of color. This thinking was historically necessary and is understandable even today, given the great curricular imbalance that continues to exist in most schools.

More recently a broader conceptualization of multicultural education has gained acceptance. It is that all students are *miseducated* to the extent that they receive only a partial and biased education. The primary victims of biased education are those who are invisible in the curriculum. Females, for example, are absent in most curricula, except in special courses on women's history that are few and far between. Although these courses are important and helpful in remediating the almost total lack of a female presence in curriculum and materials, they, too, are a double-edged sword. The message of these courses to both females and males is, as Shakeshaft has noted, that there are two kinds of history: women's history, which is peripheral, and American history, which is "real" history.[6] Working-class history is also absent in virtually all U.S. curricula. Anyon found, for example, that the content of the social studies curriculum was the *least* honest about U.S. history in the working-class schools than in all the others she observed. Also, in the working-class schools the least mention of potentially controversial topics occurred. Ironically, it was only in what she calls the "affluent professional school" and the "executive elite school" that the content of social studies instruction was more complex, sophisticated, and honest and that the curriculum and texts allowed discussions of competing worldviews and the dynamics of social class.[7] The children of the working class are deprived not only of a more forthright education but, more important, of a place in history.

Although the primary victims of biased education continue to be those who are invisible in the curriculum, those who figure prominently are victims as well. They receive only a partial education, which legitimizes cultural blinders. European American children, seeing only themselves, learn that they are the norm; everyone else is secondary. The same is true of males. And the children of the wealthy, although generally exposed to a more comprehensive view of history, learn nevertheless that the wealthy and the powerful are the real makers of history, the ones to have left their mark on civilization.

Multicultural education is by definition expansive. Because it is *about* all people, it is also *for* all people, regardless of their ethnicity, language, religion, gender, race, or class. It can even be convincingly argued that students from the dominant culture need multicultural education more than others, for they are often the most miseducated about diversity in our society. In fact, European American youths often feel that they do not even *have* a culture, at least not in the same sense that clearly culturally identifiable youths do. At the same time, they also feel that their way of living, of doing things, of believing, and of acting are simply the only possibilities. Anything else is ethnic and exotic.

Feeling as they do, these children are prone to develop an unrealistic view of the world and of their place in it. They learn to think of themselves and their group as the norm and of all others as a deviation. These are the children who learn not to question, for example, the name of "flesh-colored" adhesive strips although they are not the flesh color of three-quarters of humanity. They do not even have to think about the fact that everyone, Christian or not, gets holidays at Christmas and Easter and that other religious holidays are given little attention in our calendars and school schedules. Whereas children from dominated groups may develop feelings of inferiority based on their school experiences, dominant group children may develop feelings of superiority. Both are based on incomplete and inaccurate information about the complexity and diversity of the world in which we live, and both are harmful.

Nevertheless, multicultural education continues to be thought of by many teachers and schools as education for the "culturally different" or the "disadvantaged." Teachers in predominately European American schools, for example, may feel it is not important or necessary to teach their students anything about the civil rights movement; likewise only in scattered bilingual programs in Mexican American communities are students exposed to literature by Mexican and Mexican American authors; and only at high schools with a high percentage of students of color are ethnic studies generally taught. These are ethnocentric interpretations of multicultural education.

This thinking is paternalistic as well as misinformed. Anything remotely digressing from the "regular" (European American) curriculum is automatically considered "soft." Therefore, the usual response to make a curriculum multicultural is to water it down. Poor pedagogical decisions are then based on the premise that so called "disadvantaged" students need a watered-down version of the "real" curriculum, whereas more privileged children can handle the "regular" or more academically challenging curriculum. Gay says that the curriculum selected for diverse learners should be of a parallel *order*. For example, "if Robert Frost's and Emily Dickinson's works are used to teach the canons of good poetry for Anglo students, then the rapping routines of Run DMC and the Fat Boys are inappropriate to use as an Afro-American illustration of those same principles."[8] Although *all* students need to learn about the literature of many different cultures, her point is well taken because it is usually *only* African American students who are exposed to curriculum adaptations of this kind. Gay thus suggests that a parallel, and thus more appropriate, example would be the works of Maya Angelou and Langston Hughes. Making a curriculum multicultural should in no way dilute it; on the contrary, making it more inclusive inevitably enriches it. All students would be enriched by reading the poetry of Langston Hughes and Maya Angelou.

Multicultural education, being an alternative approach, is often considered to be most appropriate for children "at risk" of educational failure. There is a faulty conception concerning who such students are. The feeling is that students of color and those from economically oppressed families are most at risk. A comprehensive national study, however, found that between 25 and 35 percent of *all* students in the United States are seriously at risk.[9] Even these figures are considered to be artificially low. Although race, ethnicity, social class, and limited English proficiency may indeed be "risk factors" for school success, at least in terms of how schools are currently organized, most students identified as being at risk in this survey were White and middle class. Yet the term itself has become a code word for students of color from inner-city schools or poor students of all cultural backgrounds from rural and urban schools.

Students at risk of educational failure can and do come from all social and cultural backgrounds and find themselves on the periphery of the educational environment for a variety of reasons. Perhaps a more appropriate term for such students is *marginal,* as used by Sinclair and Ghory.[10] This term implies that the conditions for the failure of students are not inherent in the students themselves but rather in the learning environments created for them. By changing the environments, the so-called risk factors are reduced and marginal students again enter the educational center. A broadly conceptualized multicultural education focusing on school reform represents a substantive way of changing the curriculum, the environment, the structure of schools, and instructional strategies so that all students can benefit.

Multicultural Education Is Pervasive

Multicultural education is sometimes thought of as something that happens at a set period of the day, yet another subject area to be "covered." In a few school systems, there is even a "multicultural teacher" who goes from class to class in the same way as the music or art teacher. Although the intent of this approach may be to formalize a multicultural perspective within the standard curriculum, it is in the long run self-defeating because it tends to isolate the multicultural philosophy from everything else that happens in the classroom. By letting classroom teachers not take responsibility for creating a multicultural approach, this strategy often alienates them by presenting multicultural knowledge as somehow contradictory to all other knowledge. The schism between what is "regular" and what is "multicultural" widens. In this kind of arrangement, classroom teachers are not encouraged, through either formal in-service programs or alternative opportunities, to develop an expertise in multicultural education. It becomes exotic knowledge that is external to the "real" work that goes on in most classrooms. Given this conception of multicultural education, it is no wonder that teachers sometimes feel that it is a frill they cannot afford.

A true multicultural approach to education is pervasive. It permeates the physical environment in the classroom, the curriculum, and the relationships among teachers and students and community. It can be seen in every lesson, curriculum guide, unit, bulletin board, and letter that is sent home; it can be seen in the process by which books and audiovisual aids are acquired for the library, the games played during recess, and the lunch that is served. Seen in this way, multicultural education is a philosophy, a way of looking at the world, not simply a program or a class or a teacher. In this comprehensive way, multicultural education helps us rethink school reform.

What might this multicultural philosophy mean in the way that schools are organized? For one, it would probably mean the end of tracking, for it inevitably favors some students over others. It would also mean that the complexion of the school, both literally and figuratively, would change. That is, the entire school staff would be representative of the diversity of the immediate and outside community. Pervasiveness would probably also be apparent in the great variety and creativity of instructional strategies since students from both the dominant and other cultural groups, and females as well as males, would benefit from methods other than the traditional. The curriculum would be completely overhauled and would include the histories, viewpoints, and insights of many different peoples and both males and females. "Dangerous" topics could be talked about in classes, and students would be encouraged to become critical thinkers. Textbooks would also reflect a pluralistic perspective. Parents and community people would be more visible in the schools because they would offer a unique and helpful perspective the school would welcome. Teachers, parents, and students would have the opportunity to work together to design motivating and multiculturally appropriate curricula.

In other less global but no less important ways, the multicultural school would probably look vastly different as well. For example, the lunchroom might offer a variety of international meals, not because they are "strange" or exotic delights but because they are the foods people in the community eat daily. Sports and games from all over the world might be played, and they would not all be competitive. Letters would be sent home in the languages that parents understand. Children would not be punished for speaking their native language; on the contrary, they would be encouraged to do so and to teach their classmates and teachers as well. In summary, the school would be a learning environment in which curriculum, pedagogy, and outreach are all consistent with a broadly conceptualized multicultural philosophy.

Multicultural Education Is Education for Social Justice

All good education connects theory with reflection and action, which is what Paulo Freire defines as *praxis*.[11] In particular, developing a multicultural perspective means learning how to think in more inclusive and expansive ways, reflecting on what we learn, and putting our learning into action. Multicultural education invites students and teachers to put their learning into action for social justice. Whether debating an issue, developing a community newspaper, starting a collaborative program at a local senior center, or beginning a petition for the removal of a potentially dangerous waste treatment plant in the neighborhood, students learn that they have power, collectively and individually, to make change.

This aspect of multicultural education fits in particularly well with the developmental level of young people who, starting in the middle elementary grades, are very conscious of what is fair and what is unfair. Their pronounced sense of justice seldom has an opportunity to be channeled appropriately. The result can be anger, resentment, alienation from schooling, or simply dropping out physically or psychologically. Schools represent an ideal environment for tackling some of these important issues.

Yet as McNeil found in an ethnographic study, the educational purposes of schools are often at odds with their administrative purposes.[12] She focused on four midwestern high schools chosen for the variation in the relationship between administration and classroom instruction. McNeil was specifically interested in the ways in which the knowledge taught in schools is inevitably shaped by the school's organization. Despite their diversity, she found all four schools to be characterized by what she called "flattened content, ritualistic teaching, and disengaged students."[13]

Teachers, too, become alienated in such institutions. Given their feeling of powerlessness, they developed defensive teaching strategies:

- *Fragmentation of the curriculum;* that is, knowledge broken up into small bits and pieces, often unrelated to one another
- *Mystification,* in which the teachers' role as subject matter and classroom authority was maintained
- *Omission,* in which topics considered too controversial or complex were omitted from the curriculum
- *Defensive simplification,* that is, oversimplification of work so that students were not expected or required to expend too much effort.

Yet having high expectations, engaging students in demanding and rigorous academic work, presenting knowledge as interconnected and complex, and confronting controversial topics directly are the very approaches that would no doubt make schools more exciting and relevant for young people. By avoiding or circumventing them, the school remains antiseptic and detached from real life.

Students are often denied the opportunity to engage in learning that is related to the lives they lead in their communities. For example, Nancy Commins found that the school lives of Mexican American children were not only different but almost diametrically opposed to their home lives.[14] Although the children and their families were intimately acquainted with the issues of undocumented workers, poverty, and discrimination, the school reflected an almost total lack of awareness of these problems or at least an unwillingness to reflect them in the curriculum. The children found that what they learned at school could not be applied to their lives outside of school. In contrast, Moll's research in effective classrooms for Latino students found that teachers in these classrooms encourage their students to use personal experiences to make sense of their school experiences.[15] Topics that might be considered controversial because they revolve around community issues are commonplace in these classrooms and are used to expand the students' literacy. This might be the case, for example, in exploring issues of language discrimination, police brutality, or homelessness in the community.

The fact that social structures and power are rarely discussed in school should come as no surprise. Schools are organizations fundamentally concerned with maintaining the status quo and not exposing contradictions that make people uncomfortable in a society that has democratic ideals but where democratic realities are not always apparent. Such contradictions include the many manifestations of inequality. Yet schools are also supposed to wipe out these inequalities. To admit that inequality exists and that it is even perpetuated by the very institutions charged with doing away with it is far too dangerous an issue. Nevertheless, such issues are at the heart of a broadly conceptualized multicultural perspective because the subject matter of schooling is society, with all its wrinkles and warts and contradictions. And because society is concerned with the distribution of power, status, and rewards, education must focus on these concerns as well.

The connection of multicultural education with students' future rights and responsibilities in a democracy is unmistakable. However, many young people do not learn about these responsibilities, about the challenges of democracy, or about the important role of citizens in ensuring and maintaining the privileges of democracy. A major study on adolescents found, for example, that most youths know little about the political process and do not make connections between the actions of government and those of citizens.[16] This is precisely where multicultural education can have a great impact. Not only should classrooms *allow* discussions that focus on social justice, but they should in fact *welcome* them. These discussions might center on concerns that heavily affect culturally diverse communities—poverty, discrimination, war, the national budget—and what students can do to change them. Schools cannot be separated from social justice. Because all of these concerns are pluralistic, education must of necessity be multicultural.

Multicultural Education Is a Process

Curriculum and materials represent the *content* of multicultural education, but multicultural education is above all a *process*. First, it is ongoing and dynamic. No one ever stops becoming a multicultural person, and knowledge is never complete. Thus, there is no established "canon." Second, it is a process because it involves relationships among people. The sensitivity and understanding teachers show their students are often more important than the facts and figures they may know about the different ethnic and cultural groups. Third, and most important, multicultural education is a process because it focuses on such intangibles as teachers' expectations, learning environments, students' learning styles, and other cultural variables that are absolutely essential for schools to understand to be successful with all of their students.

However, process is too often relegated to a secondary position, because content is easier to handle and has speedier results. For instance, developing an assembly program on Black History Month is easier than eliminating tracking. Both are important, but the processes of multicultural education are generally more complex, more politically volatile, or more threatening to vested interests. Changing a basal reader is therefore easier than developing higher expectations for all students. The first involves changing one book for another; the other involves changing perceptions, behaviors, and knowledge, not an easy task.

Multicultural education must be accompanied by "unlearning" conventional wisdom as well as dismantling the policies and practices that disadvantage some students. Teacher education programs would be reconceptualized to include awareness of such intangibles as learning styles and other cultural influences on learning, the persistence of racism and discrimination in schools and society, and instructional and curricular strategies that encourage learning among a wide variety of students. Teachers' roles in the school would also have to be redefined since empowered teachers help to empower students.[17] The role of parents would no doubt need to be expanded so that the insights and values of the community could be more faithfully reflected in the school. A complete restructuring of curriculum and of the organization of schools is what is called for. The process is complex, problematic, controversial, and time-consuming but one in which teachers and schools must engage to make their schools truly multicultural.

Multicultural Education Is Critical Pedagogy

Knowledge is neither neutral nor apolitical, yet it is generally treated by teachers and schools as if it were. Consequently, what is presented to students tends to be knowledge of the lowest common denominator, that which is sure to offend the fewest and is least controversial. Nevertheless, history, including educational history, is full of great debates, controversies, and ideological struggles. The current debate concerning the canon and cultural literacy versus the need for multicultural literacy in the curriculum is one example.[18] These controversies and conflicts are often left at the schoolhouse door. Yet every educational decision made at any level, whether by a teacher or an entire school system, reflects the political ideology and worldview of the decision maker. Decisions to dismantle tracking, discontinue standardized tests, lengthen the school day, or use learning centers rather than rows of chairs all reflect a particular view of learners and of education.

It is important to understand that as teachers, all the decisions we make, no matter how neutral they may seem, may impact in unconscious but fundamental ways on the lives and experiences of our students. This is true of the curriculum, books, and other materials we provide for our students. State and local guidelines and mandates may limit what particular schools and teachers choose to teach, and this too is a political decision. What is excluded is often as telling as what is included. Because most literature taught at the high school level, for instance, is heavily male and Eurocentric, the roles of women, people of color, and those who write in other languages are thus diminished, unintentionally or not.

A major problem with a monocultural curriculum is that it gives students only one way of seeing the world. Reality is often presented in schools as static, finished, and flat. The underlying tensions, controversies, passions, and problems faced by people throughout history and today are sadly missing. To be truly informed and active participants in a democratic society, students need to learn to understand the complexity of the world and of the many perspectives involved. They have to understand that there is not only one way of seeing things, nor even two or three. A handy number to keep in mind, simply because it reflects how complex a process it really is, is 17: There are at least 17 ways of understanding reality, and until we have learned to do that, we have only part of the truth.

According to Banks, the main goal of a multicultural curriculum is to help students develop decision-making and social action skills.[19] By doing so, students learn to view events and situations from a variety of perspectives. A multicultural approach values diversity and encourages critical thinking, reflection, and action. Through this process, students can be empowered as well. It is therefore both a critical and a liberating education. Its opposite is what Freire calls "domesticating education," education that emphasizes passivity, acceptance, and submissiveness.[20] Liberating education encourages students to take risks, to be curious, and to question. Rather than expecting students to repeat teachers' words, it expects them to seek their own answers. According to Freire, education for domestication is a process of "transferring knowledge," whereas education for liberation is one of "transforming action."[21] Empowerment then means that students and teachers recognize their right and responsibility to take action. Sleeter and Grant explain as follows: "Ideally, education should help all students include a perspective of history from the students' point of view and be selected and constructed in relationship to the students' desires, visions, descriptions of reality, and repertoires of action."[22]

What does critical pedagogy mean in terms of multicultural education? A critical pedagogy ensures that cultural and linguistic diversity is acknowledged rather than suppressed, as is often the case. According to Cummins, because "transmission models" exclude and deny students' experiences, they cannot be multicultural: "a genuine multicultural orientation that promotes minority student empowerment is impossible within a transmission model of pedagogy."[23]

A few examples of how the typical curriculum discourages students from thinking critically, and what this has to do with a multicultural perspective, are in order. In most schools, students learn that Columbus discovered America; that the United States was involved in a heroic westward expansion until the nineteenth century; that Puerto Ricans were granted U.S. citizenship in 1917; that enslaved Africans were freed by the Emancipation Proclamation in 1863; that the people who made our country great were the financial barons of the previous century; and if they learn anything about it at all, that Japanese Americans were housed in detention camps during World War II for security reasons.

History, as we know, is generally written by the conquerors, not by the vanquished or by those who benefit least in society. The result is history books skewed in the direction of those who are dominant in a society. If Indian people were to write the history books, they would probably say that Columbus had invaded, not discovered, this land, that there was no heroic westward expansion but rather an eastern encroachment. Mexican Americans might include references to Aztlán, the legendary land that was overrun by Europeans during this encroachment. Puerto Rico would probably remove the gratuitous word *granted* that appears in so many textbooks and explain that citizenship was instead imposed, and it was opposed by even the two houses of the legislature that existed in Puerto Rico in 1917. African Americans would describe the active participation of enslaved Africans in their own liberation and would include slave narratives and other accounts of rebellion and resistance. Workers would no doubt credit working people rather than Andrew Carnegie with building the country and the economy. And Japanese Americans would most likely cite racist hysteria, economic exploitation, and propaganda as major reasons for their evacuation to concentration camps during World War II.

Critical pedagogy is not simply the transfer of knowledge from teacher to students, even though that knowledge may contradict what students had learned before. Thus, learning about the internment of Japanese Americans during World War II is in itself not critical pedagogy. It only becomes so when students critically analyze different perspectives and use them to understand and act on the inconsistencies they uncover. A multicultural perspective does not simply operate on the principle of substituting one "truth" or perspective for another. Rather, it reflects on multiple and contradictory perspectives to understand reality more fully. In addition, it uses the understanding gained from reflection to make changes. Thus teachers need to learn to respect even those viewpoints with which they may disagree, not to teach that which is "politically correct" but rather to teach students to develop a critical perspective about what they hear, read, or see.

Consider the hypothetical English literature book previously mentioned. Let us say that students and their teacher have decided to review the textbook to determine whether it fairly represents the voices and perspectives of a number of groups. Finding that it does not is in itself a valuable learning experience. However, if nothing is done with this analysis, it remains academic; but it becomes more meaningful if used as the basis for further action. Students might propose, for example, that the English Department order a book more inclusive of other groups for the coming year. They might decide to put together their own book, based on literature that is multicultural and with a number of perspectives. Critical pedagogy, however, does not always means that there is a linear process from *knowledge* to *reflection* to *action*. If this were the case, it would become yet another mechanistic strategy. We should not understand this reflection and action as only within the abilities of high school students. On the contrary, critical pedagogy can take place at the preschool and elementary school level as well, which has been demonstrated in a number of studies.[24]

Critical pedagogy is also an exploder of myths. It helps to expose and "de-mythify" some of the truths that we have been taught to take for granted and to analyze them critically and carefully. Justice for all, equal treatment under the law, and equal educational opportunity, although certainly ideals worth believing in and striving for, are not always a reality. The problem is that we teach them as if they were always real, always true, with no exceptions. Critical pedagogy allows us to have faith in these ideals without uncritically accepting their reality.

Critical pedagogy is based on the experiences and viewpoints of students rather than on an imposed culture. It is therefore multicultural as well because the most successful education is that which begins with the learner. Students themselves are the foundation for the curriculum. Nevertheless, a liberating education takes students beyond their own limited experiences, no matter what their background. A few examples of the connection between critical and multicultural education will demonstrate this relationship.

Many years ago, Ashton-Warner, teaching Maori children in New Zealand, found that their education was completely imposed from above.[25] The curriculum, materials, viewpoints, and pedagogy were all borrowed from a culture alien to that of the students. Because Maori children had been failed dismally by New Zealand schools, Ashton-Warner decided to develop a strategy for literacy based on the children's experiences and interests. Calling it an "organic" approach, she taught children how to read by using the words that *they* wanted to learn. Each child would bring in a number of words each day, learn to read them, and then use them in writing. Her approach was extraordinarily successful because it was based on what children knew and what they wanted to know. In contrast, basal readers, because they have nothing to do with the learners' experiences, are mechanistic instruments for what Freire calls "depositing" the educator's words in the learner.[26] The result is a severe limitation of the power of creativity and expressiveness by students.

Other approaches that have successfully used the experiences of students are worth mentioning. Heath's work is particularly noteworthy as is research by Moll and numerous projects cited by Cummins.[27] In all of the projects the children's background, language, and culture are used as the basis for their education. Rather than avoid their experiences, these programs consciously seek them out and use them as the major source of the curriculum. The result is generally a positive one.

SUMMARY

In this chapter, we have defined multicultural education by these seven characteristics:

Antiracist
Basic
Important for all students
Pervasive
Education for social justice
Process
Critical pedagogy

Given these characteristics, multicultural education represents a way of rethinking school reform because it responds to many of the problematic factors leading to school under-achievement and failure. When implemented comprehensively, multicultural education can provide an alternative that is equitable and capable of transforming the schooling of young people so that it is meaningful and responsive to their needs. Furthermore, because multicultural education is an educational process that takes into account the culture, language, and experiences of all students, it can go beyond the simple transfer of skills to include those attitudes and critical skills that have the potential to empower students for productive and meaningful lives within our democratic institutions.

This discussion leads us to an important consideration: *In the final analysis, multicultural education as defined here is simply good pedagogy.* That is, all good education takes students seriously, uses their experiences as a basis for further learning, and helps them develop into critical and empowered citizens. What is multicultural about this? To put it simply, in our multicultural society, all good education needs to take into account the diversity of our student body. That is, multicultural education is good education for a larger number of students.

Is multicultural education just as necessary in a monocultural society? We might legitimately ask whether even the most ethnically homogeneous society is truly mono-cultural, given the diversity of social class, language, sexual preference, physical ability, and other human and social differences present in all societies. In addition, our world is becoming more interdependent. Students have to understand their role in a global society and not simply in a nation. Multicultural education, therefore, is a process that goes beyond the changing demographics in a particular country. It is more effective education for a changing world.

TO THINK ABOUT

1. What is the difference between a *broadly conceptualized multicultural education* and multicultural education as defined in terms of "holidays and heroes"?
2. Why is it important that antiracism and antidiscrimination in general be at the very core of multicultural education?

3. As a proponent of multicultural education, you have been asked by the school board in your city to do a public presentation on its benefits. One of the issues the board members are certain to question you about is the conflict between multicultural education and the "basics." Prepare a presentation in which you answer these critics.

4. How are the European American students *miseducated* if they have not been exposed to a multicultural curriculum?

5. Multicultural education has often been considered an "alternative" approach. Why? Is this classification helpful or detrimental?

6. Your school has just hired a "multicultural teacher." Although you and a group of colleagues supportive of multicultural education wanted a more pervasive presence in the school than simply one teacher, you are on the hiring committee and have decided to use your influence to determine the job qualifications and job description. What should these be?

7. Think of a number of curriculum ideas that conform to the definition of multicultural education as social justice. How might students be engaged through the curriculum to consider and act on issues of social justice? Give some specific examples.

8. With a group of colleagues, think about an art, science, or math project that builds on multicultural education as critical pedagogy. How would it do so? In what activities would students be involved? How would these activities motivate them to think critically? To become empowered?

9. How would *you* define multicultural education? What would you include? Why? Define it for yourself first, and then get together with a group of colleagues for a collective definition. How do your definitions differ? Why? How might your classrooms and schools differ as a result?

NOTES

1. Meyer Weinberg, "Notes from the Editor," *A Chronicle of Equal Education*, 4, 3 (November 1982), 7.
2. Jonathon Kozol, *Death at an Early Age* (Boston, Houghton Mifflin, 1967), p. 68.
3. Michelle Fine, "Silencing in Public Schools," *Language Arts*, 64, 2 (February 1987), 157–174.
4. Jonathon Kozol, "Great Men and Women (Tailored for School Use)," *Learning Magazine*, December 1975, pp. 16–20.
5. E. D. Hirsch, *Cultural Literacy* (Boston, Houghton Mifflin, 1987).
6. Charol Shakeshaft, "A Gender at Risk," *Phi Delta Kappan*, March 1986, pp. 499–503.
7. Jean Anyon, "Social Class and School Knowledge," *Curriculum Inquiry*, 11, 1 (1981), 3–41.
8. Geneva Gay, "Designing Relevant Curriculum for Diverse Learners," *Education and Urban Society*, 20, 4 (August 1988), 327–340.
9. Jack Frymier and Bruce Gansneder, "The Phi Delta Kappa Study of Students at Risk," *Phi Delta Kappan*, October 1989, pp. 142–151.
10. Robert L. Sinclair and Ward Ghory, *Marginal Students: A Primary Concern for School Renewal* (Chicago: McCutchan Publishing, 1987).
11. Paulo Freire, *Pedagogy of the Oppressed* (New York: Seabury Press, 1970).
12. Linda M. McNeil, *Contradiction of Control: School Structure and School Knowledge* (New York: Methuen/Routledge & Kegan Paul, 1986).
13. Ibid.
14. Nancy Commins, "Language and Affect: Bilingual Students at Home and at School," *Language Arts*, 66, 1 (January 1989), 29–43.

15. Luis C. Moll, "Some Key Issues in Teaching Latino Students," *Language Arts,* 65, 5 (September 1988), 465–472.
16. S. Shirley Feldman, and Glen R. Elliott, *At the Threshold: The Developing Adolescent* (Cambridge, MA: Harvard University Press, forthcoming).
17. See McNeil, *Contradiction of Control;* Eugene García, "Attributes of Effective Schools for Language Minority Students," *Education and Urban Society,* 20, 4 (August 1988), 387–398; Michelle Fine, "Why Urban Adolescents Drop Into and Out of Public High School," in *School Dropouts: Patterns and Policies,* ed. Gary Natriello (New York: Teachers College Press, Columbia University, 1986).
18. See, for example, Hirsch, *Cultural Literacy;* Alan Bloom, *The Closing of the American Mind: How Higher Education Has Failed Democracy and Impoverished the Souls of Today's Students* (New York: Simon & Schuster, 1987); Rick Simonson and Scott Walker, eds., *Multicultural Literacy: The Opening of the American Mind* (St. Paul, MN: Greywold Press, 1988).
19. James A. Banks, *Teaching Strategies for Ethnic Studies,* 4th ed. (Boston: Allyn & Bacon, 1987).
20. Paulo Freire, *The Politics of Education: Culture, Power, and Liberation* (South Hadley, MA: Bergin & Garvey, 1985).
21. Freire, *Pedagogy of the Oppressed.*
22. Christine E. Sleeter, and Carl A. Grant, "Mapping Terrains of Power: Student Cultural Knowledge Versus Classroom Knowledge," in *Empowerment Through Multicultural Education,* ed. Christine E. Sleeter (Albany: State University of New York Press, 1991).
23. Jim Cummins, "The Sanitized Curriculum: Educational Disempowerment in a Nation at Risk," in *Richness in Writing: Empowering ESL Students,* ed. Donna M. Johnson and Duane H. Roen (White Plains, NY: Longman, 1989).
24. See, for example, Sheila D. Collins, "Discussing Controversial Topics in Early Childhood Settings," *Bulletin of the Council on Interracial Books for Children,* 14, 7 and 8 (1983), 3–5; Iris Santos Rivera, "Liberating Education for Little Children," *Alternativas,* 1 9–12 (October 1984).
25. Sylvia Ashton-Warner, *Teacher* (New York: Simon & Schuster, 1963).
26. Freire, *Politics of Education.*
27. See, for example, Shirley Brice Heath, "Questioning at Home and at School: A Comparative Study" in *Doing the Ethnography of Schooling: Educational Anthropology in Action,* ed. George Spindler (New York: Holt, Rinehart & Winston, 1982), Moll, "Some Key Issues in Teaching Latino Students"; Jim Cummins, *Empowering Minority Students* (Sacramento: California Association for Bilingual Education, 1989).

CHAPTER **9**

On Being Successful Students

OVERVIEW

The voices of the students in the ten case studies are a testament to the vitality and spirit of youth and culture. Despite a variety of conditions that might severely test the mettle and aspirations of others in similar circumstances, these youths have demonstrated a staunch determination to succeed both in school and in life in general. Because many are a minority in their communities insofar as academic success is concerned, understanding how they have succeeded in spite of the odds against them is vital. Most of them define themselves as successful students and are quite proud of this fact.

In this chapter, we will review the four major issues that emerged from the case studies. We will first explore what the students mean by success and intelligence and compare that with the expectations of schools. We will then explore the role of pride and conflict in culture and language manifested in most of these students' experiences. The important role of activities outside of the classroom in supporting students' enthusiasm for school will be investigated. Finally, the central importance of family, community, and school in developing environments for success is the final theme to be addressed. Specific examples of each of these areas will be discussed.

THE MEANING OF SUCCESS

It is interesting to note that many of the young people in the case studies have a conception of education quite distinct from that commonly held by schools. For some, being ''educated'' is directly derived from family and cultural definitions of this term. Marisol, Yolanda, and Manuel all believe that besides being good students academically, being educated means being respectful, polite, and obedient, a broader connotation typical of Latinos. Vinh also defines education in much broader terms than U.S. society in general.

He maintains that being educated means being, among other things, "nice" and "friendly," as well as listening to your teachers and doing your homework.

The role of hard work in becoming educated was mentioned by most of these students. For them, being intelligent is not an innate ability or immutable quality, something that one is born with, as intelligence is often defined in our society. On the contrary, intelligence is something that one cultivates, studies hard for, and eventually achieves. Being smart is a goal, not a characteristic. As Avi says, success is the result of hard work and confidence in oneself. Being smart is also the result of family and community support and the quality of the care shown by teachers and schools. It is, in this sense, within everyone's reach. Research shows that students who believe that intelligence is fixed tend to earn significantly lower grades than those who believe they can *become* more intelligent.[1] Beliefs about intelligence seem to be related to academic achievement.

Grades are important as an indicator of academic success in our schools, and this is true in the case of these students as well. Contrary to what many teachers and schools may believe, however, grades are not as important to these students as are other manifestations of their success. Many of them mention being satisfied with a grade that they worked hard for, even if it is not the best grade. On the other hand, Yolanda's or Fern's A's in English are not particularly satisfying to them because the classes are neither engaging nor challenging. Yolanda's social studies class and Fern's science class, both far more demanding and ones in which they did not get as high a grade, are their favorites. For many students, grades are not as important as "doing the best you can."

The purposes of education are also much broader for many of these students than the limited goals schools often set. For example, while teachers often talk in terms of future employment and career goals, many of these students see education as far more.[2] For Vinh, going to school has one purpose: to become educated. A good job is secondary. Yolanda put it most dramatically: Education for her is like eating, just as necessary and just as important. This "grand" definition of the purpose of schooling is an important one for teachers and schools to keep in mind.

For Marisol, the purpose of education is also broader. She wants to "be somebody." At present, she has only a vague notion of what this might be, but she does not confuse being educated with preparing for a job. A word should be said here, however, about the vague or romantic ideals female students tend to have regarding their future. Marisol, Yolanda, Fern, and Linda all talked about dual and seemingly contradictory career goals. Yolanda wants to be either a computer programmer or a flight attendant; Marisol, a nurse or a model; Fern, a fashion lawyer or president; and Linda, a teacher or a world-famous singer. Particularly for females, the reality of limited choices has had an impact. Most of these young women have chosen to select what to them seem the most glamorous of these choices. Besides culture, language, and social class, then, gender has an important role in mediating what students may consider realistic goals for their future.

However, their cultures should be understood not only as *limiting* their choices but also as *expanding* them. Females are often subject to limited role expectations and gender stereotyping, but they also receive affirming and powerful messages about being female from their cultures. In one study, a series of in-depth interviews with Latinas sought to determine what messages these women had received during their childhood regarding their future role in society. All ten women reported that they had been taught to be submissive, quiet, long-suffering, and patient by their mothers and grandmothers. Although these were the *verbal* messages they received, they also learned, from their mothers and grandmothers through *nonverbal* attitudes and behaviors, that women need to be resourceful, intelligent, and often stronger than men. These dual and conflicting messages were not lost on the women, all of whom were extraordinarily strong and resilient and who had learned to "take care of themselves."[3]

This research is an example of the many conflicting messages to which young people are exposed. That they may be restrictive is certainly true. However, the fact that students have chosen potential careers that are consistent with these restrictive roles does not necessarily mean that these are the only values they have internalized. As was apparent in their case studies, these young women have also learned to be incredibly determined and even stubborn about their belief in themselves. There are a multitude of values that young people need to sift through to determine which are the appropriate and more empowering choices to make. The role of schools in providing all young people with a variety of liberating role models and expectations that challenge the limiting roles assigned to them by either their own communities or by society at large is thus crucial.

Although each student is a unique individual with experiences quite different from the others and from widely diverse cultural and economic contexts, their experiences have some commonalities. The cultural values of the students and their families and their relevance for academic success are noteworthy in this regard. Their cultures may differ, but the insistence of all the families on maintaining culture and language and on providing support for academic success in a variety of ways is extraordinarily similar.

Throughout a majority of the case studies, three other issues have emerged as consistently important in the academic success of these students:

- A tenacious, although at times conflicted pride in and maintenance of culture and language
- The key role of activities outside of academics in sustaining students' enthusiasm and motivation for school
- The central importance of family, community, and school in providing environments for success

PRIDE AND CONFLICT IN CULTURE

One of the most consistent, and least expected, outcomes to emerge from these case studies has been the resoluteness with which young people maintain pride and satisfaction in their culture and the strength they derive from it. This does not mean, however, that this pride is sustained without great conflict, hesitation, or contradiction. Because the positive sense of cultural identification challenges the messages and models of an essentially assimilationalist society, it creates its own internal conflicts. However, the fact that *almost all of the students* mentioned a deep pride in their culture cannot be overlooked. Interestingly, this was not even one of the questions asked of them. The exception was Vanessa, who felt uncomfortable even describing herself in ethnic terms. The other students volunteered that their culture helped them and that they felt proud of who they were. However, Vanessa also reflected both pride and shame in her cultural background, but for different reasons.

The students mentioned the importance of their culture in a number of ways. In describing himself, James said, "First thing I'd say is, I'm Lebanese." Most of the students, in fact, defined themselves quite naturally in cultural terms, without the embarrassment that one might sometimes expect. Yolanda has no doubt that being Mexican has its benefits. Furthermore, she is aware of what some of those benefits are, particularly being bilingual. These young people seem to understand quite intuitively that their heritage informs and enriches them. Strong self-identification seemed to be understood as a value. "You gotta know who you are," is how Manuel expressed it.

Conflict and Ambivalence

However, pride in culture is neither uniform nor easy. Marisol, for instance, did not feel it was either important or necessary to take a course in Puerto Rican history. She did not even seem to think it was something that the school should offer because, as she puts it, she already knows what she should know, although it became clear that she knew virtually nothing of Puerto Rican history; in this sense, the experiences of most of the other students in the case studies were remarkably similar. Notable exceptions are Avi and James, both of whom have religious institutions on which to rely for this kind of education.

Bourdieu's theory of *cultural capital* and of the role of the schools in determining what knowledge is of most worth is illuminating here.[4] Because schools primarily reflect the knowledge and values of economically and culturally dominant groups in society, they validate and reinforce the cultural capital students from such groups already bring from home. This validation takes place through the curriculum and environment that are expressed, both overtly and covertly, in the school setting. This represents a *symbolic violence* against those groups that are devalued. The cultural model held up for all is not within easy reach of all, and only token numbers of students from less-valued groups can achieve it. If those from dominated groups learn and take on this cultural capital, along the way losing their own culture, language, and values, they may succeed. In this way, the myth of a meritocracy is maintained while few students from dominated groups are permitted to succeed. Given the rules of the game, it is surprising that as many succeed.

Some examples of the symbolic violence suffered by the students can help illustrate this point. James's culture is missing from all school activities, for example, although other, more "visible" cultures are represented. The importance of his culture is diminished through this absence. Fern's invisibility in her school and in the books and curriculum she is exposed to is another example of the devaluation of knowledge. Students often perceive that what is not taught is not worthy of learning. In contrast, the languages and cultures of Yolanda and Manuel are highly evident in their schools, and teachers often refer to them explicitly, thereby giving them even more status. The experiences of these two students in school have more closely reflected their home values. In both cases, bilingual programs were at least partly responsible.

That symbolic violence should cause conflict in students from devalued classes is hardly surprising. The situation is not unique to the United States but happens wherever one group is dominant and held up as the appropriate model. The Finns in Sweden are a case in point. Formerly colonized by the Swedes, the Finns who emigrate to Sweden are often perceived in negative and sometimes hostile ways. Neither their culture nor their language is generally valued in Swedish society. In the words of a young Finn who was educated in Sweden and went through this process, "When the idea had eaten itself deeply into my soul that it was despicable to be a Finn, I began to feel ashamed of my origins."[5] The result can be a conflict that is difficult to resolve. This particular young man concluded that such conflict was the price he had to pay: "In short, in order to live in harmony with my surroundings, I had to live in perpetual conflict with myself."[6]

For the students in these case studies, symbolic violence also seems to have worked, but only partially. For example, Marisol's idea of important school knowledge is only that which the school has deemed to be so. Only American history, not Puerto Rican history, is what counts. She also says that Puerto Ricans are "way badder" than Whites. At the same time and with what may seem to be contradictory feelings, Marisol is very proud of herself, her family, and her people in general. Her pride and satisfaction in her culture therefore become both conflicted and private. The schism between public and private becomes an irreconcilable one, much as it did for Richard Rodriguez, who speaks with both nostalgia and certainty about having to lose his language and culture to fit into the public world of the school and society:

> Without question, it would have pleased me to hear my teachers address me in Spanish when I entered the classroom. I would have felt much less afraid. I would have trusted them and responded with ease. But I would have delayed—for how long postponed?—having to learn the language of public society. I would have evaded—and for how long could I have afforded to delay?—learning the great lesson of school, that I had a public identity. . . . I continued to mumble. I resisted the teacher's demands. (Did I somehow suspect that once I learned public language my pleasing family life would be changed?)[7]

The painful alienation from family and culture is chronicled in the book *Hunger of Memory.* Rodriguez's odyssey points out the sometimes impossible task of reconciling home and school messages, which is particularly difficult for the first generation. However, although the task of trying to fit together what are at times contradictory values takes its toll, it need not always result in the complete loss of language and culture as the only alternative, as suggested by Rodriguez above. We have seen in our case studies that these successful students are struggling to maintain language and culture, in spite of the difficulty of doing so. Fern, for instance, challenges school knowledge when she says, "If there's something in the history book that's wrong, I should tell them that it is wrong."

Although they have learned to feel quite proud of themselves for many things including their culture, their dexterity in functioning in two worlds, and their bilingualism, several of these students have also learned to feel ashamed of their culture and of the people who represent it. They face the burden of having either to deny or lose their culture if they want to succeed or to keep it and fail. Sometimes students blame their families and communities for perceived failures while absolving the school of almost all responsibility. After all, they reason, the school cannot be wrong. Rich's concerns about Blacks' inability to succeed is a good example. Although he seems to understand some of the roadblocks (for he himself has experienced them), he asks, "Well, why can't *everyone* succeed in life?" He sometimes uses words to describe his community that either victimize or blame people for their failure: Blacks are "tacky," "lazy," not "professional," and used to "settling for the easiest way out," some of the very words used by those outside the community to criticize it. It is clear that as a successful student, Rich is using himself as a yardstick with which to measure others. In the process, he is not looking beyond the surface actions and behavior he sees around him. Demanding accountability from one's own community is necessary and important, but the critical analysis that must accompany it is missing. Rich's case, however, is complex. For instance, he does not place all the responsibility on his own community. He considers the role schools and teachers play by having low expectations of Black students. He has also learned that "Blacks have to work harder at things."

Vanessa's case is a particularly intriguing one in this regard. Because she is actively opposed to racism and other forms of discrimination (note her actions beginning in elementary school and her stand against heterosexism), she attempts to distance herself from her background. She already understands the very real benefits she has gained simply from being White. She does not want to claim these benefits and instead takes the position that one's culture and race are unimportant, accepting color-blindness as the ultimate goal of equity.

For others, the conflict is simply too great and they drop out, either physically or psychologically. Fine, in a study of "successful" students in a South Bronx high school, found that they were significantly *more* depressed, *less* politically aware, and *more* conformist than students who had dropped out. The dropout was more likely to be relatively nondepressed, critical of social injustice, and willing to take initiative. Fine concludes that "the price of 'success' for students who remain in school may be muting one's own voice."[8] Scollon and Scollon, in research with Indian students in Koyukon Athabascan villages of the Alaskan interior, found that these students associated the acquisition of literacy with betrayal of ethnic identity.[9] Probably the same forces were at work with African American students faced with "the burden of 'acting White,'" as reported by Fordham and Ogbu. According to these researchers, one major reason Black students do poorly in schools is that they experience great ambivalence and dissonance regarding academic effort and success. In their study of a predominately Black high school in Washington, DC, students developed group loyalty (what they called "fictive kinship") by defining some attitudes and behaviors as "White" and consequently unacceptable. The coping strategies developed by students who wanted to be academically successful and accepted by peers ranged from *underachieving in academic subjects* to *excelling in sports*, all with the purpose of hiding their academic abilities.[10]

Another way for young people to resolve this conflict, at least if they are to succeed in school, is to deny the importance of their culture *in the school setting*. At home, the culture may remain important and even necessary, especially if they wish to maintain close family relationships. At school, it becomes unimportant and superfluous.

Self-identification and Conflict

Another example of the cultural conflict some of these students feel was expressed in an inability to identify both as "American" and as belonging to their cultural group. Their sense of pride in culture precluded identification with the United States. To claim to be both is in effect to deny your background, to be a traitor to it. Manuel, for example, is quite emphatic: "I'm Cape Verdean. I cannot be an American because I'm not an American. That's it." Even somebody as seemingly "American" as James says, "Everybody else would answer, 'I'm American,' but I say, 'I'm Lebanese.' " The possibility that they could be *both* is not even considered by some of these young people. Our society has forced them to make a choice, and they have usually, although not always, made it in favor of their heritage. Although this is an extraordinarily courageous stand on their part, given their youth and the negative messages about ethnicity around them, it can also be a limiting one. The consequences of such a choice probably affect what they think they deserve and are entitled to in this society. Having no attachment, they may also feel they have no rights. That is, they may feel they have no right to claim their fair share of the power and resources of society or even to demand equality within it.

This is not to claim that most young people of their age would make similar choices. Nevertheless, it is noteworthy that these academically successful students have opted to identify, for the most part, not as "Americans" but as a member of their ethnic or national group. The relationship between a strong identification with their culture and their academic success cannot be overlooked. However, this exclusive identification as a member of their cultural group may also excacerbate the conflict of being "separate," "different," and consequently powerless.

The way that culture is maintained is also interesting to observe in these young people. In more than one case, they have maintained their "deep culture," particularly values and worldviews, often losing the more superficial aspects such as food and music preferences. These kinds of modifications are a function not only of differing messages from school and home, but also of the involvement of young people with a peer culture, with its own rituals, manifestations, and norms. As such, it represents a primary assimilating structure of our society. At the same time, we should not assume that they have lost their culture simply because they seem to act like other young people their age. For example, on the one hand, James would no doubt be considered by most people an "average American kid." Given his friends, hobbies, and life-style, this is probably true. On the other hand, his deep respect for the values of his home, his maintenance of Arabic, and his pride in and knowledge of his background all refute what might be considered the inevitable process of Americanization.

Creating New Cultures

This discussion brings us to another important role in which these young people are involved: the crucial job of creating new cultures. Their native cultures do not simply disappear, as schools and society might expect or want them to. Rather, aspects of the native culture are retained, modified, reinserted into different environments, and "reissued," so to speak, so that they are valid and workable for a new society. These young people do not totally express the original values of their cultures, nor have they been completely assimilated into the new culture. Marisol, for instance, loves rap and hip hop music, not salsa. Nevertheless, the influence of Latino (as well as other cultures) on these musical forms cannot be denied. The same can be said of the 1980s phenomenon of break dancing, a unique blend of African American and Latino music and movement transported to the U.S. urban scene.

Transformed values and behaviors resurface in sometimes surprising ways. For example, it has been convincingly documented that African American families maintain some important aspects of African culture in their child-rearing practices, values, and interactions.[11] This is not meant to suggest that African values and practices have remained intact or that they are isolated from the U.S. experience, but their impact on families and communities cannot be denied. They can be seen in such attitudes and behaviors as verbal rituals, the value of cooperation and family obligations, and the relational learning style that characterizes many African American children in school. If such important vestiges of culture can be seen in a group historically although not necessarily emotionally removed from its roots, it is clear that other ethnic and racial groups with more recent experience in the United States or those who have remained relatively isolated from the mainstream, such as American Indians, will have even greater retention of cultural values and life-styles.

The fashioning of a new culture is no easy task. It involves first the difficult and painful experience of learning to survive in an environment that may have values and behaviors at polar extremes from those in the home, for instance, the oft-cited example of Latino children looking down when being reprimanded. Whereas these children have been taught in their homes to look down as a sign of respect, in U.S. mainstream society such behavior is generally interpreted as disrespectful. Children who misbehave are expected to "take their medicine" and "look me straight in the eye." The behaviors expected at home and at school are thus diametrically opposed. Even five-year-old children are expected to understand the subtle nuances of these behaviors. They usually do, although their teachers are often completely unaware of the conflicts involved or of the great strains such competing expectations may cause. This example only scratches the surface.

The next step involved in creating new cultures is to make choices from an array of values and behaviors, selecting those that "fit" in the new society and discarding or transforming others. This process is, of course, neither conscious nor planned. Nevertheless, those who represent values and behaviors different from the mainstream are of necessity involved in this transformation every day. Whether children or adults, students or workers, they are changing the complexion, attitudes, and values of the society in which they live. In the process, they experience the pain and conflict the young people in our case studies so well demonstrated.

The important point to remember here is that U.S. society does not simply impose its culture on all newcomers. The process is neither as linear nor as straightforward as those who claim complete success for the process of *Anglo-conformity* might have us believe. Anglo-conformity refers to the pressures, both expressed and hidden, to conform to the values, attitudes, and behaviors representative of the dominant group. But the result has not been a truly pluralistic society either. Thus, although the United States is in *fact* multicultural, it is so in spite of itself; it is not the result of a goal or a desired state. Our society for the most part still reflects and perpetuates European American values and worldviews. Nevertheless, it has always reflected, albeit at times poorly or stereotypically and against its will, the values of less valued and dominated groups as well. Latino heritage, for instance, can be seen in innumerable ways, from architecture in the Southwest to the myth of the cowboy, a basically Latino creation. Jazz, widely acknowledged to be the greatest authentic U.S. music, is neither Anglo nor European American. What is "American" is neither simply an alien culture imposed on dominated groups nor an immigrant culture transposed to new soil. Neither is it an amalgam of old and new. What is "American" is the complex of interactions of old, new, and created cultures. These interactions are not benign or smooth. Often characterized by unavoidable tension and great conflict, the creation of new cultures takes place in the battlefields of the family, the community, and the schools.

Choices for Survival and Success

Creating new cultures is an exceedingly complex process. Young people are the ones most thoroughly engaged in this job, as they must face the schools every day. The role of schools, conscious or not, is to transform all students into a middle-class, European American model. One Latina student in a Boston high school has expressed it like this: "They want to *monoculture* us," she says emphatically.[12] But students, too, are changing the schools and the society. The results are not always positive nor are they always negative. They are an understandable response to an assimilationist society attempting to do away with differences.

Given the "choices" they have, students do not always make the best or most appropriate decisions. The choices are generally quite limited: either assimilation or rejection. Both are poor alternatives, according to Skutnabb-Kangas. She maintains that whereas rejection (in the form of dropping out, not taking an active part in school, or not engaging in behaviors that may lead to academic success) may seem to be an appropriate response to a system that is in effect not giving them a fair chance, if students accept this route as inevitable, they are fooling themselves into believing that they really had a choice. "Thus their rejection of a system which has as one of its goals to make them accept the unequal division of power and resources and a place at the lower end of the system, anchors them firmly exactly there, and makes it look as if it was their own choice, a choice which they celebrate."[13]

Rejection can be seen as resistance, but it cannot always be thought of as a successful strategy. This is the situation Fordham and Ogbu termed "the burden of 'acting white.' "[14] Black students, in creating what the researchers call an "oppositional culture," are in fact rejecting the only model of success offered to them, which they perceive as a White model. In the process, many of them are aiding in their own miseducation. The other choice they have, which is assimilation, often leads to shame, academic failure, and loss of identity. Young people from dominated groups often have the choice of having no choice.

Rejection, however, according to Skutnabb-Kangas, can be a *starting point* toward more permanent change. If it is combined with creating an alternative to what one is rejecting, it can serve an important purpose. For the most part, the young people in the case studies have chosen *neither* rejection *nor* assimilation. Because they are all academically successful students, it is clear that they have not rejected schooling but have "followed the rules of the game" in school. However, neither have they chosen to assimilate, as is seen in their maintenance of language, culture, and pride, although riddled with conflict, and in their very clear critique of schools and the instructional strategies used by teachers. The process is not always easy and is in fact fraught with conflict, uncertainty, and pain.

These young people are also involved in the exceedingly difficult job of creating new alternatives for achieving success in school. By refusing to accept either assimilation or rejection, they force us to look at new ways of defining success. They contradict the road to success that has generally been offered by schools and society. In the process, they create new models:

- They have held onto their culture, or at least parts of it, sometimes obstinately so.
- They are often bilingual, even demanding to use their language in school whether or not they are in a bilingual program.
- They are involved with their peers from a variety of backgrounds, with "typical American" teenage activities, tastes, and behaviors.

Thus, they are involved in the job of transforming values, in the process transforming some of the values of our society.

Messages About Language and Culture

The competing message that emerges from the case studies can be stated as follows: Culture is important, something that most of the students are proud of and maintain; but although resisting complete assimilation, they also learn that culture is also unimportant in the school environment. One intriguing lesson from this message is this: *The more students are involved in resisting assimilation while maintaining their culture and language, the more successful they will be in school.* That is, cultural maintenance, even if conflicted, seems to have a positive impact on academic success. This is obviously not true in all cases, as there are many examples of people who have felt that they had to assimilate to succeed in school. Richard Rodriguez, forced to choose between what he considered public and private worlds, is a case in point. He came to the painful conclusion that his native language and culture had no place in the public world of U.S. schools or society. We can legitimately ask whether his is a real success. More appropriately, we can ask whether it is necessary to give up part of oneself to be successful. That is the question that these young people are asking themselves and us.

In these particular case studies, successful students seem to be providing an alternative route to success. In most cases, cultural maintenance seems to have had at least a partially positive influence on academic achievement. Although it is important not to overstate this finding, it is indeed a real possibility and one that severely challenges the "melting pot" ideology that has dominated U.S. schools and society throughout this century. Similar findings, at least in terms of language maintenance, have been consistently reported by researchers in bilingual education. That is, when students' language is used as the basis for their education, when it is respected and valued, students tend to succeed in school.[15]

A small number of studies concerned with culture itself point in the same direction. For instance, in a study of successful Punjabi students, Gibson found that their parents consistently admonished them to maintain their culture and made it clear that adopting the values and behaviors of their majority peers would "dishonor" their families and communities.[16] A major study of Southeast Asian students found an intriguing connection between grades and culture: Higher grade point averages correlated with the maintenance of traditional values, ethnic pride, and close social and cultural ties with members of the same ethnic group.[17] The notion that assimilation is a necessary prerequisite for success in school or society is thus contested both by this research and by the case studies reported here. We need to caution, however, that the relationship of language and culture to learning is an extraordinarily complex issue and one that is very much affected by the context of learning. In studying linguistic and cultural influences on math learning, for example, researchers have concluded that more research must be done before a definitive relationship can be found.[18] We can probably assume that the same is true in other areas.

The research calls into question the oft-cited claim that students who are not from European American backgrounds have poor self-images and low self-esteem. It is not as simple as this. The one-sided model of "negative self-concept" has been challenged and refuted more than once.[19] We need to consider the role that schools and society in general have in *creating* low self-esteem in children. That is, students do not simply develop poor self-concepts out of the blue. Rather, they are the result of policies and practices of schools and society that respect and affirm some groups while devaluing and rejecting others. Students from dominated groups might indeed partially internalize some of the many negative messages to which they are subjected on a daily basis about their culture, race, ethnic group, class, and language, but they are not simply passive recipients of such messages. The mediating role of their families and communities and in some cases of schools (particularly, for example, through multicultural and bilingual programs) helps to contradict these negative messages and to reinforce more positive and affirming ones.

For example, James, in spite of the many negative messages about Arabs to which he has been subjected, has an incredibly strong confidence in himself. He says, with obvious pride but without arrogance, "I'm probably the smartest kid in my class." This confidence extends beyond academics. "In a lot of the things that I do, I usually do good." Fern says, "I succeed in everything I do." Yolanda likes "making my mind work." Thus, in spite of what she may hear about the supposed ignorance or laziness of Mexicans and Mexican Americans, she is certain that she indeed has a mind, that she is intelligent.

A notable exception is Vinh. He is the only student who does not consider himself successful, in spite of the fact that his grades are quite good and that he applies himself diligently to his studies. The role of language in his case should not be underestimated. His sense of academic success in Vietnam was never questioned; however, ever since coming to the United States, he has felt unsuccessful primarily because of the language barrier. His sense of success is so inextricably linked to language that it has had a profoundly negative affect on how he sees himself.

Students in these case studies also consistently mentioned that their parents taught them to be proud of their culture, that they spoke their native language at home, and that it makes them "feel proud." In addition, they mention schools that reflected their culture and language and helped them to be successful through a bilingual program and other affirming activities. Yolanda, for instance, talks about her teachers' awareness and support of her bilingualism and culture (in this case, the dancing group to which she belongs) in helping her succeed.

The conclusion that maintaining native language and culture helps students in their academic achievement turns on its head not only conventional educational philosophy but also the policies and practices of schools that have done everything possible effectively to eradicate students' culture and language in order, they maintain, for all students to succeed in school. For example, rather than attempting to erase culture and language, schools should do everything in their power to *use, affirm,* and *maintain* them as a foundation for students' academic success. School policies and practices that stress cultural pride, build on students' native language ability and use, and emphasize the history and experiences of the students' communities would be the result.

BEYOND ACADEMICS

In nearly all of the case studies, significant involvement in activities beyond academics emerges as a key ingredient in the success of students. Whether through school-related organizations, hobbies, religious groups, or other activities in which they are thoroughly engaged, students look for ways to support and sustain their school success. Often, these activities have little to do with academics. They seem to have several important roles, both academic and nonacademic, for students: keeping them on track, removing them from negative peer pressure, developing leadership and critical thinking skills, and making them feel that they belong.

Again, a notable exception is Vinh. Although he works in the summer, work does not seem to be an activity that motivates him, as would a hobby or other similar interest. Rather, it permits him to contribute to the family economy in a tangible way. Other activities that he talked about were related to maintaining literacy in Vietnamese. Perhaps this closeness to family cultural values that stress education and situate success almost exclusively in the academic sphere account for his lack of outside interests. More will be said about family support and expectations later.

Keeping on Track

One way in which activities other than school help is by keeping students "on track." That is, nonschool activities seem to focus students' attention on the importance of school while at the same time providing some relief from it. In the words of Rich, music "keeps me going." This is consistent with findings by Steinberg et al., who reviewed research on various experiences outside the classroom that may affect student achievement during the high school years. They found that participation in interscholastic athletics is more likely to enhance than interfere with high school students' academic achievement, although they found only a modest influence.[20] In our case studies, extracurricular activities seem to have a much more definitive influence, but it should be pointed out that we are not talking primarily about sports but about a much wider range of activities.

Marisol, for example, does not take part in clubs, sports, or other traditional school activities. However, she is very much involved in the Teen Clinic. This clinic, located in the high school itself, helps teenagers with information about sexuality, birth control, and parenting. Teenage pregnancy and infant mortality rates in her city are among the highest in the state and provided the impetus for starting the clinic. It is widely acclaimed as innovative and unique. Her involvement in the Teen Clinic emerges as the activity that helps Marisol keep her mind on school. She explains why she's so immersed in the work of the clinic by saying that she wants to help other students realize "what's happening out in the streets and not to put everything to waste," especially "if they're really interested in going to school and having a nice future. . . ." For Marisol, then, work at the Teen Clinic keeps her mind on the importance of going to school and succeeding.

Extracurricular activities, according to Vanessa, are "a way of releasing energy and feeling good about yourself and being in shape. And working with other people." Fern, too, is quite clear about how she uses her involvement in sports: "I compare it to stuff like when I can't get science, or like in sewing, I'll look at that machine and I'll say, 'This is a basketball; I can overcome it.' "

Shields Against Peer Pressure

The negative peer pressure to which most students are subjected can be very difficult to resist. Nevertheless, all of the students in the case studies have been quite successful in doing so. One reason has been the activities in which they have been involved, which for some act almost like a shield against negative influence. A vivid example is Marisol, who seems to view her work at the Teen Clinic as almost a magical safeguard against pregnancy. For other students as well, involvement in these school-related and community activities seems to take up nonschool time in ways that act almost as a preventive strategy for discouraging less productive, although at times more alluring, activities. This is the reason, for example, that Manuel dropped some of his friends; at just about the same time, he joined a church that takes up much of his time. Linda's devotion to music can probably be understood in this way as well.

Developing Critical Thinking and Leadership Skills

Extracurricular and out-of-school activities seem to contribute to the development of important skills, including critical thinking and leadership qualities. Through a theater workshop, which was based on students' experiences and ideas, Manuel was able to analyze critically his own experience as an immigrant to this country. This workshop provided an arena in which he could analyze more carefully and articulate consciously and clearly the pain and fear that he felt in his first years here.

James's involvement with bicycle racing, his self-acclaimed first "love" is a consuming activity in both time and attention. Before his bike accident, for example, he was riding 40 miles a day. However, James's involvement extends beyond just racing itself: He subscribes to all the related magazines, has gotten his racing license, and has been actively recruiting others interested in the sport in order to start a biking club. He is also planning to approach local bicycle merchants with the idea of obtaining financial support to sponsor the team. He will not simply ask for money, however; he intends to ask merchants to go out riding with them "to see how good we are, if we're worth, you know, sponsoring." In explaining his strategy, he says, "I wouldn't give a thousand-dollar bike to some kid that's just gonna ride around 10 mph, you know."

Avi's "work" in the synagogue is another dramatic example of how activities can help develop leadership skills. Not only does it require a great deal of study and sacrifice (not going out with his peers on Saturdays), but his involvement in the temple also makes him a role model for others in his community. Vanessa's work with a peer education group echoes this role. This group has helped her develop some important leadership qualities as well as a growing critical awareness and sensitivity to issues of exclusion and stratification. Skills related to academic achievement may be developed as a byproduct of involvement in extracurricular activities.

Belonging

The feeling of belonging, so important for adolescents, also seems to be one of the benefits of taking part in extracurricular activities. Young people will seek to "belong" and "fit in" in any way they can. Some meet this need by joining gangs or taking part in other detrimental activities in which they feel part of a "family." The students in the case studies have found positive outlets in sports, clubs, and religious activities. For many, the satisfaction of "belonging" is particularly evident in activities related to their ethnic group. Rich, for example, says he "didn't know there was a place for me" until he became involved in music. Yolanda's mother is quite strict and does not allow her as much freedom as many of her peers, so her membership in a folkloric Mexican dance group is probably an important outlet for her creative energy.

Manuel, James, Rich, and Avi have found their niche through, among other things, their church or synagogue. Their religious commitment affirms their ethnicity as well. For Manuel, a Protestant sect is much more in tune with his culture than the Catholic church typically associated with Cape Verdeans. As he so dramatically said, "I felt that God had moved there," implying that a cultural resonance was missing in the local Catholic church. James's Christian Maronite religion also provides a strong bond with his culture. Although he is at the age when many young people feel that church is an imposition, he continues to want to go. Rich combines his cultural and religious activities with his organ playing in a local Black church. And Avi actually helps to lead services and "works" in the temple.

All of these examples are graphic illustrations of how extracurricular activities in school, activities outside of school including hobbies, and religious and cultural organizations seem to support students in their academic success. Rather than detracting from their success by taking time away from homework or other school-related activities, such involvement seems to help young people positively by channeling their creative and physical energy. In some cases, these activities may also support school success. For example, the development of leadership qualities and critical thinking skills, as shown above, help students' academic skills in the classroom as well.

From these case studies, we can conclude that one important way for students to support their academic success is to seek involvement in school-related and other activities that help fill their need to belong and use their time in productive ways. Such activities help to round out the experiences of students so that they lead fuller and more realistic lives not focused solely on academics.

FAMILY, COMMUNITY, AND SCHOOL
ENVIRONMENTS FOR SUCCESS

The case studies provide ample and sometimes dramatic evidence of the importance of family, community, and school in supporting and maintaining the academic success of students. Successful students are surrounded by messages that support success, including both direct and indirect support from family, friends and activities that enhance rather than detract from success, and teachers and other school staff who care. It would appear that messages such as these are taught and repeated in the "folk theory" of success of many families of successful students.

The Crucial Role of Family

The ways in which families support and sustain students in their academic success are complex and sometimes not what one might expect, especially in non-middle-class families, who often have little experience with academic involvement or achievement. In many cases, we have seen that family cultural values themselves determine what students mean by success. Education is broadly defined by many dominated and other nonmainstream groups. This broad definition of education becomes what many young people expect from their schooling. As Vinh so emphatically stated, grades are "not important to me. Important to me is education."

Another way in which parents demonstrate their support for academic success is through high expectations. Education is highly valued and sought after by the parents of these students regardless of their economic background. In fact, in some instances, working-class and poor parents have even *more* hope in education than middle-class parents, for obvious reasons.[21] The ways in which they manifest high expectations, however, are sometimes indirect. They often cannot help their children with homework or in learning English. In addition, they often lack the "cultural capital" valued in the society at large and are therefore unable to pass it down to their children. Nonetheless, the messages they verbalize to their children are quite clear. Vinh says his uncle supports him by saying, "Next time, you should do better." "My mom says that they want me to go to school," says Yolanda. "That way, I won't be stuck with a job like them."

Such messages, although powerful, are not always enough. In many of our case studies, the young people had great respect and appreciation for their families and understood the sacrifices that had been made on their behalf. But this appreciation did not always make their school experiences any easier or more tolerable. Because their parents were not always able to give them concrete help and tangible guidance, students sometimes lacked a sense of direction. Nevertheless, in the final analysis, all of them were able to overcome such barriers. This is not true, of course, of many of their peers in similar circumstances. Manuel put it most poignantly when he said, "If I felt like I had support from my family, if they only knew the language. . . . If they were educated, I could make it big, you see what I'm saying?" Referring to the kind of help middle-class parents are able to provide for their children, he is absolutely right when he concludes, "I would've had a better opportunity, a better chance."

In spite of the hurdles some students face because of their families' lack of formal education and limited experience with the means for achieving academic success, parents have compensated by providing other critical support. In the case of students who come from different linguistic backgrounds, parents and other family members have maintained native language use in the home. This is true in all our case studies. They have done so in spite of messages to the contrary from school and from society in general. Many schools, for example, send newsletters to the home encouraging parents to speak English, rather than their native language, to their children. Resisting this advice, the parents and other family members of the students in our case have *insisted* on native language use in the home as an important means of maintaining their culture and emotional attachment to their children through family values. Such language use has also proven to be crucial in students' development of literacy and preparation for school life.[22] The more they were able to use language in a variety of ways and in diverse contexts, the more they were replicating the kinds of literacy skills necessary for successful schoolwork.

Maintenance of native language also implies maintenance of culture. These families are reiterating the message that their culture is worthy of respect, as do families who are monolingual speakers of English. In these homes as well, culture is maintained through such activities as family rituals and traditions and artifacts in the home, not to mention the even more important underlying cultural values that help inform their attitudes and behaviors on a daily basis. "Apprenticeship" in their families, and the consequent learning of culture, language, and values, seems to be a significant way in which children receive and internalize the message that they are important and worthwhile.

We have already seen that many of the students in these case studies have had to take on a role in their families of mature and responsible adults, particularly Manuel, who had to deal with doctors, hospitals, and other agencies in his father's illness. In a curious way, parents' messages about their children's worthiness are reinforced when they are compelled to take on these responsibilities. These young people have developed confidence and self-respect through interactions with the society at large on behalf of their families. They have been forced to grow up quickly, and although this means they have missed some of the pleasures of childhood, it also means that they have learned to rely on their skills and intelligence at an early age. This role has probably played a part in their success as students, in spite of the fact that it also means that they are frequently absent from school in order to assist their parents in important family matters.

Encouraging communication within the family is another way in which parents support the academic success of their children. The importance of talking with their parents about issues central to their lives was mentioned by a number of these young people. Yolanda, for example, said that she and her mother talk about "girl stuff" as well as about school and the importance of studying. Marisol also emphasized how different her parents are from others because they often talk with her and her siblings about "things that are happening nowadays. . . . They really care about us and just tell us the rights from the wrongs." For Vinh, even long-distance communication is meaningful: He writes to his parents weekly and is in turn revitalized by their messages. Linda's description of shared dinnertime in her family is a beautiful expression of the value of communication.

In numerous ways, students in these case studies made it clear that they have "dedicated" their school success to their parents, almost as a way of thanking them for the sacrifices they had made. In effect, it was their way of paying back their parents and families. Students frequently mentioned that their parents were the motivating force behind their success, even if the parents did not always completely understand or appreciate what it meant. Manuel, for example, implied that although his parents are of course proud of him, they do not really understand the significance of his graduating from high school, at least not in the same way as he does. Nonetheless, he is doing it for them, to show them (and particularly his father) that he can do it. More than one student mentioned making their parents *happy*. This focus on their parents' happiness, hardly what one would expect from sophisticated adolescents in the 1990s, is nevertheless a theme that emerged time and again.

These students often describe their parents in remarkably tender and loving ways. From Marisol's "my parents are really beautiful people" to Vanessa's "they're caring and they're willing to go against the norm," they make it clear that their parents have provided warm and close-knit environments, which have had a significant influence on their lives and on the formation of their values. Rich describes his family as "just a happy-go-lucky family" and says, "It's wonderful being a member of my family." Linda says that her parents are "always there for me, all the time" and even understands the "twisted reasons" for their rules and limits. Fern, in spite of the many problems her family has had to confront, says, "I'm gifted to have a family like this." Rather than the rebelliousness typical of so many teenagers, these young people seem to be quite happy and secure within their families. This security has probably had a significant influence on their school success.

This is not to say that parents whose children are not successful in school have *not* provided such environments. There are a multitude of complex reasons why students are successful in school, and a close and warm relationship with parents is only one of them. Although many parents provide caring and loving environments, their children may *still* be rebellious, alienated, or unsuccessful in school. A good example is Yolanda's brother, who is, as she says, "a troublemaker." He frequently has problems in school and lately in the community as well. Yet the environment their mother provides for all three of the children is the same. Other issues intervene in the complex interplay of factors that influence academic success. What Cortés calls "the societal curriculum," that is, those influences of the general society, including the mass media and gender role expectations, have to be taken into consideration.[23] Other influences may also affect school achievement: rank within family, other family dynamics including relationships among siblings, and simple personality and idiosyncratic differences. What we can say, however, is that a close and open relationship between children and their parents (or other guardians) seems to be a necessary component of school success for most students, although by itself it certainly cannot guarantee it.

Although parents and other family members are obviously prominent in the success of students, they are for the most part uninvolved in school, at least in the ways in which traditional parent involvement is defined. There are some exceptions: Fern's father never misses a school activity, and Vanessa's mother was on her local school committee. Nevertheless, most of the parents do not go to school unless called, do not attend meetings or volunteer in school activities, and are not generally members of parent organizations. In most cases, parents' uninvolvement in school was notable. This fact is somewhat surprising considering the research on the importance of parent involvement on the academic achievement of their children.[24] The fact that some of these parents do not speak English, that they themselves have not always had positive experiences in schools, and that they are inhibited by impersonal and unreceptive bureaucracies such as schools must be kept in mind. We find the same to be true, however, even with parents who are more comfortable with the school environment. For them, work schedules, child-care needs, and other necessities can probably explain their noninvolvement in the schools. Nevertheless, their children are academically successful. Parent involvement, as defined *by schools*, is not always a necessary prerequisite for student success.[25]

What accounts for this seeming discrepancy? To explain it, we need to expand the meaning of parent involvement. All of the parents of these successful students are indeed *involved*, but not necessarily as the schools might define the term. Students seem to understand this distinction, although schools may not. When these young people talk about how their parents help them, for example, they do not often mention involvement in school activities. What they do mention are their parents' role in motivating them to stay in school, being communicative with them, providing an environment of high expectations and loving support, and sacrificing their lives to help their children. They mention all of the factors we have just reviewed, and it is no wonder that they have developed such rugged determination to continue, to do well, and to "be someone."

Teachers, Schools, and Caring

Many of the students in these case studies mention particular teachers, programs, or activities in the school that have helped them succeed. The key role teachers play in the achievement of their students is not surprising. Cummins, for example, notes that teachers' roles in the school and in the community have a great impact on the education students receive.[26] The primary characteristic for the students in our case studies was "caring." Yolanda gives concrete examples of what her teachers have done to help her: "they were always calling my mom, like I did a great job. Or they would start talking to me, or they kinda like pulled me up some grades, or moved me to other classes, or took me somewhere. And they were always congratulating me." Her teachers have resolved to help students succeed, and they use a variety of strategies to reach this goal. Linda still keeps in touch with her first-grade teacher, whom she calls her mentor, and says that she is "following in her footsteps."

Students evaluate their teachers' level of caring by such factors as the time they take in teaching their students, their patience, how well they prepare their classes, and how they go about making them interesting. For example, Vinh's favorite class is one in which students can work in groups, for which the teacher has planned different themes for them to discuss. James, too, talks about caring when he says that his best teachers are those who "take the time" to listen to students and to answer all their questions. Interestingly, his favorite teacher also shows her caring by being the faculty advisor for the Helping Hand Club, which is involved in community service.

For Manuel, caring came in the form of an entire program. The bilingual program, in his case, was critical in his eventual school success. It provided a safe environment for him and other Cape Verdean students, who are a minority within a minority. Because several of the teachers are from the same community, there is an important continuity between family and school. The bilingual program also reiterated messages about the importance of home language and values because it included Cape Verdean history and culture.

In case after case, students remembered those teachers who had affirmed them, whether through their language, their culture, or their concerns. Teachers who called on students' linguistic skills or cultural knowledge were named most often. For Linda, Mr. Benson, himself "mixed," to use her expression, was both a source of academic inspiration and a mirror of her own experience. These young people could also see through some of the more superficial attempts of teachers to use the student's culture. Vinh explains it eloquently when he says that teachers "understand something *outside*. . . . But they cannot understand something inside our hearts."

The fact that the teachers who understand and call on the students' culture are often from the same background does not mean that it is only teachers from the students' ethnic group who can teach them or be meaningful in their lives. Their importance, however, cannot be underestimated. Nevertheless, many of the teachers who were singled out were in fact not from the same background. They had either learned the students' language or were knowledgeable about and comfortable with the culture, or they were simply sensitive to the concerns of young people. Marisol, for example, mentioned only one teacher to whom she could talk. This particular teacher is neither Puerto Rican nor Spanish-speaking. She is, however, someone who is sensitive to young people and can talk to them about the issues that most concern them.

The young people in these case studies have given much thought to what schools and teachers can do to help students. It is important to keep in mind that these particular students are successful in school. Thus, they can all name teachers who have made a difference in their lives. They can also describe those teaching strategies that have been successful and school practices that have helped them. These students are also critical of some teachers' lack of caring, of their consistent use of stale teaching methods, and of school policies that isolate or demoralize some of their peers. These students are among the "winners" in our schools. Yet they, too, are discontent with practices and policies that can lead to frustration and failure for great numbers of their friends. It is important that we listen to their voices.

SUMMARY

In this chapter, we have reviewed some of the major themes that emerged in the case studies. We have paid particular attention to four themes that seem to be related to the academic achievement of these students:

- A redefinition of education and success
- Pride and conflict in culture and language
- The role of activities not related to academics in sustaining school success
- The important support of family, community, and teachers

Cultural and in some cases linguistic maintenance apparently plays a key role in students' academic success. In most of these cases, language and culture have been reinforced in the home and sometimes in the school as well. When reinforced in both settings, students seem to have less confusion and ambiguity. If only valued and used in the home, students may develop more conflicted feelings, for example, James's obvious pain about the fact that his culture has been slighted time and again in so-called "multicultural" activities but his reluctance to bring it up in school. His culture's invisibility in the general school culture has had an impact on him.

The larger society also plays an important role. If young people see that their culture is devalued in such things as political initiatives to restrict the number of Puerto Ricans coming into town (as is the case with Marisol), they are certain to develop conflicted attitudes concerning their ethnic group. In spite of these sometimes harsh attacks on their culture, these successful students have been able to maintain considerable pride in their ethnic group and community. In the process, they reject both the pressure to assimilate and the pressure to give up. What they are doing is transforming culture and even language in order to "fit in," but on their own terms.

Involvement in activities outside of school also seems to play an important part in students' academic achievement. In almost all cases, successful students are involved successfully in other activities as well. Whether they are sports, social clubs, extracurricular activities in school, religious groups, or other community activities does not seem to matter. The fact that the students consistently take part in a variety of activities is what seems to make a difference. Their involvement has important benefits, including the development of leadership and other skills that reinforce their academic achievement and remove them from possible negative peer pressures.

Finally, the role of family, community, and school in providing environments for success is crucial. Each works in different, although certainly complementary, ways to motivate students to succeed. Although families from culturally dominated and economically poor communities are sometimes unable to give their children the tangible help and support dominant and economically secure families are able to, they nevertheless serve an indispensable role in their children's school accomplishments. For all the successful students we have studied, from those in the middle class to those from very poor families, they do so in the following ways:

- Maintaining native language and culture in the home
- Having high expectations of their children at all times
- Providing loving and supportive home environments
- Communicating with their children on a consistent basis

Teachers and schools also play an essential role in students' success. We have seen that teachers who care, who take time with students, and who use their students' background in teaching and communicating with them are the most successful. School policies and practices that affirm and support them are also critical. From help after school to small-group work, students were quite explicit in pointing out those classroom activities and school practices that seemed to help them learn.

In the final analysis, these successful students have pointed to the critical importance of schools and families working together to produce school achievement. In the next chapter, we will explore the specific role of schools and teachers in fostering school achievement among all students, especially those not traditionally expected to succeed.

TO THINK ABOUT

1. Why were some of the students in the case studies unable to identify both as American and as a member of their cultural group? You may want to talk with young people to gain a number of different perspectives.

2. How do you define academic success? List the characteristics that you feel define success. Do they differ from how you think most teachers define it? Do your cultural values influence your definition?

3. Think about your own culture and/or native language or that of some of your students. How have the dual manifestations of *pride* and *conflict* been apparent? Give a few concrete examples.

4. If it is indeed true that pride in culture and language are important for academic success, what does this mean for school policies and practices? Discuss a series of policies and practices that you think schools should consider to promote educational equity for all students.

5. Have you or your ethnic/racial/gender/linguistic/religious/class group been subjected to what has been called *symbolic violence*? How? Share your perceptions with other classmates.

6. According to Skutnabb-Kangas, many young people from dominated groups are faced with the impossibly difficult burden of choosing between *assimilation* and *rejection*. Give some examples of what this might mean. Can you think of more empowering alternatives?

7. Engagement in school and community activities emerged as a major support for the academic success of students in the case studies. What can schools do to promote such activities? Be specific, citing concrete examples.

8. The role of parents in providing an environment for success was highlighted by many of the students in the case studies. However, their role was often different from that which schools traditionally define as "involvement." As a teacher, how might you work with parents to help them develop environments for success?

9. "Caring" on the part of teachers, schools, and parents was pinpointed by a number of students as important to their academic success. What might schools do to give students the message that they care? How would these practices compare with current practices that you are familiar with?

NOTES

1. Research by Henderson and Diveck as cited in Carnegie Council on Adolescent Development, *Turning Points: Preparing American Youth for the Twenty-First Century* (Washington, DC: Task Force on the Education of Young Adolescents, 1989).
2. Similar conclusions have been reached by other researchers. See, for example, Carl A. Grant and Christine E. Sleeter, *After the School Bell Rings* (Philadelphia: Falmer Press, 1986); Jean Anyon, "Social Class and the Hidden Curriculum of Work," *Journal of Education*, 162, 1 (Winter 1980), 67–92; Christine E. Sleeter, "Multicultural Education Staff Development: How Much Can It Change Classroom Teaching?" paper presented at the annual meeting of the American Educational Research Association, San Francisco, March 1989.
3. The research cited was done by Pilar Muñoz and Josette Ludwig for a course I taught on Puerto Rican history and culture during the spring 1985 semester. They interviewed ten Puerto Rican women who differed in age, social class, marital status, and length of stay in the United States. In spite of these great differences, all of them reported receiving these dual messages during childhood. I am grateful to them and to the researchers for the important insights they provided on this issue.
4. Pierre Bourdieu, "The Forms of Capital," in *Handbook of Theory and Research for the Sociology of Education*, ed. John G. Richardson (New York: Greenwood Press, 1986).
5. Antti Jalava, "Nobody Told Me That I Was a Finn," in *Minority Education: From Shame to Struggle*, ed. Tove Skutnabb-Kangas and Jim Cummins (Clevedon, Eng.: Multilingual Matters, 1988), p. 164.
6. Ibid., p. 165.

7. Richard Rodriguez, *Hunger of Memory: The Education of Richard Rodriguez* (Boston: David R. Godine, 1982), pp. 19–20.

8. Michelle Fine, "Perspectives on Inequity: Voices from Urban Schools," in *Applied Social Psychology Annual IV*, ed. Leonard Brickman (Beverly Hills, CA: Sage Publications, 1983).

9. Ronald Scollon and Suzanne Scollon, *Narrative, Literacy, and Face in Interethnic Communication* (Northwood, NJ: Ablex, 1981).

10. Signithia Fordham and John U. Ogbu, "Black Students' School Success: Coping with the 'Burden of Acting White,' " *Urban Review*, 18, 3 (1986), 176–206.

11. The case has been made by Janice Hale-Benson, *Black Children: Their Roots, Culture, and Learning Styles*, rev. ed. (Baltimore: Johns Hopkins University Press, 1986). See also Asa Hilliard, "Intellectual Strengths of Minority Children," in *Teaching in a Multicultural Society: Perspectives and Professional Strategies*, ed. Doris E. Cross, Gwendolyn C. Baker, and Lindley J. Stiles (New York: Free Press, 1977); A. Wade Boykin, "The Triple Quandry and the Schooling of Afro-American Children," in *The School Achievement of Minority Children: New Perspectives*, ed. Ulric Neisser (Hillsdale, NJ: Erlbaum, 1986); Shirl E. Gilbert and Geneva Gay, "Improving the Success in School of Poor Black Children," *Phi Delta Kappan*, October 1985, pp. 133–137.

12. The video *How We Feel: Hispanic Students Speak Out* was developed by Virginia Vogel Zanger and is available from Landmark Films, Inc., in Falls Church, VA (or by calling 800-342-4336).

13. Tove Skutnabb-Kangas, "Resource Power and Autonomy Through Discourse in Conflict," in *Minority Education: From Shame to Struggle*, ed. Tove Skutnabb-Kangas and Jim Cummins (Clevedon, Eng.: Multilingual Matters, 1988), p. 262.

14. Fordham and Ogbu, "Black Students' School Success."

15. See, for example, the research cited by Jim Cummins, *Empowering Minority Students* (Sacramento: California Association for Bilingual Education, 1989); Tove Skutnabb-Kangas and Jim Cummins, eds. *Minority Education: From Shame to Struggle* (Clevedon, Eng.: Multilingual Matters, 1988); Stephen Krashen and Douglas Biber, *On Course: Bilingual Education's Success in California* (Sacramento: California Association for Bilingual Education, 1988).

16. Margaret A. Gibson "The School Performance of Immigrant Minorities: A Comparative View," *Anthropology and Education Quarterly*, 18, 4 (December 1987), 262–275.

17. Ruben G. Rumbaut and Kenji Ima, *The Adaptation of Southeast Asian Refugee Youth: A Comparative Study*, Final Report. (San Diego, CA: Office of Refugee Resettlement, September 1987).

18. Rodney R. Cocking and José P. Mestre, eds., *Linguistic and Cultural Influences on Learning Mathematics* (Hillsdale, NJ: Erlbaum, 1988).

19. See the research reviewed by Gloria Johnson Powell, "Coping with Adversity: The Psychosocial Development of Afro-American Children," in *The Psychosocial Development of Minority Group Children*, ed. Gloria Johnson Powell (New York: Brunner/Mazel Publishers, 1983). Francis Ianni, after extensive research with children from a diversity of cultural, racial, and social class backgrounds, has also reached the conclusion that minority status in and of itself has no intrinsic effect on self-regard. See *The Search for Structure: A Report on American Youth Today* (New York: Free Press, 1989). Joseph Prewitt-Díaz, in comparing Puerto Rican students in U.S. schools to a group of newly arrived Puerto Rican students, found that the latter, with one year in a bilingual program, had higher self-esteem scores than their counterparts who were not in bilingual education and not newly arrived. See "A Study of Self-Esteem and School Sentiment in Two Groups of Puerto Rican Students," *Educational and Psychological Research*, 3 (Summer 1983), 161–167. Also, Rodney W. Roth experimented with a curriculum in which the life and history of African Americans were prominently featured and found that Black students who were exposed to this curriculum developed significantly greater

Black pride than others. See "How Negro Fifth-Grade Students View 'Black Pride' Concepts," *Integrated Education*, 8 (1970), 24–27. The school's programmatic options and general attitudes in society played a more important part than did the students' inherent self-esteem in these cases.

20. Lawrence Steinberg, B. Bradford Brown, Mary Crider, Nancy Kaczmarek, and Cary Lazzaro, *Noninstructional Influences on High School Student Achievement: The Contributions of Parents, Peers, Extracurricular Activities, and Part-Time Work* (Madison: Wisconsin Center for Educational Research, National Center on Effective Secondary Schools, September 1988).

21. See the ethnographic research on literacy development in poor Black families in Denny Taylor and Catherine Dorsey-Gaines, *Growing Up Literate: Learning from Inner-City Families* (Portsmouth, NH: Heinemann, 1988); Beeman N. Phillips, "School-Related Aspiration of Children with Different Socio-Cultural Backgrounds," *Journal of Negro Education*, 41 (1972), 48–52. In addition, data collected for the *High School and Beyond* study reveal that when socioeconomic status is taken into account, Latino students have higher educational aspirations than White students; as reported in the *Tomás Rivera Center Report*, 2, 4 (Fall 1989), 9.

22. See Krashen and Biber, *On Course;* Shirley Brice Heath, "Sociocultural Contexts of Language Development," in *Beyond Language: Social and Cultural Factors in Schooling Language Minority Students* (Los Angeles: Office of Bilingual Education, California State Department of Education, Evaluation, Dissemination and Assessment Center, 1986); Nancy L. Commins, "Language and Affect: Bilingual Students at Home and School," *Language Arts*, 66, 1 (January 1989), 29–43; Jim Cummins, "The Role of Primary Language Development in Promoting Educational Success for Language Minority Students" in *Schooling and Language Minority Students: A Theoretical Framework* (Sacramento: Office of Bilingual Bicultural Education, California State Department of Education, Evaluation, Dissemination, and Assessment Center, 1981); Francois Nielsen and Roberto M. Fernandez, *Hispanic Students in American High Schools: Background Characteristics and Achievement* (Washington, DC: National Opinion Research Center, National Center for Education Statistics, 1981); Carole Edelsky, "Bilingual Children's Writing: Fact and Fiction," in *Richness in Writing: Empowering ESL Students*, ed. Donna M. Johnson and Duane H. Roen (White Plains, NY: Longman, 1989); David P. Dolson, "The Effects of Spanish Home Language Use on the Scholastic Performance of Hispanic Students," *Journal of Multilingual and Multicultural Education*, 6 (1985) 135–156. Similar findings have been reported for students in other countries; see Tove Skutnabb-Kangas and Pertti Toukomaa, *Teaching Migrant Children's Mother Tongue and Learning the Language of the Host Country in the Context of the Socio-cultural Situation of the Migrant Family* (Helsinki: Finnish National Commission for UNESCO, 1976).

23. Carlos E. Cortés, "The Societal Curriculum: Implications for Multiethnic Education," in *Education in the 80's: Multiethnic Education*, ed. James A. Banks (Washington, DC: National Education Association, 1981).

24. See, for example, Reginald M. Clark, *Family Life and School Achievement: Why Poor Black Children Succeed or Fail* (Chicago: University of Chicago Press, 1983); Anne T. Henderson, *The Evidence Continues to Grow: Parent Involvement Improves Student Achievement* (Columbia, MD: National Committee for Citizens in Education, 1987); Steinberg et al., *Noninstructional Influences on High School Student Achievement;* D. L. Stevenson, and D. P. Baker, "The Family-School Relation and the Child's School Performance," *Child Development*, 58 (1987), 1348–1357.

25. This conclusion was also reached by Margaret Gibson in her research with Punjabi students. See "The School Performance of Immigrant Minorities."

26. Cummins, *Empowering Minority Students.*

CHAPTER 10

Developing Environments That Foster High-Quality Education: The Role Of Multicultural Education

OVERVIEW

The causes of school failure for large numbers of students, as we saw in Part I, can be subsumed under two major categories:

1. Structural factors
   a. *Racism* and other forms of discrimination in society and their resultant manifestations in the schools
   b. Particular *practices and policies* in schools that are contrary to the goal of equal and high-quality education for all students
2. Cultural and linguistic discontinuities between home and school that make life in school at best uncomfortable and at worst impossible for a great many students, but most notably for those from economically oppressed, dominated, and nonmainstream groups

Any school seriously proposing to create an environment of success for all their students must address both of these overarching issues. An environment based on the principles of comprehensive multicultural education includes the curriculum; learning environment; and interactions among students, teachers, and communities, both in structural and cultural terms. It thus addresses each of these issues and moves multicultural education beyond the simplistic ''holidays and heroes,'' cultural understanding, or education for human relations approaches to a pervasive philosophical outlook based on social justice.

The case studies of ten academically successful adolescents from diverse cultural, linguistic, and economic backgrounds add to our understanding of the ways in which young people can achieve success in our schools. Their experiences provide concrete evidence that academic success defies and challenges the easy categorization and negative expectations teachers, schools, and society often have of students. Even more important, their experiences point to specific factors in the home, school, and community that have contributed to their success.

In this chapter, we will first consider the arena in which action for s cial change must take place. Although it is important to strive for equity and social j stice in education, this struggle cannot be separated from the wider society in which we live. The tensions and connections between the arenas of the school and society will be explored.

We will then focus on the themes that emerged from the case studies. The students pointed out three basic ways in which they have achieved academic success:

- Maintaining and affirming pride, even if at times conflicted, in their native language and/or culture
- Engaging in activities beyond academics in the school, home, and community
- Developing supportive environments in school, home, and community in combating negative influences and affirming the messages of success

Each of these areas will be explored further with an eye toward understanding how teachers and schools working in collaboration with families can help build these kinds of environments for success. In each case, it is important to understand that students were not simply passive recipients of schooling but rather active agents in their own success. Nevertheless, they did not achieve success on their own but in conjunction with family, peers, teachers, and schools.

MULTICULTURAL EDUCATION AND SOCIAL CHANGE: ACTION AT VARIOUS LEVELS

Ethnographic and other research evidence has documented the existence of racism and other forms of discrimination in the schools. Simply tackling these issues at the school level, however, is not enough. If we are to confront the persistence of racism and other forms of discrimination, we must do so within the broad sociopolitical context in which they occur. Racism, classism, ethnocentrism, sexism, linguicism, anti-Semitism, handicapism, and other forms of discrimination exist in schools because they exist in society. To divorce schools from society is impossible. Although schools may with all good intentions attempt to provide learning environments free from such discrimination, once students leave the classroom and building they are again confronted with an unequal society.

Teachers and schools engaged in the task of challenging social inequities need to do so with an explicit understanding on their part and that of their students that they are involved in a struggle that critiques and questions the status quo not only of schools but of society in general. Thus they will be involved in what Dickeman has called "a subversive task."[1] The balance between hope and despair is a difficult one to maintain, yet that is precisely what is called for.

It is clear that racism cannot be wiped out by schools. Nevertheless, the role of schools should not be underestimated either. It can be said that the school's unique task is to end racism *in the schools*. By developing antiracist and affirming policies and practices, schools will in effect be confronting racist and other limiting practices in other institutions as well. But this is not enough. The attack on discrimination is a many-faceted one, and schools represent only one of the arenas in which it is fought. Even if a school decides, for example, to do away with standardized tests because it considers them to be discriminatory, the implications of such a radical decision might be far-ranging and counter to the desired goals. How well their students do on such tests may in fact determine whether or not they go to college, what college they attend, and what they will study. In effect, their entire future might depend on knowing how to take tests. This being the case, the school's decision, unless well thought through and supported by other activities and policies, might in the long run be both a romantic struggle against wind-mills and detrimental to the students who most need the school's support. Once again we see that schools are not isolated but rather part of a sociopolitical context that must al-ways be taken into account.

Teachers must understand that schools exist to serve the interests of some segments of society and not others. The role of schools in channeling and preparing students from specific economic, racial, and gender backgrounds for particular slots in society is well documented.[2] In addition, the view of children as "economic resources" to be developed for the growth of the economy is also widespread.[3] Understanding these economic and political issues is necessary if teachers are to make changes that dispute not only the lim-ited expectations of schools but those of society as well. The struggle for equal and high-quality education has to be carried on not only in schools but also in communities and in the larger society. Throughout our discussion of the direction for change provided by a broadly conceptualized multicultural education, these different levels of change, that is, the classroom, school, community, and society, need to be kept in mind.

LESSONS FROM STUDENTS: MAINTAINING AND AFFIRMING PRIDE IN CULTURE

Given the two general areas we explored as causes of school failure, we can now look at them with what we have learned from our students. In this section, we will be particu-larly concerned with what we can learn from the ways in which students use their culture and language in spite of overpowering and sometimes demoralizing attitudes, behaviors, policies, and practices to the contrary.

The racism and other forms of discrimination to which students are subjected, not only in school but in the larger society as well, are evident in the case studies. Such dis-crimination is either overt, as when Marisol is not allowed to speak Spanish in class, or more subtle, as when James's culture is invisible in school activities. Yet these academ-ically successful students have not chosen to deny or forget their culture and/or language, surely an understandable response to persistent discrimination. Rather, in almost all cases, they have tended to rely on them even more strongly, although not necessarily in the school setting and sometimes with contradictory and conflicting attitudes. Their re-liance on culture and language would seem to serve as protection against the low expec-tations and sometimes outright devaluation of them by schools and society.

A few of the students had supportive school environments that not only accepted but in fact built on their culture and language. Yolanda, for instance, perceives both her elementary and her junior high schools as comfortable places because teachers called on her language and culture as valued resources. Manuel felt the same way about his bilingual program. Their experiences reiterate what was found by Tharp in a review of school achievement of students from dominated groups. In all cases of academic achievement, schools consistently supported two major practices: language development and contextualized instruction, that is, instruction based on the student's previous knowledge and experience.[4] The first lesson for schools would seem to be, then, that bilingual and multicultural programs must become integral and prominent parts of the learning environment.

Strengthening Bilingual Programs

Although bilingual education has been a vital part of the recent educational landscape for over two decades and will probably remain so for the forseeable future given the country's growing linguistic diversity, it has always been accompanied by great controversy and less than enthusiastic acceptance, sometimes even by those charged with managing such programs. Too often, for example, bilingual programs have been relegated to the space next to the boiler room in the basement or to large unused closets. Such placements are not just physical spaces but are representative of the status of these programs as well. In addition, bilingual teachers have frequently been segregated programmatically and physically from other staff, thus isolating and alienating them even more.[5] Finally, the very goal of bilingual education, that is, to serve as a temporary way station while students learn English to "quick exit" them into an all-English environment, also calls into question the value and status of such programs.

A rethinking of the very goals of bilingual education needs to take place to accord it the important role it should have in supporting English acquisition and native language maintenance, both fundamental goals of bilingual education. Not only do bilingual programs need to be in place but they also need to be visible and respected in the school environment. The importance of students' native language and of language maintenance has been denied not only in bilingual programs but in multicultural education in general. Yet its relevance was brought out many times by the students in our case studies.

Students who do not yet speak English and those who are most proficient in another language should, of course, have first priority in a bilingual program. In addition, those students from homes where a language other than English is spoken, even if they themselves seem fluent in English, need to be given the opportunity to participate in these programs, for several reasons. First, the seeming conversational English fluency of such students often misleads teachers into believing that they can handle the academic rigors of cognitively demanding work in English. This is not always the case.[6] Second, bilingualism is a worthy goal per se and a valuable resource that should be supported. The benefits of bilingualism, as we have seen elsewhere, can range from cognitive flexibility to metalinguistic awareness.[7] Doing away with the kinds of skills that will be increasingly called for in the years ahead, given our society's growing linguistic and cultural diversity, is foolhardy at best. Finally, the positive results of maintaining native language fluency in promoting the academic success of students in the case studies is abundantly clear. Even for students no longer fluent in their native language, there may be benefits in providing these programs in terms of promoting their pride and self-confidence and thus possibly influencing their school success in a positive way.

Space and funds permitting, monolingual speakers of English can and should also be included in bilingual programs. The limited research available on this type of two-way program, in which English speakers and speakers of another language are integrated in one classroom and learn both languages, suggests that it provides a powerful incentive for both groups while developing bilingualism and positive attitudes toward diversity.[8] However, these two-way programs should not become the reserve of the upper-middle class who want their children to become fluent in a second language, while students who do not speak English languish academically in English-only classrooms because of lack of funds.

Developing Comprehensive Multicultural Programs

Another key lesson from the students in our case studies is that multicultural education should be an integral part of the school experience of all students. This is not to imply that the students themselves recommended such programs. On the contrary, they hardly mentioned multicultural education at all. If they did, it was usually in the context of multicultural fairs, cookbooks, or other more superficial aspects and certainly not in the comprehensive way in which it has been defined here. Although this omission may seem curious, given the fact that they talked so much about their culture, language, and families, it simply reinforces the obvious lack of experience with multicultural education and the negative way diversity is generally viewed by schools. One major study, for example, found that the operating assumption in most schools is that differences in background and language were seen as "deficits to be corrected" and not strengths on which to build.[9] Multicultural education in most schools is reduced to making exotic masks, eating ethnic foods, and commemorating selected heroes. Thus, it should come as no surprise that students would be unaware of what multicultural education can become or how it might help them. Nevertheless, we were reminded time and again that culture and in some cases language are central to the lives of these students.

Little research has been done on the effects of multicultural education. In an early review of the research of what he called "intercultural" programs, Allport found that *indirect* approaches to the study of cultural groups seemed to be best. The most effective programs had several characteristics:

- They fostered contact and acquaintance among students of various backgrounds.
- They led to a sense of equality in social status.
- They avoided artificiality.
- They enjoyed the support of the community in which they occurred.

Allport contrasted these programs to those that focused on teaching about "group differences," which are found in most traditional curricula. He concluded that mere verbal learning or exhortation was ineffective and counterproductive and that multicultural programs that are both natural and meaningful to the lives of students are by far the most effective. He reached the conclusion that "Action is ordinarily better than mere information."[10]

Banks, in a review of programs specifically designed for "prejudice reduction," found that although children's racial attitudes can be modified if the school designs objectives and strategies for that purpose, such programs are more successful if their primary objective is to increase students' cognitive sophistication. The research also suggests that intergroup education programs, to be most effective, should not consist of what he calls "one-shot treatments."[11] Pate's research affirmed this conclusion. He found that the least effective approach was a direct "antiprejudice" teaching unit, probably because students sensed that they were being manipulated and resented it. Interestingly, he found that one of the most effective ways of reducing prejudice is not through the study of prejudice or ethnicity but rather through cooperative learning.[12] In fact, a number of research studies have demonstrated that cooperative learning not only improves academic achievement but also results in increasing cross-ethnic and cross-racial friendships among students.[13]

In general, what most research on multicultural education seems to suggest is that only by reforming the entire school environment can substantive changes in attitudes, behaviors, and achievement take place.[14] Most schools have not undergone these kinds of massive changes. Those few that have begun to modify the school culture have generally seen dramatic changes in all students.[15] In effect, the entire "culture" of the school must be changed if the impact of multicultural education is to be felt, including curriculum and materials, institutional norms, attitudes and behaviors of teachers and other staff, counseling services, the extent to which parents are welcome in the school, and the relationship of the school to the community. Practices that potentially segregate students, such as ability grouping or special education and the kind of bilingual programs that do not allow interaction among students of different backgrounds, might in fact aggravate prejudice and interethnic hostility. In contrast, cooperative learning groups, fully integrated schools, and special education and bilingual programs that allow some interaction among students of different backgrounds while still providing the important services that these students need would no doubt serve as powerful incentives against prejudice. This conclusion reinforces the definition of multicultural education as "basic" and "pervasive." It also confirms the connection between multicultural education and school reform.

The positive effect of multicultural education on helping new students adjust to the community and school and on solving issues of interethnic prejudice and hostility can be definitive. Interethnic hostility and violence are not new to schools. With the influx of large numbers of new immigrants and with few appropriate programs to prepare either communities or schools for their diversity, the problem is becoming more serious. Students' lack of understanding of cultures different from their own, the preconceptions they and their families may have brought from other countries, their internalizing of the negative ways in which differences are treated in our society, and the lack of information provided in the schools all serve to magnify the problem. Add to this the "pecking order" established in schools among different social and cultural groups and the general reluctance of schools to deal with such knotty issues, and we are left with unresolved but unremitting interethnic hostility.

The potential of multicultural education for reducing this kind of hostility is great. Howard, in reporting on the outcome of a multicultural curriculum process called Project REACH at a middle school, found that students of color reported fewer incidents of name-calling and ethnic slurs after their peers had participated in the program. In addition, students of color and those in bilingual and ESL programs demonstrated a greater sense of pride and willingness to share information about themselves.[16]

Avoiding Stereotypes

One of the central ways in which case studies help illuminate directions for action is by pointing out incongruencies and exceptions. Although it is always important to understand how culture, language, gender, and economic class influence such things as learning and communication style, it is equally crucial to understand that these factors are not *deterministic*. That is, not all Jewish students have an ethos for scholarship, not all African American students have a relational learning style, and not all Asian students are quiet and independent learners. Avi, contrary to the stereotype of the "Jewish genius," had a difficult time adjusting to his new school and had some academic problems. Vinh insisted that learning in groups while discussing themes related to students' experiences is the best way to learn.

Avi, Vinh, and the other students in the case studies help us to understand that there are as many differences within an ethnic group as there are among different groups. In so doing, they shatter stereotypes. Although in general it is good to try to understand cultural *patterns*, it is equally important to remember that such patterns are not cultural *molds*. Another lesson for schools and teachers is that cultural differences, values, and experiences merit serious study and consideration but that students should always be approached as individuals with unique personalities, experiences, and idiosyncrasies that differentiate them in important ways from one another and from others in their group.

SUPPORT BEYOND ACADEMICS

In almost every single case, the young people studied were involved in meaningful activities outside of the academic context, sometimes in the school or community and sometimes a combination of activities, including school clubs and sports, religious groups, and out of school hobbies. As we saw previously, these activities provide a variety of support for students, ranging from keeping them away from negative peer pressure to reinforcing leadership and critical thinking skills. In some cases, such activities give them an outlet that otherwise strict families allow and welcome.

Inclusive and Meaningful Activities

The first implication is that all schools, but particularly those at the secondary level, need to provide inclusive and meaningful activities that will attract a wide range of students. Although many schools do indeed provide such activities, including sports, clubs focusing on hobbies, cultural clubs, and student government, many do not. In addition, given the renewed emphasis on "the basics" that has occurred as a result of the educational reform movement of the 1980s, many reports have recommended that schools minimize extracurricular activities.[17] Many of these "reforms," particularly those focusing on "raising standards," such as longer school days and fewer so-called frills, have been felt most heavily at schools serving culturally diverse and poor students.

Even in schools that provide extracurricular activities, a majority of students are not involved in them, for many reasons, ranging from lack of funds to conflicts in schedules. For example, some sports programs, although presumably open to all, are in effect restricted to the students most able to afford them. Others meet after school and, because they provide no transportation, are really available only to those who can get home on their own or who can rely on family or friends. Students who work after school are also unable to take part in these activities. Finally, some extracurricular activities are restricted by the language and culture of students currently involved or by the perceptions of those not involved that their cultural and language differences are limitations. For example, although some Cambodian students may be quite interested in joining the soccer team, they may feel excluded because there are no other Cambodian students on the team. Or Mexican American students in a bilingual program may be interested in working on the school newspaper but may not even attempt to join because it is written completely in English.

The implications of the noninvolvement of some students in these kinds of activities have to do with equal access. It is fine for schools to say that activities are open to all students, but unless this policy is backed up with practices reinforcing it, it is meaningless. Providing ''verbal'' equal access while in reality foreclosing the possibility that some students can participate belies claims of equal opportunity. The same conditions of participation need to be established for all students. For instance, if a sports program is costly because of the required equipment, it is reasonable for the school to provide such equipment for those who cannot afford it. The same is true of transportation. If some students are closed off from activities because they do not have the same opportunity to get home from school as others, alternate means of transportation have to be provided.

Other kinds of exclusion can also be seen in terms of access. There is something seriously wrong, for example, if the newspaper staff in a culturally pluralistic school consists of only European American students. In these cases, broad-based and intentional recruitment of a diversity of students is necessary, not only by posting announcements but also by making more serious efforts to involve previously uninvolved students, such as making announcements in all the languages spoken in the school, having students from various backgrounds involved in the recruiting program, and providing alternative meaningful activities. For newspapers, a project in which students interview their families and neighbors concerning a particular issue of importance to the community might be the incentive. Involving students in the development of the school's disciplinary code in more than a superficial way might be the approach for student government. In all cases, looking for ways in which students' voices are heard and interests are considered is more likely to get them involved.

Even students' perceptions of exclusion can be understood as a problem of access. Certain activities may not exclude students *intentionally*, but the *result* is the same. Thus, if there are no activities for students who speak a language other than English, there is a problem of equal access. This is not to say that linguistic enclaves should be developed in the school, although there is an important place for language and culture clubs. Some clubs or activities that involve a diversity of students and build on that diversity are also called for. Manuel's involvement in the theater workshop is a good example. There, the various languages and cultures of students were specifically used to enrich the experiences of all those involved. Students' culture and language can be used in other activities as well, from creating a bilingual or multicultural newspaper to developing teams of sports that are popular in other cultures. Schools can do a lot more to embrace the interests and experiences of their students than is currently the case. Neglecting to do so will result in the continuation of segregated and restricted school activities.

Implications for Families and Communities

Schools are not the only institutions that can learn from the experiences of these students. Families and communities also have an important responsibility in providing meaningful outlets for young people. This is a job often carried out quite naturally by families in giving their children responsibilities in the home. In research with academically successful and unsuccessful Black students, Clark found that those who were successful were also responsible for performing household chores.[18] His explanation is that the kind of behavior necessary for developing responsibility in the home helps students in classroom situations requiring diligence, independence, and commitment. This finding was also true in our case studies. James is very much the "older brother," taking primary responsibility for his siblings while his mother is at work. Linda has a number of specific responsibilities at home. Manuel, as the mediator between family and community, plays a crucial role in his extended family.

Communities, too, can better use the creative energy and enthusiasm of young people, including volunteer work at elementary schools or day-care centers, working with the elderly, or spending time in a social service agency. Probably the best arrangements would be those coordinated by schools with community agencies or businesses, where students might get credit for services rendered. Opportunities for after-school work or community service can be provided in much more substantial ways than they currently are. The very real concerns that young people have for their communities need to be used in developing their leadership and critical thinking skills. Young people are sincerely interested in the issues affecting their communities. Vinh, for example, said that he is looking forward to a job in which he can help people; Vanessa's concern for peace and social justice is another example. There are far too few outlets for this kind of caring; even when they are available, there are few incentives for involvement.

Even religious institutions can learn from the examples seen in the case studies. When the activities such institutions offer young people are meaningful to them, they will be involved. Marisol says that church is very important to her because it is a family activity. For many of them, religion strongly reflects their cultural identification and as such serves to reinforce its importance. Yet one often finds religious institutions unaware of how to capitalize on the culture of the people in the community, neglecting to use their music, language, or cultural values in services or outreach.

Rather than detract from school success, meaningful activities in the home, school, and community that make productive use of students' time seem to support it. Particularly with adolescents, the importance of belonging and "fitting in" are best met with structured activities that at the same time allow for independence and are a vehicle for expression. This finding is reinforced with the third major lesson from the case studies: All of the successful students sought environments supportive of their success.

DEVELOPING ENVIRONMENTS FOR SUCCESS

The students in our case studies, successful in school in spite of what might be predicted to the contrary, have participated in and sought environments for success in many ways. These environments are apparent not only in school but in their homes and communities as well. Several implications emerge concerning what schools and families can do to promote the achievement of all students, not only those who are expected to succeed: the curricular and instructional adaptations made in school, the importance of communication, and the need to raise expectations for all students. We will first explore what has been called "mutual accommodation" by Díaz, Moll, and Mehan.[19]

Mutual Accommodation

A key question teachers and schools must ask themselves in their interactions with students, particularly those from diverse racial, ethnic, and linguistic backgrounds, is this: *Who does the accommodating?* The question is an important one because it gets to the very heart of how students from nondominant groups experience school every day. Dominant group students, on the contrary, rarely have to consider learning a new language to communicate with their teachers. They already speak the acceptable school language. The same is true of culture. These students do not generally have to think about their parents' life-styles and values because their families are the norm, as was seen in Vanessa's case. Students from other groups, however, have to consider such issues *every single day.* Their school experiences are fraught with the tension of accommodation that students from the dominant group could not even imagine.

Some accommodation is, of course, necessary. Without it, students and their teachers would not understand one another. If students and teachers spoke different languages at all times, operated under different goals and assumptions, and in general had varying expectations from the schools, the situation would be chaotic. Students from dominated groups and their families expect to make some accommodations, which is clear in their willingness to learn English, their eagerness to participate in school life, and in the general agreement with the "rules of the game" implicit in their contracts with the schools.

The problem is that it is generally *only* students from dominated groups and their families who are asked or forced to do the accommodating. It is noteworthy when it is the other way around. In one particular school system, which had a two-way bilingual program, for example, an evaluation after two years found that English-dominant students and their families were the ones most changed by the program. The trauma and difficulty of learning a second language was something these students had to experience firsthand to understand what their Latina and Latino classmates had been going through for years. Because they were learning in Spanish and had to confront this kind of accommodation probably for the first time in their lives, they developed a healthy respect and compassion for their Spanish-speaking peers in the program. More interaction between the two groups in the classroom, the schoolyard, and the cafeteria was visible. In addition, the English-speaking students began to appreciate the benefits of bilingualism and cited such activities as going to the local *bodega* and being able to "shop in Spanish." The resultant changes in the attitudes and behaviors of these students, and even of their families, were quite extraordinary.

The process of accommodation is evident in the case studies, too. For the most part, it has been the students who have had to make almost all of the accommodations. They have not usually questioned the need to do so; rather they have accepted it as what one has to do to get along in school. We catch glimpses of how it could be otherwise, however. Vinh speaks wistfully of how teachers understand his culture "outside" but not "something inside our hearts." He has had to do most of the accommodating by learning a new language and adjusting to a new culture, not to mention the pain of separation from his family. Although he understands that he has to do so, it has taken its toll. We can see the same thing in Marisol. Her culture and language have been almost completely missing from her formal education, and although she seems to have accepted this situation, there are moments when she does not (as when she refused to stop speaking Spanish in one of her classes). In the one instance in which she saw her Puerto Rican culture reflected in the curriculum, it made her "quite proud of myself," as she said. Linda's very definition of herself is compromised by other definitions. She had to take the time and trouble, for example, to check off "other" and write in "Black American and White American" on all her college applications.

How then can we address this issue of *who does the accommodating?* Díaz, Moll, and Mehan studied reading and writing in bilingual settings. They found that teachers' accommodations, using the students' social and linguistic resources, helped the students succeed academically. In reading, for example, teachers coordinated aspects of English reading lessons with both English and Spanish. What had previously been a painful and slow process for students was transformed into a qualitatively new and successful environment for learning. Rather than focusing on which language was used, comprehension became the lessons' primary goal. The result was a three-year jump in English reading. Similar findings were reported in a writing group. The researchers conclude that a model of "mutual accommodation" is what is called for. That is, both teachers and students need to modify their behaviors in the direction of a common goal, "academic success with cultural integrity."[20] Tharp's extensive review of programs which have been successful with previously unsuccessful dominated group students comes to the same conclusion. In his view, "accommodation without assimilation" is what seems to produce greater school achievement.[21]

The lesson for teachers and schools from the case studies and similar research is that contrary to conventional wisdom and practice, it is not students and their families who must always do the accommodating. The belief in one-way accommodation explains the general tendency among educators to view unsuccessful students as either genetically inferior or culturally deprived. When students do not automatically accommodate to the school (or other) system, their intelligence or ability or that of their families is questioned. The perspective of mutual accommodation allows schools and teachers to use the resources all students already have to work for academic success. In this model, neither the student nor the teacher expects complete accommodation; rather they work together, using the best strategies at the disposition of each.

In practice, mutual accommodation means that schools use the language and culture of students in teaching and that students use the language and culture of the school in learning. This practice can mean using the native language in instruction, designing instruction so that it takes into account the various preferred communication styles of students, and accepting and using the experiences that students have in their homes and communities as the basis for their learning. In terms of language diversity, it is what Saville-Troike calls "a mutual sociolinguistic adaptation."[22] That is, teachers need to adapt to the linguistic and cultural differences among students, and students need to understand what behavior is considered appropriate in "the subculture of the school."

In the process of mutual accommodation, both teachers and students are enriched. For example, using students' language, culture, and experiences as the basis for their teaching might mean that teachers have to expand their own repertoires. Given the absence of much that is innovative or exciting in teaching and learning approaches in schools, particularly at the high school level, expanding existing approaches is an advantage. Using the various communication styles of students also enriches all students, for they all learn to become more flexible in their learning. Furthermore, the research on cooperative learning suggests that most students benefit from a variety of approaches and that by reorganizing the social structure of classrooms, significant improvements in prosocial development, academic achievement, and race relations can be obtained.[23] Even students' attitudes and behaviors toward one another can be influenced in a positive way. In Rist's classic study of the effect of teachers' expectations on students, he found that much of the cruelty displayed by some students toward others was not inherent but a result of the social organization of the class, in which some were treated as worthwhile and smart and others were treated as "dumb" and not capable of learning.[24] Finally, providing alternate means for learning is an essentially democratic endeavor for it means expecting all students to achieve regardless of learning, language, or cultural differences.

Mutual accommodation means accepting and building on students' language and culture as legitimate expressions of intelligence and as the basis for their academic success. On the part of students and families, it means accepting the culture of the school in such areas as expectations about attendance and homework and learning the necessary skills for work in school. Through this process, both students and their families and teachers and schools are enriched. Students and their families, while being respected and accepted, can proceed with learning and achievement. Teachers and schools expand their repertoires and their way of looking at both ability and intelligence.

Communication

Students in our case studies frequently mentioned the importance of communication. At home, communication means being able to talk with their parents and families about important concerns in their lives. The importance of keeping up with their studies, pressures from peers, fears and problems facing adolescents, and negotiating for more freedom and independence were all central topics of conversation. Not all of the students were able to communicate with their families in this way. Even in these cases, however, there were other adults in their families with whom they could talk. For example, Manuel's aunt and uncle were most prominent. Clark also found that the regular occurrence of family discussions on school issues is positively correlated with high academic achievement.[25] The same has been suggested by Taylor and Dorsey-Gaines in research with poor, inner-city Black families.[26] Providing an environment for such discussions to take place, whether they concern school or not, is an important lesson for parents to consider in their interactions with their children.

Students also talked at length about teachers who made a difference in their school success. Sometimes, these were teachers from the same racial or ethnic background as the students themselves. Linda spoke emphatically about the importance of both her first-grade teacher, who was Black, and Mr. Benson, who was "mixed," just as she is. This kind of connection should be expected, given the absence of invisibility of the students' cultures and languages in much of the school environment. Issues of cultural congruence and compatibility seem to be at work here. Even such unexpected behavior as teachers' disapproval style may be firmly rooted in the values of their cultural background.[27] Students who share the same background as their teachers may be at a distinct advantage in those particular classrooms. A similar conclusion was reached by Barnhardt, who found that the academic achievement of Athabaskan Alaskan Native children rose dramatically after Native teachers began to teach them.[28]

One implication for schools is that more teachers who share the cultural background of students should be recruited. The schools' responsibility for aggressively recruiting teachers who are as diverse as the student body, something that up to now has not been given much of a national priority, is of major importance. This does not mean that only teachers from the same ethnic or racial background as students can teach them. The data concerning the rising number of culturally diverse students and the decreasing number of culturally diverse teachers suggests this is not only unrealistic but impractical as well.

All teachers, regardless of background, need to develop skills in multicultural understanding. In the study by Barnhardt, for example, the fact that the indigenous teachers organized their instruction and interacted with students in culturally appropriate ways is what seemed to have made the major difference in the students' achievement. Although ethnic group membership has a very positive impact, it is this *in conjunction with* teachers' cultural sensitivity and curricular and instructional accommodations that make a major difference. Interesting longitudinal research by Milner echoes this finding. In studying both the effect of multicultural materials and the introduction of "minority" teachers in elementary schools in two large English cities with significant "minority" populations, he found that although the race of the teacher contributed significantly to marked changes in children's attitudes, it was the *materials* that proved to be most decisive.[29] This is not to suggest that materials alone make a difference but that changing the curriculum can be a powerful incentive for positive change. It also implies that not only the teachers who are "role models" for the students can achieve these changes.

The issue of role model is a double-edged sword. Whereas teachers from students' racial, cultural, and ethnic background can make an important contribution to the school, enriching both the environment and the curriculum with their diversity, an undue burden is often placed on them. They frequently become in effect the "representative" of their race or ethnic or linguistic group on the faculty. Not only are they role models for the students, but they are also increasingly called on to deal with issues of cultural misunderstanding, to translate letters, to visit homes, to begin the school's "multicultural committee," and so on, and all of this work with no extra compensation or recognition. They become the token for their group in the school. This expectation is not only unfair to the small number of teachers who happen to be in this situation but also alleviates the school of the responsibility of meeting the needs of all of its students.

It is in the interests of all schools, given our increasing diversity, to recruit and welcome a diversity of teachers. When faculty members are diverse, multilingual, and multicultural, all students see themselves reflected. All teachers become role models for all students. The research reviewed here seems to suggest that teachers of any background can be effective with all students as long as they are *understanding, caring,* and *informed*.

Wolcott, after working in a Blackfish Village school, became aware that the critical differences between teachers and students are often based on antagonisms of cultural rather than classroom origins. He believed that teachers should assume the role of "the enemy" and students, that of "prisoner." He felt that accepting this role is in the long run more effective because it helps the teacher maintain what he called "realistic expectations" of students while acknowledging the possibility that there would be important differences in the life-styles and values of teachers and students.[30]

This is a disturbing conclusion for two reasons. First, many students are already treated exactly in this way and with far from positive results. That is, their cultures and languages are treated as if they were "foreign" and did not fit in. Consequently, the expectations teachers have of them tend to be quite low. Second, this stance implies that teachers can never be successful with their students, that students are doomed to academic failure if they are different from the mainstream. A far more reasonable approach would be for teachers to develop strategies for communicating with a wide diversity of students while having high expectations of all of them.

Another way in which teachers and schools can communicate with students is by offering help to those who do not seek it. This issue came up numerous times in the case studies: The number of successful students who had absolutely no guidance in school was astonishing. In a sense, this lack of assistance probably helped them develop extraordinary determination and self-reliance. One must contrast this lack of help to practices in private and elite public schools, where students are given any number of personalized services such as preparing for college entrance exams, selecting the right college or university based on their interests and academic records, asking for financial aid, filling out college applications and writing appropriate essays, and so on. Particularly for students who are the first in their families to go to college, such help is indispensable because their families have no prior experience with which to guide their children. The students who are most vulnerable in terms of having access to college receive the least help in schools, even when they are successful and have high hopes and aspirations for their continued schooling. That most of the students in the case studies will probably go to college, in spite of the lack of help they received, is a stunning accomplishment. One must ask, if these are the successful students, what happens to those who are unsuccessful in school?

Communication thus emerges as a key component in the kinds of environments for success schools can provide. It can be seen in the instructional and curricular strategies used by teachers, in teachers' willingness to share their experiences and background with students, in young people's opportunities to interact with their peers, or in the very services implying support and encouragement offered by schools.

Raising Expectations and Standards

The detrimental role that low expectations play in the school achievement of students, particularly those from dominated groups, has been reviewed elsewhere. Although the young people in our case studies were successful students, they brought up this point frequently as a problem in their classrooms and schools. They said that they and their classmates were treated like babies; that the work teachers gave them was undemanding; and that any work, no matter how poor, was accepted. Low expectations were not only a problem for them but for other students as well. Some may say that this is because the students in our case studies are more "intelligent" and thus could handle more demanding work than others, but this reasoning is contradicted by other research. For example,

Spring conducted a study in a small northern school system that had changed from majority White to majority Black. He found that the primary cause of decline in academic standards was *not* due to the nature of the students coming into the school but rather to the attitudes of White teachers and administrators toward them. There was a marked decline in homework assignments, a shifting of emphasis from college preparation to vocational education, and so on.[31] He concluded that it was racism rather than the demands of parents or inherent inadequacy in the students that caused the academic decline. The attitude that students are incapable of performing adequately because they happen to be Black, speak a language other than English, or come from a poor family is widespread, whether students are successful in school or not.

Lowering expectations is not always intentional. Sometimes, it is a teacher's way of accommodating instruction to student differences. Good intentions, however, do not always lead to positive results. Because such accommodations are based on the presumption that particular students are incapable of scholarly work because of language and cultural differences, they are patronizing at best. Rather than using students' skills and abilities in such accommodations, only their perceived deficits are acknowledged.

The lesson here is that expectations and standards need to be raised for all students. This does not mean conducting business as usual. High standards can be achieved in a great variety of ways and through a multitude of materials. Multicultural education means finding and using culturally, multiculturally, and linguistically relevant materials in developing students' basic skills. It also means using a variety of approaches, from peer tutoring to dramatizations, in instruction. Raising standards and expectations does not mean homogenizing instruction but creating new and different opportunities for learning for all students.

Expanding the Meaning of Parent Involvement

Very few of the parents of the successful students in these case studies are involved in school in any but the most superficial way, at least given the way that parent involvement is currently defined. Few of them volunteer their time in school, go to meetings, or even visit the school on a consistent basis. Some parents seem to be uninvolved in even the kind of home activities with their children that would seem to be important for academic success: They rarely help with homework or provide many books in the home or take the children to museums, libraries, or other environments that are said to motivate scholarly pursuits. The reasons for this uninvolvement are many, ranging from inability to speak English to limited funds to lack of previous experience with such activities to their own negative experiences with schooling.

In this way, some of the parents of these students seem to contradict much of the research on parent involvement that emphasizes the role of the family as mediator between their children and schools. Frequent interactions with the school and help with students' work are stressed in this research. In our case studies, very little of this kind of support seems to take place. Nevertheless, the students are all successful. Rather than conclude that these parents are not involved in the education of their children, we need to expand what is meant by parent involvement. We can do so by exploring the activities in which these parents *are* involved. In so doing, we can develop a more hopeful and democratic model of parent involvement within the reach of all students despite the level of their parents' schooling, their socioeconomic background, or the language spoken at home.

First, most of the parents of our students stressed the importance of going to school and going on to college. Many of the students mentioned that their parents wanted them to have a better chance, to do better than they had done, and to have the opportunity for a better job. This was a constant theme in their homes, embedded in the framework of *communication* between parents and children. The crucial issue here seems to be that the parents of successful students are able to maintain a high level of communication that affects the messages they give them. It is quite possible that parents of unsuccessful students also stress the importance of schooling, but because their message is not contextualized in a framework of open communication, their children may simply not "hear" it. Even when parents do attempt to communicate openly with their children, other factors such as negative peer pressure may get in the way. The point is that in the homes of successful students, open communication is constant.

Related to this finding, all of the students perceive their parents as loving and supportive. Although most of them also believe their parents are too strict or old-fashioned, it does not seem to detract from their feeling of closeness with their parents. The students in these case studies for the most part genuinely *like* their parents and have great respect for them. Even when students think that their parents could have helped them more, as does Manuel, they do not resent this lack of help but rather understand it and redouble their efforts to do well in school "for them." Thus, parents seem to serve not only as a motivating force but also as a model, not necessarily of educational achievement but rather of strength and resilience, something their children want to emulate.

Although most of the parents do not help with homework, they do seem to provide support by monitoring it. That is, they have expectations that their children will complete their work, they ask about homework and schoolwork frequently, and they take an interest in what their children are doing in school. They provide support in other ways also. James talked about how his mother removed his brother from a class because she was unhappy with the way the teacher was treating him. Fern described the time her father flagged down a car to take him to her school so that he would not miss a class play because of a flat tire. These are dramatic examples of how parents were willing to take risks or go to extraordinary lengths to support their children.

An important way in which parents support their children's academic success seems to be through the continued use of their native language and their continued reliance on the families' cultural values. When students came from a family who spoke a language other than English, it was always maintained as the language of communication in the home. Although English was also used in most of the homes, the salience of the native language was evident. In all cases, the cultural values of the family were emphasized, whether through religious observance; important family rites and rituals; and deep-seated values such as family responsibilities, respect for elders, or high academic aspirations. Rather than obstructing academic success, reliance on native language and culture seems to promote it.

Finally, the parents in these case studies are proud of their children and demonstrate it in a variety of ways. At the same time, they have high expectations of their children. Although they do not tend to focus on grades, they do use them as a measure of their children's effort. If they believe that their child can do better, they are quick to let them know it, in spite of the grade. From conversations with parents, it also became clear that many of their children are a source of hope for the family.

Returning to our expanded definition of parent involvement, it seems that we need to consider home activities as well as school activities. This is not meant to deny the importance of parent involvement in volunteer work, school governance, or other school-related activities. However, if we perceive parent involvement as simply what occurs in the school, the vital role that these parents have had in the school success of their children is diminished. However, we are not just concerned here with those activities traditionally equated with school success, that is, many books and toys in the home, frequent attendance at cultural activities, and so on. What we mean by home activities are intangibles: *consistent communication, high expectations, pride, understanding,* and *enthusiasm* for their children's school experiences.

These qualities seem to be at the core of the environments for success parents are best able to give their children. A synthesis of studies by Walberg reached the conclusion that what he called the "alterable curriculum of the home" is twice as predictive of academic learning as is family socioeconomic status.[32] The implication for schools is evident: Ways to use parents' hope, enthusiasm, and skills need to be explored through school and community activities that accept parents as the first and most important teachers of their children and, most important, *use the strengths and resources parents already have, especially their culture and language.* A particularly powerful example can be found in the work of Alma Flor Ada with Mexican American parents and their children.[33] Once a month, a group of parents would meet to discuss children's literature and to read the stories and poems written by their children and in some cases by the parents themselves. Although most of them had very little schooling, the impact on them has been as great as on their children. In the process of dialogue, reading, and writing, they have developed both confidence and greater abilities in using the resources at their command, particularly their language and culture, to promote the literacy of their children. As one mother said, "Ever since I know I have no need to feel ashamed of speaking Spanish, I have become strong."[34]

Parents can have a decisive effect on their children's literacy development and on their academic success in general. Schools first have to acknowledge the role parents can have in promoting success and then develop innovative strategies to use their talents, hope, and motivation. The old view that poor parents and those who speak another language or come from a dominated culture are unable to provide appropriate environments for their children can lead to condescending practices that reject the skills and resources they already have. Practices such as top-down classes on parenting, reading, nutrition, and hygiene taught by "experts" are often the result of this kind of thinking. However, when parents are perceived to have skills, strengths, and resources that can aid their children, the results are different. There is nothing wrong with information to help parents with the upbringing and education of their children if and when it is given with mutual respect, dialogue, and exchange. Otherwise, it can become another heavy-handed and patronizing strategy that does little to inspire confidence or trust.

In summary, it is safe to say that all the parents of successful students are involved in their education in a meaningful and central way. This involvement can generally be seen in intangibles such as attitudes and behaviors fostering communication, support, love, and pride. In addition, the continued use of their native language and cultural values as vehicles for such communication are probably crucial. Ways in which schools can use parents' skills, linguistic and cultural resources, and support for their children need to be explored further.

SUMMARY

In this chapter, we have considered some of the implications of the case studies for policy and practice in schools. Although improvement in education must take place at the school level, it will not necessarily lead to substantive changes in society that guarantee social justice for all. Yet the connections between schools and society cannot be denied. Schools have often been sites of protest, resistance, and change, and their role in influencing public policy can be an important one. It is necessary for teachers to understand both the tensions and the connections between change at the school and societal levels to work effectively for such change in different arenas.

The three major lessons that emerged from the case studies help us to understand the role of teachers, schools, families, and communities in working for equity in education. The responsibility of schools to strengthen bilingual and multicultural education was reviewed and relevant research in the field was presented. The role of meaningful and engaging extracurricular activities was also considered, with examples of what schools and communities can do. Finally, suggestions concerning the role of teachers and parents in providing environments for success for all students were presented, specifically, *mutual accommodation, communication, high expectations and standards,* and *expanding the meaning of parent involvement.* Although we cannot disregard the negative role of structural factors in the lack of achievement of many students, there is often common ground between teachers and families in their expectations for student learning. Nevertheless, conflicts between schools and communities arise because of lack of understanding, disrespect, and miscommunication. In the next chapter, we will consider some of the ways to bridge these gaps.

TO THINK ABOUT

1. Dickeman has suggested that teachers are engaged in "a subversive task" if they challenge the monocultural curriculum and other inequities of schools. What does she mean?
2. Think about the following four major conceptions of the goals of education:
    a. To provide students with basic skills to survive in society and become productive workers
    b. To develop productive citizens of a democracy
    c. To develop students who can become critical citizens of a multicultural society
    d. To replicate society, that is, to reproduce current structures and values
Working in four groups, explore how schools founded on one of these principles might function. What would be the differences among them? What would the curriculum, materials, administration, community outreach, and structure be like in each of these schools? Now compare each of these schools to schools with which you are familiar. What can we learn from this comparison?

3. Consider the possibility that you and a group of other staff in a new and innovative school have been given the responsibility for implementing a bilingual program for all students, both English speakers and speakers of other languages. What suggestions would you make? What are the implications for staff development, parent involvement, and scheduling? What problems and opportunities do you envision?

4. Develop a list of goals for a *comprehensive multicultural education program* in the same school. How would this school differ from others? Describe some of the activities of the school as well.

5. Think about some of the ways in which extracurricular activities in schools you know limit the participation of students. Give examples of what schools can do to become more inclusive. Consider sports, newspaper, student government, and other activities.

6. Think of schools and students you know in exploring the question *Who does the accommodating?* Give examples of what you mean. Include in your discussion issues of language, culture, class, and other differences students bring to school. How might schools and students accommodate one another's differences more fairly? Be specific.

7. You are the teacher representative on a search committee for a new teacher for your school. Develop a list of qualities or characteristics you would be looking for. Would race, ethnicity, gender, or language background make a difference? Why or why not? What if the school were very culturally diverse? Quite monocultural? Would this make a difference?

8. What do you think of Wolcott's idea that teachers with backgrounds differing from those of their students should assume the role of "teacher as enemy"? Why do you think he has proposed this view? What might be the benefits in assuming this posture? What might be the problems?

9. Although the parents of the students in our case studies have had a major influence on their children's lives, they have not always known how to provide concrete assistance. What might be the role of the school in working with parents? Give some examples of collaboration between schools and parents that would help students do better in school.

NOTES

1. Mildred Dickeman, "Teaching Cultural Pluralism," in *Teaching Ethnic Studies: Concepts and Strategies*, 43rd Yearbook, ed. James A. Banks (Washington, DC: National Council for the Social Studies, 1973).

2. See, for example, Samuel Bowles and Herbert Gintis, *Schooling in Capitalist America: Educational Reform and the Contradictions of Economic Life* (New York: Basic Books, 1976); Joel Spring, *The Sorting Machine Revisited* (White Plains, NY: Longman, 1989). For an ethnographic study that reached the same conclusion, see Kathleen Wilcox, "Differential Socialization in the Classroom: Implications for Equal Opportunity," in *Doing the Ethnography of Schooling: Educational Anthropology in Action*, ed. George Spindler (New York: Holt, Rinehart & Winston, 1982).

3. De Young, for example, has suggested that civic and business leaders in the United States have increasingly viewed children as resources to be used for economic development because they believe that sustained economic growth is necessary for national progress. See Alan J. DeYoung, *Economics and American Education: A Historical and Critical Overview of the Impact of Economic Theories on Schooling in the United States* (White Plains, NY: Longman, 1989).

4. Roland G. Tharp, "Psychocultural Variables and Constants: Effects on Teaching and Learning in Schools," *American Psychologist*, 44, 2 (February 1989), 349–359.

5. Martha Montero-Sieburth, "*Echar Pa'lante*, Moving Onward: The Dilemmas and Strategies of a Bilingual Teacher," *Anthropology and Education Quarterly*, 18, 3 (September 1987), 180–189.

6. See, for example, Virginia P. Collier, "How Long? A Synthesis of Research on Academic Achievement in a Second Language," *TESOL Quarterly,* 23, 3 (September 1989), 509–551; Jim Cummins, *Bilingualism and Special Education: Issues in Assessment and Pedagogy* (Clevedon, Eng.: Multilingual Matters, 1984).
7. Kenji Hakuta, *Mirror of Language: The Debate on Bilingualism* (New York: Basic Books, 1986); Collier, "How Long?"
8. Virginia P. Collier, "Academic Achievement, Attitudes, and Occupations Among Graduates of Two-Way Bilingual Classes," paper presented at the annual meeting of the American Educational Research Association, San Francisco, March 1989.
9. *Barriers to Excellence: Our Children at Risk* (Boston: National Coalition of Advocates for Students, 1985), p. 16
10. Gordon W. Allport, *The Nature of Prejudice* (Reading, MA: Addison-Wesley, 1954), p. 509.
11. James A. Banks, *Multiethnic Education: Theory and Practice,* 2nd ed. (Boston: Allyn & Bacon, 1988).
12. Glenn S. Pate, "Reducing Prejudice in the Schools," *Multicultural Leader,* 2, 2 (Spring 1989), 1–3.
13. See, for example, Elizabeth G. Cohen, *Designing Groupwork: Strategies for the Heterogeneous Classroom* (New York: Teachers College Press, 1986); Brenda Dorn Conard, "Cooperative Learning and Prejudice Reduction," *Social Education,* April/May 1988, pp. 283–286; Nancy Schniedewind and Ellen Davidson, *Cooperative Learning, Cooperative Lives: A Sourcebook of Learning Activities for Building a Peaceful World* (Dubuque, IA: Wm. C. Brown 1987).
14. See Pate, "Reducing Prejudice in the Schools"; Banks, *Multiethnic Education;* Allport, *Nature of Prejudice;* Raymond C. Westphal, Jr., *The Effects of a Primary-Grade Interethnic Curriculum on Racial Prejudice* (San Francisco: R & E Research Associates, 1977).
15. See, for example, the exemplary practices of some schools in dealing with immigrant students as reported in *New Voices: Immigrant Students in U.S. Public Schools* (Boston: National Coalition of Advocates for Students, 1988).
16. Gary Howard, "Positive Multicultural Outcomes: A Practitioner's Report," *Multicultural Leader,* 2, 1 (Winter 1989), 12–16.
17. DeYoung, *Economics and American Education.*
18. Reginald M. Clark, *Family Life and School Achievement: Why Poor Black Children Succeed or Fail* (Chicago: University of Chicago Press, 1983).
19. Stephan Díaz, Luis C. Moll, and Hugh Mehan, "Sociocultural Resources in Instruction: A Context-Specific Approach," in *Beyond Language: Social and Cultural Factors in Schooling Language Minority Students* (Los Angeles: Office of Bilingual Education, California State Department of Education, Evaluation, Dissemination and Assessment Center, 1986).
20. Ibid.
21. Tharp, "Psychocultural Variables and Constants."
22. Muriel Saville-Troike, "Language Diversity in Multiethnic Education," in *Education in the 80's: Multiethnic Education,* ed. James A. Banks (Washington, DC: National Education Association, 1981).
23. See, for example, Spencer Kagan, "Cooperative Learning and Sociocultural Factors in Schooling," in *Beyond Language: Social and Cultural Factors in Schooling Language Minority Students* (Los Angeles: Office of Bilingual Education, California State Department of Education, Evaluation, Dissemination, and Assessment Center, 1986); Robert E. Slavin, *Cooperative Learning* (White Plains, NY: Longman, 1983); David Johnson et al., "Effects of Cooperative, Competitive, and Individualistic Goal Structures on Achievement: A Meta-Analysis," *Psychological Bulletin,* 89 (1981), 47–62; Cohen, *Designing Groupwork; Locked In/Locked Out: Tracking and Placement Practices in Boston Public Schools* (Boston: Massachusetts Advocacy Center, March 1990).

24. Ray C. Rist, ''Student Social Class and Teacher Expectations: The Self-Fulfilling Prophecy in Ghetto Education,'' *Challenging the Myths: The Schools, the Blacks, and the Poor,* Reprint Series #5 (Cambridge, MA: Harvard Educational Review, 1971).

25. Clark, *Family Life and School Achievement.*

26. Denny Taylor and Catherine Dorsey-Gaines, *Growing Up Literate: Learning from Inner-City Families* (Portsmouth, NH: Heinemann, 1988).

27. See research cited by Shirley Hernandez Muñoz and Isaura Santiago Santiago, ''Toward a Qualitative Analysis of Teacher Disapproval Behavior,'' in *Theory, Technology, and Public Policy on Bilingual Education,* ed. Raymond V. Padilla (Rosslyn, VA: National Clearinghouse of Bilingual Education, 1983).

28. C. Barnhardt, '' 'Tuning In': Athabaskan Teachers and Athabaskan Students,'' in *Cross-Cultural Issues in Alaskan Education,* Vol. 2, ed. R. Barnhardt (Fairbanks: University of Alaska, Center for Cross-Cultural Studies, 1982).

29. David Milner, *Children and Race: Ten Years On* (London: Ward Lock Educational, 1983).

30. Harry F. Wolcott, ''The Teacher as an Enemy,'' in *Education and Cultural Process: Anthropological Approaches,* 2nd ed., ed. George D. Spindler (Prospect Heights, IL: Waveland Press, 1987).

31. Joel Spring, *American Education* (White Plains, NY: Longman, 1985).

32. H. J. Walberg, ''Improving the Productivity of America's Schools,'' *Educational Leadership,* 41 (1984), 19–27.

33. Alma Flor Ada, ''The Pajaro Valley Experience,'' in *Minority Education: From Shame to Struggle,* ed. Tove Skutnabb-Kangas and Jim Cummins (Clevedon, Eng.: Multilingual Matters, 1988).

34. Ibid.

CHAPTER 11

Affirming Diversity: Implications for Schools and Teachers

OVERVIEW

The implications of the case studies stress the central role of schools in fostering academic success for all students. Multicultural education represents a promising means to achieve this goal. This is not to say that it can wipe out social inequality or student underachievement. No program or educational philosophy can make such grandiose claims. However, if one of the primary purposes of education is to give young people the skills, knowledge, and critical awareness to become productive members of a diverse and democratic society, multicultural education as broadly conceptualized can be the philosophical underpinning guiding this effort.

Affirming Diversity, the title of this book, is at the very core of multicultural education. It implies that cultural, linguistic, and other differences can and should be accepted, respected, and used as a basis for learning and teaching. Rather than maladies to be cured or "problems" to be confronted, differences are an important and necessary starting point for learning and teaching and can enrich the experiences of students and teachers. In this chapter, we will consider two concrete issues suggested by the case studies in exploring what it means to affirm diversity. The first concerns expanding the definition of *American,* and the second focuses on a model of multicultural education that emerges from the seven characteristics defined in Chapter 8.

EXPANDING DEFINITIONS: WHAT IT MEANS TO BE AMERICAN

As we saw quite poignantly in some of the case studies, a number of students had great difficulty in accepting a split concept of self (what has commonly been called the "hyphenated American"). In our society, one is either American or foreign, English-speaking or Spanish-speaking, Black or White. The possibility that one could be at the same time Spanish-speaking and English-speaking, Vietnamese and American, or Black and White is hardly considered. A case study of Lowell, Massachusetts by Kiang quotes a Cambodian who expressed this sentiment with obvious pain: "When they say 'American,' they don't mean us—look at our eyes and our skin."[1]

The designation of American is generally reserved for those who are White and English-speaking. Others, even if here for many generations, are still seen as quite separate. This point was brought out rather humorously in the old "Barney Miller Show" when Jack Soo, who played a police officer of Japanese American heritage, answers the inevitable question, "Where are you from?" so often asked of Asians, with the unexpected reply, "Omaha." In this way, he challenged the view of Asians as foreign. No matter how many generations they have been here and regardless of whether they speak only English and have little contact with their native heritage, Asians are not generally accorded the designation American. The same would not be true of a European American, even a relatively recent arrival. The issue of race in being accepted as a "real" American is far more salient than years of residence or even language spoken.

Racism has always been a mediating force in the acceptance or rejection of groups in U.S. society. It is not uncommon to see references to *Americans, Blacks,* and *Latinos,* as if they were mutually exclusive. If a book refers in general to "Americans," whether about history, child psychology, geography, or literature, the cover picture, majority of illustrations, and content will be almost exclusively White. Only if the book concerns what might be considered a deviation from the "norm," as would be the case if it were about African American literature or the psychological development of Latino children, do the pictures and content reflect these groups.

The issue of self-identification is a complicated one because it involves not only cultural but also, and probably primarily, political issues. Thus, it is quite understandable that some Indians prefer not to be called American, given the history of their treatment and abuse by the U.S. government. The same can be said of some Puerto Ricans, who refuse to think of themselves as Americans because of the colonial exploitation of Puerto Rico. As pointed out in the previous chapter, such refusal may have negative consequences, especially if those who are already disenfranchised become even more alienated from the sources of power and change available to them.

The definition of *American* as currently used effectively excludes the least powerful. As such, it legitimizes control and hegemony in cultural, economic, and political terms of what has been called "preferred" over "nonpreferred" groups.[2] Thus, it must be rejected. Our present and future diversity demands an expanded and *inclusive* definition, not hyphenated Americans, implying split and confused identities. *African-American* might imply a bifurcated identity, whereas *African American* signifies that a new definition is possible, one that stresses not confusion or denial but acceptance and transformation of what it means to be an American.

Americanization in the past has always implied *Angloization.* It meant not only learning English but also forgetting one's native language; not only learning the culture but also learning to eat, dress, talk, and even behave like the European American model. As so movingly expressed by a writer talking about the process experienced by Jews in New York some 80 years ago, "The world that we faced on the East Side at the turn of the century presented a series of heartbreaking dilemmas."[3] To go through the process meant the inevitable loss of a great part of oneself in the bargain.

These heartbreaking dilemmas still exist today, as we have seen in the case studies. At the turn of the century, the choice was generally made in favor of assimilation. The choices, although no less difficult today, are not as limited as they once were. The civil rights and related liberation movements have led to more freedom in maintaining native language and culture. The great number and diversity of immigrants into the United States during the past two decades, unequalled except at the beginning of the century, has also changed the complexion of our country. Between 1980 and 1990, legal immigration alone was almost 9 million, equaling that of 1900–1910.[4] Such changes are having a profound impact on the meaning of assimilation. *Americanization* can no longer mean assimilation to a homogeneous model. Consequently, to continue using *American* to refer exclusively to those of European heritage makes little sense.

The students currently enrolled in our schools are in some ways more fortunate than previous students: They have more freedom in maintaining their language and culture. Nevertheless, the choice of having no choice is still largely true. On the one hand, if they choose to identify with their culture and background, they may feel alienated from this society; on the other hand, if they identify with U.S. (generally meaning European American) culture, they feel like traitors to their family and community. The choices are still heartbreaking ones for many students.

As they currently exist, these choices are quite clear-cut and rigid: One is either true to oneself and family or one is American. This can be compared to what Lambert has called "subtractive bilingualism," that is, the kind of bilingualism that develops at the expense of one's native language.[5] This kind of bilingualism means that one does not really become "bilingual" at all but rather is in the transition between being monolingual in one language to being monolingual in another, although sometimes vestiges of the original language may remain. In the same way, multiculturalism is subtractive to the extent that one is in transition from being monocultural in one culture to being so in another.

The opposite of subtractive multiculturalism can be called *additive multiculturalism*. Just as children who have reached full development in two languages enjoy cognitive advantages over monolinguals, we can speculate that those who have reached a state of *additive multiculturalism* also enjoy advantages over monoculturals, including a broader view of reality, feeling comfortable in a variety of settings, and multicultural flexibility.[6]

Expanding the definition of *American* may help students and others facing the dilemma of fitting into a multicultural society. Such an expansion is not meant to force-fit everyone under the general heading. It is meant instead to expand the choices people have in making an accommodation between cultural and linguistic and social and national identification. In this way, and with a range of possibilities, the students in our case studies, as well as others, might have more of a choice than before, creating a variety of means by which to self-identify. European Americans would no longer be the only "Americans."

There is an inherent and natural tension between Americanization, with its commonly accepted meaning of assimilation, and keeping one's culture and language. As we approach the beginning of the twenty-first century, however, the question shifts a bit. No longer a choice of whether one *should* assimilate or not, the question now becomes, How far can society, and the institutions of society such as schools, be pushed to accommodate the changing definition of *American?* It is probably the first time in our history that this question has been asked in more than a rhetorical way. The fact is that new challenges are being posed daily to the view of the United States as a monolithic and monocultural society, as seen in the wide use of languages other than English by an increasing percentage of the population, the ever greater demands for bilingual education in scores of languages, and the ease and conviction with which growing numbers of people are claiming their heritage as important resources to be nurtured and maintained.

The fact that this question can be posed at all places us in a unique historical moment. In the past, such possibilities could probably not even be considered. Brumberg, in his study of the public school experiences of East European Jews in New York City at the beginning of the twentieth century, maintains that given their historical context and Americanizing mission, the schools probably could not have behaved other than they did. Bilingual education, for instance, was out of the question. He also claims, however, that even today there is a built-in conflict of interest if the same institution, that is, the school, attempts to acculturate students to a dominant culture and language and at the same time instructs them in what he calls an "alternative language and lifestyle."[7] For students from the dominant culture, this is not an alternative at all but simply a replication of the life-styles, values, culture, and language of their home. Students whose families represent languages and cultures different from the dominant one are at a disadvantage.

This view of schools as the inevitable assimilators of students must be challenged. The boundaries of pluralism, formerly delimited by an Anglocentric definition, are being disputed daily. Given the different social and historical context in which we are living, schools need to accommodate diversity in more humane and sensitive ways than they have in the past. Formerly, just one major option existed, and it was quickly, if not always eagerly, seized by most immigrants: quick assimilation into the so-called melting pot. In an insightful essay on the rise of pluralism, Greenbaum proposes two reasons why assimilation occurred so quickly in the past: one was *hope* and the other was *shame*. Hope contributed in a major way in holding out the promise of equality, economic security, and a safe haven from war and devastation. "Most important is the fact that the main fuel for the American melting pot was shame. The immigrants were best instructed in how to repulse themselves; millions of people were taught to be ashamed of their faces, their family names, their parents and grandparents, and their class patterns, histories and life outlooks."[8]

This has not been the situation in the United States alone. In other countries with large numbers of immigrants, there are similar pressures. Skutnabb-Kangas explores what the pressure to assimilate has meant on an international level: "This static and ethnocentric view, where the whole burden of integration is on the incomer alone, and where the dominant group's values are presented as somehow 'shared' and 'universal,' rather than particularistic and changing, like all values are, still prevails in many countries."[9] Schools and society are being pushed beyond their limits as new demands and questions are posed because these limits are no longer acceptable to a growing number of people. The students in our case studies, for example, are challenging the view of assimilation by force. Not content to accept past restrictions, they provide evidence that an evolution is taking place. Although still caught in the conflict and uncertainties of how to expand their possibilities, these young people are increasingly sure of who they are and determined to keep their identity.

LEVELS OF MULTICULTURAL EDUCATION AND SUPPORT

If indeed we do not accept the limits that society and schools impose, we need to consider how multicultural education can be incorporated in a natural and global way into the curriculum and instruction. First, we will explore how one starts on this multicultural journey. Then we will propose four levels of multicultural education and compare them with monocultural education.

Starting Out

How does a school or a teacher start a multicultural program? If we say that multicultural education must be comprehensively defined, pervasive, and inclusive, it does not mean that only a full-blown program qualifies. Because multicultural education is a process, we need to understand that it is in constant flux. That is, it is never quite finished. Given the fact that multicultural education is critical pedagogy, it must of necessity always be changing and dynamic. A static "program-in-place" or a slick packaged program is contrary to the very definition of multicultural education.

Let me illustrate with an example from a junior high school English teacher in a community of European American (primarily Irish, French, and Polish) and Puerto Rican students.[10] When asked how she included a multicultural perspective in her teaching, she replied that she has not yet reached that level. Rather, she said, her classroom had what she called "bicultural moments." She was very supportive of multicultural education and used curriculum and instructional strategies that emerged from this perspective, but she felt that the children in her classes did not even know about their own or one another's backgrounds, let alone about the world outside their communities. Thus, in her curriculum she focused on exploring, through reading and writing, the "little world" of their own communities before venturing beyond it. Her reasoning was logical: If students do not even understand themselves, their families, and their communities, how can they appreciate others of different backgrounds?

An example of a "bicultural moment" in writing concerned the journals her students kept. One of the central themes was the family, and what they wrote was later used as the basis for class discussions. A particularly vivid example involved two adolescent boys, one Irish American and the other Puerto Rican, and their perspectives and feelings toward their baby sisters. The Irish American boy complained about what a brat his little sister was. The way in which he described her was full of tenderness, although hidden under the crusty surface of a boy trying to conceal such feelings. The Puerto Rican boy's journal, in contrast, was consciously sentimental. He described in great detail just how beautiful and wonderful his baby sister was and concluded that everyone in his family thanked God for sending her to them. Both of these boys loved their sisters and both were poetic and loving in their descriptions of them, but they expressed their love in widely different ways. Although not claiming that one was an Irish American and another was a Puerto Rican "way" of feeling, this teacher was nonetheless using these differences as a basis for students' understanding that the same feelings are often expressed in distinct ways and that different families operate in unique but valid ways. This bicultural moment was illuminating for all students. It served to expand both students' literacy and their way of thinking. For the teacher, to "begin small" meant to use the experiences and understandings students bring to class rather than exotic or irrelevant curriculum that is meaningless to them.

This is a message worth remembering. In our enthusiasm to incorporate a multicultural philosophy in our teaching, we can sometimes forget that our classrooms are made up of young people who usually know very little about their own culture or that of their classmates. Starting out small, then, means being sensitive to these bicultural moments and using them as a beginning for more wide-ranging multicultural education.

Afrocentrism and Its Role in a Multicultural Perspective

Related to the issue of biculturalism is the development of what has recently been called *Afrocentrism*,[11] which refers to a philosophical outlook and values based on African cultures. In some ways, it is a direct response to *Eurocentrism*. This philosophy has become particularly visible in the schools. Afrocentric curricula and educational environments have gained importance in the recent past because traditional classrooms in the United States are based on European American standards and values and thus tend to put African American children at a disadvantage. This is true in the content of the curriculum, where African Americans are missing, to a lack of understanding of students' communication styles by most teachers.

Hale-Benson, for example, has suggested that African American children would be more successful in schools based on African cultural norms. According to her, *ideology, method, and content* are the three components that must change for a curriculum to be meaningful to Black children.[12] She has developed a model emphasizing Afrocentric language and communication skills; development of positive attitudes toward learning and school; and African American studies embedded in the curriculum. A number of Afrocentric schools have been developed that use such a model. The reasoning behind these schools is that since African American children (particularly males) are being failed wholesale by traditional schools, it is important that students' culture, values, language, and communication patterns serve as the basis for their education. A number of these schools designed especially for Black males are staffed almost entirely by Black male teachers, presumably because so many boys are lacking such role models in their lives.

Given the experience of African American students in traditional school settings, the reasoning behind Afrocentric schools is understandable. It is important to emphasize that Afrocentric schools are but one example of multiculturalism: they stress *one* cultural outlook and are thus specifically aimed at alleviating the educational disadvantages of one group that has traditionally been disenfranchised and miseducated by schools. It is not clear if students from other cultural backgrounds would benefit from programs of this type. Nevertheless, Afrocentric schools are one option within a *multicultural continuum*. Just as *bicultural moments* represent a step away from a Eurocentric curriculum, an Afrocentric perspective is another response to a curriculum that is not working for large numbers of students. The challenge for us as a society is to work toward a truly comprehensive and multicultural perspective that works for *all* of our students, while along the way responding to the very real educational needs of *some* of our students.

Becoming a Multicultural Person

Developing truly comprehensive multicultural education takes many years, in part because of our own monocultural education. Most of us, in spite of our distinct cultural and/or linguistic backgrounds, were educated in monocultural environments. We seldom have the necessary models for developing a multicultural perspective. We have only our own experiences, and these have been overwhelmingly Eurocentric, English-speaking, and imposed. Sleeter, for example, in a review of related literature, found that because teachers share a pervasive culture and set of practices, there are limits to the extent to which they can change *without concurrent changes in their context.*[13]

Becoming a multicultural teacher, therefore, first means becoming a multicultural person. Without this transformation of ourselves, any attempts at developing a multicultural perspective will be shallow and superficial. But becoming a multicultural person in a society that still emphasizes the model of an educated person in a monocultural framework is not easy. It means reeducating ourselves in several ways.

First, *we simply need to learn more,* for example, by reading a variety of materials and going to many culturally pluralistic activities. It means looking for books and other materials that inform us about people and events we may know little about. Given the multicultural nature of our society, those materials are available, although sometimes they need to be sought out because we have learned not to see them.

Second, *we need to confront our own racism and biases.* It is impossible to be a teacher with a multicultural perspective without going through this process. Because we are all products of a society that is racist and stratified by gender, class, and language, we have all internalized some of these messages in one way or another. Sometimes, our racism is unconscious, as in the case of a former student of mine who referred to Africans as "slaves" and Europeans as "people" but was mortified as soon as she realized what she had said. Sometimes, the words we use convey a deep-seated bias, as when a student who does not speak English is characterized as "not having language," although she may speak her native language quite fluently. Our actions also carry the messages we have learned, for example, when we automatically expect that our female students will not do as well in math as our male students. Our own reeducation means not only learning new things but also unlearning some of the old. The process is a difficult and sometimes painful one. It is nevertheless a necessary part of becoming multicultural.

Third, *becoming a multicultural person means learning to see reality from a variety of perspectives.* Because we have often learned that there is only one "right answer," we have also developed only one way of seeing things. A multicultural perspective demands just the opposite. We need to learn to approach reality from a variety of perspectives. Reorienting ourselves in this way can be exhausting and difficult because it means a dramatic shift in our worldview. After going through this process, however, we can turn with renewed vigor to our schools and classrooms to remake them into multicultural environments.

Although the transformation of individuals from being monocultural to being multicultural will not by itself guarantee that education will become multicultural, it would certainly lay the groundwork for it. As one teacher who is thoroughly multicultural in outlook and practice told me, "Since I've developed a multicultural perspective, I just can't teach in any other way. " That is, her philosophical outlook is evident in the content she teaches, the instructional strategies she uses, the environment in her classroom, the interactions she has with students and their parents, and in the values she expresses in her school and community. Wurzel maintains that it is necessary to go through seven "stages of the multicultural process":

- Monoculturalism
- Cross-cultural contact
- Cultural conflict
- Educational interventions
- Disequilibrium
- Awareness
- Multiculturalism

His argument that cross-cultural conflict is both inevitable and a positive element in the process of learning is equally helpful.[14] According to this perspective, no growth can really take place until we begin questioning our own cultural values.

We now need to consider several different levels of multicultural education and how they might be operationalized in the school.

A Model of Multicultural Education

A monocultural perspective represents a fundamentally different framework for understanding differences than does a multicultural one. Even a multicultural perspective, however, has a variety of levels of attitudes and behaviors. I would classify them into at least four levels: *tolerance; acceptance; respect;* and *affirmation, solidarity,* and *critique.* Although these are necessarily static and arbitrary categories, they are used only in an effort to understand how multicultural education might be manifested in schools in a variety of ways. A model ranging from monocultural to comprehensive multicultural education will be proposed. The levels will be considered vis-à-vis the seven characteristics of multicultural education proposed previously. We can then explore how multicultural education, as a process, takes a variety of forms in different settings. In addition, we will be reminded that a truly comprehensive multicultural education demands attention to many components of the school environment.

Tolerance is the first level. To be tolerant means to have the capacity to bear something, although it may be at times unpleasant. To tolerate differences means that they are endured, although not necessarily embraced. We may learn to tolerate differences, but this level of acceptance can be quite shaky. What is tolerated today may be rejected tomorrow. Tolerance therefore represents the lowest level of multicultural education in a school setting. Yet many schools have what they consider very comprehensive mission statements that stress only their "tolerance" for diversity. They may believe that this is an adequate expression of support, although it does not go very far in multicultural understanding. In terms of school policies and practices, it may mean that linguistic and cultural differences are borne as the inevitable burden of a culturally pluralistic society. Programs that do not build on but rather replace differences might be in place, for example, ESL programs. "Black History Month" might be commemorated with an assembly program and a bulletin board. The life-styles and values of students' families, if different from the majority, may be considered to require understanding but modification.

Acceptance is the next level of dealing with diversity. If we accept diversity, it means that we at the very least acknowledge differences without denying their importance. In concrete terms, programs acknowledging students' languages and cultures would be visible in the school. These might include a transitional bilingual program that uses the students' primary language at least until they are "mainstreamed" to an English-language environment. It might also mean celebrating some differences through such activities as multicultural fairs and cookbooks. In a school with this level of multicultural diversity, a time may be set aside weekly for "multicultural programs." Communication with parents through newsletters and so on would be carried on through their native language.

Respect is the third level of multicultural education. Respect means to admire and hold in high esteem. When diversity is respected, it is used as the basis for much of the education offered. It might mean offering programs of bilingual education that use students' native language not only as a bridge to English but also throughout their schooling. Frequent and positive interactions with parents would take place. In the curriculum, students' values and experiences would be used as the basis for their literacy development. Students would be exposed to different ways of approaching the same reality and would therefore expand their way of looking at the world. *Additive multiculturalism* would be the ultimate goal for everybody.

Affirmation, solidarity, and *critique* represent the very highest level of multicultural education. It means accepting the culture and language of students and their families as legitimate and embracing them as valid vehicles for learning. It also means understanding that culture is not fixed or unchangeable, and thus one is able to critique its manifestations and outcomes. Because multicultural education is concerned with equity and social justice for all people, and because basic values of different groups are often diametrically opposed, conflict is inevitable. Passively accepting the status quo of any culture is inconsistent with multicultural education. As eloquently expressed by Kalantzis and Cope, "Multicultural education, to be effective, needs to be more active. It needs to consider not just the pleasure of diversity but more fundamental issues that arise as different groups negotiate community and the basic issues of material life in the same space—a process that equally might generate conflict and pain."[15]

Multicultural education without critique implies that cultural understanding remains at the romantic or exotic stage. If we are not able to transcend our own cultural experience through reflection and critique, we cannot hope to understand and critique that of others. Without critique, the possibility that multicultural education might be used to glorify reality into static truth is a very real danger. Thus there has been vigorous criticism of the way in which multicultural education has been conceptualized and implemented in the past: "The celebration of ethnicity in intercultural education can (but need not . . .) in fact function both as a new more sophisticated type of control mechanism and as a pacifier, to divert attention from social and economic inequality."[16] This criticism by

Skutnabb-Kangas points out how diversity often skirts the issue of racism and discrimination. In some schools, *diversity* is a more euphemistic substitute for dealing with the very real issues of exclusion that many students face. Racism needs to be confronted head-on, and no softening of terms will help. However, when *diversity* is understood in the more comprehensive way described above, it can lead to inclusion and support of all people.

In the school, affirmation, solidarity, and critique mean using the culture and language of all students in a consistent, critical, comprehensive, and inclusive way. It goes beyond creating ethnic enclaves that can become exclusionary and selective, although for disenfranchised communities, this is certainly a step in the process. It means developing *multicultural* settings in which all students feel reflected and visible, for example, through two-way bilingual programs in which the languages of all students are used and maintained meaningfully in the academic setting. The curriculum would be characterized by multicultural sensitivity and inclusiveness, offering a wide variety of content and perspectives. Teachers' attitudes and behaviors would reflect only the very highest expectations for all students, although they would understand that students might express their abilities in very different ways. Instructional strategies would also reflect this multicultural perspective and would include a wide variety of means to teach all students. Parents would be welcomed and supported in the school as students' first and most important teachers. Their experiences, viewpoints, and suggestions would be sought out and incorporated into classroom and school programs and activities, They, in turn, would be exposed to a variety of experiences and viewpoints different from their own, which would help them expand their horizons.

Other ways in which these four levels might be developed in schools are listed in Table 11.1 on pages 280–281. Of course, multicultural education cannot be categorized as neatly as this chart would suggest. This model simply represents a theoretical way of understanding how different levels of multicultural education might be visible in a school. It also helps to highlight how pervasive a philosophy it must be. Although any level of multicultural education is preferrable to that offered by a monocultural perspective, each level challenges with more vigor a monolithic and ethnocentric view of society and education. As such, the fourth level is clearly the highest expression of multicultural education.

The fourth level is also the most difficult to achieve for some of the reasons mentioned previously, including the lack of models of multicultural education in our own schooling and experiences. It is here that we are most challenged by values and life-styles different from our own and with situations that severely test the limits of our tolerance. For instance, dealing with people who are different from us in hygienic practices, food preferences, and religious rites that we may find bizarre can be trying. It is also extremely difficult and at times impossible to accept and understand cultural practices that run counter to our most deeply held beliefs. For example, if we believe strongly in equality of the sexes and have in our classroom children whose families value males more highly than females, or if we need to deal with parents who believe that education is a frill and not suitable for their children, or if we have children in our classes whose religion forbids them to take part in any school activities except academics—all these situations test our capacity for affirmation and solidarity. And well they should, for we are all the product of our cultures and thus have learned to view reality from the vantage point of the values they have taught us.

Culture is not static; neither is it necessarily positive or negative. The cultural values and practices of a group of people represent their best strategies, at a particular historical moment, for negotiating the environment and circumstances in which they find themselves. What some groups have worked out as appropriate strategies may be considered unsuitable or even barbaric and uncivilized by others. Because each cultural group proceeds from a different context, we can never reach total agreement on the "best" or most appropriate ways in which to lead our lives. In this sense, culture needs to be approached with a relativistic framework, not as something absolute.

Nevertheless, it should also be stressed that above and beyond all cultures there are human and civil rights that need to be valued and maintained by all people. These rights guarantee that all human beings are treated with dignity, respect, and equality. Sometimes the values and behaviors of a group so seriously challenge these values that we are faced with a dilemma: to reject it or to affirm the diversity it represents. If the values we as human beings hold most dear are ultimately based on extending rights rather than negating them, we must decide on the side of those more universal values.

It is not always easy to determine how to resolve conflicts revolving around cultural differences. Such resolution is sometimes impossible. For one, the extent to which our particular cultural lenses may keep us from appreciating differences can be very great. For another, some values may be irreconcilable. In the majority of cases, however, some accommodations that respect both cultural values and basic human rights can be found. Because societies have generally resolved such conflicts in only one way, that is, favoring the dominant culture, few avenues for negotiating differences have been in place. Multicultural education, although at times extremely difficult, painful, and time-consuming, can help provide one way of attempting such negotiations.

SUMMARY

In this chapter, we have considered two issues that have implications for multicultural education: the definition of *American* and the different levels multicultural education may have. Both focus on education as expansive, inclusive, and comprehensive, compared to monocultural education, which tends to be limiting, exclusive, and restricted.

Anything less than a program of comprehensive multicultural education will continue to shortchange some students in our schools. Our society has promised all students an equal and high-quality education, but educational results have belied this promise. Students most victimized by society, that is, those from economically poor and culturally and linguistically dominated groups, are also the most vulnerable in our schools. Their status there tends to replicate the status of their families in society in general. Unless our educational system confronts inequity at all levels and through all school policies and practices, we will simply be proceeding with business as usual. Affirming diversity in no way implies that we merely celebrate differences. On the contrary, issues of racism and inequality must be confronted head-on in any comprehensive program of multicultural education. *Diversity* is no substitute for antiracism and should not be used as such. In the final chapter, we will consider specific strategies and approaches that build on the multicultural perspectives described here.

TABLE 11.1   Levels of Multicultural Education

Monocultural Education	Characteristics of Multicultural Education	Tolerance
Racism is unacknowledged. Policies and practices that support discrimination are left in place. These include low expectations and refusal to use students' natural resources (such as language and culture) in instruction. Only a sanitized and "safe" curriculum is in place.	**Antiracist/ Antidiscriminitory**	Policies and practices that challenge racism and discrimination are initiated. No overt signs of discrimination are acceptable (name-calling, graffiti, blatantly racist and sexist textbooks or curriculum, etc.). ESL programs are in place for students who speak other languages.
Defines education as the 3 R's and the "canon." "Cultural literacy" is understood within a monocultural framework. All important knowledge is essentially European American. This Eurocentric view is reflected throughout the curriculum, instructional strategies, and environment for learning.	**Basic**	Education is defined more expansively and includes attention to some important information about other groups.
No attention is paid to student diversity.	**Pervasive**	A multicultural perspective is evident in some activities, such as Black History Month and Cinco de Mayo, and in some curriculum and materials. There may be an itinerant "multicultural teacher."
Ethnic and/or women's studies, if available, are only for students from that group. This is a frill that is not important for other students to know.	**Important for All Students**	Ethnic and women's studies are only offered as isolated courses.
Education supports the status quo. Thinking and acting are separate.	**Education for Social Justice**	Education is somewhat, although tenuously, linked to community projects and activities.
Education is primarily content: who, what, where, when. The "great White men" version of history is propagated. Education is static.	**Process**	Education is both content and process. "Why" and "how" questions are tentatively broached.
Education is domesticating. Reality is represented as static, finished, and flat.	**Critical Pedagogy**	Students and teachers begin to question the status quo.

Acceptance	Respect	Affirmation, Solidarity, and Critique
Policies and practices that acknowledge differences are in place. Textbooks reflect some diversity. Transitional bilingual programs are available. Curriculum is more inclusive of the histories and perspectives of a broader range of people.	Policies and practices that respect diversity are more evident, including maintenance bilingual education. Ability grouping is not permitted. Curriculum is more explicitly antiracist and honest. It is "safe" to talk about racism, sexism, and discrimination.	Policies and practices that affirm diversity and challenge racism are developed. There are high expectations for all students; students' language and culture are used in instruction and curriculum. Two-way bilingual programs are in place wherever possible. Everyone takes responsibility for racism and other forms of discrimination.
The diversity of lifestyles and values of groups other than the dominant one are acknowledged in some content, as can be seen in some courses and school activities.	Education is defined as that knowledge that is necessary for living in a complex and pluralistic society. As such, it includes much content that is multicultural. *Additive multiculturalism* is the goal.	Basic education is multicultural education. All students learn to speak a second language and are familiar with a broad range of knowledge.
Student diversity is acknowledged, as can be seen not only in "Holidays and Heroes" but also in consideration of different learning styles, values, and languages. A "multicultural program" may be in place.	The learning environment is imbued with multicultural education. It can be seen in classroom interactions, materials, and the subculture of the school.	Multicultural education pervades the curriculum; instructional strategies; and interactions among teachers, students, and the community. It can be seen everywhere: bulletin boards, the lunchroom, assemblies.
Many students are expected to take part in curriculum that stresses diversity. A variety of languages is taught.	All students take part in courses that reflect diversity. Teachers are involved in overhauling the curriculum to be more open to such diversity.	All courses are completely multicultural in essence. The curriculum for all students is enriched. "Marginal students" no longer exist.
The role of the schools in social change is acknowledged. Some changes that reflect this attitude begin to be felt: Students take part in community service.	Students take part in community activities that reflect their social concerns.	The curriculum and instructional techniques are based on an understanding of social justice as central to education. Reflection and action are important components of learning.
Education is both content and process. "Why" and "how" questions are stressed more. Sensitivity and understanding of teachers toward their students are more evident.	Education is both content and process. Students and teachers begin to ask, "What if?" Teachers empathize with students and their families.	Education is an equal mix of content and process. It is dynamic. Teachers and students are empowered. Everyone in the school is becoming a multicultural person.
Students and teachers are beginning a dialogue. Students' experiences, cultures, and languages are used as one source of their learning.	Students and teachers use critical dialogue as the primary basis for their education. They see and understand different perspectives.	Students and teachers are involved in a "subversive activity." Decision-making and social action skills are the basis of the curriculum.

TO THINK ABOUT

1. What do you see as the difference between *African-American* and *African American?* Is is simply a punctuation difference or does the hyphen create a different perception of these terms?
2. Define *American*.
3. Three different models for understanding pluralism or the lack of it are these:
     • *Anglo-conformity*—All newcomers need to conform to the dominant European American, middle-class, and English-speaking model.
     • *"Melting pot"*—All newcomers "melt" to form an amalgam that becomes American.
     • *"Salad bowl"*—All newcomers maintain their languages and cultures while combining with others to form a "salad," which is our uniquely U.S. society.
     In three groups, take one of the above and argue that it represents the dominant ideology in U.S. society. Give concrete examples. Afterward, in a large group, decide if one of these ideologies is really the most apparent and successful. Give reasons for your conclusions.
     How would you critique each of these ideologies? What are the advantages and disadvantages of each?
4. How would you identify a person who has developed what I called *additive multiculturalism?* How might that individual be different from one who is monocultural? Give some examples.
5. Do schools have a role to play in assimilating students to society? Why or why not? If so, how do they do it? Can it be done through a process that respects and affirms them at the same time?
6. Based on your experience, give some examples of "bicultural moments." If you have not had any, propose a classroom activity that might result in some.
7. Take a position, pro or con, on the debate concerning Afrocentric schools. Are such schools defensible? Do they exacerbate inequality in our society? Will they help students? Are they necessary? What other alternatives are possible?
8. In a small group, explore ways in which teachers can become *multicultural people*. Propose specific examples in their attitudes, beliefs, and behaviors.
9. You and a group of your colleagues are responsible for initiating discussions on becoming a multicultural school. Although many staff members are firmly committed to the idea, one of the issues you feel needs to be explored is confronting the biases and racism of the staff itself. What do you plan to do? Give a proposed time line for the process you develop.
10. Evaluate schools you are familiar with in terms of the model of multicultural education I have proposed. Consider the curriculum; materials; interactions among staff, students, and community; and the entire environment for living and learning in the school.

NOTES

1. Peter Nien-Chu Kiang, *Southeast Asian Parent Empowerment: The Challenge of Changing Demographics in Lowell, Massachusetts*, Monograph #1. (Boston: Massachusetts Association for Bilingual Education, 1990).
2. Antonia Pantoja and Barbara Blourock, "Cultural Pluralism Redefined," in *Badges and Indicia of Slavery: Cultural Pluralism Redefined*, ed. Antonia Pantoja, Barbara Blourock, and James Bowman (Lincoln, NE: Study Commission on Undergraduate Education and the Education of Teachers, 1975).
3. Words of Morris Raphael Cohen, cited in Stephan F. Brumberg, *Going to America, Going to School: The Jewish Immigrant Public School Encounter in Turn-of-the-Century New York City* (New York: Praeger, 1986), p. 116.

4. As cited by John B. Kellogg, "Forces of Change," *Phi Delta Kappan*, November 1988, pp. 199–204.
5. W. E. Lambert, "Culture and Language as Factors in Learning and Education," in *Education of Immigrant Students*, ed. A. Wolfgang (Toronto: OISE, 1975).
6. See Virginia P. Collier's analysis of research on academic achievement and second language development: "How Long? A Synthesis of Research on Academic Achievement in a Second Language," *TESOL Quarterly*, 23, 3 (September 1989), 509–531.
7. Brumberg, *Going to America*.
8. William Greenbaum, "America in Search of a New Ideal: An Essay on the Rise of Pluralism," *Harvard Educational Review*, 44 (August 1974), 411–440.
9. Tove Skutnabb-Kangas, "Legitimating or Delegitimating New Forms of Racism: The Role of Researchers," *Journal of Multilingual and Multicultural Development*, 11, 1 and 2 (1990), 77–100.
10. I am grateful to Susan Barrett for this wonderful example.
11. See, for example, Molefi Asanti, *Afrocentrism: The Theory of Social Change* (Trenton, NJ: Africa World Press, 1988).
12. Janice E. Hale-Benson, *Black Children: Their Roots, Culture, and Learning Styles*, rev. ed. (Baltimore: Johns Hopkins University Press, 1986).
13. She also found that much more than a series of workshops was needed to provide all that teachers needed to learn about diversity. See Christine E. Sleeter, "Multicultural Education Staff Development: How Much Can It Change Classroom Teaching?" paper presented at the annual meeting of the American Educational Research Association, San Francisco, March 1989.
14. Jaime Wurzel, "Multiculturalism and Multicultural Education," in *Toward Multiculturalism: A Reader in Multicultural Education*, ed. Jaime Wurzel (Yarmouth, ME: Intercultural Press, 1988).
15. Mary Kalantzis and Bill Cope, *The Experience of Multicultural Education in Australia: Six Case Studies* (Sydney: Centre for Multicultural Studies, Wollongong University, 1990).
16. Skutnabb-Kangas, "Legitimating or Delegitimating New Forms of Racism."

CHAPTER **12**

Multicultural Education in Practice

OVERVIEW

The purpose of this chapter is to consider strategies and approaches that teachers and schools can use to affirm and support students in becoming, in Manuel's words, "all that they can be." Because the major purpose of any good education is student learning, we will explore how multicultural education can provide a sound basis for all students, females and males from a variety of backgrounds, to achieve to their potential.

As you will recall, the definition of multicultural education in Chapter 8 was derived from an exploration of a number of factors that may help explain why some students do not succeed in school: racism and other forms of discrimination, structural factors in schools, and the negative ways in which cultural and linguistic differences are viewed in the school. The approach in this chapter will be to parallel Chapters 3 to 6 of Part I, using the same issues as a basis for our discussion. This will take the form of what Freire has called "problem-posing,"[1] in which the problems themselves become the focus of a search for possible solutions. That is, they will be used as the organizational framework for considering approaches and strategies that can counteract the negative environments many students face in school. We will go back to the following issues:

- Racism, discrimination, and expectations of students' achievements (Chapter 3)
- Structural factors in schools (Chapter 4)
- Cultural issues (Chapter 5)
- Linguistic diversity (Chapter 6)

Suggestions for putting multicultural education into practice will be made within each of these broad categories. Because multicultural education here is viewed in a com-

prehensive way and in a sociopolitical context, we will steer clear of approaches and strategies that deny, trivialize, or otherwise demean cultural, linguistic, social, and other
differences. Likewise, because there has been a historic tendency to view teachers within
the "factory model" as mass production workers unable to develop creative and empowering strategies for their classrooms, teachers' ideas and experiences will be the basis of
this chapter. Rather than answers or prescriptions for "prejudice reduction" or simple
"cultural awareness" lessons, the focus will be on providing a framework so that teachers themselves can make the curriculum reflect the communities of which they are a part
and the larger society in which we all live. Although some specific recommendations will
be made, they should be seen as guidelines for developing a multicultural environment
that welcomes all students rather than as static recipes for multicultural lessons.

It is impossible to become instantly multicultural. Attempts to do so are sometimes
comical and frequently counterproductive and superficial. However, teachers can do a
little bit every day and work toward implementing change systematically, which is probably more effective in the long run. In addition, each teacher and/or each school is different in outlook, culture, and especially student body. Thus the emphasis in this chapter
will be on teachers' and students' development of multicultural approaches that best meet
the needs of their particular setting. After making a number of suggestions in each of the
categories in the organizational framework, specific situations and problems for teachers
to work on will be presented. At the end of the chapter, a number of resources that may
help teachers in further developing a multicultural classroom environment will be recommended. A variety of novels focusing on the ethnic experience in the United States is
included. These books are recommended both as teachers' resources and as literature for
high school students. Books such as these are frequently helpful in giving concrete information about different cultural groups and providing an authentic voice on the dilemma of coming of age and the interconnections among ethnicity, culture, gender, and
class. They are one graphic and important way to learn about the kinds of issues faced by
many students in U.S. classrooms.

COUNTERACTING RACISM, DISCRIMINATION, AND LOW EXPECTATIONS

Racism, discrimination, and low expectations of student abilities are considered together
because they affect one another so profoundly. We will explore several ways in which this
interaction takes place and then propose a number of strategies for addressing them.

Our biases are bound up with those of society at large in myriad ways, even in the
way in which we learn to approach differences. Not dealing with children's curiosity
about differences in skin color, facial features, or hair textures is a good example. There
is a stubborn reluctance to address these issues head-on because by doing so, we feel
that we are drawing unneeded attention to them. Children quickly pick up the message
that talking about or even acknowledging these kinds of differences is a negative thing.
The problem is that these issues *do* get addressed, but generally in secretive and destructive ways. Name-calling, rejection, and other manifestations of hostility can be
the result.

IMPLICATIONS OF DIVERSITY FOR TEACHING AND LEARNING

Expectations are bound up with the biases we have learned to internalize. If we expect children who come from economically poor communities to be poor readers, we may reflect it in modifications we make in the way we teach them. Similarly, if we expect girls to be passive and submissive, we may teach them as if they were. Although our teaching approaches are either frequently unconscious or developed with the best of intentions, the results can be disastrous. We have seen many vivid examples throughout this book. Thus, having good intentions or even caring deeply about students is not enough. We need to consider our biases, which even the most enlightened teachers carry with them, every day that we step foot into the classroom. We are sometimes shocked when others point out to us, for instance, that we call on the girls in our class less often than the boys or that we accept slovenly work from some students and not from others. African American and Latino students have often stated that teachers were happy with a C from them in math, say, whereas they expected higher grades from other students in the class. We cannot mandate, of course, that teachers develop high expectations for all students or that schools become antiracist, antisexist institutions overnight, but we can suggest changes in the educational environment that help promote these processes.

Promoting and Actively Working Toward Creating a Diverse Staff

Although individual teachers cannot usually affect the hiring practices of schools by themselves, they can join others to work for a racially, ethnically, gender-balanced, and linguistically diverse staff. When positions are available, they can lobby for the inclusion of job qualifications that make it clear that diversity is an important criterion for consideration. This is true for all positions throughout the school and is particularly important for underrepresented groups, such as women in top administrative posts. As has been stated previously, there is no easy one-to-one correlation between students' self-image and the number of staff or faculty from diverse groups. Nevertheless, schools in which the teaching staff is primarily European American and the administration is heavily male, whereas the student body and kitchen staff are overwhelmingly Mexican American and female, for example, may send a powerful, albeit unintended, message about the second-class status of some students and staff.

Teachers can suggest that aggressive outreach efforts be used to locate a diverse staff. These can include public notices, so that parents and other community members are informed of openings; postings in community centers and local businesses; announcements in local newspapers; and notices sent to local radio stations. These notices should be translated into the major languages spoken in the community.

What Can You Do?
- If the student body is very heterogeneous but the teaching staff is not, what can you do to encourage more diversity on the staff? What if no openings are currently available, but you and others are concerned about the cultural imbalance of students to staff? List some creative ways to make your school more multicultural, using current resources.
- Use the same scenario, but change one ingredient: Both the teaching staff and student body are quite *homogeneous*. Why is it important to diversify the teach-

ing staff? Create another list of activities to help a more homogeneous school become multicultural.

Making Differences and Similarities an Explicit Part of the Curriculum

Focusing on human differences and similarities can begin as early as the preschool years, for example, dealing with skin color, hair texture, and other physical differences and similarities. Rather than telling White children that it is not polite to say that Black children have "dirty" skin, the teacher can use this statement as a basis for making skin differences an explicit part of the curriculum: using individual photographs of the children for a bulletin board on all the beautiful colors of children in the class, pictures from magazines of people from all over the world, stories that emphasize the similarities in human feelings across all groups, and dolls that represent a variety of racial and ethnic groups as well as both genders.

Teachers can develop a "class culture" or "school culture" so that the school is truly a community. For example, some activities and rituals should be required for all students, such as having local or national school heroes representing a variety of backgrounds; having all students learn songs, poems, or speeches from several cultures; and having all students take part in local history projects that explore the lives, experiences, and accomplishments of many different people. On the individual classroom level, a teacher might develop a *Classtory* (a history of the class). It can include the pictures and biographies of each member of the class with information about their culture, the languages they speak, and the things they like to do with friends and family. In this way, children learn that history is not simply what has happened in the past to "important" people but something that they and their communities are involved in making every day. Activities such as these do not browbeat the concept of similarities and differences into children's heads but develop them as natural images.

With older students, focusing on multicultural literature that depicts the reality of women and men of many groups is an effective strategy. Curriculum guides that discuss the history and culture of particular groups are also helpful, and these can be used in conjunction with guides that discuss a variety of groups.

With all students, from preschool through high school, it is important to create a physical environment that affirms differences. This environment can include a variety of pictures and posters, wall hangings from different cultures or models made by the students, maps and flags from all over the world, bulletin boards of celebrations of special days that feature multicultural themes, exhibits of art from around the country and the world, and a well-stocked multicultural and gender-balanced library. When students are working quietly, music representing different cultures can be played. The game corner can include a variety of games, from checkers to Parchese to Mankala to dominoes. Different languages can also be represented on bulletin boards and posters, with translations in English.

What Can You Do?
- Focus on your specific curriculum. How can you make similarities and differences an explicit part of your curriculum? If you are a subject matter specialist, list the topics that you will be teaching in the next month. If you are an

elementary or preschool teacher, list the themes or topics you will be teaching. How can you make them more explicitly multicultural and antisexist? Write down specific ideas, along with resources to help you accomplish this task. Work with a colleague to do the necessary research and share the results. You may want to develop one or more actual lesson plans in detail as a starting point.

- Think about the resources you have in your school and your classroom. Develop an environment that is physically multicultural. Write down as many concrete ideas as you can think of or actually draw the floor plan of your classroom (and school), indicating where and how resources that are multicultural might best be used.

Making Racism and Discrimination an Explicit Part of the Curriculum

Focusing on similarities and differences alone does not guarantee that racism will disappear. Because racism and other forms of discrimination are generally hushed up or avoided in the curriculum, they become uncomfortable topics of conversation in the school. Making racism and discrimination an explicit part of the curriculum can be a healthy and caring way to deal with these painful issues.

Even young children can take part in discussions on racism and discrimination. While many teachers believe that young children should not be exposed to the horrors of racism at an early age, they are overlooking the fact that many children suffer the effects of racism or other forms of discrimination every day of their lives. Making it an explicit part of the curriculum, for all children, helps them deal with it in productive rather than negative ways. Examples can be found in work with young children in critical pedagogy and in discussing controversial issues.[2]

The name-calling that goes on in many schools provides an opportunity for teachers and students to engage in dialogue. Rather than dealing with these as "isolated incidents" or as the work of a "few troublemakers," as is often done, making them an explicit part of the curriculum places them as systemic problems in society in general and in schools in particular. Then both teachers and students are forced to name, confront, and work through the racism, sexism, heterosexism, and so on that are implicit in these activities. This step can take any form, from "circle" or "sharing time" to actual lessons on name-calling.

Developing strategies that focus on barriers to student achievement can be very successful with specific groups. Bell describes one such process that emerged from an ethnographic research project in an urban elementary school. Designed to explore the experiences of fifth- and sixth-grade girls, the project used consciousness raising as a means to empowerment. Using "generative themes," a key Freirian approach, a team of researchers and students identified and explored several problems as the focus of their deliberations. By the end of the year, the girls had developed both a more critical understanding of sexism in schools and society and an awareness of some of the ways to confront it.[3]

What Can You Do?
- Stereotypes of racial and cultural groups, women, social classes, and disabled people, among others, are all around us. Develop some ways in which to make

these an explicit part of the curriculum. Locate appropriate materials and describe how you would have students go about countering the stereotypes they see.

• Most teachers have witnessed name-calling and racist and exclusionary behavior in their schools. Think back to the last such incident you saw. How was it handled? Would you handle it any differently now? How would you make it an explicit part of the curriculum? What materials might you use to help you?

• How might you use stories in the news to bring up issues of racism and other forms of discrimination? Develop a number of activities, related to your subject area and grade level, that focus on current news in which stereotyping, racism, or exclusion can be found.

CHANGING SCHOOLS: RESTRUCTURE AND RENEWAL

As became abundantly clear in Chapter 4, structural factors in the schools themselves exacerbate the problems of social inequality. In fact, they sometimes reproduce societal inequalities in schools as well. Although changing a few structures in the schools cannot guarantee equity, it can set the stage for promoting equal and high-quality education for all students.

We will consider each of the structures reviewed in Chapter 4 to develop strategies for restructure and renewal in the schools.

Tracking

If tracking is acknowledged to be a problem in promoting education for all students in a democratic society, de-tracking schools is the first step, although it is not enough. Very often, students seem to track themselves, selecting courses that they feel are most appropriate for them. This kind of self-awareness is both important and necessary, but it is too often based on negative expectations that students have learned to have for themselves. The decision to de-track is often made in a top-down manner, with teachers having little or no say in the process. In addition, schools are often de-tracked with little planning or preparation for alternative groupings. Because of growing class size in many schools and because heterogeneous classes are often unwieldy, teachers may end up regrouping by ability in their classrooms. The problems associated with tracking often reappear under a different guise.

Professional development activities are an important consideration here. Most teachers have professional days they can use to attend conferences, meetings, or other schools. Visiting schools that have successfully de-tracked is an effective activity for teachers whose schools are contemplating doing so.

Teachers can be instrumental in recommending topics focusing on tracking, de-tracking, and alternative kinds of grouping for staff development sessions. A group of interested colleagues might ask for the opportunity to prepare staff seminars in which they share ideas for de-grouping that they have developed in their own classrooms.

Because tracking also occurs in extracurricular activities, schools need to refocus their efforts to make clubs and other organizations appealing to a wider range of students.

The school newspaper, for instance, is generally thought of as an activity for only highly intellectual students ("nerds"), whereas sports are seen as the domain of so-called "jocks." Ironically, activities and clubs such as these frequently perpetuate the social class groupings that students develop in the school instead of helping to counter the stereotypes on which they are based. Extracurricular and other activities were important in the academic success of the ten students in our case studies, as they are to many students. Nevertheless, they are often seen as exclusive clubs with limited membership. Although no message saying "You need not apply" is purposely given, many students read an implicit message in the recruitment policies and activities of some clubs and organizations.

What Can You Do?

- If your school and/or classroom is not de-tracked, what can you do to avoid the negative effects of tracking in your classroom? Create some alternative ways of grouping your students that are not ability-based. Develop relevant activities for the groups.

- Work with a colleague or colleagues to set up interclass groups based on criteria other than ability (e.g., specific projects, hobbies, or interests). Develop relevant activities for each group.

- Are there classrooms in your school (including special education, bilingual, and ESL) that are substantially separate from the others? Develop a plan to work with some of the teachers in those classrooms. Ask if they would like to develop a collaborative project that might be of mutual interest to the children. Activities focused on interdisciplinary academic areas with a potential for multicultural learning (the ecology of the community or the inadequacy of housing and the plight of the homeless) would probably be more successful than those based strictly on "cultural awareness" because the students would all be involved in exploring specific community problems and attempting to find solutions. Build this activity into your curriculum on an ongoing basis. What ideas do you have for a project of this kind? Write down the themes and some approaches you might use with the students.

- Let us say that you and some of your colleagues have the opportunity to develop a staff development session focusing on alternative grouping strategies. How would you develop it? How would you present it? How might you use cooperative groups with participants to illustrate your point?

Testing

Standardized testing has become a mainstay of the educational scene in the United States. Tests are used to place students; assess their progress; remove them from programs; and admit them into top tracks, gifted and talented programs, special education, bilingual classes, and so on. They exert a powerful influence on most educational decisions. Given this power, tests and the testing industry need to be monitored closely, evaluated rigorously, and/or challenged. The specific strategies that each school and school district chooses to engage in may vary, depending on how they use tests, whether the tests are grossly biased or not, and the testing skills that students already have. There are two basic strategies here: Either oppose or challenge the use of tests, or focus more attention on test taking and how to use it to the advantage of the students.

Because the effects of testing, particularly standardized testing, are so often negative, particularly for poor students and students of color, one strategy is to challenge the use of tests in the first place. With a group of interested colleagues and parents, teachers might approach the local school committee and ask that standardized tests be kept to a minimum, that the results be used in more appropriate ways, and that students not be jeopardized because of the results of such tests.

Alternatively, teachers might decide that given the pervasiveness of testing and the power it exerts on the options of young people, their energy might be better spent in teaching students how to take tests more effectively. For the time being, crucial decisions that will affect the lives of students are being based, at least partially, on test results. This fact was brought home quite clearly in the strategy used by Jaime Escalante, the calculus teacher in Garfield High School in East Los Angeles, as dramatized in the film *Stand and Deliver*. In affluent schools and neighborhoods, students learn specific test-taking skills that help them do very well on tests. If this option is selected, curriculum committees at the elementary level or high school departments might decide to focus more of their attention on these skills in the curriculum.

What Can You Do?
- Assess the reality of your school and community. Find out how standardized tests are used and how other criteria may be better employed. Determine which of the strategies described above is the most appropriate one for your school. Get together with colleagues to decide how to proceed.

The Curriculum

Because the curriculum in most schools is skewed toward a European American perspective, it excludes the lived realities and perspectives of many students. Textbooks and other materials reinforce this bias, making the development of an inclusive curriculum even more difficult. Scrapping the existing curriculum, however, is usually neither feasible nor practical. Several general strategies, using both the existing curriculum and an emerging one, may help to turn this situation around.

Teachers can use the current curriculum as the basis for helping students develop both a more critical perspective and better research skills. For example, if a class is studying the Revolutionary War, students can examine the experiences of African Americans, Native Americans, women, loyalists, and others whose perspectives have generally been excluded from the curriculum. When studying the Industrial Revolution, they can explore the role of the emerging workers' movement, children and young women factory workers, and the impact of European immigration on the rise of the cities. They can also focus on this era by studying the emergence of scientific discoveries through inventions by African Americans during the late nineteenth century.

When teaching different mathematical operations, teachers can ask students to investigate how they are done in other countries. Teachers can bring appropriate materials, such as an abacus, to class and demonstrate their use.

If traditional U.S. holidays are used as a source for the curriculum, teachers can try to include other perspectives. For example, when Columbus Day is approaching, teachers can discuss the concept of ''discovery'' with students so that they understand that this was the perspective of the Europeans, not the Indians. Alternative activities can focus on October 12 as the encounter of two worldviews and histories rather than on the ''discovery'' of one world by another. Similar activities can be planned for Thanksgiving, considered by many Indians to be a day of mourning. However, the tendency to associate automatically holidays from different cultures that happen to fall around the same time as parallel holidays should be avoided. Hanukkah is *not* parallel to Christmas. It has always been a relatively minor holiday that has recently received a lot more attention so that it parallels Christmas. The attempt to make it fit into this framework uses the Christian holiday as the standard, and is thus resented by some Jews. In any event, feedback and suggestions from parents and other community members will make the holiday curriculum as inclusive as possible.

An emerging multicultural curriculum can be created by using the experiences, cultures, and languages of all the students in the class. Students should be encouraged to bring their culture into the classroom through a variety of ways, for example, a program in which all parents are invited to collaborate by teaching the class a particular talent, interest, or hobby. These talents do not have to be culture-specific. For instance, a parent who is a seamstress may teach the children how to sew a hem. Although this talent may not be particularly Asian or Latina, for example, it is nevertheless important for all students to see that people from all backgrounds have talents and worthwhile experiences.

These activities are particularly effective at the early elementary level, but sometimes they are equally relevant for secondary students studying a particular subject. For example, older students studying calligraphy can invite a local Chinese artist to give them some pointers. Of if they are learning about operating a small business, they may want to invite a local barber or beautician from the community.

An oral history project can focus on the students and their home experiences. For example, for a multicultural library, students collect stories, poems, and legends from their families, either tape-recorded or written down. All the stories and poems can be collected, illustrated, bound, and placed in the library. More elaborate activities might include dramatizations for the school assembly, videotaping parents and other community members reciting the poems and stories, and developing a program whereby older students read the stories to children in the kindergarten and first grade.

What Can You Do?

- Look at the next unit you plan to teach. Think of some ways in which you can make it more inclusive, while taking care not to make it scattered and irrelevant. Develop a number of activities that are more reflective of the backgrounds of the students in your class, school, and community. If you work in a community that is not very diverse, think of how you might make your unit more inclusive and still meaningful for your students.

- How can you develop an oral history in your class based on the subject you are studying? Plan a unit that uses the talents and experiences of people in the community as a basis for the curriculum. Develop lessons in which you teach your students the specifics of identifying subjects, interviewing, transcribing, and developing a final product. Think of how you can integrate this project into the rest of your curriculum.

Pedagogy

The case studies in this book highlighted the fact that the standard pedagogy used in many schools is unappealing to most students. The students provided specific suggestions for making schools more interesting.

Although textbooks may be important teaching and learning tools, they often become the entire curriculum and are used as the only basis of pedagogy in the class, to the exclusion of other materials. Other resources can become the focus of study, including audiovisual materials such as camcorders and cameras, guest speakers, and other reading material.

Even more important, however, is to develop a variety of approaches that will engage the majority of the students. Although a straight lecture, what has been called "chalk and talk," may be appropriate sometimes, it is a strategy that perceives students as passive learners and receptacles of knowledge. It is also culturally inappropriate for many students. To help make them more active learners as well as to provide a multiculturally sensitive learning environment, teachers should encourage group work; individualized tasks; research; peer tutoring; cross-age tutoring; and group reflection, dialogue, and action projects in the school and community, such as volunteer activities at a senior center, working with a local day-care center, or a letter-writing campaign about a community issue (e.g., the need for a traffic light at a nearby intersection).

What Can You Do?
- Develop one new teaching strategy to begin using with your class. Start slowly, teaching students how to work in new ways. Often, alternative strategies are not successful simply because students are not taught how to approach them. In addition, we sometimes change the way we do things so radically that chaos ensues. If you can add new strategies or approaches to your repertoire on an ongoing and consistent basis, your pedagogy can undergo substantial changes within a year.

- Ask students to give you suggestions on your instruction. What is it that they like? What do they dislike? How would they change the classroom? The materials? What would they do to make it more interesting to them? Just as the students in our case studies were never at a loss for ideas to make learning more "fun" or relevant, your students will have many suggestions as well.

- Review the research on the KEEP Project (see Chapter 5). Using your own students, devise instructional modifications that may be in keeping with their cultural backgrounds. Try changing your classroom to reflect these modifications, little by little. Do they make a difference? How? If not, why not?

Physical Structure

There are many things in our physical environment that we can do little about. There are others that we can change, however. Some of these are in our classrooms and some are outside of it.

Teachers should make their classrooms as inviting and comfortable as possible. In the younger grades, this can mean having interesting activity corners, a cozy place to read, a number of comfortable chairs, and a place for group work. In the older grades, a quiet place for individual work sends the message that learning is an important activity. Placing seats in a horseshoe arrangement at certain times is an appropriate strategy for involving more students in a discussion.

It is unfortunate that many teachers in secondary schools feel that decorating the room is unnecessary. Even older students appreciate a cheerful and educational environment in which posters, maps, pictures, books, and music are an indispensable part of the environment.

Outside the classroom, teachers may want to address some of the policies that make school an uninviting place. For instance, when children cannot have recess outside because of inclement weather and instead have to sit in the auditorium quietly, this is a sure way to invite misbehavior. Alternative activities in the gym will allow students to use their energy in more productive ways and be better prepared for the work of learning when they return to class.

What Can You Do?

- Look around your classroom. Is it an inviting place? What can you do to make it more so? How can you use children's experiences, interests, and backgrounds in creating a good space in which to work? Think of their learning styles, languages, and talents in creating a space that makes them want to come to school.

- Consider your bulletin boards and other places for exhibits or projects. What are they like and how could they be better utilized? Involve your students in planning and implementing an improved physical space in your classroom.

- What can you do outside your classroom? What is it about the physical space that particularly bothers you? Is it graffiti, garbage in the yard, or an overall unappealing aspect to the school? Develop an action plan to involve students, other staff, and community members in cleaning or repairing some aspect of the school environment. You might decide on a tree-planting project for the front yard or a plan to paint the halls with children's murals. Whatever the project, involve as many people as possible so that the school is truly representative of the community it serves.

Disciplinary Policies

Disciplinary policies and procedures are usually developed to provide an atmosphere of purpose and order. Invariably, however, they function to exclude some students from a meaningful education, for any number of reasons. Insensitivity to cultural, linguistic, and social differences interact with racism, discrimination, and expectations of student achievement to produce an environment in which some students are bound to succeed and others are doomed to fail. Teachers in particular and schools in general can approach disciplinary policies and practices in creative ways to avoid some of these results.

Students, whenever possible, should help determine disciplinary policies and practices. Rather than relying on those who happen to be on the Student Council, generally a rather limited group of students, a forum should be selected in which a broad range of student voices will be heard. This forum can include academic classes, assemblies, and other student activities.

Schools can determine how disciplinary policies and practices affect some students unfairly by looking at rates of detention, suspension, and assignments to "special" classes or alternative programs for those who have been identified as having behavior problems. If students in these programs are overwhelmingly from one social or racial group or gender, schools need to take appropriate precautions to avoid both the appearance and the reality of discrimination.

What Can You Do?

- Create class rules with your students. Think of how they must be stated in positive rather than negative terms. Focus on privileges rather than on punitive consequences.

- Monitor your own behavior with your students. Do you tend to be more patient with some students than with others? Are you quicker to assign detentions or take other disciplinary measures with some students than with others? Do you use sarcastic, menacing, or negative language with some students? Select a day or a week in which to evaluate your behavior, using checklists and field notes to determine *who*, *how*, and *when* you discipline. Next, select a day or week in which you consciously try to change that behavior.

- Be sensitive to how some students are more negatively affected by some disciplinary practices than others. For example, if a student is consistently assigned to detention after school and misses work as a result, he or she might be losing needed family income. Think of a number of alternative and more positive strategies for affecting behavior.

- Encourage parents and other community members to participate on committees in which disciplinary policies are discussed. In your own classroom, invite parents to discuss their perceptions of school policies with you.

Limited Role of Students

Students are often uninvolved in decisions affecting their schooling. Involvement in such decisions need not be limited to high school students in the top tracks. Students at all levels, from preschool through high school, can help determine the direction of their schooling in a great many ways. Nevertheless, care should be taken to provide *meaningful* student involvement rather than tokenism. Placing students on school committees in which they have little interest and no experience simply to have student involvement often backfires. They soon drop out and in the process may reinforce teachers' perceptions that they are too young or immature to be involved in decision making. The lesson here is that when they feel their input is important and meaningful to them, students will take part. Teachers and schools need to plan accordingly.

Students often have hobbies or other interests that are invisible in school. Making them visible is one way of engaging students. For instance, crafts that are familiar and culturally meaningful can be incorporated into the arts curriculum. Students can also be encouraged to tell stories and legends with which they are familiar to their classmates.

"Circle" or "sharing time" or some other such mechanism can be used to encourage students in dialogue, even at the high school level. Dialogue such as this not only ensures that all students are heard but also helps teachers discover what students are interested in so that they can develop a more inclusive curriculum.

What Can You Do?
- Set aside a specific time once a week to plan the curriculum with your students. Younger students may only be able to give you very general suggestions, but these should be considered and incorporated when possible. Older students can be more articulate in naming issues, within the broader outlines of your subject matter, that they would like to study.

- Ask students to bring in favorite objects or hobbies to use as the basis for particular lessons. They can prepare the lessons themselves and teach the other students in the class or in a small group. Examples of topics they might choose include how to care for a gerbil, the fun of stamp collecting, how to make dumplings, learning how to write in Arabic, flags from around the world, learning greetings in Japanese, composing music raps, and so on.

- Develop a social action project with your students. Working in groups, have them decide on problems or issues in the school or community in which they would like to be engaged (anything from homelessness to not being able to chew gum in school) and for which they develop an action plan. Depending on how they are approached, social action projects can take anywhere from a week to an entire academic year and can be interdisciplinary in scope. In the process, the community becomes the primary source of the curriculum.

Limited Role of Teachers

Like students, teachers are often disempowered within the school. Although they usually have some control over the curriculum they implement in their own classrooms, the broad outline is often legislated from a central office. Requirements for testing and other mandated activities may further rob the curriculum of its individualized character. Teachers are not always consulted when decisions about student placement, curriculum, or the purchase of materials are made. They are often made to feel as if their jobs are not given much respect.

Promoting professionalism in the field of teaching is an important responsibility for all school staff, at the classroom, school, department, and school system levels. In many cases, released time from the classroom is essential for this important work to take place.

Teachers need to be involved in the important work of curriculum design and implementation, either through school or central system curriculum committees. A corollary to curriculum development is the involvement of teachers in decisions regarding the purchase of educational materials.

Teachers and other staff members can be consulted when new teachers are to be hired. Serving on interviewing committees, helping to determine job qualifications, and ensuring that affirmative action is taken into consideration are all important functions in which teachers' involvement is essential.

What Can You Do?

- Develop allies in the struggle to set up educational environments that promote the learning of all students. These allies can include teachers, other staff in the school, parents, and students. The involvement of other teachers with whom you work and interact every day is especially crucial. A support group of this kind can have many roles. For example, you might become a study group that meets once a week to discuss a mutual concern, say, the disciplinary policy in the school. By focusing on a problem such as this, teachers and others can read, discuss, and learn from colleagues and then use this knowledge as a basis for suggestions to change the policy.

- Visit other classrooms and schools that are becoming more multicultural. Share your perceptions of these visits with colleagues.

- Set up a "buddy system" with a trusted colleague to help you grow professionally. Develop a system in which you visit one another's classrooms and reflect together on teaching styles, curriculum, and the general climate in your classrooms. Plan to meet at least once a week to review new thoughts, materials, and curriculum. Do some team teaching and plan some mutually interesting projects together.

Limited Parent and Community Involvement

Many parents are uninvolved in the day-to-day life or in the overall policy development of the school. However, most are involved in the education of their children through the values they have fostered at home and in the implicit and explicit expectations they have of them. All of the ways in which parents are involved need to be fostered by schools and teachers so that parents learn that they are an essential component of the educational process.

Although parents who are not involved in the actual school should not be penalized for it, they can be encouraged to become involved. This is not the only involvement that should be honored, however. A two-pronged approach in which home and school activities are given equal value is probably best.

Teachers and schools can communicate with parents on a consistent basis, through a weekly or monthly newsletter, phone calls, meetings at school or home, or a combination of these methods. When school meetings are to take place, child care, translations into languages spoken by the parents, and transportation can be provided. Teachers can encourage parents to bring into the classroom activities and materials that are meaningful to them and their children. In this way, the curriculum will be more reflective of the students and their communities.

What Can You Do?

- Begin a class newsletter to send home to parents. Include work representative of all the students. If parents speak a language other than English, have students work together to translate portions of the newsletter into their home language.

- Invite parents to class to share a particular talent that is related to the curriculum you are teaching. To get a better idea of what these talents are, during the first weeks of class ask parents to indicate any special skills they may have (whether or not they feel these might be of interest to children). For example, a waitress can teach students how to set a table correctly; a homemaker may want to demonstrate how to balance a checkbook; another parent may share a musical talent.

- Develop a strategy for parent and community outreach. Include strategies and materials for encouraging parents to become more involved.

RESPECTING AND AFFIRMING CULTURAL DIFFERENCES

Culture and cultural diversity are at the very core of a multicultural perspective. Many of the suggestions up to now focus on ways to respect and celebrate cultural differences. We will consider a few more specific examples of how cultural diversity can be affirmed in schools and classrooms.

Because students' culture often has an impact on how they learn, teachers need to become aware of differences in learning and how these can be accommodated in the classroom. It is important always to ask the question, *Who does the accommodating?* Is it always students from dominated cultures? To counteract this tendency, it is helpful to match the learning preferences of students with specific relevant activities. Students who are comfortable working in groups should have the opportunity to do so; so should students who are not used to this style of working. The point is not to segregate students according to their preferences but rather to develop skills in all students so that they are comfortable with a broad range of activities.

Teachers can investigate other out-of-school activities that students like to engage in. Some students, for example, love to perform; others like to express themselves through art. Use these activities in the school to motivate the students to learn school-related subjects.

What Can You Do?
- Ask your students to talk about their culture from time to time. Even young students can do so, although in a more limited way than older ones. The point of this activity is to help make students' cultures visible in the school. Using their culture as a point of reference, they learn that

  Everybody has a culture.

  Their culture is important and valued in the school.

  Their culture can provide a solid basis for their education.

  Rather than their culture being perceived as a source of shame or embarrassment, this activity helps to make culture a source of pride and empowerment.

- Encourage students to share their culture with others. Artifacts from home, cultural traditions that they celebrate, books and stories, and important people in their lives can all be brought into the school to help make the curriculum more inclusive.

- Interviewing can be used as a teaching strategy. Students can interview one another as well as family and community members. Develop a unit based on this strategy. How can the results of such interviews be used in the curriculum? Think of different content areas and other strategies that can be developed.

- Because so many people are first- to third-generation newcomers to the United States, the immigrant experience is a rich source of inspiration for the curriculum. How might you use this experience? Develop a series of interdisciplinary lessons based on the students' stories and those of their parents and grandparents. Be specific and include the objectives, materials, and strategies that you would use with your particular grade level.

LINGUISTIC DIVERSITY AS A RESOURCE

The languages and dialects that students speak can and should be made an explicit part of the curriculum if we are to give them the message that language diversity is valued in our schools. Rather than viewing linguistic diversity as a deficit, we need to see it as an asset on which further learning can be built. A number of activities can help us do so.

Teachers should learn to say each child's name correctly. They should not make Marisol *Marcy* or Vinh *Vinny*. Given the pressure to conform that all students face, it is too easy to let their names be changed in order to fit in. Although learning a lot of names in different languages may be time-consuming for teachers, it is not difficult and is an important first step in affirming who students are rather than who we may want them to become.

Student language should be accepted without immediate correction, including language from both new speakers of English and those who speak another variety of it. Overcorrection can intimidate both kinds of students. Although it is necessary for all students to learn standard English, especially those who have been traditionally denied higher-status learning, it is equally important for teachers to accept and value their language. Rather than directly correcting students' language, teachers can model standard English in their responses or statements. Students soon pick up the message that there are different ways of saying the same thing and that some of these ways are more appropriate in some settings than in others. Linda Howard's case study provides a powerful example of this code switching.

What Can You Do?
- Think about students in your classes who speak a language other than English. Ask them to teach you and the other students some words in the language. Use these words in the classroom context. Write them up and put them on bulletin boards or use them in homework or project assignments.

- Learn another language. If you have a great many Khmer-speaking students, for example, learning their language would go a long way in showing them how you value it. Going through the process of learning another language also allows teachers to demonstrate genuine solidarity with students who have to learn a second language. If you have students who speak a variety of languages, learn at least some phrases in each of the languages. Students are usually delighted when teachers show a real interest in their language, even if they stumble over words and phrases.

- Even if you do not speak a language other than English, encourage your students to do so. Think of ways in which you might do so to best advantage in your classroom. You might, for example, encourage some small-group work, peer tutoring, or parent volunteers.

- Ask students to bring in poems, stories, legends, or songs in their native language. They might want to teach these to their classmates. Have them available (in written form or on tape) for other students to read or listen to.

SUMMARY

In this chapter, we have reviewed the factors leading to school failure or achievement for students from diverse backgrounds as proposed in Part I. These factors have been used to suggest actual classroom strategies and approaches based on the principles of multicultural education suggested in Chapter 8. The emphasis throughout the chapter has been to encourage teachers to develop strategies and approaches for their particular students and the communities in which they teach. In this way, incorporating a multicultural perspective becomes a natural outgrowth of the lives of the students for whom it is planned.

The purpose here is not to suggest that multicultural education is a simplistic or superficial set of activities, materials, or approaches. On the contrary, a packaged series of lesson plans is in direct conflict with the goals of a comprehensive multicultural education. If the purpose of education, however, is to prepare young people for productive and critical participation in a democratic and pluralistic society, the activities, strategies, and approaches we use with them need to echo these concerns. Schools, as currently structured, do little to prepare students for this future. The structure, curriculum, and pedagogical approaches in most schools tend to contradict these goals. Likewise, the stratification of society cannot be overlooked as affecting in a direct way the school experience of students. The cultural and linguistic differences students bring to school, along with how these differences are perceived, are other crucial factors that need to be addressed through the curriculum and instruction. It is only by addressing all of these issues in a systematic way through the curriculum and instruction that meaningful changes can be made.

In the final analysis, multicultural education is a moral and ethical issue. Our student body is becoming more diverse than ever before, representing more racial, cultural, linguistic, and social class differences. Our ability to understand these differences and to use them in constructive ways, is still quite low. In addition, the world in which we find ourselves calls for adults who are critical thinkers and who can confront and resolve complex issues such as ethnic polarization, nuclear disarmament, and rampant racism in sensitive and ethical ways. If we believe that all students are capable of brilliance, that they can learn at high levels of achievement, and that the cultural and linguistic resources they bring to school are worthy of respect, affirmation, and solidarity, multicultural education represents a far more principled approach for our schools than does monocultural education.

FOR FURTHER READING

PROFESSIONAL RESOURCES

The following resources represent some of the many curricula and other materials available in multicultural education. Not meant to be an exhaustive list, it is a representative sample of curricula that suggest ways to develop a multicultural perspective in different grade levels, subject areas, themes, and with a variety of ethnic groups.

Banks, James A. *Teaching Strategies for Ethnic Studies,* 5th ed. Boston: Allyn & Bacon, 1991. This book, a classic in the field of multicultural education, presents level-specific lesson plans that focus on different ethnic groups. Also included are a variety of useful resources such as children's books, professional references, and audiovisual materials on various groups.

Cohen, Elizabeth G. *Designing Groupwork: Strategies for the Heterogeneous Classroom.* New York: Teachers College Press, 1986. A helpful guide, combining the theory and practice of collaborative groupwork for classrooms. The author focuses on the intellectual and social goals of grouping and suggests strategies for preparing students for cooperative groupwork by planning it in stages and making certain every student has a part.

Connecticut Education Association. *Violence, The Ku Klux Klan, and the Struggle for Equality.* New York, NY: Council on Interracial Books for Children, and the National Education Association, 1981. An informational and instructional kit for bringing the history of the Klan into the secondary classroom, it includes background information, lesson plans, and an annotated bibliography.

Council on Interracial Books for Children. *Winning Justice for All.* New York: Women's Educational Equity Act Program, 1980. A curriculum for upper elementary grades that includes lessons on stereotyping, sexism, and racism and how to counteract them. Three filmstrips accompany the curriculum.

Grant, Carl A., and Christine E. Sleeter. *Turning on Learning: Five Approaches to Multicultural Teaching.* Columbus, OH: Merrill, 1989. A book of 48 model lesson plans in several subject areas for grades 1–12 in multicultural education, using the five approaches in Christine E. Sleeter and Carl A. Grant, *Making Choices for Multicultural Education: Five Approaches to Race, Class, and Gender* (Columbus, OH: Merrill, 1988).

McGinnis, James, and other contributors. *Educating for Peace and Justice: National Dimensions.* St. Louis, MO: Institute for Peace and Justice, 1985. A teachers' manual about peace and justice for elementary school through college. Contains lessons, materials, and background information differentiated by level on nonviolent conflict resolution, institutional violence, peace and justice in the school, racism, sexism, and multicultural education, among others.

Márquez, Roberto, and Sonia Nieto. *Literature and Society of the Puerto Rican People.* New Brunswick, NJ: Rutgers University Press, 1983. A curriculum on Puerto Rican literature (either directly written in English or translated into English from the original Spanish) for the secondary school, this manual can be used with either Spanish or English speakers. Includes a curriculum outline, sample lessons, selected bibliography, and other resources.

Ramsey, Patricia G., Edwina Battle Vold, and Leslie R. Williams. *Multicultural Education: A Source Book.* New York: Garland, 1989. A source book containing essays and annotations on several issues related to multicultural education including multicultural programs, curricula, and strategies.

Schneidewind, Nancy, and Ellen Davidson. *Open Minds to Equality.* Boston: Allyn & Bacon, **1983.** A source book of strategies and activities for the elementary and middle school level on discrimination based on race, gender, class, and age.

Wade, Rahima Carol. *Joining Hands: From Personal to Planetary Friendship in the Primary Classroom.* Tucson, AZ: Zephyr Press, **1991.** A source book of ideas on friendship and how to achieve it. The book begins with a personal exploration of the meaning of friendship and then works through relationships in the classroom and the extension of friendship into the larger world.

Zanger, Virginia Vogel. *Face to Face: The Cross-Cultural Workbook.* Rowley, MA: Newbury House, **1985.** A workbook for intermediate and advanced ESL students to explore U.S. life by learning about cultural similarities and differences. Uses structured interviews with other students and includes questionnaires, background information, and relevant vocabulary exercises.

NOVELS ON THE ETHNIC AND IMMIGRANT EXPERIENCE

Novels often provide an authentic and engaging way with which to explore issues of inclusion and exclusion, the pain and fear of immigration and racism, and the triumph of the human spirit in the face of obstacles. The following is a representative sample of novels and autobiographical accounts that focus on coming of age in the United States from a variety of perspectives. Some of them are also appropriate for the English or history curricula in high schools. Novels not only help to make the curriculum more multicultural but also can be used to provide all students with realistic and often dramatic examples of experiences that are quintessentially American, although they may be very different from their own.

Anzaldúa, Gloria. *Borderlands La Frontera: The New Mestiza.* San Francisco: Spinsters/Aunt Lute Book Company, 1987. (Mexican)

Arnow, Harriette Louisa. *The Dollmaker.* New York: Macmillan, 1954. (Appalachian)

Baldwin, James. *Go Tell It on the Mountain.* New York: Laurel/Dell, 1985; originally published in 1953. (African American)

Bulosan, Carlos. *America Is in the Heart.* Seattle: University of Washington Press, 1973; originally published in 1946. (Filipino)

Curran, Mary Doyle. *The Parish and the Hill.* New York: Feminist Press at the City University of New York, 1986. (Irish)

Di Donato, Pietro. *Christ in Concrete.* New York: Bobbs-Merrill, 1939. (Italian)

Dorris, Michael. *A Yellow Raft in Blue Water.* New York: Henry Holt, 1987. (American Indian)

Kingston, Maxine Hong. *Woman Warrior.* New York: Knopf, 1976. (Chinese)

McKay, Claude. *Home to Harlem.* Boston: Northeastern University Press, 1987; originally published in 1928. (Jamaican)

Medina, Pablo. *Exiled Memories: A Cuban Childhood.* Austin: University of Texas Press, 1990. (Cuban)

Morrison, Toni. *The Bluest Eye.* New York: Holt, Rinehart & Winston, 1970. (African American)

Mukherjee, Bharati. *Jasmine.* New York: Grove Weidenfeld, 1989. (Hindu-Indian)

Rivera, Edward. *Family Installments: Memories of Growing Up Hispanic.* New York: William Morrow, 1982. (Puerto Rican)

Roth, Henry. *Call It Sleep.* Paterson, NJ: Pageant Books, 1960; originally published in 1934. (Jewish)

Smith, Betty. *A Tree Grows in Brooklyn.* New York: Harper & Row, 1943. (Irish and German)

Szymusiak, Molyda. *The Stones Cry Out: A Cambodian Childhood.* New York: Hill & Wang, 1986. (Cambodian)

Thomas, Joyce Carol, ed. *A Gathering of Flowers: Stories About Being Young in America.* New York: Harper & Row, 1990. (young adult; multicultural)

Uchida, Yoshiko. *Picture Bride.* Flagstaff, AZ: Northland Press, 1987. (Japanese)

Although the list is of necessity quite limited, numerous other novels can be located through the library and bookstores. In addition, the following resources focus on books with a multicultural perspective that can be used with younger children as well.

Harris, Violet. *Using Multicultural Literature in the Classroom.* Norwood, MA: Christopher-Gordon Publishers, 1992.

Pytowska, Ewa, and Gail Pettiford Willett. *A Quest for Belonging: Empowering Adolescents Through Multicultural Literature.* Boston: Intercultural Training Resource Center and Savanna Books, 1989.

Rudman, Masha Kabokow. *Children's Literature: An Issues Approach,* 3rd ed. White Plains, NY: Longman, forthcoming.

NOTES

1. Paulo Freire, *Pedagogy of the Oppressed* (New York: Seabury Press, 1970).
2. For two enlightening and empowering examples of education for young children that is both multicultural and liberating, see Sheila D. Collins, "Discussing Controversial Topics in Early Childhood Settings," *Bulletin of the Council on Interracial Books for Children,* 14, 7 and 8 (1983), 3–5; Iris Santos Rivera, "Liberating Education for Little Children," *Alternativas,* 1, 9–12 (October 1983–January 1984), 5–7.
3. Lee Anne Bell, "Changing Our Ideas About Ourselves: Group Consciousness Raising with Elementary School Girls as a Means to Empowerment," in *Empowerment Through Multicultural Education,* ed. Christine E. Sleeter (New York: State University of New York Press, 1991).

Glossary

Ableism. Discriminatory beliefs and behaviors directed against people with disabilities.

African American Language (AAL). Also called *Black English* or *Ebonics, AAL* refers to the language system characteristically spoken in the African American community. According to Williams, the term "acknowledges its African cultural roots, identifies its geographical residence, and reflects the linguistic integrity of this effective communication system." See Selase W. Williams, "Classroom Use of African American Language: Educational Tool or Social Weapon?" in *Empowerment Through Multicultural Education,* ed. Christine E. Sleeter (New York: State University of New York Press, 1991), p. 204.

Afrocentrism. A philosophical outlook and values based on African and African American cultures.

Ageism. Discriminatory beliefs and behaviors directed against people because of their age.

Anti-Arab discrimination. Discriminatory beliefs and behaviors directed against Arabs.

Anti-Semitism. Discriminatory beliefs and behaviors directed against Jews.

Bilingual education. Generally refers to an educational approach that involves the use of two languages of instruction at some point in the student's school career. Other terms associated with bilingual education follow: **Bilingual/bicultural education.** The cultures associated with the primary and second languages are also incorporated into the curriculum. **Immersion bilingual education.** Students are immersed in their second language for a year or two before their native language is introduced as a medium of instruction. By their fifth or sixth year of schooling, they may be receiving equal amounts of instruction in both languages. **Maintenance (or developmental) approach.** A comprehensive and long-term method that uses both students' native and second languages for instruction. The primary objective of this approach is to build on and develop students' literacy in their native language and extend it to their second language as well. Students could remain in such a program throughout their schooling. **Submersion bilingual education.** Also called "sink or swim," this approach, as used in the United States, places students in a totally English-language environment without using their native language and related literacy experiences as a basis for instruction. **Two-way bilingual education.** A program model for integrating students whose native language is English with those for whom English is a second language. The purpose of this approach is to develop bilingualism in both kinds of students. **Transitional approach.** Students receive all or most of their content area instruction in their native language while learning English as a second language. As soon as it has been determined that they can benefit from the monolingual English-language curriculum, they are "exited" out of the program. The primary objective of this approach is to teach students English as quickly as possible so that they can continue their education in a monolingual, or "mainstream," program.

Bilingualism. There are two kinds of bilingualism: **Additive.** Second-language learning that builds on previous literacy in the first language. **Subtractive.** Second-language learning that ignores previous literacy in the first language and thus detracts from developing more extensive literacy in the new language.

Classism. Discriminatory beliefs and behaviors based on differences in social class, generally directed against those from poor and/or working-class backgrounds.

Communication style. How individuals interact with one another and the messages they send, intentionally or not, through their behaviors.

Cultural capital. The knowledge that is associated with the dominant group and thus has most status in a society. As defined by Bourdieu, it can exist in three forms: dispositions of the mind and body; cultural goods such as pictures, books, and other material objects; and educational qualifications. According to him, this is the best hidden form of the hereditary transmission of capital. See Pierre Bourdieu, "The Forms of Capital," in *Handbook of Theory and Research for the Sociology of Education,* ed. John G. Richardson (New York: Greenwood Press, 1986).

Culture. The ever-changing values, traditions, social and political relationships, and worldview shared by a group of people bound together by a combination of factors that can include a common history, geographic location, language, social class, and/or religion.

Curriculum. The organized environment for learning in a classroom and school. The curriculum includes both *expressed* elements (usually written down in the form of goals, objectives, lesson plans, and units and included in educational materials such as textbooks) and *hidden* elements (i.e., the unintended messages, both positive and negative, in the classroom and school environments).

Deficit theories. Theories that hypothesize that some people are deficient in intelligence and/or achievement either because of *genetic inferiority* (because of their racial background) or because of *cultural deprivation* (because of their cultural background and/or because they have been deprived of cultural experiences and activities deemed by the majority to be indispensable for growth and development).

Educational equity. Beyond equal educational opportunity, educational equity is based on fairness and promotes the real possibility of equality of outcomes for a broader range of students.

English as a Second Language (ESL). A systematic and comprehensive approach to teaching English to students for whom it is not a native language. It is an important component of bilingual programs in the United States but can exist by itself as well.

Equal education. Providing the same resources and opportunities for all students, while at the same time using the skills, talents, and experiences they bring as a valid starting point for further schooling.

Ethnocentrism. Discriminatory beliefs and behaviors based on ethnic differences.

Ethnography. Educational research that is qualitative in nature and uses anthropological methods such as fieldwork, interviewing, and participant observation in studying schools and students.

Eurocentric curriculum. Curriculum that focuses on the values, life-styles, accomplishments, and worldviews of Europeans and/or European Americans.

Heterosexism. Discriminatory beliefs and behaviors directed against gay men and lesbians.

Linguicism. According to Skutnabb-Kangas, this term refers to "ideologies and structures which are used to legitimate, effectuate and reproduce an unequal division of power and resources (both material and non-material) between groups which are defined on the basis of language." See Tove Skutnabb-Kangas, "Multilingualism and the Education of Minority Children," in *Minority Education: From Shame to Struggle,* ed. Tove Skutnabb-Kangas and Jim Cummins (Clevedon, Eng.: Multilingual Matters, 1988), p. 13.

Low-incidence populations. Legally refers to a group of speakers of a language other than English too small to be entitled to a bilingual program. In most states with mandated bilingual education laws, the minimum number of students who speak a particular language for whom the local school district must have a program is 20.

Marked language. A language or language system not highly valued by the society at large.

Minorities. The distinctions made between different kinds of minorities by John Ogbu. See "The Consequences of the American Caste System," in *The School Achievement of Minority Children: New Perspectives,* ed. Ulric Neisser (Hillsdale, NJ: Erlbaum, 1986). **Castelike or involuntary minorities.** Those incorporated into a society against their will. In the United States, this term generally refers to American Indians, African Americans, Mexican Americans, and Puerto Ricans, all of whose ancestors were either conquered or enslaved. **Voluntary or immigrant minorities.** Those who have chosen freely to emigrate to another society.

Multicultural education. A process of comprehensive and basic education for all students. Multicultural education challenges and rejects racism and other forms of discrimination in schools and society and accepts and affirms the pluralism (ethnic, racial, linguistic, religious, economic, gender, etc.) that students, their communities, and teachers represent. Multicultural education permeates the curriculum and instructional strategies used in schools, as well as the interactions among teachers, students and parents, and the very way that schools conceptualize the nature of teaching and learning. Because it uses critical pedagogy as its underlying philosophy and focuses on knowledge, reflection, and action (praxis) as the basis for social change, multicultural education furthers the democratic principles of social justice.

Multiculturalism. There are two kinds of multiculturalism: **Additive.** Learning that builds on previous knowledge and experiences in the first culture. **Subtractive.** Learning that ignores previous knowledge and experiences in the first culture and thus detracts from developing more extensive knowledge and awareness of other cultures.

Pluralism. There are three basic models for understanding pluralism in our society: **Anglo-conformity.** A model of pluralism based on the concept that all newcomers need to conform to the dominant European American, middle-class, and English-speaking majority. **Cultural pluralism** (alternatively called *salad bowl, mosaic,* or *tapestry*). A model based on the premise that all newcomers have a right to maintain their languages and cultures while combining with others to form a new society reflective of all our differences. **Melting pot.** A model that maintains that differences need to be wiped out to form an amalgam that is uniquely American but without traces of the original cultures.

Praxis. The process of connecting reflection with action in the pursuit of knowledge and social change. See Paulo Freire, *Pedagogy of the Oppressed* (New York: Seabury Press, 1970).

Racism. According to Meyer Weinberg, a system of privilege and penalty based on one's race. It consists of two facets: a belief in the inherent superiority of some people and inherent inferiority of others, and the acceptance of the way goods and services are distributed in accordance with these judgments. See "Introduction," in *Racism in the United States: A Comprehensive Classified Bibliography* (New York: Greenwood Press, 1990).

Resistance theory. As applied to schools, this term refers to the way in which students actively or passively resist learning. Reasons for this resistance may be varied, from cultural or linguistic differences to perceptions that the knowledge taught is meaningless and imposed. It can take a variety of forms, from acting out to refusing to complete school work or other assignments to dropping out altogether. Although resistance is rarely intentional, it can be extremely effective either in disrupting or preventing learning or in developing alternative ways of coping within schools.

Self-fulfilling prophecy. Term coined by Merton to refer to the way that students perform based on what teachers expect of them. See Robert Merton, "The Self-Fulfilling Prophecy," *The Antioch Review*, 8 (1948), 193–210.

Sexism. Discriminatory beliefs and behaviors directed against women.

Symbolic violence. As used by Bourdieu, this term refers to the way in which the power relations of the dominant society are maintained in the school primarily through the curriculum. See Pierre Bourdieu, *Outline of Theory and Practice* (Cambridge: Cambridge University Press, 1977).

Tracking. The placement of students for instruction with others of equal or matched ability (homogeneous groups).

Bibliography

Ada, Alma Flor. "The Pajaro Valley Experience." In *Minority Education: From Shame to Struggle*. Edited by Tove Skutnabb-Kangas and Jim Cummins. Clevedon, Eng.: Multilingual Matters, 1988.

Allport, Gordon W. *The Nature of Prejudice*. Reading, MA: Addison-Wesley, 1954.

Anyon, Jean. "Social Class and the Hidden Curriculum of Work." *Journal of Education*, 162, 1 (Winter 1980), 67–92.

Anyon, Jean. "Social Class and School Knowledge." *Curriculum Inquiry*, 11, 1 (1981), 3–41.

Apple, Michael W. *Ideology and Curriculum*. London: Routledge & Kegan Paul, 1979.

Apple, Michael W. *Teachers and Texts: A Political Economy of Class and Gender Relations in Education*. Boston: Routledge & Kegan Paul, 1986.

Apple, Michael W., and Lois Weis, eds. *Ideology and Practice in Schooling*. Philadelphia: Temple University Press, 1983.

Aruri, Naseer H. "The Arab-American Community of Springfield, Massachusetts." In *The Arab-Americans: Studies in Assimilation*. Edited by Elaine C. Hagopian and Ann Paden. Wilmette, IL: Medina University Press International, 1969.

Asanti, Molefi, *Afrocentricity: The Theory of Social Change*. Trenton, NJ: Africa World Press, 1988.

Ashton-Warner, Sylvia. *Teacher*. New York: Simon & Schuster, 1963.

Au, Katherine H. "Participant Structures in a Reading Lesson with Hawaiian Children." *Anthropology and Education Quarterly*, 11, 2 (1980), 91–115.

Baez, Tony. "Desegregation and Bilingual Education: Legal and Pedagogical Imperatives." *Bulletin of the Council on Interracial Books for Children*, 17, 3 and 4 (1986).

Bagley, Christopher, Kanka Mallick, and Gajendra K. Verma. "Pupil Self-Esteem: A Study of Black and White Teenagers in a British School." In *Race, Education and Identity*. Edited by Gajendra K. Verma and Christopher Bagley. New York: St. Martin's Press, 1979.

Banks, James A. "Ethnicity, Class, Cognitive and Motivational Styles: Research and Teaching Implications." *Journal of Negro Education*, 57, 4 (1988), 452–466.

Banks, James A. *Multiethnic Education: Theory and Practice*, 2nd ed. Boston: Allyn & Bacon, 1988.

Banks, James A. *Teaching Strategies for Ethnic Studies*, 4th ed. Boston: Allyn & Bacon, 1987.

Banks, James A., and Cherry A. McGee Banks. *Multicultural Education: Issues and Perspectives* Boston; Allyn & Bacon, 1989.

Baratz, Stephen S., and Joan C. Baratz. "Early Childhood Intervention: The Social Science Base of Institutional Racism." In *Challenging the Myths: The Schools, the Blacks, and the Poor*, Reprint #5. Cambridge, MA: *Harvard Educational Review*, 1971.

Barnhardt, C. " 'Tuning In': Athabaskan Teachers and Athabaskan Students." In *Cross-Cultural Issues in Alaskan Education*, Vol. 2. Edited by Ray Barnhardt. Fairbanks: University of Alaska, Center for Cross-Cultural Studies, 1982.

Barriers to Excellence: Our Children at Risk. Boston: National Coalition of Advocates for Students, 1985.

Bastian, Ann, Norm Fruchter, Marilyn Gittell, Colin Greer, and Kenneth Haskins. *Choosing Equality: The Case for Democratic Schooling*. New York: New World Foundation, 1985.

Bennett, Christine I. *Comprehensive Multicultural Education: Theory and Practice*. Boston: Allyn & Bacon, 1986.

Bennett, Kathleen P. "Doing School in an Urban Appalachian First Grade." In *Empowerment Through Multicultural Education*. Edited by Christine E. Sleeter. Albany: State University of New York Press, 1991.

Bennett, Kathleen P., and Margaret D. LeCompte. *The Way Schools Work: A Sociological Analysis of Education*. White Plains, NY: Longman, 1990.

Bereiter, Carl, and S. Englemann. *Teaching Disadvantaged Children in the Preschool*. Englewood Cliffs, NJ: Prentice Hall, 1966.

Beyond Language: Social and Cultural Factors in Schooling Language Minority Students. Los Angeles: Office of Bilingual Education, California State Department of Education, Evaluation, Dissemination, and Assessment Center, 1986.

Bikson, T. K. "Minority Speech as Objectively Measured and Subjectively Evaluated." ERIC 1974 ED 131135.

Blanchard, Evelyn Lance. "The Growth and Development of American Indian and Alaskan Native Children." In *The Psychosocial Development of Minority Group Children*. Edited by Gloria Johnson Powell. New York: Brunner/Mazel Publishers, 1983.

Bloom, Allan. *The Closing of the American Mind: How Higher Education Has Failed Democracy and Impoverished the Souls of Today's Students*. New York: Simon & Schuster, 1987.

Bloome, David, ed. *Classrooms and Literacy*. Norwood, NJ: Ablex Publishing, 1989.

Bloome, David, ed. *Literacy and Schooling*. Norwood, NJ: Ablex Publishing, 1987.

Bond, Horace Mann. "Two Racial Islands in Alabama." *American Journal of Sociology*, 36 (1930–1931), 554.

Bourdieu, Pierre. "The Forms of Capital." In *Handbook of Theory and Research for the Sociology of Education*. Edited by John G. Richardson. New York: Greenwood Press, 1986.

Bourdieu, Pierre. *Outline of Theory and Practice*. Cambridge: Cambridge University Press, 1977.

Bowles, Samuel, and Herbert Gintis. *Schooling in Capitalist America: Educational Reform and the Contradictions of Economic Life*. New York: Basic Books, 1976.

Bowser, Benjamin P., and Raymond G. Hunt. *Impacts of Racism on White Americans*. Beverly Hills, CA: Sage Publications, 1981.

Boykin, A. Wade. "The Triple Quandry in the Schooling of Afro-American Children." In *The School Achievement of Minority Children: New Perspectives*. Edited by Ulric Neisser. Hillsdale, NJ: Erlbaum, 1986.

Braddock, Jomills H., II. *Tracking: Implications for Student Race-Ethnic Subgroups*, Report No. 1. Baltimore: Johns Hopkins University, Center for Research on Effective Schooling for Disadvantaged Students, February 1990.

Britzman, Deborah P. "Cultural Myths in the Making of a Teacher: Biography and Social Structure in Teacher Education." *Harvard Educational Review*, 56, 4 (November 1986), 442–456.

Brophy, J. E., and T. Good. *Teacher-Child Dyadic Interaction: A Manual for Coding Classroom Behavior*. Austin: Research & Developmental Center for Teacher Education, University of Texas, 1969.

Brown, Ann L., Annemarie Sullivan Palincsar, and Linda Purcell. "Poor Readers: Teach, Don't Label." In *The School Achievement of Minority Children: New Perspectives*. Edited by Ulric Neisser. Hillsdale, NJ: Erlbaum, 1986.

Brown, James S., and Harry Schwarzweller. "The Appalachian Family." In *Appalachia: Its People, Heritage, and Problems*. Edited by Frank S. Riddel. Dubuque, IA: Kendall/Hunt Publishing, 1974.

Brumberg, Stephan F. *Going to America, Going to School: The Jewish Immigrant Public School Encounter in Turn-of-the-Century New York City*. New York: Praeger, 1986.

Bryk, Anthony S., and Yeow Meng Thum. "The Effects of High School Organization on Dropping Out: An Exploratory Investigation." *American Educational Research Journal*, 26, 3 (Fall 1989), 353–383.

Buriel, Raymond, and Desdemona Cardoza. "Sociocultural Correlates of Achievement Among Three Generations of Mexican American High School Seniors." *American Educational Research Journal*, 25, 2 (1988), 177–192.

Campos, J., and R. Keatinge. "The Carpinteria Language Minority Student Experience: From Theory, to Practice, to Success." In *Minority Education: From Shame to Struggle*. Edited by Tove Skutnabb-Kangas and Jim Cummins. Clevedon, Eng.: Multilingual Matters, 1988.

Carew, Jean V., and Sara Lawrence Lightfoot. *Beyond Bias: Perspectives on Classrooms*. Cambridge, MA: Harvard University Press, 1979.

Carnegie Council on Adolescent Development. *Turning Points: Preparing American Youth for the Twenty-First Century*. Washington, DC: Task Force on the Education of Young Adolescents, 1989.

Castellanos, Diego. *The Best of Two Worlds*. Trenton: New Jersey State Department of Education, 1983.

Cazden, Courtney B. "Social Context of Learning to Read." In *Comprehension and Teaching: Research Reviews*. Edited by J. T. Guthrie. Newark, DE: International Reading Association, 1981.

Cazden, Courtney B., and Ellen L. Leggett. "Culturally Responsive Education: Recommendations for Achieving *Lau* Remedies." In *Culture and the Bilingual Classroom: Studies in Classroom Ethnography*. Edited by Henry T. Trueba, G. P. Guthrie, and Katherine H. Au. Rowley, MA: Newbury House, 1981.

Cazden, Courtney B., and Catherine E. Snow, eds. *English Plus: Issues in Bilingual Education*. Special Issue of *The Annals of the American Academy of Political and Social Sciences*, 508 (March 1990).

"Children of Intermarriage." *New York Times*, June 20, 1984, C1.

Churchill, Ward. "White Studies: The Intellectual Imperialism of Contemporary U.S. Education." *Integrated Education*, 19, 1 and 2 (January 1982), 51–57.

Clark, Reginald M. *Family Life and School Achievement: Why Poor Black Children Succeed or Fail*. Chicago: University of Chicago Press, 1983.

Cocking, Rodney R., and José P. Mestre, eds. *Linguistic and Cultural Influences on Learning Mathematics*. Hillsdale, NJ: Erlbaum, 1988.

Cohen, Elizabeth G. *Designing Groupwork: Strategies for the Heterogeneous Classroom*. New York: Teachers College Press, 1986.

Coleman, James S., Thomas Hoffer, and Sally Kilgore. *High School Achievement: Public, Catholic and Private Schools Compared*. New York: Basic Books, 1982.

Collier, Virginia. "Academic Achievement, Attitudes, and Occupations Among Graduates of Two-Way Bilingual Classes." Paper presented at the annual meeting of the American Educational Research Association, San Francisco, March 1989.

Collier, Virginia. "How Long? A Synthesis of Research on Academic Achievement in a Second Language." *TESOL Quarterly*, 23, 3 (September 1989), 509–531.

Collins, Sheila D. "Discussing Controversial Topics in Early Childhood Settings." *Bulletin of the Council on Interracial Books for Children,* 14, 7 and 8 (1983), 3–5.

Commins, Nancy L. "Language and Affect: Bilingual Students at Home and at School." *Language Arts,* 66, 1 (January 1989), 29–43.

Committee on Policy for Racial Justice. *Visions of a Better Way: A Black Appraisal of Public Schooling.* Washington, DC: Joint Center for Political Studies Press, 1989.

Conard, Brenda Dorn. "Cooperative Learning and Prejudice Reduction." *Social Education,* April/May 1988, pp. 283–286.

Cortés, Carlos E. "The Education of Language Minority Students: A Contextual Interaction Model." In *Beyond Language: Social and Cultural Factors in Schooling Language Minority Students.* Los Angeles: Office of Bilingual Education, California State Department of Education, Evaluation, Dissemination, and Assessment Center, 1986.

Cortés, Carlos. "The Societal Curriculum: Implications for Multiethnic Education." In *Education in the 80's: Multiethnic Education.* Edited by James A. Banks. Washington, DC: National Education Association, 1981.

Crawford, James. *Bilingual Education: History, Politics, Theory, and Practice.* Trenton, NJ: Crane Publishing, 1988.

Crawford, James. "Immersion Method Is Faring Poorly in Bilingual Study." *Education Week,* 5 (April 23, 1986), 1, 10.

Cross, Doris E., Gwendolyn C. Baker, and Lindley J. Stiles. *Teaching in a Multicultural Society: Perspectives and Professional Strategies.* New York: Free Press, 1977.

Cross, William E., Jr. *Shades of Black: Diversity in African-American Identity.* Philadelphia: Temple University Press, 1991.

Cummins, Jim. *Bilingualism and Special Education: Issues in Assessment and Pedagogy.* Clevedon, Eng.: Multilingual Matters, 1984.

Cummins, Jim. *Empowering Minority Students.* Sacramento: California Association for Bilingual Education, 1989.

Cummins, Jim. "Linguistic Interdependence and the Educational Development of Bilingual Children." *Review of Educational Research,* 49 (Spring 1979), 222–251.

Cummins, Jim. "The Role of Primary Language Development in Promoting Educational Success for Language Minority Students." In *Schooling and Language Minority Students: A Theoretical Framework.* Sacramento: Office of Bilingual Bicultural Education, California State University, Evaluation, Dissemination, and Assessment Center, 1981.

Curry, Lynn. *Learning Styles in Secondary Schools: A Review of Instruments and Implications for Their Use.* Madison: National Center on Effective Secondary Schools, University of Wisconsin, 1990.

Daniels, Harvey A., ed. *Not Only English: Affirming America's Multilingual Heritage.* Urbana, IL: National Council of Teachers of English, 1990.

Delgado-Gaitán, Concha. "Parent Perceptions of School: Supportive Environments for Children." In *Success or Failure? Learning and the Language Minority Student.* Edited by Henry T. Trueba. Cambridge, MA: Newbury House, 1987.

Dennis, Rutledge M. "Socialization and Racism: The White Experience." In *Impacts of Racism on White Americans.* Edited by Benjamin P. Bowser and Raymond G. Hunt. Beverly Hills, CA: Sage Publications, 1981.

Deyhle, Donna. "Learning Failure: Tests as Gatekeepers and the Culturally Different Child." In *Success or Failure? Learning and the Language Minority Student.* Edited by Henry T. Trueba. Cambridge, MA: Newbury House, 1987.

DeYoung, Alan J. *Economics and American Education: A Historical and Critical Overview of the Impact of Economic Theories on Schooling in the United States.* White Plains, NY: Longman, 1989.

Díaz, Stephan, Luis C. Moll, and Hugh Mehan. "Sociocultural Resources in Instruction: A Context-Specific Approach." In *Beyond Language: Social and Cultural Factors in Schooling Language Minority Students.* Los Angeles: Office of Bilingual Education, California State Department of Education, Evaluation, Dissemination, and Assessment Center, 1986.

Dickeman, Mildred. "Teaching Cultural Pluralism." In *Teaching Ethnic Studies: Concepts and Strategies,* 43rd Yearbook. Edited by James A. Banks. Washington, DC: National Council for the Social Studies, 1973.

Divoky, Diane. "The Model Minority Goes to School." *Phi Delta Kappan,* November 1988, pp. 219–222.

Dixon, C. N. "Teaching Strategies for the Mexican American Child." *Reading Teacher,* 30 (1976), 141–145.

Dolson, David P. "The Effects of Spanish Home Language Use on the Scholastic Performance of Hispanic Students." *Journal of Multilingual and Multicultural Development,* 6 (1985), 135–156.

Dornbusch, Sanford M., Philip L. Ritter, P. Herbert Leiderman, Donald F. Roberts, and Michael J. Fraleigh. "The Relation of Parenting Style to Adolescent School Performance." *Child Development,* 58 (1987), 1244–1257.

Edelsky, Carole. "Bilingual Children's Writing: Fact and Fiction." In *Richness in Writing: Empowering ESL Students.* Edited by Donna M. Johnson and Duane H. Roen. White Plains, NY: Longman, 1989.

Edmonds, Ron. "Characteristics of Effective Schools." In *The School Achievement of Minority Children: New Perspectives.* Edited by Ulric Neisser. Hillsdale, NJ: Erlbaum, 1986.

The Education of Hispanics: Status and Implications. Washington, DC: National Council of La Raza, 1987.

Eisner, Elliot W. "The Ecology of School Improvement." *Educational Leadership.* 45, 5 (February 1988), 24–29.

Ekstrom, Ruth B., Margaret E. Goertz, Judith M. Pollack, and Donald A. Rock. "Who Drops Out of High School and Why? Findings from a National Study." In *School Dropouts: Patterns and Policies.* New York: Teachers College Press, Columbia University, 1986.

England, Robert E., Joseph Stewart, Jr., and Kenneth J. Meier. "Excellence in Education: Second Generation School Discrimination as a Barrier." *Equity and Excellence,* 24, 4 (Summer 1990), 35–40.

Epstein, Joyce L., and Susan L. Dauber. *Teacher Attitudes and Practices of Parent Involvement in Inner-City Elementary and Middle Schools,* Report 33. Baltimore: Center for Research on Elementary and Middle Schools, Johns Hopkins University, March 1989.

Equal Educational Opportunities Act of 1974, 20 U.S.C. 1703 (f).

Erickson, Frederick. "Qualitative Methods in Research on Teaching." In *Handbook of Research on Teaching,* 3rd ed. Edited by Merlin C. Wittrock. New York: Macmillan, 1986.

Erickson, Frederick. "Transformation and School Success: The Politics and Culture of Educational Achievement." *Anthropology and Education Quarterly,* 18, 4 (December 1987), 335–356.

Erickson, Frederick, and Gerald Mohatt. "Cultural Organization of Participant Structures in Two Classrooms of Indian Students." In *Doing the Ethnography of Schooling: Educational Anthropology in Action.* Edited by George D. Spindler. New York: Holt, Rinehart & Winston, 1982.

Everhart, Robert. *Reading, Writing, and Resistance.* Boston: Routledge & Kegan Paul, 1983.

Farrell, Edwin, George Peguero, Rasheed Lindsey, and Ronald White. "Giving Voice to High School Students: Pressure and Boredom, 'Ya Know What I'm Sayin?' " *American Educational Research Journal,* 25, 4 (Winter 1988), 489–502.

Feagin, Joe. *Racial and Ethnic Relations.* Englewood Cliffs, NJ: Prentice Hall, 1978.

Federal Education Funding: The Cost of Excellence. Washington, DC: National Education Association, 1990.

Feistristzer, E. Emily. *Teacher Crisis: Myth or Reality? A State-by-State Analysis, 1986*. Washington, DC: National Center for Education Information, 1986.

Feldman, S. Shirley, and Glen R. Elliott. *At the Threshold: The Developing Adolescent*. Cambridge, MA: Harvard University Press, forthcoming.

Felice, Lawrence G. "Black Student Dropout Behavior; Disengagement from School Rejection and Racial Discrimination." *Journal of Negro Education*, 50 (1981), 415–424.

Fernández, Ricardo R., and Gangjian Shu. "School Dropouts: New Approaches to an Enduring Problem." *Education and Urban Society*, 20, 4 (August 1988), 363–386.

Fine, Michelle. "Perspectives on Inequity: Voices from Urban Schools." In *Applied Psychology Annual IV*. Edited by Leonard Bickman. Beverly Hills, CA: Sage Publications, 1983.

Fine, Michelle. "Silencing in Public Schools." *Language Arts*, 64, 2 (February 1987), 157–174.

Fine, Michelle. "Why Urban Adolescents Drop Into and Out of Public High School." In *School Dropouts: Patterns and Policies*. Edited by Gary Natriello. New York: Teachers College Press, Columbia University, 1986.

Fordham, Signithia, and John U. Ogbu. "Black Students' School Success: Coping with the 'Burden of Acting White.'" *Urban Review*, 18, 3 (1986), 176–206.

Foy, Colm. *Cape Verde: Politics, Economics and Society*. London: Pinter Publishers, 1988.

Freire, Paulo. *Pedagogy of the Oppressed*. New York: Seabury Press, 1970.

Freire, Paulo. *The Politics of Education: Culture, Power, and Liberation*. South Hadley, MA: Bergin & Garvey, 1985.

Frymier, Jack, and Bruce Gansneder. "The Phi Delta Kappa Study of Students at Risk." *Phi Delta Kappan*, October 1989, pp. 142–151.

García, Eugene. "Attributes of Effective Schools for Language Minority Students." *Education and Urban Society*, 20, 4 (August 1988), 387–398.

Gardner, Howard. *Frames of Mind*. New York: Basic Books, 1983.

Gay, Geneva. "Designing Relevant Curriculum for Diverse Learners." *Education and Urban Society*, 20, 4 (August 1988), 327–340.

Gerber, David A. *Anti-Semitism in American History*. Urbana: University of Illinois Press, 1986.

Gibson, Margaret A. "The School Performance of Immigrant Minorities: A Comparative View." *Anthropology and Education Quarterly*, 18, 4, (December 1987). 262–275.

Gilbert, Shirl E., and Geneva Gay. "Improving the Success in School of Poor Black Children." *Phi Delta Kappan*, October 1985, pp. 133–137.

Gilliland, Hap. "The Need for an Adapted Curriculum." In *Teaching the Indian Child: A Bilingual/Multicultural Approach*. Edited by Jon Reyhner. Billings: Eastern Montana College, 1986.

Ginsburg, Herbert. "The Myth of the Deprived Child: New Thoughts on Poor Children." In *The School Achievement of Minority Children: New Perspectives*. Edited by Ulric Neisser. Hillsdale, NJ: Erlbaum, 1986.

Ginsburg, Herbert. *The Myth of the Deprived Child: Poor Children's Intellect and Education*. Englewood Cliffs, NJ: Prentice Hall, 1972.

Giroux, Henry A. "Theories of Reproduction and Resistance in the New Sociology of Education: A Critical Appraisal." *Harvard Educational Review*, 53 (1983), 257–293.

Giroux, Henry A. *Theory and Resistance in Education: A Pedagogy for the Opposition*. South Hadley, MA: Bergin & Garvey, 1983.

Glenn, Charles Leslie, Jr. *The Myth of the Common School*. Amherst: University of Massachusetts Press, 1988.

Gollnick, Donna M., and Philip C. Chin. *Multicultural Education in a Pluralistic Society*, 3rd ed. New York: Maxwell Macmillan International Publishing Group, 1990.

Goodlad, John I. *A Place Called School*. New York: McGraw-Hill, 1984.

Gougis, Reginald A. "The Effects of Prejudice and Stress on the Academic Achievement of Black

Americans." In *The School Achievement of Minority Children: New Perspectives*. Edited by Ulric Neisser. Hillsdale, NJ: Erlbaum, 1986.

Gould, Stephen Jay. *The Mismeasure of Man*. New York: Norton, 1981.

Gouldner, Helen. *Teachers' Pets, Troublemakers, and Nobodies: Black Children in Elementary Schools*. Wesport, CT: Greenwood Press, 1978.

Grant, Carl A., and Christine E. Sleeter. *After the School Bell Rings*. Philadelphia: Falmer Press, 1986.

Grant, Carl A., and Christine E. Sleeter. *Turning on Learning: Five Approaches for Multicultural Teaching*. Columbus, OH: Merrill, 1989.

Greeley, Andrew M. *Catholic High Schools and Minority Students*. New Brunswick, NJ: Transaction Books, 1982.

Greenbaum, William. "America in Search of a New Ideal: An Essay on the Rise of Pluralism." *Harvard Educational Review*, 44 (August 1974), 411–440.

Grossman, Herbert. *Educating Hispanic Students: Cultural Implications for Classroom Instruction, Classroom Management, Counseling, and Assessment*. Springfield, IL: C. C Thomas, 1984.

Guidelines for Selecting Bias-Free Textbooks and Storybooks. New York: Council on Interracial Books for Children, 1980.

Hahn, Andrew. "Reaching Out to America's Dropouts: What to Do?" *Phi Delta Kappan*, December 1987, pp. 256–263.

Hakuta, Kenji. *Bilingualism and Bilingual Education: A Research Perspective*, Number 1. Washington, DC: National Clearinghouse for Bilingual Education, Spring 1990.

Hakuta, Kenji. *Mirror of Language: The Debate on Bilingualism*. New York: Basic Books, 1986.

Hale-Benson, Janice E. *Black Children: Their Roots, Culture, and Learning Styles*. Baltimore: Johns Hopkins University Press, 1982.

Hamayan, Else V., and Ron Perlman. *Helping Language Minority Students After They Exit from Bilingual/ESL Programs*. Washington, DC: National Clearinghouse for Bilingual Education, Spring 1990.

A Handbook for Teaching Portuguese-Speaking Students. Sacramento: Office of Bilingual Bicultural Education, California State Department of Education, 1983.

Haney, Walter. "An Estimation of Immigrant and Immigrant Student Populations in the United States as of October 1986." Background paper for the Immigrant Student Project, Boston College, Boston, 1987.

Harris, Violet, ed. *Teaching Multicultural Literature in Grades K–8*. Norwood, MA: Christopher-Gordon Publishers, 1992.

Heath, Shirley Brice. "Questioning at Home and at School: A Comparative Study." In *Doing the Ethnography of Schooling: Educational Anthropology in Action*. Edited by George Spindler. New York: Holt, Rinehart & Winston, 1982.

Heath, Shirley Brice. "Sociocultural Contexts of Language Development." In *Beyond Language: Social and Cultural Factors in Schooling Language Minority Students*. Los Angeles: Office of Bilingual Education, California State Department of Education, Evaluation, Dissemination, and Assessment Center, 1986.

Heath, Shirley Brice. *Ways with Words*. New York: Cambridge University Press, 1983.

Henderson, Anne T. *The Evidence Continues to Grow: Parent Involvement Improves Student Achievement*. Columbia, MD: National Committee for Citizens for Education, 1987.

Hilliard, Asa G. "Intellectual Strengths of Minority Children." In *Teaching in a Multicultural Society: Perspectives and Professional Strategies*. Edited by Doris E. Cross, Gwendolyn C. Baker, and Lindley J. Stiles. New York: Free Press, 1977.

Hirsch, E. D. *Cultural Literacy: What Every American Needs to Know*. Boston: Houghton Mifflin, 1987.

Hispanic Education: A Statistical Portrait 1990. Washington, DC: National Council of La Raza, 1990.

Howard, Gary. "Positive Multicultural Outcomes: A Practitioner's Report." *Multicultural Leader,* 2, 1 (Winter 1989), 12–16.

Hurtado, Aída, and Raúl Rodriguez. "Language as a Social Problem: The Repression of Spanish in South Texas." *Journal of Multilingual and Multicultural Development,* 10, 5 (1989), 401–419.

Iadicola, Peter. "Schooling and Symbolic Violence: The Effect of Power Differences and Curriculum Factors on Hispanic Students' Attitudes Toward Their Own Ethnicity." *Hispanic Journal of Behavioral Sciences,* 5, 1 (1983), 21–43.

Ianni, Francis A. *The Search for Structure: A Report on American Youth Today.* New York: Free Press, 1989.

Jackson, Gregg, and Cecilia Cosca. "The Inequality of Educational Opportunity in the Southwest: An Observational Study of Ethnically Mixed Classrooms." *American Educational Research Journal,* 11 (1974), 219–229.

Jalava, Antti. "Nobody Told Me That I Was a Finn." In *Minority Education: From Shame to Struggle.* Edited by Tove Skutnabb-Kangas and Jim Cummins. Clevedon, Eng.: Multilingual Matters, 1988.

Jensen, Arthur R. "How Much Can We Boost I.Q. and Scholastic Achievement?" *Harvard Educational Review,* 39 (1969), 1–123.

Johnson, David W., Geoffrey Maruyama, Roger Johnson, Debora Nelson, and Linda Skon. "Effects of Cooperative, Competitive, and Individualistic Goal Structures on Achievement: A Meta-Analysis." *Psychological Bulletin,* 89 (1981), 47–62.

Johnson, Donna M., and Duane H. Roen. *Richness in Writing: Empowering ESL Students.* White Plains, NY: Longman, 1989.

Jones, Aaron. "Why Being Bilingual Is Important to Me and My Family." *NABE News,* February 1, 1991.

Jones, James M. "The Concept of Racism and Its Changing Reality." In *Impacts of Racism on White Americans.* Edited by Benjamin P. Bowser and Raymond G. Hunt. Beverly Hills, CA: Sage Publications, 1981.

Jordan, Brigitte. "Cosmopolitan Obstetrics: Some Insights from the Training of Traditional Midwives." *Social Science and Medicine,* 28, 9 (1989), 925–944.

Kagan, Spencer. "Cooperative Learning and Sociocultural Factors in Schooling." In *Beyond Language: Social and Cultural Factors in Schooling Language Minority Students.* Los Angeles: Office of Bilingual Education, California State Department of Education, Evaluation, Dissemination, and Assessment Center, 1986.

Kalantzis, Mary, and Bill Cope. *The Experience of Multicultural Education in Australia: Six Case Studies.* Sydney: Centre for Multicultural Studies, Wollongong University, 1990.

Kamin, Leon J. *The Science and Politics of I.Q.* Hillsdale, NJ: Erlbaum, 1974.

Katz, Michael B. *Class, Bureaucracy, and the Schools: The Illusion of Educational Change in America.* New York: Praeger, 1975.

Keller, Gary S., and Karen S. van Hooft. "A Chronology of Bilingualism and Bilingual Education in the United States." In *Bilingual Education for Hispanic Students in the United States.* Edited by Joshua Fishman and Gary Keller. New York: Teachers College Press, 1982.

Kellogg, John B. "Forces of Change." *Phi Delta Kappan,* November 1988, pp. 199–204.

Kiang, Peter Nien-Chu. *Southeast Asian Parent Empowerment: The Challenge of Changing Demographics in Lowell, Massachusetts,* Monograph #1. Boston: Massachusetts Association for Bilingual Education, 1990.

Kozol, Jonathon. *Death at an Early Age.* Boston: Houghton Mifflin, 1967.

Kozol, Jonathon. "Great Men and Women (Tailored for School Use)." *Learning Magazine,* December 1975, pp. 16–20.

Krashen, Stephen, and Douglas Biber. *On Course: Bilingual Educator's Success in California.* Sacramento: California Association for Bilingual Education, 1988

Lambert, Wallace E. "Cultural and Language as Factors in Learning and Education." In *Education of Immigrant Students.* Edited by A. Wolfgang. Toronto: OISE, 1975.

Lambert, Wallace E. "An Overview of Issues in Immersion Education." In *Studies on Immersion Education: A Collection for U.S. Educators.* Sacramento: Office of Bilingual Education, California State Department of Education, 1984.

Lambert, Wallace E. "The Two Faces of Bilingual Education." *Focus,* Number 3. Rosslyn, VA: National Clearinghouse for Bilingual Education, 1980.

Landry, Walter J. "Future *Lau* Regulations: Conflict Between Language Rights and Racial Non-discrimination." In *Theory, Technology, and Public Policy on Bilingual Education.* Edited by Raymond V. Padilla. Rosslyn, VA: National Clearinghouse for Bilingual Education, 1983.

Latino Youths at a Crossroads. Washington, DC: Children's Defense Fund, 1990.

Lau v. Nichols. 414 U.S. 563. St. Paul, MN: West Publishing, 1974

Lee, Edmund W. "Chinese American Fluent English Proficient Students and School Achievement." *NABE Journal,* 13, 2 (Winter 1989), 95–111.

Lee, Valerie E., and Anthony S. Bryk. "Curriculum Tracking as Mediating the Social Distribution of High School Achievement. *Sociology of Education,* 61, 2 (April 1988), 78–94.

Lessow-Hurley, Judith. *The Foundations of Dual Language Instruction.* White Plains, NY: Longman, 1990.

Lightfoot, Sara Lawrence. "The Teacher as Central Figure." In *Beyond Bias: Perspectives on Classrooms.* Edited by Jean V. Carew and Sara Lawrence Lightfoot. Cambridge, MA: Harvard University Press, 1979.

Lipsitz, Joan. *Successful Schools for Young Adolescents.* New Brunswick, NJ: Transaction Books, 1984.

Little Soldier, Lee. "Cooperative Learning and the Native American Student." *Phi Delta Kappan,* October 1989, pp. 161–163.

Locked In/Locked Out: Tracking and Placement Practices in Boston Public Schools. Boston: Massachusetts Advocacy Center, March 1990.

Longstreet, Wilma S. *Aspects of Ethnicity: Understanding Differences in Pluralistic Classrooms.* New York: Teachers College Press, Columbia University, 1978.

McCarthy, Cameron, and Michael W. Apple. "Race, Class and Gender in American Educational Research: Toward a Nonsynchronous Parallelist Position." In *Class, Race and Gender in American Education.* Edited by Lois Weis. Albany: State University of New York Press, 1988.

McDermott, Ray P. "Achieving School Failure: An Anthropological Approach to Illiteracy and Social Stratification." In *Education and Cultural Process: Anthropological Approaches,* 2nd ed. Edited by George D. Spindler. Prospect Heights, IL: Waveland Press, 1987.

McDermott, Ray P. "The Cultural Context of Learning to Read." In *Papers in Applied Linguistics: Linguistics and Reading,* Series I. Edited by Stanley F. Wanat. Arlington, VA: Center for Applied Linguistics, 1977.

McDermott, Ray P. "Social Relations as Contexts for Learning in School." *Harvard Educational Review,* 47, 2 (May 1977), 198–213.

McIntosh, Peggy. "Understanding Correspondence Between White Privilege and Male Privilege Through Women's Studies Work." Paper presented at the annual meeting of the National Women's Studies Association, Spelman College, Atlanta, June 25, 1987.

McNeill, Linda M. *Contradictions of Control: School Structure and School Knowledge.* New York: Methuen/Routledge & Kegan Paul, 1986.

Marín, Gerardo, and Barbara Vanoss Marín. "Methodological Fallacies When Studying Hispanics." *Applied Social Psychology,* 3 (1983), 99–117.

Massachusetts General Laws 1971, 441:71A et seq.

Matute-Bianchi, María E. "Ethnic Identities and Patterns of School Success and Failure Among Mexican-Descent and Japanese-American Students in a California High School: An Ethnographic Analysis." *American Journal of Education*, 95, 1 (1986), 223–255.

Mejia, Daniel. "The Development of Mexican-American Children." In *The Psychosocial Development of Minority Group Children*. Edited by Gloria Johnson Powell. New York: Brunner/Mazel Publishers, 1983.

Merrian, Sharan B. *Case Study Research in Education: A Qualitative Approach*. San Francisco: Jossey-Bass, 1988.

Merton, Robert. "The Self-Fulfilling Prophecy." *The Antioch Review*, 8 (1948), 193–210.

Miller, Julie A. "Native-Language Instruction Found to Aid LEPs." *NABE News*, 14, 3 (December 1, 1990), 1, 3.

Milner, David. *Children and Race: Ten Years On*. London: Ward Lock Educational, 1983.

Mizio, Emelicia. "The Impact of Macro Systems on Puerto Rican Families." In *The Psychosocial Development of Minority Group Children*. Edited by Gloria Johnson Powell. New York: Brunner/ Mazel Publishers, 1983.

Moll, Luis C. "Some Key Issues in Teaching Latino Students." *Language Arts*, 65, 5 (September 1988), 465–472.

Moll, Luis C., and Stephen Díaz. "Change as the Goal of Educational Research." *Anthropology and Education Quarterly*, 18, 4 (December 1987), 300–311.

Molnar, Alex. "Racism in America: A Continuing Dilemma." *Educational Leadership*, 47, 2 (October 1989), 71–72.

Montero-Sieburth, Martha. "*Echar Pa'lante*, Moving Onward: The Dilemmas and Strategies of a Bilingual Teacher." *Anthropology and Education Quarterly*, 18, 3 (September 1987), 180–189.

Muller, Thomas, and Thomas Espenshade. *The Fourth Wave*. Washington, DC: Urban Institute Press, 1985.

Muñoz Hernández, Shirley, and Isaura Santiago Santiago. "Toward a Qualitative Analysis of Teacher Disapproval Behavior." In *Theory, Technology, and Public Policy on Bilingual Education*. Edited by Raymond V. Padilla. Rosslyn, VA: National Clearinghouse for Bilingual Education, 1983.

"The NABE No-Cost Study on Families." *NABE News*, February 1, 1991.

Nakanishi, Don T., and Marsha Hirano-Nakanishi, *The Education of Asian and Pacific Americans: Historical Perspectives and Prescriptions for the Future*. Phoenix, AZ: Oryx Press, 1983.

National Commission on Secondary Education for Hispanics. *"Make Something Happen": Hispanics and Urban School Reform*. Washington, DC: Hispanic Policy Development Project, 1984.

National Indochinese Clearinghouse. *A Manual for Indochinese Refugee Education, 1976–1977*. Arlington, VA: Center for Applied Linguistics, 1976.

Natriello, Gary, ed. *School Dropouts: Patterns and Policies*. New York: Teachers College Press, Columbia University, 1986.

Natriello, Gary, Edward L. McDill, and Aaron M. Pallas. *Schooling Disadvantaged Children: Racing Against Catastrophe*. New York: Teachers College Press, 1990.

Neill, D. Monty, and Noe J. Medina. "Standardized Testing: Harmful to Educational Health." *Phi Delta Kappan*, May 1989, pp. 688–697.

Neisser, Ulric, ed. *The School Achievement of Minority Children: New Perspectives*. Hillsdale, NJ: Erlbaum, 1986.

New Voices: Immigrant Students in U.S. Public Schools. Boston: National Coalition of Advocates for Students, 1988.

Nielsen, Francois, and Roberto M. Fernández. *Hispanic Students in American High Schools: Background Characteristics and Achievement*. Washington, DC: National Opinion Research Center, National Center for Education Statistics, 1981.

Nieto, Sonia. "Excellence and Equity: The Case for Bilingual Education." *Bulletin of the Council on Interracial Books for Children*, 17, 3 and 4 (1986).

Nieto, Sonia. "Self-Affirmation or Self-Destruction: The Image of Puerto Ricans in Children's Literature Written in English." In *Images and Identities: The Puerto Rican in Two World Contexts*. Edited by Asela Rodríguez de Laguna. New Brunswick, NJ: Transaction Publications, 1987.

Nieto, Sonia. "We Speak in Many Tongues: Linguistic Diversity and Multicultural Education." In *Multicultural Education for the Twenty-First Century*. Edited by Carlos F. Díaz. Washington, DC: National Education Association, 1991.

Nine-Curt, Carmen. *Nonverbal Communication in Puerto Rico*. Cambridge, MA: Evaluation, Dissemination, and Assessment Center, 1977.

Oakes, Jeannie. *Keeping Track: How Schools Structure Inequality*. New Haven, CT: Yale University Press, 1985.

Ogbu, John U. "The Consequences of the American Caste System." In *The School Achievement of Minority Children: New Perspectives*. Edited by Ulric Neisser. Hillsdale, NJ: Erlbaum, 1986.

Ogbu, John U. "Variability in Minority School Performance: A Problem in Search of an Explanation." *Anthropology and Education Quarterly*, 18, 4 (December 1987), 312–334.

Ogbu, John U., and M. E. Matute-Bianchi. "Understanding Sociocultural Factors: Knowledge, Identity and School Adjustment." In *Beyond Language: Social and Cultural Factors in Schooling Language Minority Students*. Los Angeles: Office of Bilingual Education, California State Department of Education, Evaluation, Dissemination, and Assessment Center, California State University, 1986.

On Creating a Hispanic America: A Nation Within a Nation? Washington, DC: Council on Inter-American Security, 1986.

Orfield, Gary. *Working Paper: Desegregation of Black and Hispanic Students for 1968–1980*. Washington, DC: Joint Center for Political Studies, 1982.

Oritz, Flora Ida. "Hispanic-American Children's Experiences in Classrooms: A Comparison Between Hispanic and Non-Hispanic Children." In *Class, Race and Gender in American Education*. Edited by Lois Weis. Albany: State University of New York Press, 1988.

Ovando, Carlos J. "Teaching Science to the Native American Student." In *Teaching the Indian Child: A Bilingual/Multicultural Approach*. Edited by Jon Reyhner. Billings: Eastern Montana College, 1986.

Ovando, Carlos J., and Virginia P. Collier. *Bilingual and ESL Classrooms: Teaching in Multicultural Contexts*. New York: McGraw-Hill, 1985.

Padilla, Raymond V., ed. *Theory, Technology, and Public Policy on Bilingual Education*. Rosslyn, VA: National Clearinghouse on Bilingual Education, 1983.

Pantoja, Antonia, and Barbara Blourock. "Cultural Pluralism Redefined." In *Badges and Indicia of Slavery: Cultural Pluralism Redefined*. Edited by Antonia Pantoja, Barbara Blourock, and James Bowman. Lincoln, NE: Study Commission on Undergraduate Education and the Education of Teachers, 1975.

Pate, Glenn S. "Reducing Prejudice in the Schools." *Multicultural Leader*, 2, 2 (Spring 1989), 1–3.

Paulston, Christina Bratt. *Bilingual Education: Theories and Issues*. Rowley, MA: Newbury House, 1980.

Peng, Samuel B., William B. Peters, and Andrew J. Kolstad. *High School and Beyond: A National Longitudinal Study for the 1980's: A Capsule Description of High School Students*. Washington, DC: U.S. Department of Education, Office of Educational Research and Improvement, 1981.

Persell, Caroline Hodges. *Education and Inequality: The Roots and Results of Stratification in America's Schools*. New York: Free Press, 1977.

Persell, Caroline Hodges. "Social Class and Educational Equality." In *Multicultural Education: Issues and Perspectives*. Edited by James Banks and Cherry A. McGee Banks. Boston: Allyn & Bacon, 1989.

Philips, Susan Urmston. *The Invisible Culture: Communication in Classroom and Community on the Warm Springs Indian Reservation.* White Plains, NY: Longman, 1982.

Philliber, William W., and Clyde B. McCoy, eds. *The Invisible Minority: Urban Appalachians.* Lexington: University Press of Kentucky, 1981.

Phillips, Beeman N. "School-Related Aspirations of Children with Different Socio-Cultural Backgrounds." *Journal of Negro Education,* 41 (1972), 48–52.

Powell, Gloria Johnson. "Coping with Adversity: The Psychosocial Development of Afro-American Children." In *The Psychosocial Development of Minority Group Children.* Edited by Gloria Johnson Powell. New York: Brunner/Mazel Publishers, 1983.

Powell, Gloria Johnson, ed. *The Psychosocial Development of Minority Group Children.* New York: Brunner/Mazel Publishers, 1983.

Prewitt-Díaz, Joseph O. "Home-School Discrepancies and the Puerto Rican Student." *Bilingual Journal,* 5, 2 (Winter 1980), 9–12.

Prewitt-Díaz, Joseph O. "A Study of Self-Esteem and School Sentiment in Two Groups of Puerto Rican Students." *Educational and Psychological Research,* 3 (Summer 1983), 161–167.

Quality Education for Minorities Project. *Education That Works: An Action Plan for the Education of Minorities.* Cambridge: Massachusetts Institute of Technology, January 1990.

Racial and Ethnic Dropout Rates in New York City: A Summary Report. New York: ASPIRA, 1983.

Ramirez, J. David. *Final Report: Longitudinal Study of Structured English Immersion Strategy, Early-Exit and Late-Exit Transitional Bilingual Education Programs for Language Minority Children.* Washington, DC: Office of Bilingual Education, 1991.

Ramirez, Manuel, and Alfredo Castañeda. *Cultural Democracy, Bicognitive Development and Education.* New York: Academic Press, 1974.

Ramsey, Patricia G. *Teaching and Learning in a Diverse World: Multicultural Education for Young Children.* New York: Teachers College Press, Columbia University, 1987.

Red Horse, John. "Indian Family Values and Experiences." In *The Psychosocial Development of Minority Group Children.* Edited by Gloria Johnson Powell. New York: Brunner/Mazel Publishers, 1983.

Reissman, Frank. *The Culturally Deprived Child.* New York: Harper & Row, 1962.

Reyhner, Jon. "Native American Languages Act Becomes Law." *NABE News,* 14, 3 (December 1, 1990).

Reyhner, Jon, ed. *Teaching the Indian Child: A Bilingual/Multicultural Approach.* Billings: Eastern Montana College, 1986.

Rist, Ray C. "Student Social Class and Teacher Expectations: The Self-Fulfilling Prophecy in Ghetto Education." *Challenging the Myths: The Schools, the Blacks, and the Poor,* Reprint Series #5. Cambridge, MA: Harvard Educational Review, 1971.

Rivera, Charlene, ed. *Language Proficiency and Academic Achievement.* Clevedon, Eng.: Multilingual Matters, 1984.

Rodriguez, Clara E. *Puerto Ricans: Born in the U.S.A.* Boulder, CO: Westview Press, 1991.

Rodriguez, Richard. *Hunger of Memory: The Education of Richard Rodriguez.* Boston: David R. Godine, 1982.

Romero, Arturo. "The Mexican-American Child: A Socioecological Approach to Research." In *The Psychosocial Development of Minority Group Children.* Edited by Gloria Johnson Powell. New York: Brunner/Mazel Publishers, 1983.

Rosenfeld, L. B. "An Investigation of Teachers' Stereotyping Behavior: The Influence of Presentation, Ethnicity, and Social Class on Teachers' Evaluations of Students." Prepared for the National Institute of Education (DHEW), Washington, DC: ERIC, 1973, ED 090172.

Rosenthal, Robert. "*Pygmalian* Effects: Existence, Magnitude, and Social Importance." *Educational Researcher,* 16, 9 (December 1987), 37–41.

Rosenthal, Robert, and Lenore Jacobson. *Pygmalion in the Classroom*. New York: Holt, Rinehart & Winston, 1968.

Roth, Rodney W. "How Negro Fifth-Grade Students View 'Black Pride' Concepts." *Integrated Education*, 8 (1970), 24–27.

Rubovitz, Pamela C., and Martin L. Maehr. "Pygmalian in Black and White." *Journal of Personality and Social Psychology*, 25, 2 (1973), 210–218.

Rumbaut, Ruben G., and Kenji Ima. *The Adaptation of Southeast Asian Refugee Youth: A Comparative Study*, Final Report. San Diego: Office of Refugee Resettlement, September, 1987.

Ryan, William. *Blaming the Victim*. New York: Vintage Books, 1972.

Sadker, David, and Myra Sadker. *Year 111: Final Report, Promoting Effectiveness in Classroom Instruction*. Contract No. 400-80-0033. Washington, DC: National Institute of Education, March 1984.

Santos Rivera, Iris. "Liberating Education for Little Children." *Alternativas*, 1, 9–12 (October 1983–January 1984), 5–7.

Sarason, Seymour B. *The Culture of the School and the Problem of Change*, 2nd ed. Boston: Allyn & Bacon, 1982.

Sarason, Seymour B. "Jewishness, Blackishness and the Nature-Nurture Controversy." *Psychology and Social Action: Selected Papers*. New York: Praeger, 1982.

Saville-Troike, Muriel. "Language Diversity in Multiethnic Education." In *Education in the 80's: Multiethnic Education*. Edited by James A. Banks. Washington, DC: National Education Association, 1981.

Schaefer, Richard T. *Racial and Ethnic Groups*, 3rd ed. Glenview, IL: Scott, Foresman, 1988.

Schniedewind, Nancy, and Ellen Davidson. *Cooperative Learning, Cooperative Lives: A Sourcebook of Learning Activities for Building a Peaceful World*. Dubuque, IA: Wm. C. Brown, 1987.

Schneidewind, Nancy, and Ellen Davidson. *Open Minds to Equality*. Boston: Allyn & Bacon, 1983.

Schooling and Language Minority Students: A Theoretical Framework. Sacramento: Office of Bilingual Bicultural Education, California State University, Evaluation, Dissemination, and Assessment Center, 1981.

Scollon, Ronald, and Suzanne Scollon. *Narrative, Literacy, and Face in Interethnic Communication*. Norwood, NJ: Ablex Publishers, 1981.

Shakeshaft, Charol. "A Gender at Risk." *Phi Delta Kappan*, March 1986, pp. 499–503.

Simon, Rita J., and Howard Alstein. *Transracial Adoptees and Their Families*. New York: Praeger, 1987.

Simonson, Rick, and Scott Walker, eds. *Multicultural Literacy: The Opening of the American Mind*. St. Paul, MN; Greywolf Press, 1988.

Sims, Rudine. *Shadow and Substance: Afro-American Experience in Contemporary Children's Fiction*. Champaign, IL: National Council of Teachers of English, 1982.

Sinclair, Robert L., and Ward Ghory. *Marginal Students: A Primary Concern for School Renewal*. Chicago: McCutchan, 1987.

Sindell, Peter. "Some Discontinuities in the Enculturation of Mistassini Cree Children." In *Education and Cultural Process: Anthropological Approaches*, 2nd ed. Edited by George Spindler. Prospect Heights, IL: Waveland Press, 1987.

Sirotnik, Kenneth A., and Jeannie Oakes, ed. *Critical Perspectives on the Organization and Improvement of Schooling*. Boston: Kluwer-Nijhoff Publishing, 1986.

Skutnabb-Kangas, Tove. "Legitimating or Delegitimating New Forms of Racism: The Role of Researchers." *Journal of Multilingual and Multicultural Development*. 11, 1 and 2 (1990), 77–100.

Skutnabb-Kangas, Tove, and Jim Cummins, eds. *Minority Education: From Shame to Struggle*. Clevedon, Eng.: Multilingual Matters, 1988.

Skutnabb-Kangas, Tove, and Pertti Toukomaa. *Teaching Migrant Children's Mother Tongue and Learning the Language of the Host Country in the Context of the Socio-cultural Situation of the Migrant Family.* Helsinki: Finnish National Commission for UNESCO, 1976.

Slavin, Robert E. *Ability Grouping in Elementary Schools: A Best Evidence Synthesis.* Baltimore: Johns Hopkins University, Center for Effective Elementary Schools, 1986.

Slavin, Robert E. *Cooperative Learning.* White Plains, NY: Longman, 1983.

Slavin, Robert E., Nancy A. Madden, Nancy L. Karweit, Barbara J. Livermon, and Lawrence Dolan. "Success for All: First-Year Outcomes of a Comprehensive Plan for Reforming Urban Education." *American Educational Research Journal,* 27, 2 (Summer 1990), 255–278.

Sleeter, Christine E. *Empowerment Through Multicultural Education.* Albany: State University of New York Press, 1991.

Sleeter, Christine E. "Multicultural Education Staff Development: How Much Can It Change Classroom Teaching?" Paper presented at the annual meeting of the American Educational Research Association, San Francisco, March 1989.

Sleeter, Christine E., and Carl A. Grant. "Race, Class, Gender and Disability in Current Textbooks." In *The Politics of the Textbook.* Edited by Michael W. Apple and Linda K. Christian-Smith. New York: Routledge & Chapman Hall, 1991.

Sleeter, Christine E., and Carl A. Grant. "A Rationale for Integrating Race, Gender, and Social Class." In *Class, Race, and Gender in American Education.* Edited by Lois Weis. New York: State University of New York Press, 1988.

Snow, Richard E. "Unfinished Pygmalion." *Contemporary Psychology,* 14 (1969), 197–200.

Spindler, George D. "Why Have Minority Groups in North America Been Disadvantaged by Their Schools?" In *Education and Cultural Process: Anthropological Approaches,* 2nd ed. Edited by George D. Spindler. Prospect Heights, IL: Waveland Press, 1987.

Spindler, George, ed. *Doing the Ethnography of Schooling: Educational Anthropology in Action.* New York: Holt, Rinehart & Winston, 1982.

Spindler, George, ed. *Education and Cultural Process: Anthropological Approaches,* 2nd ed. Prospect Heights, IL: Waveland Press, 1987.

Spring, Joel. *American Education.* White Plains, NY: Longman, 1985.

Spring, Joel. *The Rise and Fall of the Corporate State.* Boston: Beacon Press, 1972.

Spring, Joel. *The Sorting Machine Revisited: National Educational Policy Since 1945.* White Plains, NY: Longman, 1989.

Stein, Annie. "Strategies for Failure." *Challenging the Myths: The Schools, The Blacks, and the Poor,* Reprint Series #5. Cambridge, MA: Harvard Educational Review, 1971.

Steinberg, Laurence, Patricia Lin Blinde, and Kenyon S. Chan. "Dropping Out Among Minority Youth." *Review of Educational Research,* 54, 1 (Spring 1984), 113–132.

Steinberg, Laurence, B. Bradford Brown, Mary Cider, Nancy Kaczmarek, and Cary Lazzaro. *Noninstructional Influences on High School Student Achievement: The Contributions of Parents, Peers, Extracurricular Activities, and Part-Time Work.* Madison: University of Wisconsin Center for Educational Research, National Center for Effective Secondary Schools, September 1988.

Stevenson, David L., and David P. Baker. "The Family-School Relation and the Child's School Performance." *Child Development,* 58, 5 (October 1987), 1348–1357.

Stodolsky, Susan S., and Gerald Lesser. "Learning Patterns in the Disadvantaged." In *Challenging the Myths: The Schools, the Blacks, and the Poor,* Reprint Series #5. Cambridge, MA: Harvard Educational Review, 1971.

Stonequist, Everett V. *The Marginal Man: A Study in Personality and Culture Conflict.* New York: Russell & Russell, 1961.

"Stuck in the Horizon: A Special Report on the Education of Native Americans." *Education Week,* August 2, 1989, pp. 1–16.

Suarez-Orozco, Marcelo M. " 'Becoming Somebody': Central American Immigrants in U.S. Inner-City Schools." *Anthropology and Education Quarterly,* 18, 4 (December 1987), 287–299.

Sue, Stanley, and Robert Chin. "The Mental Health of Chinese-American Children." In *The Psychosocial Development of Minority Group Children.* Edited by Gloria Johnson Powell. New York: Brunner/Mazel Publishers, 1983.

Suzuki, Bob H. "The Education of Asian and Pacific Americans: An Introductory Overview." In *The Education of Asian and Pacific Americans: Historical Perspectives and Prescriptions for the Future.* Edited by Don T. Nakanishi and Marsha Hirano-Nakanishi. Phoenix, AZ: Oryx Press, 1983.

Swain, Merrill. "Bilingual Education for the English-Speaking Canadian." In *Georgetown University Round Table on Languages and Linguistics 1978: International Dimensions of Bilingual Education.* Edited by James Alatis. Washington, DC: Georgetown University Press, 1978.

Takaki, Ronald. *Strangers from a Different Shore: A History of Asian Americans.* New York: Penguin Books, 1987.

Tam Thi Dang Wei. *Vietnamese Refugee Students: A Handbook for School Personnel.* Cambridge, MA: National Assessment and Dissemination Center, 1980.

Taylor, Denny, and Catherine Dorsey-Gaines. *Growing Up Literate: Learning from Inner-City Families.* Portsmouth, NH: Heinemann, 1988.

Terman, Lewis. *The Measurement of Intelligence.* Boston: Houghton Mifflin, 1916.

Texas Dropout Information Clearinghouse. *Parent and Community Involvement: Information Is a Key to Dropout Prevention.* Austin, TX: Education Agency, Fall 1989.

Tharp, Roland G. "Psychocultural Variables and Constants: Effects on Teaching and Learning in Schools." *American Psychologist,* 44, 2 (February 1989), 349–359.

Tomás Rivera Center Report, 2, 4 (Fall 1989).

Trankina, Frank J. "Clinical Issues and Techniques in Working with Hispanic Children and Their Families." In *The Psychosocial Development of Minority Group Children.* Edited by Gloria Johnson Powell. New York: Brunner/Mazel Publishers, 1983.

Troike, Rudolph. "Research Evidence for the Effectiveness of Bilingual Education." *NABE Journal,* 3 (1978), 13–24.

Trueba, Henry T., ed. *Success or Failure? Learning and the Language Minority Student.* Cambridge, MA: Newbury House, 1987.

Tucker, G. R. "Implications for U.S. Bilingual Education: Evidence from Canadian Research." *Focus,* Number 2, Rosslyn, VA: National Clearinghouse for Bilingual Education, 1980.

Tyack, David B. *The One Best System. A History of American Urban Education.* Cambridge, MA: Harvard University Press, 1974.

U.S. Bureau of the Census. *Condition of Hispanics in America Today.* Washington, DC: U.S. Department of Commerce, 1983.

U.S. Bureau of the Census. *Current Population Survey: Consumer Income Series.* Washington, DC: U.S. Department of Commerce, 1982.

U.S. Bureau of the Census. *We, the First Americans.* Washington, DC: U.S. Government Printing Office, December 1988.

U.S. Commission on Civil Rights, *Teachers and Students: Differences in Teacher Interaction with Mexican-American and Anglo Students.* Washington, DC: U.S. Government Printing Office, 1973.

"U.S. English—A Common Language Benefits Our Nation and All Its People," Washington, DC: U.S. English, n.d.

U.S. General Accounting Office, *Bilingual Education: A New Look at the Research Evidence,* Washington, DC: U.S. Government Printing Office, March 1987.

"U.S. History Textbooks: Help or Hindrance to Social Justice?" *Bulletin of the Council on Interracial Books for Children,* 15, 5 (1984), 3–8.

Valdiviese, Ray, and Cary Davis, *U.S. Hispanics: Challenging Issues for the 1990s.* Washington, DC: Population Trends and Public Policy, December 1988.

Valentine, Charles A. "Deficit, Difference, and Bicultural Models of Afro-American Behavior." *Challenging the Myths: The Schools, the Blacks, and the Poor,* Reprint Series #5. Cambridge, MA: Harvard Educational Review 1971.

Vega, William A., Richard L. Hough, and Annelisa Romero. "Family Life Patterns of Mexican-Americans." In *The Psychosocial Development of Minority Group Children.* Edited by Gloria Johnson Powell. New York: Brunner/Mazel Publishers, 1983.

Visions of a Better Way: A Black Appraisal of Public Schooling. Washington, DC: Joint Center for Political Studies, 1989.

Vogt, Lynn A., Cathie Jordan, and Roland G. Tharp. "Explaining School Failure, Producing School Success." *Anthropology and Education Quarterly,* 18, 4 (December 1987), 276–286.

Vuong G. Thuy. "The Indochinese in America: Who Are They and How Are They Doing?" In *Education of Asian and Pacific Americans: Historical Perspectives and Prescriptions for the Future.* Edited by Don T. Nakanishi and Marsha Hirano-Nakanishi. Phoenix, AZ: Oryx Press, 1983.

Waggoner, Dorothy. "Foreign-Born Children in the U.S. in the Eighties." NABE *Journal,* Fall 1987, pp. 23–49.

Walberg, Herbert J. "Improving the Productivity of America's Schools." *Educational Leadership,* 41, 8 (May 1984), 19–27.

Walsh, Catherine E. *Pedagogy and the Struggle for Voice: Issues of Language, Power, and Schooling for Puerto Ricans.* New York: Bergin & Garvey, 1991.

Warren, Richard L. "Schooling, Biculturalism, and Ethnic Identity: A Case Study." In *Doing the Ethnography of Schooling: Educational Anthropology in Action.* Edited by George Spindler. New York: Holt, Rinehart & Winston, 1982.

Weekly Compilation of Presidential Documents, 27, 16 (April 22, 1991), 468-472.

Wehlage, Gary G., and Robert A. Rutter. "Dropping Out: How Much Do Schools Contribute to the Problem?" In *School Dropouts: Patterns and Policies.* New York: Teachers College Press, Columbia University, 1986.

Weinberg, Meyer. *A Chance to Learn: A History of Race and Education in the U.S.* Cambridge: Cambridge University Press, 1977.

Weinberg, Meyer. *Because They Were Jews: A History of Anti-Semitism.* Westport, CT: Greenwood Press, 1986.

Weinberg, Meyer. "Notes from the Editor." *A Chronicle of Equal Education,* 4, 3 (November 1982).

Weinberg, Meyer. *Racism in the United States: A Comprehensive Classified Bibliography.* Westport, CT: Greenwood Press, 1990.

Weis, Lois, ed. *Class, Race and Gender in American Education.* Albany: State University of New York Press, 1988.

Wells, Amy Stuart. *Hispanic Education in America: Separate and Unequal.* New York: ERIC Clearinghouse on Urban Education 59, Teachers College, Columbia University, 1989.

Westphal, Raymond C., Jr. *The Effects of a Primary-Grade Interethnic Curriculum on Racial Prejudice.* San Francisco: R & E Research Associates, 1977.

Wilcox, Kathleen. "Differential Socialization in the Classroom: Implications for Equal Opportunity" and "Ethnography as a Methodology and Its Application to the Study of Schooling: A Review." In *Doing the Ethnography of Schooling: Educational Anthropology in Action.* Edited by George D. Spindler. New York: Holt, Rinehart & Winston, 1982.

Willett, Jerri. "Contrasting Acculturation Patterns of Two Non-English Speaking Preschoolers." In *Success or Failure? Learning and the Language Minority Student.* Edited by Henry T. Trueba. Cambridge, MA: Newbury House, 1987.

Williams, Melvin D. "Observations in Pittsburgh Ghetto Schools." *Anthropology and Education Quarterly,* 12 (1981), 211–220.

Williamson, Joel. *New People: Miscegenation and Mulattoes in the United States.* New York: Free Press, 1980.

Willig, Ann C. "A Meta-Analysis of Selected Studies on the Effectiveness of Bilingual Education." *Review of Educational Research,* 55 (1985), 269–317.

Wilson, William Julius. *The Truly Disadvantaged: The Inner City, the Underclass, and Public Policy.* Chicago: University of Chicago Press, 1987.

Wineburg, Samuel S. "The Self-Fulfillment of the Self-Fulfilling Prophecy: A Critical Appraisal." *Educational Researcher,* 16, 9 (December 1987), 28–37.

Winkler, Karen J. "Researcher's Examination of California's Poor Latino Population Prompts Debate Over the Traditional Definitions of the Underclass." *The Chronicle of Higher Education,* October 10, 1990, pp. A5, A8.

Wise, Fred, and Nancy Brown Miller. "The Mental Health of the American Indian Child." In *The Psychosocial Development of Minority Group Children.* Edited by Gloria Johnson Powell. New York: Brunner/Mazel Publishers, 1983.

Witkin, Herman A. *Psychological Differentiation.* New York: Wiley, 1962.

Wolcott, Harry F. "The Teacher as an Enemy." In *Education and Cultural Process: Anthropological Approaches,* 2nd ed. Edited by George Spindler. Prospect Heights, IL: Waveland Press, 1987.

Women and Minorities in Science and Engineering. Washington, DC: National Science Foundation, 1988.

Wurzel, Jaime S. *Toward Multiculturalism: A Reader in Multicultural Education.* Yarmouth, ME: Intercultural Press, 1988.

Yao, Esther Lee. "Working Effectively with Asian Immigrant Parents." *Phi Delta Kappan,* November 1988, pp. 223–225.

Young, John, and John Lum. *Asian Bilingual Education Teacher Handbook.* Cambridge, MA: Evaluation, Dissemination, and Assessment Center, 1982.

Zogby, James J. "When Stereotypes Threaten Pride." *NEA Today,* October 1982, p. 12.

Index